Contents

Raising the Corporate Umbrella

Raising the
Corporate Umbrella

Corporate communication in the 21st century

Philip J. Kitchen

and

Don E. Schultz

palgrave

First published 2001 by
PALGRAVE
Houndmills, Basingstoke, Hampshire RG21 6XS and
175 Fifth Avenue, New York, N.Y. 10010
Companies and representatives throughout the world

PALGRAVE is the new global academic imprint of
St. Martin's Press LLC Scholarly and Reference Division and
Palgrave Publishers Ltd (formerly Macmillan Press Ltd).

ISBN 0-333-92639-0 hardcover

This book is printed on paper suitable for recycling and made from fully managed and sustained forest sources.

A catalogue record for this book is available from the British Library.

Library of Congress Cataloging-in-Publication Data

Kitchen, Philip J.
  Raising the corporate umbrella : corporate
  communications in the 21st century /
Philip J. Kitchen, Don E. Schultz.
    p. cm.
  Includes bibliographical references and index.
  ISBN 0-333-92639-0 (cloth)
    1. Business communication. 2. Chief executive
officers. 3. Communication International.
4. Competition, International. I. Schultz, Don E. II. Title

HF5718 .K57 2001
658.4'5—dc21
                                          2001033118

Editing and origination by
Aardvark Editorial, Mendham, Suffolk

10 9 8 7 6 5 4 3 2 1
10 09 08 07 06 05 04 03 02 01

Printed and bound in Great Britain by
Creative Print & Design (Wales), Ebbw Vale

List of figures

List of tables

Notes on contributors

Philip J. Kitchen is the Martin Naughton Professor of Business Strategy, specializing in Marketing at the Queen's University School of Management and Economics, Belfast. There, he teaches and carries out research in marketing management, marketing communication, corporate communication, promotion management, and international communications management. He is Founding Director of the Executive MBA program. Before Queen's he was Senior Lecturer in Marketing and Founder and Director of the Research Centre for Corporate and Marketing Communications within the Department of Marketing at Strathclyde University. Prior to university life he worked as a Regional Manager for a national firm before entering higher education as a mature student. A graduate of the CNAA (B.A.Hons) initially, he received Masters degrees in Marketing from UMIST (M.Sc.) and Manchester Business School (M.B.Sc.) respectively, and his Ph.D. from Keele University. Since 1984 he has been active in teaching and research in the communication domain. He is Founding Editor and is now Editor-in-Chief of the *Journal of Marketing Communications* (Routledge Journals, 1995). He is Editor of *Public Relations: Principles and Practice* (International Thomson, 1997, 2000), and *Marketing Communications: Principles and Practice* (1999). He is co-author of *Communicating Globally: An Integrated Marketing Approach* (2000) with Don Schultz of Northwestern University (NTC Business Books, Chicago and Macmillan Business, London). He is also co-editor of *Marketing: The Informed Student Guide* (2001), with Tony Proctor (International Thomson, London).

Dr. Kitchen has contributed to such journals as the *International Journal of Advertising, Journal of Advertising Research, Journal of Marketing Management, European Journal of Marketing, Marketing Intelligence and Planning, Journal of Marketing Communications, ADMAP,*

Journal of Nonprofit and Public Sector Marketing, International Journal of Bank Marketing, Journal of Corporate Communications, Small Business and Enterprise Development, Creativity and Innovation Management, Journal of Business Ethics, and, numerous practitioner journals. Dr. Kitchen founded, organized, and chaired the 1st International Conference on Marketing and Corporate Communications and was Editor of the Proceedings (Keele, 1996, Strathclyde, 1998). This Conference is now an annual event (Antwerp, Belgium, 1997; Glasgow, Scotland 1998; Salford, England, 1999; Erasmus Universiteit, The Netherlands, 2000; Queen's University, 2001). Dr. Kitchen serves on the Editorial Advisory Board of the *Journal of Marketing Management* and is a Review Board Member for *Marketing Intelligence and Planning* and *Corporate Communications: An International Journal.*

He has presented papers on marketing management, corporate or marketing communications in England, Scotland, Czech Republic, Estonia, France, Germany, Belgium, Portugal, Australia, New Zealand, Spain, the Republic of Ireland, Northern Ireland, Israel, and in the United States.

Kitchen is also active in the professional arena. He is a member of the Measurement Academic Advisory Panel (MAAP) with Hill & Knowlton which involves leading academics from the U.S.A., Europe and Australia. This group seeks to bring a robust academic dimension to H&K thinking across a wide range of measurement evaluation tools.

Don E. Schultz is Professor (Emeritus) of Integrated Marketing Communications (IMC) at the Medill School of Journalism, Northwestern University, Evanston, IL, U.S.A. Professor Schultz and his colleagues pioneered the first graduate program in IMC. He is also President of his own marketing communication and management firm – Agora Inc., in Evanston, Illinois. Professor Schultz has consulted, lectured, and held seminars on marketing, marketing metrics, marketing communication, branding, advertising, sales promotion and other communications topics in North and South America, Europe, the Middle East, Australia, New Zealand, and Asia. He was Founding Editor of the *Journal of Direct Marketing,* and has published nine books including *Integrated Marketing Communications* (1992) which he co-authored with Stanley Tannenbaum and Robert Lauterborn. His landmark text *Measuring Brand Communications ROI* written with Jeffrey Walters has revolutionized the entire field of marketing communication and branding measurement. It was published by the Association of National Advertisers in New York (1997). His 5th edition of *Strategic Brand Communication Campaigns* (with Beth Barnes) was published in the Fall of 1999. *Communicating Globally: An Inte-*

grated Marketing Approach (with Phil Kitchen) was published by NTC Business Press and Macmillan Business in Spring (2000).

Professor Schultz is a prolific writer. He has published over 100 articles, research papers and studies in scholarly journals around the world. He is a regular columnist for *Marketing News* and *Marketing Management*, both published by the American Marketing Association. He is on the editorial review board of a half-dozen scholarly journals published around the world. He also publishes in the professional press as well in publications ranging from *Advertising Age* to *Direct*.

Schultz is also active in the professional arena. He sits on the Board of Directors of Penton Media, Cleveland, OH; Insignia Systems, Minneapolis, MN; dunnhumby, London; Brand Finance plc., London and The Simon Richards Group, Melbourne, Australia. He is also on the advisory boards of a large range of new technology and start-up companies such as Zefer, Boston, Recipio, San Mateo, CA, Sixtyseven Kilocycles, Chicago and others.

Ted Zorn (Ph.D.), author of Chapter 2, is Professor and Chair of the Management Communication Department, University of Waikato, Hamilton, New Zealand. His research and teaching focus on organizational influence processes, especially leadership and change communication. He is currently Editor of *Management Communication Quarterly* (Sage Publications) and Chair of the Organizational Communication Division of the National Communication Association, U.S.A.

Cees B.M. van Riel (Ph.D.), co-author of Chapter 3, is Professor of Corporate Communication and Director of the Corporate Communication Centre at the Rotterdam School of Management, Erasmus University Rotterdam, The Netherlands. He is also European Director of the Reputation Institute. His research focuses on the interaction between corporate strategy and reputation management. He has published numerous papers in such journals as *Management Communication Quarterly* and *Public Relations Review*. His book *Principles of Corporate Communications* was published by Prentice Hall International in 1995 followed by other monographs. He is one of the Founding Editors of the international journal *Corporate Reputation Review*.

Guido Berens, co-author of Chapter 3, is a doctoral candidate at the Erasmus Research Institute of Management of Erasmus University, Rotterdam, The Netherlands. His research focuses on the influence of corporate reputation on companies' relationships with stakeholders. His background is in cognitive psychology.

Richard J. Varey (Ph.D.), author of Chapters 4 and 10, is Director of the Corporate Communication Research Unit, a research group of the School of Management at the University of Salford. Prior to his academic career he ran his own consultancy business and continues to deal with senior managers on a wide range of communication issues. He has written widely on management, strategic marketing, marketing and quality management, internal marketing, service quality, and communication management, for management and business publications, as well as academic journals and conferences. His books include: *Internal Marketing: Directions for Management*, Routledge, London, 2000 (with Lewis, B); and *Marketing Communication: A Critical Introduction*, Routledge, London, forthcoming. He is a member of the editorial boards of the *Journal of Communication Management*, the *Journal of Marketing Communications*, *Corporate Reputation Review*, and *Corporate Communications: An International Journal*. He is a member of the advisory committee of the International Corporate Communication Institute.

Jim Garrity, author of Chapter 6, is Senior Vice President, Corporate Marketing, where he heads the Corporate Marketing Division of First Union in Charlotte, North Carolina. With First Union since 1997, he oversees all aspects of marketing for the corporation. Prior to First Union, Jim was the Vice President of Communications at Compaq for five years. At Compaq Jim managed marketing communications for North America and led global marketing communication strategy. Prior to Compaq, Jim spent over 20 years at IBM in a variety of sales and marketing management positions. His last position at IBM was Director of Advertising, IBM, U.S.A.

Jim is a member of the Association of National Advertisers Board of Directors, served as ANA Chairman in 1998 and is the founder and current chairman of ANA's New Technologies Committee.

Marilyn S. Roberts, author of Chapter 7, is an Associate Professor and Assistant Dean for the Division of Graduate Studies and Research in the College of Journalism and Communications at the University of Florida. She earned a Bachelor's degree in journalism from Southern Methodist University, a Master's in Mass Communication from Abilene Christian University, and a Ph.D. in Communication from the University of Texas at Austin. She has taught international and cross-cultural advertising for nearly a decade. In 1999 and 2000, she supervised the United States/Canadian Regional Champion winning teams in the International Advertising Association's InterAD student competition. She has served as chair of the American Academy of Advertising's International Advertising Education

Committee. Prior to returning to her doctoral work, Dr. Roberts owned and operated an advertising and public relations firm in Texas.

Thomas L. Harris is a management consultant, educator, author, journalist and former public relations agency principal. He is managing partner of Thomas L. Harris & Company, a public relations management consultancy that serves corporations and public relations firms. He was Adjunct Professor of Integrated Marketing at the Medill School of Journalism, Northwestern University for 14 years. Previously, he was principal of Golin/Harris International, one of the largest public relations firms in the world. He is the author of three books on public relations: *The Marketer's Guide to Public Relations*; *Choosing and Working with Your Public Relations Firm*; and, *Value-Added Public Relations*. He was the winner of the 2000 Gold Anvil Award, the highest award presented by the Public Relations Society of America. Tom has contributed Chapter 8.

James E. Lukaszewski, author of Chapter 9, advises, coaches, and counsels the men and women who run very large corporations and organizations. He is a specialist in trouble-shooting tough, touchy, sensitive corporate communications issues. He helps prepare spokespersons for crucial public appearances. James has authored several books including: *Influencing Public Attitudes: Strategies that Reduce The Media's Power*; *Executive Action: Crisis Communication Management System*; *War Stories and Crisis Communication Strategies, An Anthology*; *Crisis Communication Planning Strategies: A Workbook*; and *Media Relations During Emergencies*.

He has also published 19 unabridged monographs on critical communication subjects since 1994, and more than 130 articles and book chapters. He sits on the review board or editorial board for *Public Relations Journal*, *PR News*, *PR Reporter*, and was the first crisis columnist for the PRSA's member publication: *PR Tactics*. A member of several distinguished PR associations, he has worked in executive positions for leading PR companies, until founding the Lukaszewski Group in 1989. James is a graduate of Metropolitan State University, and has completed the MIT-Harvard Public Disputes Program: "Dealing With An Angry Public."

Shekar Swamy is President, R K SWAMY BBDO Advertising Limited, India. In this capacity he oversees the operation of India's seventh largest advertising agency, servicing clients such as Adidas, Bayer, Citizen, Henkel, Mercedes-Benz, Sara Lee and Sony Corp. He is a Member of the Executive Board of BBDO Asia Pacific. He is a Visiting Professor at the Integrated Marketing Communications Department, Northwestern University, U.S.A., where he teaches a module titled: "Global Marketing Communications." He holds a B. Com., MBA (University of Delhi) and MS (Advertising-Northwestern University). His total work experience of 20 years spans several countries and covers a wide spectrum of brand and corporate communication issues. Shekar is the author of Chapter 11.

Anders Gronstedt, Ph.D., co-author with Don Schultz of Chapter 12, is the CEO of the Gronstedt Group, a marketing training firm with offices in Superior Colorado and Stockholm, Sweden. His firm develops executive seminars and web-based training methods for sales, service, and other front-line workers to better integrate marketing and communications. A former member of the graduate Integrated Marketing Communications faculty at the University of Colorado, Dr. Gronstedt is a world-renowned management consultant, speaker, and author. His book: *The Customer Century: Lessons from World-Class Companies in Integrated Marketing and Communications*, Routledge, 2000, was selected as the "must read" in February 2001, and *AdWeek* recently excerpted the first chapter of the book.

Acknowledgements

With grateful thanks to our outstanding group of contributors, for sharing their knowledge, expertise and experience not only with the readers of this text but with the lead authors as well. The bringing together of this world-class group of academics and practitioners to develop a common view of corporate communications in the beginning of the 21st century in terms of structure, practice and management is likely without equal. We are indebted to the various authors and their associates who helped provide the content for this text. Their expertise and cooperation have been invaluable.

We also acknowledge with gratitude the many individuals, companies, and authors who have assisted us by providing case illustrations, vignettes, and other materials and in allowing these to be cited and shared.

We also thank the many students who, through their questions and comments in the classrooms and research labs across several continents, have helped us sharpen and refine our corporate communication concepts, techniques and approaches. And, we must also acknowledge the literally thousands of practitioners who through workshops, seminars and symposia around the world have forced us to test our theories against the real world of marketplace practice.

To all of you, thanks for your help, your guidance, your support and most of all your encouragement to formally define the field of corporate communication, what it is and what it should be, as we move forward in a dramatically different arena than the past.

Chapter

Raising the corporate umbrella – the 21st-century need

philip j. kitchen and don e. schultz

ILLUSTRATION

"Pressure to Perform Better Grows on Companies' CEOs"

Introduction

Impatient investors and unforgiving directors are increasingly pinning the blame for their corporate woes on the chief executive.

Procter & Gamble's Durk Jager was a recent example of a high-profile executive whose crown turned to thorns amid a plunging share price and loss of confidence in 2000.

Mr Jager was, as of June 2000, the *36th* U.S. chief executive to be axed in *that month* – an average of six top management changes every business day, according to executive employment consultancy Challenger, Gray, and Christmas.

Why is this happening?

John Challenger, chief executive, says shareholders and boards are giving their chiefs the choice of boosting the bottom line or the boot. "It's like managing a soccer club – a couple of bad decisions and the fans will not suffer them staying. The sacking mentality is spreading like a virus," he says.

A recent survey found that shareholders consider improving financial performance is a chief executive's top priority. More than seventy percent want their chief executive to boost returns, compared with three percent who are more interested in long-term performance.

I

Darrel Rigby, a director of the management consultants Bain & Co., adds: "This is not a fad. Institutional investors are also becoming pushier toward boards of directors."

The Sword of Damocles

The chief executives of computer companies are the most likely to be axed, followed by those managing financial services companies and industrial products. But, *no sector is spared and no chief executive is invulnerable to the pressure.*

The average tenure of a U.S. chief executive has halved to about four or five years during the past decade, says Challenger. But the tenure was even shorter for the incumbents of some of the United States' most promising jobs.

Procter & Gamble's Mr Jager lasted 17 months. Richard Huber, the former Aetna boss, was sacked after two and a half years, while Coca-Cola booted its chief executive, Doug Ivester in April after only one year. Other blue chip with a revolving door in the chief executive suite during the past year include Mattel, where the chief left after only three years, and Revlon, where the chief left after two.

Boosting investors' expectations and failing to achieve the expected financial results is a bad omen, according to Challenger.

Recent high-profile sackings or early departure *have also coincided with a long-term slide in the stocks' share price and increasing boardroom impatience with prospects,* he adds. Another danger sign is *failing to sell a convincing story to the board and analysts.* This could be bad news for Daimler-Chrysler's chairman, Jurgen Schrempp, and its U.S. controller, James Donlon. The company seems to be running out of gas when the auto industry is booming. Applying the same criteria, Richard Brown, chief executive of Electronic Data Systems, the world's number two computer services company might also be feeling uncomfortable. The stock plunged 25% on Friday.

Challenger said: "Being a chief executive is now a short-lived and very precarious job."

... to be continued with "Jager's Legacy to be Erased at Procter & Gamble." See end illustration.

Source: The Scotsman, Monday 12 June 2000, Business Section, p. 19; used with permission. Article provided by Duncan Hughes, New York.

Introduction

CEOs under fire; plunging share prices; loss of investor confidence; sacking senior executives; revolving boardroom doors; failing to tell or sell convincing stories ... All these points are illustrative of the need for chief executive officers, board level personnel, corporate communication directors and managers, and the organizations they represent to communicate effectively with stakeholders who could impact upon organizational performance. All are part and parcel of the fiercely enhanced competitive environment of the 21st-century globalized marketplace.

In our recent book *Communicating Globally: An Integrated Marketing Approach* (Schultz and Kitchen, 2000), we stated that the challenge facing organizations the world over is the need for a transitioning process. Transitions in production and manufacturing. Transitions in logistics and distribution. And, most importantly, transitions in marketing and communication. It is simply not feasible to continue to use marketing and communication approaches developed for and in the Industrial Age in an arena of globalization, electronic commerce, instantaneous communication and the like.

We argued in that book that the best mechanism for making the transition in marketing and communication was (and is) the integration of all efforts, that is, the development of process, of systems, of coordination. In short, the integration of all forms of marketing communication both inside and outside the organization. We also suggested many ideas, tools, models, concepts, and measurement devices to ensure that – in the marketing communication domain at least – CEOs, senior marketing executives, marketing managers, brand managers, and all those organizations servicing their needs were equipped with the appropriate tools to compete effectively in this new marketplace. These tools, concepts, and ideas are necessary when organizations are faced with the need to transition from where they are now, to where they need to be in the newly wired globally integrated world of the 21st century (see Figure 1.1).

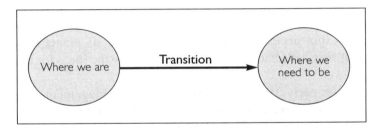

Figure 1.1 Transition is the challenge

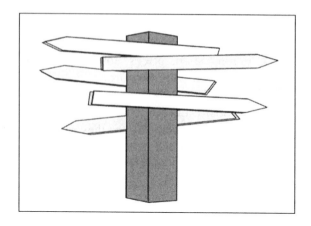

Figure 1.2 Directionless digression

But we still felt that we had not addressed all of the necessary organizational communication issues. There was and still is a gap in the development and practice of marketing and communication. Our study of many texts – both academic and practitioner – which offered structure and direction for all forms of communicating being done at the corporate level, suggested a diversity of operations which when summed resembled a scenario of the man who mounted his horse and rode off – *in all directions* (see Figure 1.2).

This type of structureless, or at least unfocused approach, in today's world, is of little value. Today, organizations – multinational, global or national and even local – are inevitably cast in the role of communicators. While many are not terribly well skilled in the field, they are nevertheless required by modern business situations to become so, and fail to do so at their peril.

In this book we still proclaim the virtues of integrated marketing and communication approaches, but from a different overarching corporate perspective. A perspective that suggests that the corporation is at least as important as the products or services it vends. A perspective that says the firm and its outputs are tremendously influenced by the perceptions of its stakeholders, not necessarily the actual output of its plants or service centers. But first, let's backtrack and explain where the ideas for this book came from.

Back in the early 1990s, a leading guru of management thought – Professor Charles Handy then of London Business School – published a book titled *The Empty Raincoat*. The title refers to a sculpture seen by

Professor Handy in an open-air sculpture garden in Minneapolis. Of the three shapes created by Judith Shea, the dominant shape was a bronze raincoat, standing upright, but with no one inside it. For Handy, the empty raincoat served as a paradox for the apparent emptiness of much that was done in the name of technological, industrial, or post-industrial "progress." In this book, we will use Handy's paradox in a different way. To us, the empty raincoat seems to personify the apparent "emptiness" of so many corporate entities. Emptiness in the sense that the firm may seem to be cold, distant, unfeeling, and often unrelated to the customers and consumers it desires to serve. In the drive for globalization, too many times the corporate parent has disappeared leaving a group of unidentified brand children to prove their worth and value. For example, in the consumer-oriented world of the 21st century, it is not just the brands that these corporations manage and market that are important to consumers, but the corporations themselves. In today's world, executives and managers at all levels, from the CEO downwards, must reach out and communicate *not only with customers and consumers* from whom they expect to extract sales and profits, but also with various related and involved publics and stakeholders – each of whom can impact markedly on both short-term and long-term market share and profit performance. Thus the corporation, in our view, has become a brand that also needs to be "marketed," or, put another way, *communicated* for in our view, most marketing is communication and most communication is essentially marketing.

What we mean by "raising the corporate umbrella" is that senior executives, led by the CEO, need to conceive and present the organization in such a way that it not only protects and nurtures all the individual brands and customer relationships within its portfolio, but that the organization stands for something other than an anonymous faceless profit-taking corporate entity. Such an organization and its total meaning, that is, its "corporate umbrella" cannot be hoisted by empty corporate entities. The corporation can only be communicated when its managers understand and practice a total integrated communication program that puts reality and realism inside the firm that can then be communicated outside to the various stakeholders and those who have or might have a relationship of some sort with the firm. The goal of this text is to put flesh on the bones of the corporation and raise the corporate umbrella in such a way that:

(a) it acts as a forcefield metaphor – nurturing, protecting, and providing the resource-fertile environment to grow individual brands and stakeholder relationships as valuable and potentially irreplaceable assets.

(We reiterate our premise that brands are "owned" by customers and consumers even though they may be "managed" by organizations.)

and

(b) it acts as a metaphor in terms of the way it can be operationalized at the corporate level. In other words, integrated communication acts like the ribs of an umbrella in that the various communication activities of the firm support the overall communication system. Lose or mismanage one of the communication "ribs" such as crisis management or corporate advertising and the whole communication coverage of the organization becomes unstable and exposed to the stormy winds of change.

The contextual background

The most recognizable development in business and management today is the globalization of markets for products and services (Kitchen, 1999). For many businesses and industries, business extends well beyond the national marketplace. Even those businesses which doggedly proclaim national focus are still impacted upon and affected by global economic and competitive forces. The reality is that communication and technology, taken as a double-edged sword of convergence, have created a global marketplace. Globalization, though an undoubted reality for many smaller nation states such as Sweden prior to 1980, has enjoyed continuous development since these days. Dunning, writing in 1993, astutely commented that by the early 1990s, the decision-making nexus of multinational companies:

> had come to resemble the central nervous system of a much larger group of inter-dependent, but less formally governed activities, aimed primarily at advancing the globally competitive strategy and positioning of the core organization.

And yet, what is meant by the term "multinational"? Automatically, we think of corporations such as Kodak, Nestlé, Coca-Cola, Microsoft, Unilever, IBM, De Beers, General Motors, Nike, and Ford. From photography to pharmaceuticals, cola to computers, soap to software, and diamonds to detergents, the markets addressed by these corporations span the entire world – a world dominated by three major regional markets – the U.S.A./Canada, Europe, and the Pacific Rim area, led by Japan. Every multinational organization aims to advance its already remarkable global position – either in market value, market share, revenue, or profit terms – by means of global strategy and global positioning. Yet, these huge corporations are not the only firms competing globally. Craig and Douglas (1995), writing before the wave of dot.com companies had crashed on the beach of unresponsive global markets, indicated the emergence of the new breed of "mini-multinationals" which "target specialty niche or what increasingly are being called 'vertical markets' worldwide." Today, they are found in such areas as precision instruments, medical equipment, computer peripherals, steel, chemicals, and a host of other "industries." Their strategy is similar to that of the giant multinationals, to advance globally in terms of competitive strategy and to position their organization appropriately in their selected arenas. For either multi, mini, or "wannabe" multinationals – the real question is how do firms advance competitive strategy and positioning globally? Dunning (1993) continues:

> it does this by combining its *organizational resources* with those it acquires from other firms; second by its technology, product and marketing strategies; and third, by the nature of the alliances it concludes with other firms (italics added).

Notice the threefold focus of gaining and retaining global competitive advantage: organizational resource; control over technology and marketing; and strategic alliances. Each of these can and does relate to communication at the marketing and the corporate level. But corporations also need to:

- take full advantage of economies of scale and scope arising from global integration. This includes significant economies arising from experience and learning curve effects in both manufacturing and marketing

- have a proper understanding of differences in supply capabilities and consumer needs in different countries. This understanding would be derived from nationally and internationally integrated databases which monitor supply and demand (current and future) side capabilities and needs

- use the experience gained in global and national markets to strengthen the resource base of the firm as a whole (adapted from Bartlett and Ghoshal, 1998).

As shown in Figure 1.3 the resource base of the business is being continually strengthened by information from both the supply and demand

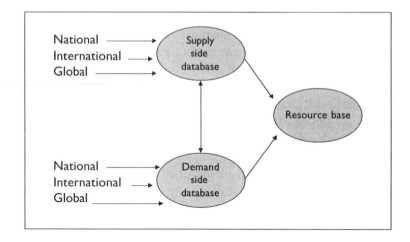

Figure 1.3 Strengthening the resource base

side. Information not just about labor, capital, and technology, but also information about markets, customers, consumers, and stakeholders or publics. Part of this information will constitute an image of the company, what it is, what it does, what it stands for, who its personalities may be – and this image impacts on organizational performance in the markets or constituencies where the business competes or seeks to compete. The resource base of the organization then links to what the organization actually does to develop and sustain corporate identity and corporate relationships and to protect and nurture the strategic business units and individual brands within its portfolio. But, the raising of corporate identity must depend upon balance – balance between globalization, localization, and learning experience will ... vary according to the nature and range of products produced (or services marketed), where they are produced, and firm specific characteristics. It will also depend on the channels of knowledge within the enterprise and the way in which decisions are taken (paraphrased from Dunning, 1993).

Businesses will not all be at the same stage of development, nor may global corporations wish to present themselves globally in all markets. Indeed, in our experience, most organizations go through various stages in their movement from strictly local to global giants.

Corporate strategy and senior decision-making means that businesses will range along various continuums from local to global dependent on contextual circumstance in terms of market factors and organizational culture. But, as stated earlier, the aim is always to enhance the competitive strategy and position of the core organization and to build and strengthen relationships with customers and publics (Kitchen, 1997).

But questions arise. The evidence from a variety of perspectives indicates that globalization of business, markets, technology, and communication is positioned on a steeply ascending learning curve. Businesses and executives are responding to these changes and developments, some rapidly, some more slowly. The major function of corporate strategy is to maintain or enhance competitive performance and to generate and bind to the organization customers and consumers that provide the necessary income flows for the firm to survive. Naturally, the lion's share of corporate strategy, by dint of necessity, generally is devoted to marketing activities. Our argument (Schultz and Kitchen, 2000) is that this is spearheaded by globally integrated marketing communication and well planned and executed communication programs among all important publics and stakeholders. But behind every brand, and every strategic business unit and indeed every local operation, is the corporation. What does it stand for? What is known regarding its overall profile? Where and how does it compete? Against whom? What does it contribute over and above marketing exchanges? How can its personality be best represented? In the eyes of which stakeholders or publics? We turn to some of these questions now.

Raising the corporate umbrella

It has been argued that a multinational or global firm's personality and image will become the biggest factors in consumer choice between its products and services and those selected from competitors (Eales, 1990; Melewar and Saunders, 1998, 2000). We agree with this premise, but personality and image do not just impact on consumer choice and behavior, but also on a variety of publics or stakeholders, whose views and behaviors can markedly impact on overall corporate performance and simultaneously exert a positive or negative influence on consumers, governments and shareholders.

If one seeks to raise a corporate umbrella over the basketful of individual brands within an organization, the question then becomes ... *in what way is the business, the organization, the corporation ... a "brand" in its own right*? Admittedly, the question arises from the long series of studies that relate to making brands recognizable. But, in today's world, the corporation commonly must be visible, and visibility requires planning, forethought, vision, and most of all, flawless execution. Raising the corporate umbrella requires:

■ development and articulation of a coherent integrated corporate vision where the central concept is corporate brand identity. This brand identity requires an internal organizational brand building focus, that rests inexorably on accurate measurement of external brand image studies among key stakeholders (adapted from Kapferer, 1992, 1996)

■ recognition that a strong corporate brand is a strategic asset for the corporation or firm. It may add value to product brands in terms of globally integrated marketing communication; may attract potential employees; fortify trust in share values in terms of investor relations (van Riel, 1997, 2000); or fulfill a host of other corporate communication objectives in relation to key stakeholders.

Such a corporate brand has been described by van Riel (1997) as:

> a set of values perceived as typical for a specific company in the eyes of a variety of stakeholders. Naturally the subsets of attributes linked to the corporate brand will differ according to the nature of the relationship every stakeholder group has with the company. Financial audiences will focus on financial aspects, consumers on products, etc.

van Riel, citing Schultz et al. (1993), then makes the crucial point that:

> *the power of a corporate brand will increase* **if various stakeholders perceive the same** (or at least similar) **basic values as crucial in their appreciation of the company**. Consistency avoids contradictions, limits fragmentation, increases recognition of a company, resulting in a higher degree of familiarity and appreciation.

In the world of marketing it is noted that over time, product differentiation tends to reduce in firm after firm and industry after industry (Porter, 1980). The same phenomenon is noted in service companies and industries. For many firms, developing and building corporate identity or corporate branding has become a desirable necessity. Consumers in many advanced western markets have become less gullible, less trusting, and they have a desire to know of the corporations behind the brands that they purchase and consume. Thus, the corporate brand (as it is perceived) has become an important determinant of purchase intent and behavior. Let's explore the concept of basic values further by using the corporate umbrella concept (see Figure 1.4).

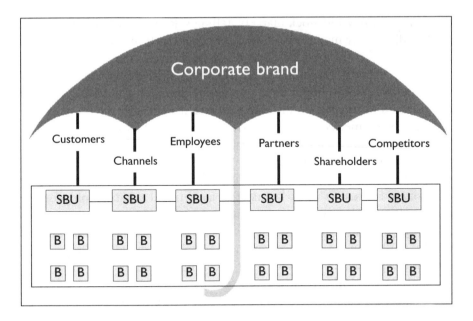

Figure 1.4 Raising the corporate umbrella

This figure represents the corporate umbrella concept raised as a protective nurturing device held over the strategic business units and individual brands within its portfolio. Each element of the "umbrella" needs to be decoded.

The handle of the umbrella is placed or should be placed in the hands of the senior operational officer of the corporation. This may mean either the chief executive officer or executive chairman of the board of directors of the corporation. The title is not as important as the fact that the individual (and it usually is an individual) has executive authority, as empowered by the articles of association and the board of directors, to develop and implement communication and operational strategy on behalf of the corporation. However, few individuals have been with today's multinationals since their inception. Exceptions to this include Richard Branson the Virgin CEO, and Anita Roddick, Founder and CEO of The Body Shop. Above many other aspects of the CEO's role, communication to a wide range of publics or stakeholders is crucial to organizational success and development, and will impact markedly on SBU growth and development, and brand performance.

The stem of the umbrella represents the core values that have become associated with the organization over time. In the initial and closing illustration to this chapter, the "reign" of Durk Jager was cut short by poor performance on world stock markets, falling sales and profitability, and an evident distrust by major shareholders of departure from traditional values. Hence Lafley's "back to the future" approach in the closing illustration. The essence of all corporate brand relationships is trust. Where there is trust, market values remain high, purchasers remain loyal, and employees are attracted to stay within the company and sustain and support its development over time. According to Micklethwait and Wooldridge (1997), trust can only be sustained if fairness is built into the heart of operational and strategic policy. However, if an organization is seen to be patently unfair, this destroys trust and a spiraling downward cycle of distrust can be encountered. Trust is most keenly felt as betrayal when employees are disheartened and communicate their negative impressions to other listening and impressionable publics. One recent example is the lack of trust in the Labour government and its leadership in the U.K. The empowerment of spokesmen for Tony Blair, the Prime Minister, who are known for applying the philosophy of spin-doctoring – the modern day equivalent of Machiavellianism – lies behind the loss of votes, a greater mistrust among the electorate in terms of politics, politicians, and the political process, and of course dissenting voices within the leadership and rank and file of the Labour Party. We have been reminded recently by Gronstedt (2000) that:

> communicating the vision with words alone will lead management down the path of slogans and exhortations.
>
> No matter how impeccable the rhetoric of top management is, or how frequently it is repeated, employees and stakeholders listen to their actions more than their words. It is management's actions that determine if the vision becomes a force of corporate unity or a source of employee criticism.

Ind (1998) also reminds us that core values stem usually from the convictions of a founder, are reinforced or amended by experience, and nurtured by key groups within an organization. Only if these values assist in achieving organizational goals do they tend to become firmly embedded. Values need to be:

- indicative of strategic intent
- widely shared in terms of aspiration
- obsessed with winning
- exhibit consistency of purpose over time.

Values that do not exhibit these characteristics tend to have a negative impact on the organization over time. Likewise an obsession with winning, if pursued in a way that treats employees as dispensable cogs in the machine, or consumers as yet more fish in the marketing sea, will not exercise a leadership position in today's or tomorrow's global markets.

The ribs of the umbrella refer to the integrated communication activities of the firm in support of the overall communication system. Lose, mismanage, or damage one of the communication "ribs" such as crisis management or corporate advertising (see Figure 1.6) and the whole communication coverage of the organization becomes unstable in the winds of change as indicated in Figure 1.5, allowing turbulence to impact on strategic business units and brands.

The breakage of one of the ribs reduces the ability of the overarching umbrella concept to protect the organization against the prevailing competitive environment. Stakeholders, likewise, become uneasy about organizational ability to deliver on the core values and mission of the organization.

However, Figure 1.4 also illustrates that corporate image can be impacted by the performance of a strategic business unit or one of the brands within its portfolio. As strategic business units exert a powerful influence over the brands within their own ambit so they also interact with customers, channels, and competitors, and may adversely affect other strategic business units also. Hence the need for integrated corporate communication activities, so that corporate values permeate every level of the organizational structure. This facet of integrated communication will be discussed further in Chapter 5.

Figure 1.5 Exposed to the winds of change

The 21st-century need

The 21st century will be one of tremendous change and diversity (Keegan, 2000). By the year 2010, the world's population will have risen to 7.2 billion (currently 6.1 billion); world GNP per capita will approximate $40,537 billion (currently $30,169 billion) of which the triad areas U.S.A./Canada, Pacific Rim, led by Japan, and the European Community will attract about 48 percent (currently 58 percent). Almost irrespective of the distribution and widening of world markets, multinationals will be poised to take full advantage of market and marketing opportunities on a global scale. By 2010 the manufacturer-driven marketplace, and the distribution-driven marketplace will have been dwarfed in comparison (cited in Schultz and Kitchen, 2000) with the global marketplace, which is characterized by interactivity. The most obvious characteristic of the interactive marketplace is that buyers, customers, consumers, and stakeholders will have significantly greater access to information than in any previous phase of economic and social development. Corporations will be more visible than ever before. They will have to exercise social responsibility to a greater extent than ever before. All businesses, irrespective of the location of corporate headquarters, will have to build real relationships with real stakeholders. Note the word "real" – *not* outbound, based on spin, rhetoric, and one-way communication, but based on a correct understanding of the dynamics of served markets and constituencies throughout the world in which the organization is competing.

Overview and plan of the book: constituent elements decoded

The book has been developed for practitioners and students who wish to develop knowledge, skills, and insight in global corporate communication. Here, we will draw upon the views, opinions, expertise, and in-depth knowledge of a range of practitioners, consultants, and teachers in this new dynamic area. Each of them is actively involved in their area of expertise. Each either has developed or is developing a global knowledge via their relationships with leading national, multinational or global organizations. But, given the early stage in the field of building and implementing corporate communication as it strives to become a profession, note that it is:

shaped by its tools. The professions of advertising and marketing, our theories, practices, and even the basic sciences that it draws on are determined by the tools at its disposal at any time. (Harris, 1997)

Figure 1.6 illustrates the architectural framework or the tools available to develop skills and insight into raising the corporate umbrella.

- This chapter provides the basic rationale and structural overview of the book.

- In Chapter 2 Ted Zorn places communication leadership where it rightly belongs – in the hands of the chief executive officer. The concept of "talking heads" suggests that CEOs not only have the task of leading and directing the corporation, but also of communicating with confidence with the various stakeholders and publics who constitute the organization's sphere of influence and who often raise major social questions about the firm. Done effectively and well this can make a significant difference in today's congested and often contentious marketplace(s). This chapter explains the problems and challenges facing CEOs and those who assist them, then suggests strategies for meeting these challenges.

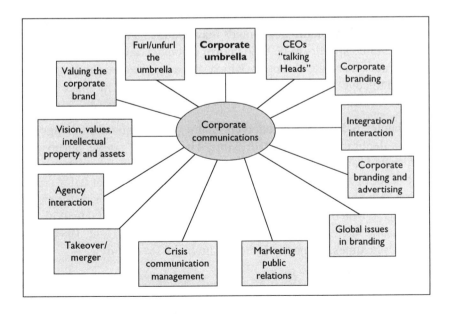

Figure 1.6 Transition is the challenge

■ In Chapter 3 Cees van Riel (1995) – who has offered singular leadership in the field of corporate communication – and Guido Berens address the distinguishing characteristics of the building blocks of corporate identity and its (hopefully) clearly mirrored reflection – corporate image. Image has been generally accepted as the "picture of how an organization is perceived by target groups," while identity has to do with the way an organization presents itself to its target audiences or publics. A main aim of this chapter is to provide insight into the question of whether the corporate branding strategy of a multi-business company should be focused on uniformity or variety. The authors provide and discuss the SIDEC model, which can be an important aid in solving this question.

■ In Chapter 4 Richard Varey addresses the issue of responsive and responsible managerial practices inside corporate communication management. He suggests that communication be repositioned away from simply transmissive to aggressively participatory. The old battles associated with "turf wars," adversarialism, and imperialism need to be replaced with interaction, integration, and development of internal consistency to be effective in the globalized world of the 21st century.

■ In Chapter 5 the editors further develop the subject of integrated communication and integrated marketing communication. This is not an "either–or" scenario. For some organizations the brand *will* be the organization, for others, individual brands may reside in a corporate entity that on face value appears to be little known among certain crucial publics or constituencies. The extent to which the corporate umbrella can be opened to cover all aspects of the organization, and the rationale for that "umbrella coverage," will be developed and explained here.

■ In Chapter 6 Jim Garrity unravels many of the critical challenges of corporate branding and advertising. The biggest single purpose of corporate branding is to build recognition, especially for organizations that need, or appear to need, "umbrella identification" that is for corporations who have widely diversified or broad product lines or for organizations in which there are potential significant levels of public criticism such as the nuclear power conglomerates (Grunig and Hunt, 1984). But, as Jim illustrates, corporate branding involves several areas:

■ branding versus advertising
■ from branding to integrated marketing communication
■ building a corporate brand from a product base
■ going to the next level

■ extending the brand
■ benchmarking best practices
■ cohesiveness.

■ Marilyn Roberts tackles the issues concerning corporate communication in an expansive and expanding globalization of markets in Chapter 7. As was discussed earlier in the book, much of business in today's world is carried out in a global marketplace. Improved communication and accelerated technological developments have underpinned the emergence of the global marketplace and the implications of this affect every facet of business performance and activity. Products, services, customer patterns or profiles, communication strategies, and organizational images either *are global* now, or have the potential to be such in the future. This chapter utilizes the findings from the Global Best Practices Study. Among those who participated were BBDO Worldwide, Bozell Worldwide, Grey International, J. Walter Thomson, McCann-Erickson Worldwide, Saatchi & Saatchi, TBWA, and Young and Rubicam Advertising.

■ Tom Harris, the author of *The Marketer's Guide to Public Relations* (1993), addresses the topic of how marketing public relations can be used as part of the corporate umbrella in Chapter 8. Many corporations employ the same public relations and advertising agencies to build not only individual brand imagery but also enhance the corporate identity program. The issue of interaction between corporate and marketing communication activities cannot be neatly dichotomized into separatist functional activities. Instead they are mutually interactive, synergistic, and mutually reinforcing. Harris illustrates these points in detail in his discussion.

■ Issues and crises can upset the most carefully crafted corporate communication identity program. Despite the armor plating of many corporate entities, like the Titanic the hull can be breached and disaster threatened by unconsidered eventualities and ill-timed and unplanned processes. Jim Lukaszewski shows how a well-earned corporate reputation can vanish in minutes if no plans are in place to deal with all potential issues and crises *before and while* they occur. There is really no substitute for clear and well articulated values which become the hallmark of proactive corporate social responsibility. Chapter 9 is targeted toward practitioners in the global marketplace and their senior managers who must be able to recognize and proactively respond to the risks that arise from corporate and employee interaction with significant constituencies or stakeholders locally and globally. Given the nature of crisis communication and the related ethical issues, this chapter is the longest in the book.

■ The theme of threats and opportunities to corporate communication is continued in Chapter 10 by Richard Varey. No stock-market quoted organization is ever free from the specter of potential takeover, even when this comes in the welcome guise of future merged growth potentialities. The issue of preparedness and indeed protection from unwanted advances is addressed here and how communication can be used to protect the firm or to provide rationale for proactive programs. Clearly, there are some interesting stories to tell and rationales to explore. A number of roles are identified for corporate communication management and the professional manager of communication in preventative and action measures.

■ In Chapter 11, Shekar Swamy addresses the nature of the corporation, its great commercial purpose, and how these huge organizations act as engines of prosperity and growth. However, such organizations – in their very genesis – have inherent adversarial relations with various constituents. The questions tackled here include: how can communication assist in aligning those various divergent views? And, how can external agencies help in reducing corporate vulnerability? Other significant issues in the relationship between corporations, agencies, and external publics are also addressed here.

■ Anders Gronstedt has recently addressed many significant communication issues in *The Customer Century* (2000). Here in Chapter 12, Don Schultz and Anders address the significant issues of "vision, values, intellectual property, and assets." These issues connect closely with other chapters in the text. Admittedly, most business organizations have been built on the basis of vision – rapidly supported by raw materials in the form of labor and capital, land, factories, and buildings. These elements of business building are still of vital import. But, real wealth is not generated by these elements. Instead, wealth and success in the 21st century will be built on the potentialities, and actualities of the human mind – knowledge, experience, understanding, and capabilities. But, we emphasize the fact that while corporate leaders – CEOs – will be able to show their way ahead in terms of visioning, and be privileged, as was Winston Churchill to give the shout that energized the [nation], intellectual capital is within the potentiality of every member of the corporation. All have something to contribute. But businesses have value, not just to themselves, but to a broad range of stakeholders. How can corporate communication develop or deliver the value(s) inherent in the corporation? That is the question tackled here.

■ Chapter 13 addresses the value of the corporate brand and how much actual financial worth it comprises. However, a very real issue tackled here is what convinces senior management or the financial community to make brand investments? Here, Don Schultz describes a practical approach, acceptable to both management and the financial community, to brand valuation. It is described in layman's terms as far as possible, so that the process is transparent and all calculations are fairly obvious.

■ Finally, we conclude with Chapter 14. As the book began with the transliterated metaphor (of Handy's empty raincoat), we end with it. We have indicated throughout the text that values, trust, responsibilities, and relationships are inherent to our process of "raising the corporate umbrella." In this chapter we ostensibly close one somewhat worn and torn corporate umbrella, admittedly associated with success in the 20th century. Recast, reconstituted, and rebuilt, we then unfurl the new corporate umbrella which organizations need in the 21st century. The ribs of this latter "umbrella" are, however, not seen as prescriptive and each corporate communication manager and those responsible for corporate communication will have to review them and see how they fit his or her specific organization, or can be adapted in relation thereto.

Both corporate and marketing communication need to be used in terms of "raising the corporate umbrella." Interaction and integration between these two vital strands of communication lead to synergistic outcomes. Please note, however, that we are not advocating that the corporate umbrella be unfurled to its maximum extent over all organizational activities throughout the world, unless this is the strategic desirable outcome from corporate values and mission. For most values, the umbrella concept will be applied in the same way that globalization is applied now ... that is, raise the corporate umbrella wherever strategically and tactically possible. In some cases, it may be necessary, however, to retain focus on a strategic business unit name and the gamut of related individual brands. Indeed brand architecture whether global or local is a key element in holding all the "ribs" of the corporate umbrella together.

Summary and conclusion

This chapter has:

- indicated the current performance pressures on CEOs and the centrality of CEO communication

- shown the need for organizations to transition from where they are now to where they need to be

- developed the corporate umbrella concept in terms of the handle, stem, cloth, and ribs

- described the fiercely competitive contextual and critically sensitive stakeholder environment

- shown how the resource base of the firm can be strengthened

- described how inadequacy in terms of developing the umbrella concept can allow the organization to be afflicted by environmental storms in the context of the 21st century

- outlined the structural architecture of the text.

We now invite readers to travel the road of corporate communication with us. In the following pages the conceptual ideas will be unfolded more fully. We will draw upon expert views in the domain of corporate communication. Our aim is to provide an accurate map of the terrain which corporations and their leading personnel need to traverse in their quest for survival, growth and profitability in the 21st century.

ILLUSTRATION

"Jager's Legacy to be Erased at Procter & Gamble"

Introduction

The methods of Procter & Gamble's ex-chief executive, Durk Jager, who departed P&G in June 2000, were ultimately too ambitious even for an industry known for its ruthless competition. His whirlwind 17 months at the top put the United States' largest producer of household goods on a path for change that turned into a dead-end.

The lasting legacy?

The new chiefs made it known within hours of Jager's departure that they would systematically dismantle his heritage and return to traditional values. Alan Lafley, a 23-year veteran of the company has taken over as chief executive with John Pepper, Mr Jager's predecessor and rival, called out of retirement to become chairman.

Historical background

Mr Jager, who served with the company for 29 years before taking the top post in January last year, had the shortest tenure of any chief executive in the company's 163-year history. His style produced inconsistent results and created friction on both Wall Street and at the company's head office in Cincinnati.

New kid on the block?

Mr Lafley wasted no time in spelling out his back-to-the-future agenda to get profits back on track after two straight quarters of disappointments and a $75 billion drop in market value. He said: "It is clear we changed too much too fast. As a result, we did not make enough tough choices to balance top and bottom-line growth." He also flagged a review of the company's longer-term growth plans. "The transition that we expected to take about a year to complete is clearly going to take a year longer."

But Mr Lafley's core problem of delivering strong and sustainable growth will not go away.

The core problem

Mr Jager's plan, code-named Operation 2005, was to almost double sales and earnings in the next five years by streamlining operations and focusing on new products. It called for the cutting of 15,000 jobs, the closure of ten plants, centralizing management, and putting more resources into promoting products and getting them to market quickly.

But the company's earnings continued to drop as sales slowed. The strong dollar also hurt P&G's revenue in Europe. In January 2000, its market value fell $38 billion after botched merger talks with drug giants Warner Lambert and American Home Products. Two months later, P&G warned that its third-quarter profits would be smaller than expected and shares suffered another

ILLUSTRATION (cont'd)

30 percent drop. Last week's warnings that it would not meet earnings forecasts pushed the share value down to 1997 levels. On Friday 9th June 2000, the share price closed at $53 compared with a 52-week high of $118.

Watch this space

Clearly Mr Lafley is to be faced with a number of strategic and operational issues. Many of these revolve around the need to communicate change effectively with a number of key stakeholders. Can this be done? Certainly, yes.

Will it be done? Let's check again in eighteen months time.

Source: The Scotsman, Monday 12 June 2000, Business Section, p. 19; used with permission (subtitle, headings and endnote added). Article provided by Duncan Hughes and Jon Rees.

Acknowledgement

We gratefully acknowledge our thanks to *The Scotsman* for permission to include the two articles cited in the text of this chapter.

Talking heads: the CEO as spokesperson

2

ted zorn

Stephen Tindall and The Warehouse

Stephen Tindall is founder and CEO of The Warehouse, the most successful department store in New Zealand. From humble beginnings with just one store and three employees in 1982, The Warehouse has grown to about 90 stores in New Zealand in 2001. In 2000 the company expanded into Australia by buying a chain of 130 stores that are being re-branded to The Warehouse's name and design. Growth and profits are impressive. The company increased its net profit 30% to NZ$70 million in the most recent fiscal year. Average annual sales growth since 1997 has been 20% and its net earnings growth 26%. As a dramatic illustration of its success, New Zealand's total department store sales increased by about $94 million in 1998, of which $93 million came from The Warehouse. Tindall was chosen as the Deloitte/*Management* Executive of the Year in 1998, and The Warehouse as the Deloitte/*Management* company of the year in 2000.

A Warehouse store is immediately recognizable as a large "Red Shed" and its slogan, "The Warehouse: Where everyone gets a bargain," is, as one writer put it, now as well known in New Zealand as the national anthem (Tapsell, December 1998). Tindall himself is something of a national icon. Recently named *Management* magazine's most popular leader (Tapsell, April 1998), Tindall is widely respected for the growth and financial success of The Warehouse, but he is known for much more than that.

He also has a unique approach to being the spokesperson for the company: "My job is to try now and nurture the leadership in the company and the well-being through our 'people come first' philosophy and make sure it goes right through the organization ... I see it as more important to be with our people rather than just waving the company's flag with the big people we trade with" (Tapsell, April 1998).

However, that doesn't mean Tindall stays out of the public eye. Quite the contrary, he is often in the news explaining some innovative Warehouse policy, such as parallel importing, the application of new technology, or employee-friendly practices. Just as often, he ends up not directly speaking about The Warehouse at all, but about sustainable, socially responsible business practices or investing in a new technology start-up venture. Tindall and The Warehouse were high-profile founding members of the New Zealand Business Council for Sustainable Development (NZBCSD) as well as New Zealand Businesses for Social Responsibility (NZBSR).

Tindall gets an enormous amount of positive press for the Warehouse's success and for his enthusiastic endorsement of causes and initiatives that have popular appeal. Certainly The Warehouse benefits from its association with these causes and initiatives. That is, consumers are attracted not only to the prospect of getting a bargain, but also to the pro-environment, pro-employee, and pro-New Zealand image projected by Tindall and Warehouse practices. One issue here, given the expansion to Australia is how the pro-New Zealand element of this image will have to be altered, given the almost traditional competitiveness of the two cultures. The same issue has also affected The Body Shop in their expansion, especially in the U.S.A. market (see illustration in Chapter 4). However, insofar as New Zealand is concerned, even in Tindall's communication that is not directly promoting The Warehouse, he builds the brand identity of the company. In fact, I would argue that perhaps his most powerful brand-building communication does not even mention The Warehouse. This is in line, of course, with many other corporate CEOs whose image extends beyond that of the corporation they represent, while nonetheless impacting favorably upon it.

Source: Author.

Introduction and overview

In Chapter 1, the CEO is described as holding the handle of the umbrella, that is, serving as the primary person to raise the corporate umbrella. This is a useful analogy, because it points to the CEO as the focal point or driving force behind the corporate communication process. But the CEO often does much more than raise the umbrella so that others may speak for them. There are many examples of CEOs such as Stephen Tindall, Anita

Roddick, Jack Welch, and Richard Branson who, by the force of their personalities and communication, create and help sustain a strong and attractive corporate image that appeals to a host of stakeholders, including customers, investors, and employees. Moreover, such corporate leaders come to represent for stakeholders and the wider public not only their specific companies, but also sets of values and positions on prominent issues of the day. Sam Walton, the ex-Wal-Mart CEO, now deceased, was another excellent corporate communicator.

There is also a danger here in that the "raising the umbrella" analogy, or indeed any focus on overt strategic communication, can suggest an insincere posing for the purpose of promotion or persuasion, creating cynicism rather than a positive response from stakeholders. This insincerity needs to be avoided at all costs, as customers, clients, or stakeholders will soon "wise up" to anything that smacks of spin-doctoring or Machiavellianism. Raising the corporate umbrella, if it is to mean anything means coordinating and pulling together, so that the same values are portrayed *not just in words, but in all the organization seeks to do*. Rhetoric is no substitute for delivery. Tindall, for example, has been particularly successful in coming across as authentic, recently being referred to as "the Mr Nice Guy of New Zealand Business" (*National Business Review*, 19 May 2000).

In this chapter, I will demonstrate that CEOs face a number of dilemmas, or what I will refer to as dialectical tensions, in their communication. Managing these tensions is an ongoing challenge for all CEOs, and there is no one recommended strategy that fits all situations. However, the communication of some CEOs, such as Stephen Tindall who has been particularly effective, can illustrate effective strategies for managing these tensions. The aim of this chapter is to explain the problems or challenges facing the CEO as spokesperson for the organization, then to suggest some strategies for meeting these challenges.

To achieve this aim, I will first discuss CEO communication in the context of the contemporary business environment. Then, I will explain briefly a framework for analyzing CEO communication, including some of the key dialectical tensions CEOs face in communicating with multiple stakeholders. Finally, I will identify some important tools for managing these tensions, and the lessons to be garnered for corporate communicators. While the focus throughout the chapter is the CEO, implicit in the chapter is the idea that corporate communication professionals must understand the CEO's communication situation and work closely with the CEO to craft appropriate communication strategies. Thus, the analytical tools should be helpful not only to CEOs themselves, but also to corporate communication professionals as they work to assist CEOs.

The context of CEO communication

While many people in organizations today enact leadership roles, the CEO is typically the most visible. Serving as spokesperson for the organization is only one leadership role, but it is a particularly prominent and important one. As spokesperson, the CEO typically sets the tone, suggests a culture, and establishes a vision. That is, CEOs shape the context within which other organizational stakeholders (including other leaders) operate. When Jack Welch said that General Electric divisions would return 20 percent growth each year, that had a powerful framing effect on the entire company; that is, it created a frame through which to view almost all other aspects of the company. However, at the same time, the CEO is today operating in a business and social context that is different from previous eras.

Chapter 1 illustrated some important factors to consider in understanding the context of the CEO serving as the organization's spokesperson. These include the globalization of markets, increased pressures for short-term financial returns, and increased pressures on CEOs to produce such returns and tell convincing stories to create positive stakeholder perceptions. Undoubtedly, CEO public utterances also impact the financial markets. Lofty statements of unfulfilled intent have often returned to haunt such firms as Xerox, Price Line, and Procter & Gamble. In addition to these changes in business conditions are a number of broad social trends that are important to recognize, particularly the move to a post-traditional society, loss of assumed roles, and the move to negotiated meanings, rather than assumed meanings.

The social critic Norman Fairclough (1992, 1995) has identified several trends or characteristics of our "post-traditional" society with implications for the study of CEO, or more broadly, leadership communication. Most basic to this chapter is his claim that there has been a loss of assumed roles, identities, and relationships in moving from traditional to post-traditional society. Rather than a fixed feature of roles and positions as was the case in pre-modern times, identities and relationships today are negotiated (Fairclough, 1995). Thus, organizational stakeholders do not simply assume and accept an identity, but are searching and negotiating for one (or more). Nor do they assume relational definitions based on tradition, but personally and socially construct relational definitions. These trends make the negotiation of identities and relationships central to contemporary leadership communication. Both the CEO's identity and the identities of stakeholders are open to negotiation.

It is obvious, of course, that leaders today rarely assume their positions because of tradition or heritage. Instead, persons aspiring to leadership must negotiate meanings for who they are, who they are capable of becoming, and what their role as leader entails. Less obviously, it means that the negotiation of stakeholders' identities and relationships presents both a challenge and an opportunity for contemporary leaders. Since these are not fixed, stakeholders cannot be assumed to see themselves in set ways (for example as followers), nor their relationship to another person as leader–follower.

On the other hand, it does mean that people are searching for positive identities and relationships. Negotiating desirable identity and relational definitions then becomes a key influence and motivational opportunity for aspiring leaders. In fact, most contemporary theories of leadership implicitly suggest the importance of these processes. For example, transformational leadership theories suggest that leaders make followers feel like "winners" or "champions" (Bass 1985; Kouzes and Posner, 1987). That is, CEOs, via their communication, can suggest positive identities for staff, consumers, and corporate partners. Stephen Tindall's implicit message can be seen as "Associate with us and you can be part of a noble experiment to change business practices for the better" – thus suggesting an attractive identity for stakeholders.

Fairclough also argues that the role of discourse, or communication, in society has changed. Because we don't simply accept our social station as in traditional societies, but attempt to create identities and relationships via our communication, highly developed communication skills are critical. Thus we see an increased demand for "emotional labour" (Hochschild, 1983) and "communicative labour" (Fairclough, 1995) in organizations today. Effective leaders – particularly in highly visible positions such as that of the CEO – must be skilled communicators. Also, it is important to recognize that corporate communication personnel (especially the "czar") have to assist or advise the CEO in terms of identifying critical communication areas and directing the dialogue. A handsome or pretty face will only go so far these days. As is made plain in this chapter, it is simply not enough just to make a few cogent comments from time to time. These must be fundamentally related to the core values associated with the corporation and what it stands for in society.

Fairclough (1992) further indicates that the nature of social interaction has changed. For example, he describes a movement toward "informalization" in interaction, meaning that a key feature of much contemporary communication is the removal of overt power markers, thus masking the power imbalances typical of relationships such as CEOs have with stakeholders. The use of first names instead of formal titles is a clear example. In part, these trends are required for the delicate practices of negotiating identities and relationships in post-traditional society. Thus, contemporary leadership communication is likely to take on an egalitarian, interactive (versus one-way) nature. The chatty, down-home style of former Chrysler CEO Lee Iacocca comes to mind, especially when compared with the almost wooden television appearances of the Ford Chairman following the Firestone debacle. In politics this trend is readily apparent when the president or prime minister is expected to "be like us" and be likeable, while at the same time being held to high standards. With trends toward the globalization of culture, this trend is likely to be felt worldwide, but will certainly be more prominent currently in cultures Hofstede (1991) described as "low power distance," such as most English-speaking countries. In high-power distance countries such as Japan, the CEO's role has to change from one in which CEOs are rarely ever seen or heard from, to one in which they may make more substantive visible contributions to overall market performance. The recent (1999) Asean meltdown seemed to indicate that the only role played by CEOs, as some corporations encountered collapse, was that of publicized sorrow, in sackcloth and ashes.

Also characteristic of contemporary society is the increase of promotional discourse, including the seepage of the communicative practices of advertising into other realms of social life. Of course, this is due in part to the fact that identities and relationships are not fixed and must be negotiated. This suggests that contemporary leaders must engage in self-promotion to create constructions of themselves as leaders, more so than leaders in traditional societies. Research suggests that effective leaders often consciously manage the impressions they convey (Gardner and Avolio, 1998; Gardner and Cleavenger, 1998). The examples of well known corporate CEOs appearing in television and print commercials are indicative of this trend. For example, Dave Thomas, Wendy's CEO in the U.S.A., has done more television commercials than any other corporate spokesperson.

In part because of the importance of discourse in contemporary society and because of the value placed on promotional discourse to secure desired identities and relationships, we have seen the emergence of what Fairclough describes as the "technologization" of discourse. The existence of this chapter – in essence a treatise on what characterizes effective CEO communication – is evidence for this trend. That is, the fact that we are studying leadership communication and trying to identify the "technology" (or techniques) of effective CEO communication is exactly what Fairclough is referring to. The proliferation of leadership research (including the emergence of a journal specifically devoted to leadership studies) and "how to" leadership books in recent years are indicative of this trend. Habermas (1984) described this as the replacement of communicative practices by strategic practices.

A result of technologization of practices influenced by progressive informalization is "synthetic personalization," that is, a trend toward being personal and friendly in our communication for the purpose of achieving some personal or corporate goal. The standardized smile and pleasant comments we get from sales and service personnel are evidence of this. Obviously, synthetic personalization creates the potential for increased cynicism and questioning of authenticity (Fairclough, 1992). And, the cynicism makes the creation of a leadership identity characterized by sincerity and authenticity more of a challenge – and all the more important.

A final dimension of the contemporary context of CEO communication is the trend toward "marketization," or the introduction of market-oriented thinking into nearly every domain of public (and sometimes private) life (Fairclough, 1995). A key part of marketization is the glorification of traditional business values, such as free-market competition, expanding market share, and bottom-line (economic) focus. Thus, institutions such as churches, universities, and hospitals develop market plans and talk about members, students, and patients as "customers" they need to woo and serve. Alongside the marketization trend is something of a backlash against it, with people not only questioning the marketization of non-businesses, but criticizing the unquestioned acceptance of market logic in businesses as well. The backlash is due to the infusion of promotionalism into nearly every aspect of our lives, as well as to our unease with the fact that so many organizations seem to have narrowed their sense of purpose and self-definition to the market-oriented goals of growth and profit. The growth of organizations such as Business for Social Responsibility and the protests at recent meetings of the World Trade Organization are evidence of this backlash.

The above analysis suggests that CEOs today must excel at communication, and that a key facet of their communication is constructing positive relationships between themselves and the organization, on the one hand, and stakeholders on the other, as well as positive identities for the organization, themselves, and all stakeholders. These trends further suggest that the nature of leadership communication is likely to take on several characteristics, such as informal and self-promotional qualities, and that it is being "technologized" – or, carefully and strategically crafted – by those studying it and practicing it.

But, as we have seen, technologization and marketization have heightened cynicism among stakeholders, and have simultaneously heightened the value of organizations that seem sincere in their efforts to stand for more than just profit and growth at all costs.

A constructive-dramaturgical theory and transformational leadership

In previous writing (Zorn, 1995), I have explained a theoretical framework – constructive-dramaturgical theory (or, CDT) – that can be useful in analyzing the communication of CEOs. In brief, CDT suggests that communicators negotiate meanings for important phenomena – in particular, their identities and relationships. Leaders, such as CEOs, work to influence stakeholders' meanings. Of course, for the CEO, they should have a well experienced team of individuals skilled in corporate communication to draw upon for advice, and tactics in how to portray meanings most appropriately. For, for CEOs and stakeholders, meanings for the organization and its products and/or services are particularly important. However, these cannot be easily separated from the identities and relationships of the communicators (in this case, the CEO and stakeholders). Their perceptions of the organization and its products and services are loosely bound up in how they view themselves and each other (that is, their relationships and identities). For example, consider customers at a store with a well established brand and well known CEO, like The Body Shop. Customers will likely find it difficult to separate the organization and its products and services from how they think of themselves (Do I think of myself as socially conscious? Would I consider myself an environmentalist?), how they think of Anita Roddick (Is she sincere? Is she a model business leader or a bit of a crackpot?), and how they think of their relationship to Anita Roddick (Do we share the same values? Do I like what she stands for?). Branding and relationship marketing are based on the idea that our perceptions of products and services are intertwined with our identities and relationships vis-à-vis the people and companies we do business with.

A second claim of CDT is that we construct meaning using schemas, or mental models, the most basic of which is the personal construct – a bi-polar dimension of judgment, such as good–bad, rich–poor, or secure–insecure. Third, a particularly important higher level schema is role-identities. Each of us has a number of role-identities, or ways we would like to think about ourselves in particular roles (for example loving father, talented professional). Fourth, since role-identities are inherently unstable – that is, I might like to think of myself as a talented professional, but I'm not so sure sometimes – we constantly seek support for them. So, we seek evidence that we are in fact the kind of person we desire to be in a particular role. Such evidence is typically sought from self-assessments or via the way others communicate with us.

The final important component in CDT is relational dialectics, which occur in all relationships. A relational dialectic is a dynamic force – a tension – in the relationship that suggests two appealing extremes that push and pull us in the relationship. Dialectics are relational forces that are both interdependent and mutually negating. That is, both poles of a dialectic are desirable, yet enhancing one is at the expense of the other. For example, the most basic dialectic in relationships is autonomy–connection. We want to be connected to others and at the same time we desire personal autonomy, or freedom of action. But the more autonomy we seek, the less connection we tend to have, and vice versa. Thus, we work to increase connection, or closeness, in valued relationships, yet doing so often impinges on our autonomy. This is true of close personal relationships as well as business relationships. For example, I may act to increase my connection to a particular airline by joining its frequent passenger program or its VIP airport lounge club, yet doing so pressures me to give up some autonomy – that is, the free choice I have in choosing airlines when I want to travel. (I manage this particular dialectic by being a member of several airlines' frequent passenger programs!) This push and pull effect creates the dynamic nature of relationships and communication. We pursue a desired goal such as connection, only to find if we get too much of it, we want the other extreme, autonomy.

Relational dialectics are prominent in our thinking about particular relationships; that is, they suggest prominent personal constructs that we use to create meaning. In our dealings with others, these dialectics are frequently used in making sense of, and choices in, relationships.

The dialectics that characterize leader–stakeholder relationships (as with all kinds of relationships) will, to some degree, be specific to the relationship in question. However, since relationships in part reflect cultural forces, certain dialectics will be prevalent within particular cultures. Leader–stakeholder relationships in most western cultures (at least) will be characterized by the dialectics presented in Figure 2.1. Each of these will be explained briefly below.

Connection–autonomy

Connection–autonomy is the most fundamental dialectic in relationships. That is, relationships by definition imply connection, which we seek to

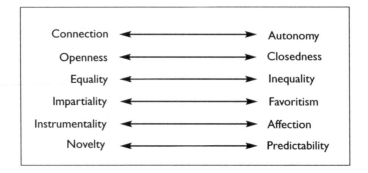

Figure 2.1 Key relational dialectics in CEO communication

establish and enhance in valued relationships; yet at the same time, relationships are made up of individuals who value personal freedom, identity, and autonomy. This dichotomy is prevalent in leader–stakeholder relationships, albeit in somewhat different manifestations. Leaders and stakeholders obviously are connected, and both will typically value a certain degree of autonomy. In fact, as Brown and Levinson (1987) have forcefully shown, the need for autonomy is fundamental to human existence and thus we strive to avoid impeding others' autonomy in our communication (for example by making requests rather than issuing orders). And, contemporary leadership models encourage leaders to foster both a close connection with followers and to empower followers to act autonomously. These leadership models emphasize shared values and vision as the basis for connection between leader and follower, and thus, the basis for influence. Followers are then empowered to act "autonomously," meaning to make their own decisions, but to be guided by the shared values and vision. Thus the autonomy they experience – empowerment – is constrained by the basis of their connection – vision and values. Similarly, organizational leaders attempt to foster close connections to valued customers and investors while at the same time recognizing their freedom to choose business elsewhere.

Regardless of the specifics of their circumstances, leaders and stakeholders will experience the connection–autonomy dialectic in some form. Their experience of the dialectical tension is likely to make connection–autonomy a primary dimension used in perceiving their relationship. This construct will in turn figure prominently in the role-identities each forms around the leader–stakeholder relationship. That is, one important dimension of judgment regarding how the CEO performs as leader is likely to be in terms of the kinds of connection formed with stake-holders and the degree to which he or she allows autonomy in relation to stakeholders when acting. This dimension (among others) will guide the CEO's choices in how to perform leadership actions, for example whether to intervene when staff are experiencing difficulty or when market research indicates customers are doing business with competitors.

Furthermore, anticipating a similar set of concerns among stakeholders, leaders and their advisors will make choices to influence stakeholders' experience of connection with and autonomy from the leader. Effective CEO/spokespersons communicate in a way that make us feel connected to them, their companies, and their products and services, without threat-ening autonomy. Stakeholders are likely to be motivated (for example to follow or support a vision) when their interaction produces a relationship in which they feel appropriately connected with and autonomous from the leader. Since both poles of the dialectic are desirable, and since the partic-ular balance will be specific to individuals and relationships, "effective" leader–stakeholder interaction is a dynamic, ongoing process of adapting and adjusting to this tension. Corporate communication professionals must be tuned in to stakeholders' changing perceptions of this balance, and advise the CEO accordingly.

Openness–closedness

A second important dialectic is openness–closedness. Effective leaders attempt to empower stakeholders with information they need and want, and attempt to develop relationships and systems that foster open lines of communication. Thus the appeal of openness. Yet, as with all human beings, leaders and stakeholders value their privacy, or closedness. Add-itionally, CEOs are privy to certain information that they choose not to disclose. And, as ample research on supervisor–subordinate commun-ication has demonstrated, workers at lower levels are reluctant for many reasons to communicate information – particularly bad news – upward.

For CEOs and communication professionals, a sense of being open with stakeholders is important. This can come through in their communication, such as the self-disclosing (and often self-deprecating) stories Lee Iacocca (former head of Chrysler) told about himself (Seeger, 1994) or via prac-tices such as open-book management. Stephen Tindall got good press for being very open about the difficulties The Warehouse had with its infor-mation systems in the mid-1990s. And he announced in 1998 that his annual reports would be changed to a "warts and all" format, providing information not only on the company's achievements, but also information on where it had fallen short on its goals.

Even though openness may seem to be the more important pole of this dialectic, a certain amount of closedness is also frequently desirable. CEOs, often experiencing intense scrutiny from the press, want to maintain a certain amount of privacy. Corporate communication professionals often serve as a buffer to allow CEOs some privacy, or distance, from the press. Likewise, stakeholders today are concerned about their privacy, particularly companies gathering information on them via unobtrusive, electronic means.

Equality–inequality

Equality–inequality is a dialectic that has emerged in research on relationships at work (Bridge and Baxter, 1992; Zorn, 1995), but not in non-work relationships. Burns (1978) argued that transforming leadership results in a "relationship of mutual stimulation and elevation that converts followers into leaders" (p. 4), and this theme of elevating followers, and encouraging them to take initiative and act autonomously, runs strong in contemporary leadership literature. The trend discussed above toward the informalization of discourse also points to this tension (Fairclough, 1992, 1995). That is, leaders often downplay status differences, thus enhancing perceptions of equality. Stephen Tindall and the late Sam Walton (former CEO of Wal-Mart) have been known for dressing informally and visiting their stores often, chatting with workers and pitching in to do work that needs doing. Yet, as long as leaders lead and followers follow, there is an inherent inequality in the relationship, and the desire for role clarity may make a certain amount of inequality desirable as well. Thus, in striving for an effective balance, CEOs and their communication advisors should look for ways to break down the barriers between CEOs and stakeholders, creating egalitarian relationships. Yet, they must simultaneously be mindful that stakeholders will expect the CEO to be "leader-like" (that is, unequal) when difficult decisions need to be made, such as in crises.

Impartiality–favoritism

Impartiality–favoritism (Bridge and Baxter, 1992) is also present in many leader–stakeholder relationships. As Bridge and Baxter argue, organizations "are typically guided by a moral order that involves the equitable treatment of everyone" (p. 203); thus the desirability of the impartiality pole. On the other hand, if as I have argued here, CEOs influence through negotiating and supporting valued role identities, stakeholders may also want to feel special or privileged, and effective leaders need to appeal to that need.

A former student who worked as an intern in the Clinton White House once told me that Bill Clinton made everyone he talked to feel special, as if they had his undivided attention. This is an excellent description of an effective handling of the impartiality–favoritism dialectic. On the one hand, the person being talked to feels special, at least for the moment. On the other hand, if everyone gets to feel special, the leader can't be accused of (unfair) favoritism.

Instrumentality–affection

Rawlins (1989) described the dialectic of instrumentality–affection in his research on adult friendships. This dialectic recognizes the tension between caring for another as an end in itself versus as a means to an end. Leaders and stakeholders sometimes develop genuine affection for each other. However, their relationships are eminently instrumental as well, in that a prominent aspect of their relational definition is the achievement of some set of goals. Given Fairclough's conclusions about synthetic personalization characterizing contemporary discourse, the instrumentality–affection tension is likely to be prominent. That is, the close connection established by charismatic leaders with stakeholders is likely to be valued and, at the same time, questioned for its authenticity. We have all experienced the situation in which we question someone acting in a friendly manner. "What does she want this time?" we might ask. CEOs and corporate communication advisors need to be careful not to be seen to be connecting with stakeholders purely for the purpose of some gain, such as a photo opportunity or smoothing the way in order to ask for some major sacrifice on the part of stakeholders.

Novelty–predictability

A final dialectic to consider is novelty–predictability. This is a tension in nearly any communication and nearly any relationship. In the context of "raising the corporate umbrella," CEOs must have enough predictability – or consistency – in their messages to establish what they and their companies stand for. Yet, when communication becomes too predictable, people cease to pay attention to it. Herb Kelleher, CEO of Southwest Airlines, is notorious for doing the outrageous – such as dressing up as Corporal Klinger (from the television show *M.A.S.H.*) at a company Christmas party. So, there's novelty in his communication. Yet, he consistently (or predictably) communicates the corporate values for which Southwest Airlines has become known, such as a sense of fun and a commitment to customer service (Freiberg and Freiberg, 1996).

Summary of dialectics

The value of a dialectics approach is that it forces us to avoid being simplistic. It forces us to consider that we can't follow a simple, prescriptive list of rules in our communication, because we and our audiences often desire goals, or end states, that are to some degree conflicting. CEOs therefore face a complex situation. Not only do they have multiple stakeholder groups to address, each group (and indeed, each individual) wants *both* autonomy and connection, *both* novelty and predictability, and so on.

Strategies for managing dialectics

Of course, there are no simple formulas for managing such complex situations. However, a number of tools are available to the CEO in communicating his or her message including listening, sensitivity, and relationship management. Corporate communication professionals must also be aware of these strategies and work with CEOs to guide their communication.

Certainly an important starting point is listening and sensitivity to the dialectical tensions that characterize CEO–stakeholder relationships. Being sensitive to dialectical tensions means staying in close contact with stakeholders to gauge their needs, desires, and concerns vis-à-vis the various dialectics. Market research, employee surveys, and other formal means of tapping stakeholder perceptions are important, and these are ways by which the corporate communication professional can be especially helpful to CEOs. But at least as important for the CEO is regular personal contact to listen and experience stakeholders' responses. Since dialectics are continually in flux, the astute communicator constantly monitors and adjusts, striving for the right balance.

The importance of sensitivity to dialectical tensions further suggests the need to develop strong relationships with key stakeholders. Ulmer (in press) demonstrates how establishing strong relationships with key stakeholders enables CEOs to weather difficult times, since stakeholders who have been courted during good times often become supporters and advocates rather than adversaries when times are tough. Many infamous cases of organizational crises such as the *Exxon Valdez* disaster or the Union Carbide disaster in Bhopal, India are examples of important stakeholders (such as local communities) being ignored or mistreated pre-crisis, only to find they become effective and costly adversaries post-crisis. Monsanto, Coca-Cola, and Firestone are also recent examples of how stakeholders can be misaligned with (apparent) failure in corporate (CEO) communications.

Framing

A set of tools that are critically important to any leader are what Fairhurst and Sarr (1996) refer to as framing. If CEOs are constantly negotiating and managing meanings with stakeholders, they must become skilled at framing issues and situations in ways that encourage stakeholders to view these issues and situations in ways favorable to the leader and organization. All events are open to multiple interpretations, and effective CEOs and other corporate communicators work proactively to frame situations in particular ways. The importance of framing becomes especially obvious in crises. Aaron Feuerstein, CEO of Malden Mills, a textile company based in the northeastern U.S.A., faced a particularly challenging crisis when a fire destroyed his textile mill. There are many ways he could have framed his response to the crisis. He could have taken the opportunity to frame it as "the last straw" that drove him to move his company to another location with cheaper labor costs, as nearly all his competitors had done. He could have framed it in terms of searching for someone to blame. Instead, as one newspaper reported:

> With one of his buildings still burning behind him, the 69-year-old owner of Malden Mills ... spoke the words everyone in the [community] wanted to hear ... "We're going to continue to operate in Lawrence ... We had the opportunity to run to the south many years ago. We didn't do it then, and we're not going to do it now." (Milne, 1995, p. B50, *The Boston Globe* December 12, 1995)

Feuerstein framed the response as a commitment to his workers and the community (Ulmer, in press).

Importantly with tools such as framing, the words spoken must correspond with action. That is, as important as the spoken communication is, even the most skilled framing can backfire if it is seen in stark contrast to the CEO's other actions. At least, there must be close enough correspondence for the words to be credible. As Ulmer showed in his analysis of the Malden Mills crisis, Feuerstein's words were consistent with a long pattern of words and actions demonstrating commitment to stakeholders both before and after the crisis. There are a number of specific framing tools CEOs can use in their communication. Fairhurst and Sarr (1996) provide a detailed analysis of framing tools such as metaphors, jargon, contrast, spin, and stories. These are depicted in an adapted form in Table 2.1.

Table 2.1 provides a brief explanation of framing approaches. For example, contrast is a technique used to describe something in terms of its opposite. It can be useful to emphasize the importance or unusual nature of a choice. One of the unusual actions Feuerstein took in the aftermath of the Malden Mills fire was to pay hourly employees their full salaries even

Table 2.1 Framing tools					
Tool	Metaphors	Jargon/ Catch- phrases	Contrast	Spin	Stories
Function	Show subject's likeness with something else	Frame a subject in familiar terms	Describes subject in terms of its opposite	Puts a subject in positive or negative light	Frame a subject by example
Major use	Desire for subject to take on new meaning	Familiar references can enhance meaning	To differentiate, show what subject is *not*	Reveal subject's strengths or weaknesses	Attract attention, build rapport
Dangers	Mask alternative meanings	May seem trite, cliché, overused	Meaning may be skewed by poor contrast	Spin may be too far removed from reality to be believable	Mask alternative meanings
Example	"We treat our staff like family"	"This new program is a game-breaking initiative"	"We could have rested on our laurels or continued to improve"	"The problems we experienced were actually a blessing"	"Let me describe what happened when I visited our Wellington store last week"

Source: Adapted from Fairhurst and Sarr, 1996.

while many of them could not work due to the fire's damage to the mill. A month after he had first promised to pay salaries for 30 days to unemployed workers the first time he announced:

> I am happy to announce to you that we will once again – for at least 30 days more – pay all of our employees. And why am I doing it? I consider the employees standing in front of me here the most valuable asset that Malden Mills has. I don't consider them as some companies do as an expense that can be cut. (Ulmer, in press)

The contrast here – asset versus expense – draws attention to the fact that his values and actions stand in stark contrast to those of the many companies who were rapidly downsizing in the 1990s.

Strategic ambiguity and common starting points

One strategy that seems perhaps obvious to recommend is for CEOs to be clear and consistent in their messages. However, while that is often good advice, recalling the discussion about dialectics should provide a caution here. There has been perhaps an overemphasis on clarity and consistency of corporate (including leadership) communication in both practitioner and academic literature. Eisenberg's (1984) theory of strategic ambiguity and van Riel's (1995) theory of common starting points both point to the fact that sometimes in corporate communication, ambiguity and flexibility are actually preferable to clarity and consistency. Essentially, both theories point to the tension that all communicators feel between being clear and understood on the one hand, and on the other, allowing flexibility of interpretation. They also point to the fact that the values underlying specific messages may be more important than specific directives or explanations.

Strategic ambiguity is important because leaders (like other communicators) often seek to accomplish multiple goals in their communication. In a single message, a CEO might want to inform and persuade the audience while simultaneously creating a certain identity or image for himself/herself and the organization, suggest identities for various stakeholders (for example valued employees, trusted partners), and suggest particular kinds of relationships among the organization, various stakeholders, and himself/herself. To achieve all this requires a certain degree of ambiguity that allows "reading in" to the message. In essence, strategic ambiguity allows the CEO to appeal effectively to multiple audiences that may have different concerns and needs (Ulmer, 2000).

Obviously, there are potential ethical dilemmas in using strategic ambiguity if the intent is purely to be vague, to manipulate, or escape blame. The theory of common starting points (CSPs) suggests that consistency with underlying values is what helps overcome such dilemmas (Leitch, 1999). Leitch and Motion (1999) show how the New Zealand firm Mainfreight uses CSPs to allow a wide range of corporate messages to be conveyed. On the surface, these messages may look conflicting, even contradictory; yet they are consistent with an underlying set of values. Similarly, CEOs such as Stephen Tindall may speak on a wide range of topics and may come across as inconsistent and contradictory if they are not anchored by a set of stable, core values. As Eisenberg (1984) pointed out, organizational values may be expressed at "levels of abstraction at which agreement can occur" (p. 231).

Conclusion

Given the current social and business context, CEOs cannot escape their role as corporate spokesperson. To be effective, they must communicate with a wide range of stakeholders, managing each set of relationships to achieve corporate goals. Since communication involves negotiating meanings – not just delivering them pre-packaged to a passive audience – CEOs, and those corporate communication professionals who work with them, must be vigilant in monitoring the dialectical tensions that characterize such relationships, and must develop communication skills for managing these tensions strategically. Corporate communication professionals can play an important role in advising and monitoring CEO communication to assess the degree to which CEOs achieve an appropriate balance, and working with CEOs to achieve corporate communication goals by using the strategies proposed above.

The "Good Bloke" of New Zealand Business

One CEO who is often mentioned in the same sentence with Stephen Tindall is Dick Hubbard. Hubbard is founder and CEO of Hubbards Foods, a New Zealand-based company that makes breakfast cereals. Hubbard has been the most vocal spokesperson, and like Tindall, a founding member, of the New Zealand Business for Social Responsibility (BSR). Also like Tindall, Hubbard is a founding member of the New Zealand Council for Sustainable Development. Thus, he has worked to make the Hubbards brand mean something more than just breakfast cereal.

Only 10 years old, Hubbards Foods has had substantial success, becoming New Zealand's third largest cereal maker and with annual turnover of NZ$25 million. In the year 2000, Hubbards broke into two large overseas markets, getting contracts to supply cereal to Woolworths' 350 Australian supermarkets and Tesco's supermarkets in the U.K., both of which should mean substantial long-term growth.

The breakfast cereals themselves are noteworthy. Hubbard, with a background in food product development and marketing, created his original "Hubbards Fruitful Breakfast" and has gradually expanded the number and variety of cereals. The common themes – the brand – is the inclusion of fruit in most cereals and colorful, artistically sophisticated packaging. One cereal is linked in name to the Outward Bound program and a share of its profits go to Outward Bound.

Hubbards is well known for socially responsible and employee friendly practices. For example, the company makes a point of hiring long-term unemployed workers. Ten percent of profits are directed into charitable causes and another 10 percent into employee profit-sharing.

Hubbard himself is an energetic spokesperson for the company and for his causes – notably, BSR. He travels around New Zealand extensively giving speeches to various groups on BSR and related issues. Also, all Hubbards' cereals include a copy of the *Clipboard*, a brief newsletter that Dick Hubbard writes himself. Included in the *Clipboard* are articles on new products, BSR and related issues, and customer concerns (such as sugar content of cereals), as well as inspirational stories and poems. A recent *Clipboard* article described the staff's trip to Samoa. About 80 percent of the company's employees are Samoan, and as a 10th anniversary gift to employees, the company took the entire staff – over 100 workers – for a week-long holiday and cultural experience in Samoa. Another recent *Clipboard* explained

ILLUSTRATION (cont'd)

Hubbard's reflections on a recent union dispute followed by an article on the company's new profit-sharing scheme.

Recently, Hubbard was named an Officer of the New Zealand Order of Merit (an award established after knighthoods were discontinued in New Zealand) for his services to business and the community.

Hubbard is not without criticism, however. In early 2000, the company engaged in a much publicized dispute with the Service and Food Workers Union, which protested the company's pay rates. After four days of negotiation, the dispute was settled. But the negative publicity led to some angry words exchanged between the union organizers and Hubbard, and also provided an opportunity for a few shots from other potentially prompted adversaries.

Hubbard's philosophical nemesis is Roger Kerr of the Business Roundtable. Kerr said the trouble showed the danger of being "holier than thou" (Hubbard, 2000). Hubbard, on the other hand, said in a recent *Clipboard* that the "family" was stronger than ever as a result of the dispute and maintained that his belief in unions was as strong as ever.

Acknowledgement

I would like to thank George Cheney and the Editors for their helpful advice on earlier drafts of this manuscript.

Balancing corporate branding policies in multi-business companies

cees b.m. van riel and guido berens

Conflicting Views about Corporate Branding

The CEO/Chairman looked once more at the letter he had just drafted for his management team and strategic business unit directors. It was a great letter – in his opinion. It formulated why the company had to change the multi-branding strategy into a more uniform approach. The arguments were crystal-clear: it would increase familiarity for the company; it would be more attractive for the labor market; communications could be spread across the corporate entity; and, the shareholders would appreciate cost reductions that could be gained by the revised strategy. He also thought, personally, that it would be advantageous because his friends at the golf club would get a better impression of the company he was responsible for as well.

Three days after the letter was sent, the first reactions reached his office. The CEO was surprised to see little enthusiasm for his ideas. Was this something one ought to expect in an international company? It was quite peculiar to see that while everyone could benefit from the new strategy, no one seemed to be overly enthused and supportive of the revised strategy. The one irritating exception was the kind letter of the business unit in Luxembourg, just the one that he intended to sell shortly, due to its low profit rates. But, real support should have come from the blue chips, not from business units that were first in line as potential disinvestments.

Three weeks later, criticism had intensified. One of his most regarded executives resigned. This executive openly stated in an interview with a national newspaper that he loved being an entrepreneur and would never accept a job where "corporate headquarters" determined everything. Critical letters, sometimes anonymous, bombarded his office. The CEO understood he had to do something to avoid further damage. The next day he called a well-known firm of international corporate communications consultants. They recommended holding a meeting with all members of the management team as soon as possible. The purpose of this meeting would be twofold. Firstly, to enable them to express their concerns. Secondly, to announce a systematic approach to involve managers in the decision-making processes that would help steer the corporate branding issue.

They also recommended including a presentation with examples of other firms who had passed through similar experiences. Not in terms of describing the final outcome, but, by focusing mainly on the processes they went through internally and externally. The discussions with the consultancy made it clear to the CEO that it was of crucial importance to get support from his own business unit management first, before expressing anything about an intensified use of a corporate umbrella externally.

In the event, the presentation by the consultancy about the procedures applied by various competitors in dealing with similar problems in front of the critical audience of business unit managers was evaluated quite positively. The managers were especially enthusiastic about the fact that they were to play a serious role in the decision-making processes to choose a uniform or more variety focused style of corporate branding

The consultant leading the presentation explained that in finding an answer to the question of whether the emphasis in the corporate branding strategy of a multi-business company should be placed on "uniformity" or "pluriformity," the so-called SIDEC model can be used as an important aid *internally*. SIDEC stands for Strategy, Internal organization, Driving forces, Environment and Corporate branding strategy. The presupposition underlying the SIDEC model is that the final voice in favor of a particular type of corporate branding strategy is determined by considering the homogeneity of the corporate strategy, the internal organization of the company, the driving forces on group and strategic business unit levels, and the homogeneity of the environment in which the company operates.

Three months after the data were gathered according to the logic of the SIDEC model, the CEO stated in an interview with a journalist of the corporate employees' magazine that he "felt that the company had avoided a lot of internal damage by listening carefully to the arguments provided by the managers within the company before making a final decision about the new branding strategy."

Source: Authors.

Introduction and overview

Corporate identity and corporate image are often thought of as closely related. Corporate identity can be defined as a company's *self-presentation*, that is, the managed cues or signals that an organization offers about itself to stakeholders. Corporate identity is thus the manifestation of the organization's characteristics, that is, the abstract and relatively constant features that distinguish it from other organizations. Identity is conceived as the totality of a company's behavior, communication, and symbolism (Birkigt and Stadler, 1986; van Riel, 1995). Symbolism concerns the use of logos, house styles, staff outfits, and other visual cues. These cues promote recognition of a company and can help express its business philosophy. However, symbols are generally thought to be less important components of identity than the company's communications and – especially – actual organizational behavior.

Corporate identity signals are received and processed by the company's stakeholders, who gradually develop an *image* of the organization, that is, a set of meanings by which the organization is known (Dowling, 1986). This set of meanings can also be called the *reputation* of the company. The image or reputation of a company is thought to be a close reflection of its behavior, communication, and use of symbols (that is, its identity), though there may well exist a strategic gap between planned identity and received image.

As stated, identity is not the only determinant of corporate image. Images are also often derived from hearsay (news reports, stories from friends), from stereotypes related to the industry in which the company is active, to its country of origin or to business in general. Furthermore, the relationship between identity and image is reciprocal: identity influences image, but image can also influence identity.

Nevertheless, choices related to identity (that is, to behavior, communication, and symbols) can be an important means to create a favorable image among stakeholders, which can in turn have a positive influence on bottom-line performance. However, these choices are not always easily made. They not only depend on consideration of the desired external image, but also on internal decision-making. In particular, large disagreements often arise between corporate and business unit management of a multi-business company concerning the choice of a corporate branding strategy. Corporate level management often refers to the company's strength and size in defending a uniform brand strategy, while business unit management often refers to the value of their own brand in their market in defending a pluriform approach. Thus, in determining what is the best choice in a specific situation, it may not be sufficient to consider only the desired or actual image of the company. From an academic and also the practitioner's point of view, it is important to gain insight into the question whether emphasis in the corporate branding strategy of a multi-business company should be placed on uniformity or variety. In this chapter, the so-called SIDEC model is presented, which can be an important aid in finding an answer to this question.

Until now, the attention of both academics and practitioners has mainly been devoted to the considerations for determining a branding strategy at the product or individual brand level. Authors like Aaker (1991), Kapferer (1992), Keller (1993), and Sullivan (1990) pay extensive attention to the advantages and disadvantages of horizontal and vertical brand stretching (line extensions, brand extensions and style brands). However, studies on so-called "sourcing effects" (see for example, the *Brand Power Study* by Young & Rubicam, 1994) show that buyers increasingly display the need for *knowing the source*, that is, the organization behind a (product) brand (for example Brown and Dacin, 1997; Maathuis, 1999). Furthermore, brand policies arise from decision-making processes within an organization. Thus, non-product related issues, concerning both internal and external groups, are likely to influence choices regarding brand strategy. Until now, the literature has not systematically considered the considerations that lead to the establishment of a particular corporate branding strategy. The aim of the SIDEC model is to offer guidelines for choosing a strategy, analogous to the aim of the literature on brand extensions for choosing brand strategies on the product level.

SIDEC model

SIDEC stands for **S**trategy, **I**nternal organization, **D**riving forces, **E**nvironment and **C**orporate branding strategy. The SIDEC model is displayed in Figure 3.1. The presupposition of the model is that the final voice in favor of a particular type of *corporate branding strategy* is determined by considering the homogeneity of the corporate *strategy* and *driving forces* at group and business unit level, the way in which the *internal organization* takes place, and the homogeneity of the *environment* in which the business operates. In the remainder of this chapter, we consider these four independent variables of the SIDEC model, in order to be able to conclude with the consequences of the four factors on the corporate branding strategy.

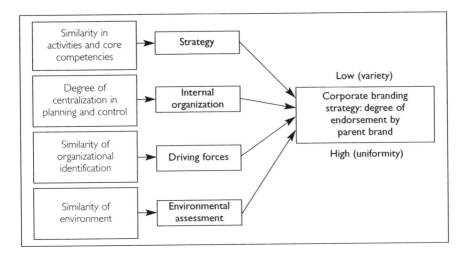

Figure 3.1 The SIDEC model

Strategy

Following Mintzberg and colleagues, *strategy* can be described as "the pattern or plan that integrates an organization's major goals, policies, and action sequences into a cohesive whole" (Mintzberg, Quinn and Ghoshal, 1998). In case of a complex, diversified company, the question is: which strategy should function as the input for the communication strategy? Should the strategy of the head office or the strategies of the business units be taken as the central guiding principle?

In answering the question whether, and if so, to what extent, one can communicate in a consistent fashion about the whole or "merely" about particular parts of a company, it is important to have insight into the degree to which there is a *strategic fit* between the company's center and its individual parts. In line with Jemison and Sitkin (1990), "strategic fit" can be described as "the degree to which the operational businesses augment or complement the parent's strategy and thus makes identifiable contributions to the financial and non-financial goals of the parent" (and vice versa). More specifically, we recommend paying attention to the related sub-questions.

1. Is there complementarity regarding the *scope* of the activities among the company's various divisions?

2. Is there complementarity in the way in which the company's objectives are *implemented*?

3. Is the distinctive power (for example with regard to *core competence*) created by all the business units together or is it concentrated in one single division?

Complementarity of scope

"Scope" is viewed by Johnson and Scholes (1989) as one of the key factors in strategic decision-making. Scope refers to the nature and the spreading of the activities, in other words, those literal and figurative borders within which the company operates. The larger the coherence between the present product/market combinations in a company is, the more it seems desirable to make the strength of the entire organization clear in a uniform way to external target groups. This is indeed often true for a "focused" company, but in "related differentiated" companies, matters often are more complicated (Porter, 1985). "Related" can refer to the control of the entire production chain (think for instance of large agricultural companies that sell everything, from seed, corn, fodder to consumer end products such as milk, meat, and so on) or to the existence of only a few connections. If there is complete chain control, it seems undesirable to extensively inform all involved parties on this, because one could be perceived as a too powerful block. If the threat of evoking feelings of fear in buyers or for instance suppliers is less prominent, it is indeed advisable to make the rationale behind the coherence in the portfolio clear and thus to communicate about the totality.

Complementarity of implementation style

It is not only important to map the coherence of the company's activities, but also to gain insight into the way in which the various divisions realize their objectives, for example arrogantly, risk avoiding, aggressively, and so on. Large differences in market approach, in particular if they are readily observable to important stakeholders of the company (for instance, because the activities take place within the same geographical area), make it more complicated to communicate a similar message externally about both the whole *and* the constituent parts. For companies that work in a uniform way, with regard to product quality and/or market approach, the best strategy is to communicate unequivocally with respect to both the totality and the divisions.

Complementarity of core competencies

A core competence is the whole of the acquired knowledge and experience in the organization (Prahalad and Hamel, 1990). It involves accumulated knowledge, skills, attitudes and problem-solving methods that are deep-rooted in groups of people in the organization. In choosing a corporate branding strategy, an important question is whether the parent company and the business units have similar core competencies. A good example of a core competence that is shared throughout an organization is the HRM policy of 3M aimed at constant technological innovation. Right from the start, 3M has propagated and realized a worldwide policy, in which each R&D employee is allowed to freely spend 15 percent of his/her time on inventing a new product or another kind of innovation from which the company could draw benefit.

Companies that actively possess core competencies can make clear to both external and internal target groups what the added value of the "parent behind the brand" is (Campbell, Goold, Alexander, 1995). Core competencies in fact prove the added value of the entire company, both to the market ("when Philips endorses it, it must be good"), and to internal target groups ("without the R&D capacity of IBM Armonk, the sales organization is not able to offer advanced products"). In both cases, it indicates what the added value is of belonging to a conglomerate of companies.

In case of a "natural" symbiosis of the above-mentioned central issues, a "strategic fit" is present. However, this is often a fit on paper; that is, it exists in abstraction (in notes, in the minutes of meetings, in the heads of people and so on). This does not imply that it can actually be realized (implementation problem). In variation of a well-known saying, it can be claimed that "where there's a will, there is a strategic fit!" The critical test is not whether a strategic fit can be found at all, but whether there is an *organizational fit*, that is, whether measures have been taken which make it possible to successfully realize the stated intentions (Datta, 1991).

Companies such as 3M, which possess an evident organizational fit, have an ideal point of departure to flesh out the profiling of the company in a consistent way, both on an authorized level and on the business unit (BU) level. If, however, large gaps exist between the strategy of the Center and those of the BUs, it is more sensible to leave the communication strategy as much as possible to the individual divisions and to communicate on corporate level merely on a "low profile" basis, and then only with corporate target groups or stakeholders.

Internal organization

A company's strategy, as well as the employed styles of management and the "administrative practices, cultural practices, and personnel characteristics of the operational businesses" (Jemison and Sitkin, 1990), are the result of an internal negotiation process and not solely of the wishes of "the masters voice," that is, the view of the top management alone. After all, various groups within a company strive primarily for the realization of their self-interest and only secondarily for the discharge of one's duty that arises from group membership.

The various interest groups in a company can be regarded as "political coalitions" (March, 1988) which together, whether reluctantly or not, must find a solution to the curious paradox that companies should be large (because of the benefits of large-scale production) as well as small (because of the advantages of decentralized entrepreneurship). In doing so, both technocratic and atmospheric aspects play a part. The technocratic side involves the way in which the head office guides and controls the business units (centralization or decentralization). The atmospheric aspect concerns the degree to which a conflict arises between the wishes of the head office to exert influence on business units, and the need for the latter to bear responsibility.

The extent to which it is possible and desirable to coordinate activities in the domain of communication runs parallel to the way in which coordination mechanisms in general are employed in a company (Laforet and Saunders, 1999). When planning generally is centralized, this will likely also be the case for the planning and monitoring of communication efforts. The most extreme form of centralization of communication is working with a central communication budget. This seldom proves to be employed by organizations of considerable size and diversity (van Riel and van den Broek, 1992). However, companies increasingly start working with so-called coordinating organs and common starting points (CSPs) in the domain of communication, central values that function as a basis for "translations" into all forms of communication used by a company (van Riel, 1995).

Driving forces

The foregoing discussion has mainly dealt with characteristics on an abstract organizational level (congruity relating to strategy and coordinating systems). The third part of the SIDEC model focuses not on characteristics of the organization as a whole, but on the characteristics of individuals, namely congruity concerning the driving forces that affect the daily activities of the employees. Since the real distinctive power of a company is determined by the behavior of its own employees, this third part of the SIDEC model should be considered to be one of the most crucial issues with respect to decisions concerning communication strategy.

The driving forces behind the behavior of people in a company can be mapped by means of the Hierarchical Meaning Structure Analysis method of van Rekom (1998). On the basis of this method, which is applicable qualitatively as well as quantitatively, insight is gained into the nature of the "values" which are employed by employees in the company's various divisions while performing their daily activities. The method yields information about the business unit level as well as the level of the whole concerning the possible differences and similarities relating to behavior of employees. In case of a high degree of similarity with respect to the nature of the value patterns – between the various business units as well as between the business unit and the whole – it is less complicated to employ a uniform approach in the communication strategy than it would be in the reversed situation.

In addition to information about the driving forces, it is also important to consider a related variable, that is, personal identification with the company. Identification can be described as "the perceived oneness with an organization and the experience of the organization's successes and failures as one's own" (Mael and Ashforth, 1992). Identification can be motivated by matters such as affiliation, feelings of safety, self-development, social acceptance or recognition, prestige or status, and value congruity between the person and the organization.

A high degree of identification is, according to Mael and Ashforth (1992), positively connected to employees' motivation to make an effort at successfully realizing the company's objectives (identification as "performance-indicator"). However, they also point out the negative consequences of a too high identification with the company, as this could also lead to an exaggerated form of dependence with respect to the company (the pathologies of overly dependent organizational members).

A potential cause of organizational identification that has received a lot of attention in the literature is perceived external prestige. It is thought that the degree of identification is higher when organizational members believe that important outsiders (such as consumers, shareholders, or the general public) hold the organization in high esteem. Indeed, several researchers have found a significant effect of perceived external prestige on organizational identification (Mael and Ashforth, 1992; Bhattacharya, Rao and Glynn, 1995; Fisher and Wakefield, 1998).

Employees can identify with at least two organizational levels: the corporate level and their own business unit level. In practice, identification can take place with a variety of objects: section, working group, division, international organization, and so on. In choosing a communication strategy for the entire organization, one should thus consider the internal differences with respect to the degree of identification between the various organizational levels.

Recently Smidts, van Riel, and Pruyn (2000) have developed a measuring instrument for organization identification (the so-called ROIT). By means of this instrument, insight can be gained into the degree of identification of employees with not only their own business unit, but also on the corporate level. Four possibilities can arise, represented in Figure 3.2.

Particularly when employees have a strong identification with their own business unit and a low identification with the parent company, a uniform approach in communication is not desirable. It often involves (financially) strong business units that consider themselves the "milch cows" of the company. However, strong identification between the business unit and the parent company makes the choice for a uniformity approach more likely.

Analogous to the terminology employed above (strategic fit and organizational fit), this third part of the SIDEC model involves the tracing of the "driving forces fit" on the level of the individual employees. However, insight into the individual driving forces of staff members in an organization "only" yields information about the state of affairs on a particular moment in the life cycle of a company. It would be fatalistic to assume that this could not be changed. It seems likely that a professional approach in the domain of employee communication can bring about an actual change in negative situations. Some evidence for this assumption is given in the aforementioned ROIT study (Smidts et al., 2000).

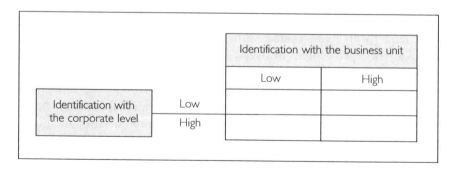

Figure 3.2 Identification and organizational level

Environment

In deciding on the nature of the emphasis to be placed in the corporate branding strategy, the next question deals with the environment of the parent company and the business units. The environment of a company can be defined at three levels: the level of specific tasks, the level of the industry, and the general level (Fahey and Narayanan, 1986). The following questions concerning the environment of business units and the parent company can be relevant for determining corporate branding policies.

1. Are there differences in the *definitions* of the environment between business unit and corporate level, and between the individual business units?

2. Are there differences in the way in which the parent company and the business units are *regarded* by the environment?

3. To what degree is there a desire from the environment to *know* the company behind the business units?

Differences in definitions of environment

For each environmental level (task, industry, and general), a classification of the relevant stakeholders can be made. This can for instance be done by employing the "linkage-model" of Grunig and Hunt (1984), which distinguishes five types of stakeholders: enabling (shareholders, government), functional output (customers, distributors), functional input (employees), normative (peers with which the company cooperates), and diffused (community, media). A survey can then be drawn up for each organizational division wherein it can be worked out per target group how one "assesses" the nature of the dependence relationship with this target group. This involves matters such as the characterization of clients and prospects with respect to their perceptions and preferences regarding the products and services offered by the organization. It also involves matters such as the nature of the competition, the kind of distribution channels and the influence of legislation as imposed by authorities. This can be displayed in a matrix as represented in Table 3.1.

When business units operate in an environment that is significantly different from the environments of other business units or the environment of the corporate level, a uniform corporate branding approach will likely be undesirable. For example, when business units of the same company that target different consumer segments (such as Seat and Skoda) use the

Table 3.1 Environment, organizational division and target group categories

	Parent company			Business unit		
	Task Environment	Industry Environment	General Environment	Task Environment	Industry Environment	General Environment
Characterization of clients/prospects						
Nature of competition						
Nature of distribution channels						
Nature of legislation						

same brand name, this could cause disapproval among (some of) these consumers. Likewise, the use of a uniform branding strategy could cause disapproval of distributors when some business units use a distribution system and other business units sell directly to the customers, as is often the case in insurance companies

When the environments have been defined, *priorities* are established for each organizational level. This can be achieved by assessing each stakeholder group's power, legitimacy, and urgency (Mitchell et al., 1997). Naturally, this can also be different for each division, so that one (or several) categories of target groups could be informed in a different way by what is in principle the same organization. This could entail that one receives too many, too few or even contradictory messages of the same company.

Differences in esteem by the environment

In determining corporate branding policies, it is not only important to know what stakeholder groups are relevant for the different business units and the corporate level, but also what image those stakeholders have of each different part. When a group of stakeholders is much more familiar with a particular business unit and holds much more favorable associations with the business unit than with the corporate level (as could be the case with consumers), a uniform branding strategy could be counterproductive for this group of stakeholders. Conversely, when the corporate level is better known and esteemed than a particular business unit (for example by investors), a uniform strategy would be desirable. The reason for this is that familiarity with a brand and the favorableness of stakeholders' image of the brand are necessary preconditions for achieving commercial success (Keller, 1993).

Demand for transparency from the environment

Of particular relevance here is the observation that stakeholders, including consumers, are increasingly demanding organizations to disclose their identity (for example van Riel, 2000). Furthermore, it has been shown that information about company strategy and identity can strongly influence a company's relationships with its stakeholders, for example by influencing consumers' product decisions (Brown and Dacin, 1997; Maathuis, 1999). It can, therefore, influence performance. In situations in which the demand for transparency is high, a uniformity approach would (other things being equal) be a likely choice, as it identifies the organization behind the business units.

Corporate branding strategy

When sufficient information has been gathered about the four areas discussed above (strategy, internal organization, driving forces and environment), it is possible to make a sophisticated choice regarding the accent to be applied in a company's corporate branding strategy. Thereby, a strategy framework for the total communication of a company will be established.

Theoretically, two extremes in the corporate branding strategy can be chosen: the uniformity model (the corporate level and the business units are positioned and profiled identically), and the variety model (all are positioned and profiled differently). In practice, policies can also be positioned between these extremes, creating a continuum. Brand policies can thus be characterized by the degree of endorsement by the parent company, that is, the degree to which the parent company "backs up" its business units' communication efforts. The continuum can be divided in four categories, that is, no endorsement, weak endorsement, medium endorsement, and strong endorsement. This is displayed and illustrated in Table 3.2.

In the uniformity model (high degree of endorsement), tight guidelines with respect to communication are imposed by the top of the organization. Uniformity is chosen concerning naming, symbolism and sometimes even concerning content (what should be communicated) and design/style (how it should be communicated). Examples are IBM, Chrysler, ABN AMRO, and (recently) Fortis.

In the variety model (no endorsement) the company chooses to leave the communication (how and what) completely free on the BU level. On the holding level, messages will be communicated only and very reservedly with financial target groups. In practice, this leads to a multiform brand strategy within the various product market combinations on business unit level. This model often occurs within financial holdings. Examples are Unilever and Procter & Gamble, whose business unit and product brands (for example Omo, Van den Bergh) display no (prominent) reference to the parent company.

When using a medium or a low degree of endorsement, the company strikes a subtle balance between emphasizing the security-providing power of the "parent behind the brand" in the background, in combination with the profiling of the individual business unit, which is autonomous within a

Table 3.2 Continuum of endorsement

	No endorsement (variety)	Weak endorsement	Medium endorsement	Strong endorsement (uniformity)
Visualization	"Business unit name"	"Business unit name" member of "parent company" (logo)	"Parent company name" (logo) "Business unit name"	"Parent company name" (logo) "Specialization"
Example	Barings	Barings "Member of ING (lion)"	ING (lion) Barings	ING (lion) investment banking
Corporate branding strategy	Stand-alones, low degree of parent visibility, high degree of autonomy at business unit level, avoiding spill-over effects	Low degree of parent visibility, used by companies in a transition phase of complete autonomy towards integration into an integrated market approach	High degree of parent visibility, no consistent fit with the key elements of the corporate message, applied in "greenfields" or in more mature markets where competitors already have achieved a strong position	High parent visibility, high degree of identification with corporate level, high degree of transparency, strict coordination of communication strategy, showing the strength of the group

certain margin. Thus, when using a "medium" endorsement, communication efforts could contain a roughly equal mix of a business unit's own communication elements and corporate elements. For example, the ING Group uses some brands that show the ING corporate brand next to the business unit brand and have varying degrees of autonomy regarding communication policies (for example ING Barings). This strategy is used primarily in new markets (for example "greenfields"), in which the parent company is still relatively unfamiliar. When one wants to draw even less attention to the parent company, for example in a transition phase from variety to uniformity, a weak endorsement (for example Primerica, a member of Citigroup) could be used.

It should be realized that this continuum (or fourfold division) is purely theoretical, since no company could or would like to meet only one of the categories of this typology. As a matter of fact, it would be better to speak of a main course determined by the company, and side courses to be chosen for particular business units where necessary. Thus, it could occur that, because of the considerations of the SIDEC model, some business units of a company are treated as in the uniformity model, while other business units of the same company are treated as in the variety model. For example, in the ING Group, some business units show no endorsement by the Group (for example Nationale-Nederlanden), some show a minimal degree of endorsement (for example BBL, whose logo is underlined in orange to indicate its group membership), and some show a medium degree of endorsement (for example ING Barings).

In the literature on corporate identity, a similar classification of corporate branding policies is employed (Kammerer, 1989; Olins, 1989; Biggar and Selame, 1992). However, the existing typologies, in particular the well-known threefold division of Olins, mainly deal with the visualization, especially the choice of the name and the logo with which the company as a whole wishes to present itself externally. This concerns the extent to which one wishes to *reveal* the "parent behind the brand."

Another aspect of communication strategy is, however, the degree to which a company wishes to exert influence on the question of what will be communicated with respect to the total communication strategy. This concerns the crucial role that common starting points could play as a reference point concerning content in determining the bandwidth within which a company can and should communicate with various types of target groups.

The visual and content aspects of communication policies are often related, but not always. For example, some of the ING Group's American brands (for example ING Life of Georgia, ING Equitable Life) prominently show their membership of the ING Group, but have a high degree of freedom in the content of their communication efforts, because of their need to adapt to the local market.

Conclusion

From the preceding discussion, it should be clear that internal considerations can provide important guidelines for answering the question to what degree (if at all) the "parent" of a multi-business company should be visible in the communication efforts of its business units. On the abstract level of the whole organization, these considerations concern the internal organization and similarities in strategy between business units and the parent company. On the level of individual employees, important considerations concern differences in driving forces and organizational identification. Although the SIDEC model focuses mainly on internal considerations, it is important to realize that an assessment of relevant developments in the environment should also play a significant role in determining corporate branding policies. In particular, assessment of the images of the parent company and the business units is an indispensable tool for making careful decisions.

When a company decides to reveal the "parent" behind one or more business units, it should make clear who and what this "parent behind the brand" is. In other words, it is then important to establish the identity of the parent company. This can be done by clarifying the nature of the activities of the entire company, and by establishing central values, which can be used as starting points for communication and behavior towards relevant target groups. In choosing such values, it is advisable to search for a mix of the internal ideals and driving forces (inside-out perspective) and the actual corporate image existing among external target groups (outside-in perspective). Although this chapter has been mainly concerned with the inside-out perspective, we do realize that the outside-in perspective is just as important for establishing corporate branding strategy.

Hopefully this chapter has clarified that the introduction of a corporate umbrella does not necessarily mean that a uniform corporate branding strategy is the best solution. It would be advisable to organizations with complex organizational structures and large differences in the nature of the product/market combinations to develop their corporate branding strategy in a balanced manner. That is, with tolerance for exceptions, but with firmness with regard to the mutually determined starting points by which the "parent behind the brand" should be profiled by the business units.

Corporate Branding: Experiences of an IT Firm

Information technology is a booming business. In many countries examples can be found of business start-ups that have flourished fast into serious challengers of those who controlled the market before. The burden of normal management problems which the old economy firms seem to have experienced, also hit these new economy firms the moment their scale became mature. One of the problems these firms have to solve is a communication problem. Not only how to develop a competitive advantage by distinctive and appealing communication, but also by paying attention to the question of which name to reveal behind all services that are and will be offered to the market.

A Dutch firm, Caesar, went through a similar process. This fast growing firm offers four different (at first sight) services. The managers within all units are supposed to be fully responsible for their own performance. However, they all feel that one day their services will be more appreciated if all business units can build on one strong company behind the brands. The management team applied the SIDEC model method in their decision-making process in addition to an external assessment where similar attributes were measured among their key clients. In contrast to the case description that was presented at the beginning of this chapter, Caesar's CEO immediately wanted to involve his managers. But he made it clear from the beginning that he didn't see any argument to intensify a corporate umbrella over all communication of the Caesar business. However, he changed his mind when all managers in the business units urged him to accept a stronger endorsement with one corporate brand, based on the results of both the internal survey (based on the SIDEC model) and external information (using the SIDEC attributes and testing them among clients). Interesting are the results of the discussions among managers based on an assessment of the actual and desired parent visibility and content agreement.

The need to be supported by a more uniform corporate brand intensified when external market research showed that clients would appreciate a more uniform corporate umbrella too:

	Optimit	Oreade	Propago	TrainIT
Is it an advantage that business unit X, Y, Z belongs to the Caesar Group? (5 point scale)	4.25	4.20	4.15	4.31

As a consequence, the Caesar Group decided to apply a strong endorsement by the corporate brand in their future communication.

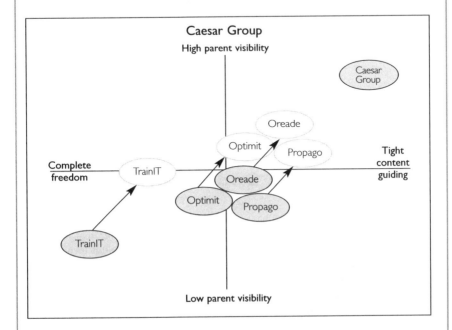

Figure 3.3 The Caesar Group

Chapter 4

Responsive and responsible communication practices: a pluralist perspective

richard j. varey

Integrity Through Integration – The Body Shop

Why is it that The Body Shop has such a strong brand that positions the firm with apparently "honest" products? A brand position moreover that is associated with environmental concern and social justice? Could integrated communication be the answer? If one were to ask founder Anita Roddick about The Body Shop's efforts to craft and use integrated communication, she would likely counter with a query about the meaning of the question. Yet, The Body Shop has apparently succeeded in managing business and workplace communication as an authentic aspect of its corporate culture. Corporate image stems from clear and solid values that visibly operate within the company, and not just from the "creative" pen of an advertising or public relations agency. This reinforces the distinction raised by Zorn in Chapter 2 between solid values and the doctrine of spin.

In part, the company competes on its ethical stance towards the environment and employment – its customers buy not just products but also *buy into* a set of values. And, employees and customers are more likely to be activists than those of many other retailers. For example, when I suggested that The Body Shop had adopted cause-related marketing, Anita Roddick counter-claimed that they "market causes" (Varey, 1996b).

Modern business managers have need to face the reality that economic success requires unifying the interests of their partners, labor, the public, governments, and investors as well as satisfying customers. We can think of it as a "corporate community" in which each of these stakeholders or constituencies benefits by contributing to their common success. The Body Shop and many other progressive companies have amply demonstrated that this concept works beautifully (Halal and Varey, 1999). But, this requires much more integrated management than has been pursued in the orthodox structures of many traditional corporations (see Chapter 1).

Environmental communication is viewed not just as a trendy add-on, but as a cultural and educational enterprise: "We use our shops worldwide as 'arenas of education' ... We preach and teach; we educate and inform ... We prefer to give staff information about the products, anecdotes about the history and derivation of the ingredients, and funny stories about how they came on to Body Shop shelves. We want to spark conversations with our customers, not browbeat them to buy." (Roddick, 1992, p. 23, p. 25).

This education is accomplished through the provision of a variety of messages which differ in their technical complexity, message length, target audience, message substance, and terminology, communicated through different communication channels. Simple information is provided on a product's packaging, through shop windows, or through in-store posters. More complex information is provided by leaflets. Complex information is given to consumers through talks held by The Body Shop managers at local community meetings, through factory tours, or through detailed "values reports" which can be ordered by mail or read via the Internet.

Educational communication that helps consumers to learn develops credibility for The Body Shop: "What we have tried to do is establish credibility by educating our customers, giving them intelligent information about where ingredients come from, how they are tested and what they are used for. It humanizes the company, making customers feel they are buying from people whose business practices they know and trust." (Roddick, 1992, p. 27).

The Body Shop has approached ethical management on a much broader basis than just environmental issues. It has also encompassed fair trade, animal rights, human welfare and social justice issues. The credibility of the environmental communication was further enhanced through cooperating with pressure groups. Campaigns are advertised through shop window displays and in-store leaflets. Through its numerous campaigns with Greenpeace, Friends of the Earth, and so on, The Body Shop gained something like an indirect pressure group endorsement.

But, by the late 1990s, The Body Shop began to lose some of its pressure group support. This was an indirect consequence of its conversion into a plc and its aggressive expansionist internationalization strategy, especially into the U.S. market, which did succeed in exporting its franchising approach to the U.S. However, its ethical business philosophy, which was an important factor of its corporate success in the U.K., did not receive the same type of response in the U.S.A. market. The main reason for this failure lay in the cultural–historical nature of its business philosophy. In the U.K., credibility developed over decades, in line with the business culture and history of The Body Shop: the small beginning in Brighton; the step-by-step expansion; and accompanying media coverage on The Body Shop's community programs and campaigns with environmental pressure groups. Because of the cultural–historical nature of credibility, it is difficult to "export" it into another country; rather, it has to be rebuilt from scratch in new markets, and this may take a lengthy period of time.

In the U.S.A., The Body Shop appeared to be just another cosmetics retailer. One consequence of the failure of The Body Shop to develop its ethical profile in the U.S. was that it had to resort to more conventional communication techniques, such as advertising, which were avoided in the U.K. Differences between the educational communication in the home market and its communication abroad revealed an inconsistency in The Body Shop's management approach. Ultimately, such inconsistency began to negatively filter back to the U.K. market, undermining The Body Shop's friendly relationship with pressure groups.

Now, corporate restructuring and a new management team have taken on the task of repositioning The Body Shop in an international business arena. How will the move to traditional marketing and public relations management impact on the corporate image of the company? Notably, Anita Roddick claims "a concern for the big world beyond cosmetics" and to run her business according to female principles. She sees these as: "Caring; Making intuitive decisions; Not getting hung up on hierarchy; A sense of work as part of life, not separated from it; and, Putting your labour where your love is" (Roddick, 1992). The November 1996 Body Shop catalogue contained the line "To dream of the person you'd like to be is to waste the person you are." Could this way of thinking and working provide a strategic imperative for the communication function?

Source: Author.

Introduction

This chapter aims to examine the issue of integrated (total) corporate communication management. To do this requires a pluralistic perspective considering many related concepts. These include: differentiation, specialization, fragmentation, coherence, professionalism, encroachment, colonization, imperialism, and integration.

There is evidence of continuing and accelerating differentiation all around us. Executives need to focus on integration as the primary means of enhancing corporate capacity to serve stakeholders responsively and responsibly in a competitive marketplace. Integrated diversity is necessary for responsive and responsible managerial practice. At the same time, there is a related need for organizations of all types to accomplish competitive differential advantage. The best way in which this can be achieved, at least in light of the mores of contemporary society, seems to be to grow companies by organic growth, merger, or acquisition (see also Chapter 9). Thus communication is not simply *transmissive*, as it would be in a steady state scenario, but also needs to be *aggressively participatory*. Communicating is necessary to strategic development and is associated with coherent management. Or, put another way, strategic integration or coherent organization, not just a tool for objective information transmission.

One rib supporting the corporate umbrella is that corporate communication be seen as a managerial system that recognizes the interrelations between marketing, public relations (including employee relations), and management. The managerial system, in today's world, consists of organizing *with leadership* in the face of aggressive determined differentiation and competitiveness.

Integration, imperialism, and encroachment

Herbert Spencer (1897/1968, and 1971), in his "functionalism," sets out the concept of evolution: the process of increasing differentiation (specialization of functions) and integration (mutual inter-dependence of structurally differentiated parts and coordination of their functions). Generally, as evolution continues the trend is toward complexity. In the struggle for survival, only those survive who adapt to their changing environment. Spencer's argument can readily extend to organizations, especially in the complex business world of the 21st century. Leaving aside the issue of evolution, which rightly belongs to business historians, in this chapter, I intend to explore specific issues associated with the problem of integration. Two major issues concern territorialism and imperialism.

Turf wars arise with territorialism – when each department has its own agenda, builds up adversarial relationships with other departments, then competes for budget allocation and/or kudos, if necessary cannibalizing other departments to succeed. Intra-corporate groups compete for power. This is perhaps the principal barrier to integration.

The other corporate phenomenon is cultural imperialism. Some educators and practitioners see specialized (in traditional terms) groups of communicators – marketing and public relations – as enemies rather than allies (see Lauzen, 1991, for example). Turf wars erupt when one group intrudes on the activities traditionally "owned" by the other group. Such imperialism – a spirit of sovereignty over an empire – is manifested in the one-sided glorification of a particular ideology leading to the legitimization of the subordination of others – a form of "ethnocide" – for example marketing is the most important discipline, PR is pre-eminent, and so on (see Kitchen, 1995; Kitchen and Moss, 1995).

Tempers really come to the boil when "foreign" specialists are assigned to manage the function – the act of encroachment.

Is there a solution to the potential barriers occasioned by these three issues?

Corporate evolution and integrated diversity

Wilber (1995, 1996) indicates that differentiation is natural, but that not recognizing the need for integration is perhaps the greatest failing of contemporary management. Today, many executives are paying little attention to integration or are pursuing unification or standardization as if they were integration (Schultz and Kitchen, 2000). The result of too little attention to integration is dissociation, which is commonly shown in scenarios concerning loyalty, cooperation, corporate identity, and so on. Organization design efforts treat the problem as one of individual participation ("hearts and minds"), or skills (performance), or processes (systems) while the real need is to reconceive communication as a cultural phenomenon in the realm of collective understanding.

Corporate Communication can be seen as a managing perspective that treats communication as a mode of managing and as intersubjective, concerned with "We," rather than as an internal or external event or thing ("It" – objective). Communication occurs within the social groupings we call corporations and markets. We need to think in terms of consciously interacting social groups (or stakeholders), rather than the activities and words as communication. Note how prevalent it is to hear of "communication" when referring to objects such as letters, posters, memos, reports, speeches, advertisements, and so on, which when delivered to another person are supposed to constitute "communication."

Corporate communication needs to become a "We" knowledge-rich environment for purposive social groups. "Communication" per se remains the poor "It." In other words, a substitute for what people really want. Take a look at your annual employee survey and your Investors in People (IIP) audit report if you don't believe me!

As van Riel (2000) has shown, the various communication specialists operating in the corporation have a communication responsibility – to contribute to creating sustainable corporate stories which resonate positively with internal and external stakeholders. But often corporate stories, presumably developed in an integrated manner, can be forestalled in practice by several factors. These include systems of influence in corporations: turf wars and so on.

The politics of internal coalitions

Integration is rarely a natural condition. Mintzberg (1983) developed a compelling and useful framework for understanding systems of influence in corporations. The corporate game of *empire building* is a solo game played by middle managers to enhance their power bases by acquiring subordinates and sub-units to create independent sovereignties with spheres of influence. Several political means may be employed in order to influence. People may have privileged access to influential others, especially those who design the corporate superstructure. People may gather privileged information through gate-keeping and centrality (being able to operate at the intersections of important flows of internal communication, and thereby gain power). Legitimate systems of influence may be used, as well as political skills. Much depends on the effort expended by a manager in influencing.

Empire building is about the growth of the manager's own unit, requiring, except in exceptional circumstances of major corporate growth, the take-over of existing functions and positions. Managers are motivated for autonomy and achievement since power, status, and rewards increase as the unit they manage grows. The empire building game is played to competitively acquire territory (psychological territory is a sphere of influence) and associated rights through the positions and units that contain them, since rewards are based on the number of subordinates and resources allocated, and decisions are delegated on the basis of positions the manager controls. Positions and units provide constituencies of political supporters, so the politicking manager seeks to build coalitions. The drive for autonomy leads not only to expansion but also to balkanisation. The corporation becomes increasingly divided (differentiated) to allow maximum discretion to each unit in the middle range of the management system. Operating units are driven to aggrandizement.

Authority and ideology are forces for cohesion, whereas claims to special *expertise* provide resistance against cohesive organization. Politicking deploys illegitimate power coupled with conflict and, often, the clandestine voice of "players." The authority system uses legitimate/formal power in the form of personal and bureaucratic control of subordinates by superiors. Members are required, in the interests of the corporate body, to participate and to suspend their own (individual) voice. The system of ideology (the traditions, beliefs, and stories of members) draws on members' loyalty in suspending their own voice except in support of the corporation. The *expertise* system, on the other hand, distributes power unevenly, requiring mutual adjustment based on the skills and knowledge of "experts." Professional operators can band together to exercise group power through the system of politics or power of their external professional coalitions (for example, the Chartered Institute of Marketing, the Institute of Public Relations, and so on). This force undermines (opposes) alliance-building. Traditionally, practitioners have erected strong barriers between the long-established communication disciplines (public relations, employee relations, advertising, direct marketing, sales promotion, and so on), managing these separately with different (and often inconsistent and conflicting) goals, objectives, and budgets. Often, effectiveness and efficiency suffer by this fragmented way of managing.

There are ways to protect a power base. The norm of secrecy is a good one. Protective myths are useful. The specialist's knowledge base can be protected by controlling training and recruitment. And, the ace up the sleeve is to deny the competence of any outsider. Professionals flaunt their expertise by emphasizing the uniqueness of their skills and knowledge, the importance of these to the corporation, and the inability to replace them. Non-professionals feign expertise. Their influence is then derived from their political will exerted and their political ("communication"?) skill, rather than technical knowledge or skills.

Communication is seen by too many as synonymous with information, and it is still a maxim of myopic management practice that knowledge is power. It is no mystery, then, that communication specialists seek power through their privileged positions and expertise, and are aggrieved when this is denied by those in authority.

The IABC Excellence Study (Dozier et al., 1995) showed that communication departments are powerful (influential) due to their support from the dominant coalition of the corporation, thus enabling them to contribute to strategic planning. But, this influence is derived also through their strategic contributions. Excellence in managing communication requires knowledge of the business as well as managerial and technical expertise.

A collective (corporate) managing system

Traditional departments and narrow specialist groups tend to operate in institutional "silos" in competition: for supremacy; to protect their "turf"; to secure credibility; for "a seat at the boardroom table"; to secure "the ear of the dominant coalition"; or simply for resources. An alternative model of integrated communication systems seeks to build bridges between "islands of communication," and to eventually establish new task groupings, perhaps by way of cross-functional working in the interim. As organizations re-engineer working arrangements and formal structure around value-producing business processes, so they should re-engineer their communication management into a truly corporate (sub) system for managing.

Departments should not be allowed to seek independence, and the concern of managers should not be encroachment, but how to remove barriers to real cooperative working so that "communicating" can add value to business enterprise. The integrated approach does not promote the engagement of non-specialists in competition to manage traditional communication departments. Rather it seeks to foster greater recognition of corporate dependencies and the need for wider interaction and participation in constructing meanings, identity, and knowledge (Deetz, 1992), and compatible goals. Stronger more direct linkages are required between those who need to communicate and those who are charged with enabling and facilitating these interactions. A value-creation perspective (of managing) on the departmentalization issue is required if the power-control assumptions and desires of the traditionalist manager (enacting constraining managerialism) are to be overcome for the benefit of the corporate community. This will require that managers recognize communications as central to the work of the enterprise community. Such an approach, if tackled using the umbrella metaphor, can enable reconciliation of social and economic interests, for business is in reality a socio-economic institution upon which all are dependent, and may allow the vista of a "life ethic" to temper the debilitating effects of the mutation of citizens into consumers. Corporate performance is determined by various factors as shown in Figure 4.1.

These factors indicate that the interests of the few (corporate owners, managers, and their customers) are no longer universally given greater value than the interests of the many (all other stakeholders). Arrogant managers who do not value relationships and stakeholders' interests (or even stakeholders themselves), and do not value leadership and other

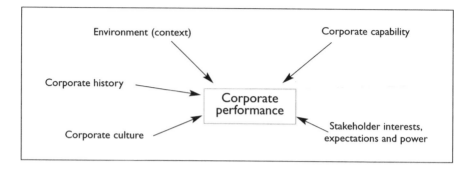

Figure 4.1　Determinants of corporate performance

change-oriented practices will find it more difficult to keep their license to operate (that is, employment).

Corporate learning can be constrained by "informational insulation" brought about through close cultural proclivity. Despite the endeavors of senior management, traditional organizational departmentalism/functionalism can create a multi-cultural climate within the corporation's management structure. This is exemplified by departmental jargon which acts as shorthand within the cultural group and as a device for exclusion of those outside the group. The shape and progress, therefore, of corporate learning and corporate development are wholly dependent on overcoming the disparate cultural catalysts of information insulation. This will only be achieved through the adoption of a cultural synthesis engendered by an overarching communication system (Swan et al., 2000).

Institutional economists would argue that any organization is a meanings system and information processor. Communication structure is conditioned by the culture of an organization. The systems and processes of communication not only enable, but also limit, the forms of communication, and this impacts upon attitudes to, and the resulting quality of, information and knowledge upon which the organization bases its decisions. In other words, "islands of communication" have poorly developed or ineffective bridges between the specialist groups. The resultant silos of specialist interests are the result of large-scale mechanization and its associated inherent specialization. The corpus is functionally divided in a rigid hierarchical form of organization. Each department or function attends to one or a few audiences – usually shareholders and senior executives are dominant in receiving attention in this step-by-step "parcel post" managerial approach to communication. If organizational communication is taken as an evolutionary, culturally dependent process of co-producing knowledge and creating relationships, then organizational performance must be open to improvement. The development of a *learning consciousness* could provide for a learning environment as a source of sustainable competitive advantage. But only if a shift can be made from "Fordist" task allocation to specialist multi-functionalism.

This paradigm shift is a prerequisite to encouraging departmental specialists to be flexible and disencumbered of the rhetoric of inertia by developing a mutually agreed language within established "zones of meaning" (Heath, 1994). These zones can only be based on social learning, determined by what the group need to learn in order to maintain relationships. Therefore, relationships should be envisioned as collaborative projects encouraging constant re-evaluation, refinement and modification of "zones." Without a successful "web of social learning," firms are failed human institutions. Corporate communication provides a synthesized approach to elaborating, maintaining and progressing zones of shared meaning. Corporate communication can thus be conceptualized as an integrated managing system comprising the essential managing processes. Learning consciousness, that is understanding of the concepts of learning and "learning management," becomes a critical element of each process. Learning, and potential restructuring, in relation to stakeholders and publics (internal and external) are essential to future managerial thought and behavior.

An alternative paradigm of employee–employer relations requires that organizational competence and capability are deliberately developed through the establishment of the internal structures and processes of an enterprise culture. Members of the organization are thereby influenced to act to ensure that competitive advantage is created and maintained. *Internal marketing* and internal public relations are integrators of business functions within an organization, and can achieve coordination of the parts of the organization around compatible purposes. This develops the customer paradigm and ensures that marketing and quality management are not separate management functions, and the differing perspectives on customer needs and quality perceptions are rationalized by reducing interfunctional conflicts in communicating and joint responsibilities to each other. This urges an explicit market and community focus in non-marketing functions and the sharing of customer satisfaction goals. This "de-departmentalization" of functions may be seen operationally in cross-functional problem-solving and briefing teams.

Dialogical communication establishes mutual understanding and trust in staff–management relations, and between functional departments. Cooperation is a critical success factor in building necessary organizational culture and capability. Senior managers often have misguided assumptions about their organization's culture and this can seriously undermine change programs. Internal marketing drives interactive (that is, intersubjective) communication to help overcome resistance to change (see Varey and Lewis, 2000, for further discussion of the organization design aspect of internal marketing as a management strategy).

Dialogical (but not two-way monological) communicating can establish mutual understanding and trust (but not necessarily total agreement) between managers and workers, between functional departments, and between provider and customer, and sufficient acceptance to enable action to be taken. A shift from control-driven to value-driven organization as well as a shift from the individual to the collective level of management is evident. Employees are then no longer seen by managers as raw materials that need to be "managed." Cooperation is a critical success factor in building the necessary organizational culture and capability. But, as Richard Dawkins has pointed out, cooperative behavior is not natural to humans and has to be learned.

Integration has often been taken to mean the consolidation (merger) of communication departments. However, this consolidation process has been on (and perhaps off) the management agenda for many years – mostly for cost-reduction reasons. The contemporary agenda has evolved such that the drivers for a reinvented communication management system are the increasingly competitive global business environment; electronic media; and the emerging partnership (cooperation) between many interested publics. The role of the communication manager is to orchestrate the total process of business communication so that the corporation itself is communicated. Lauer (1995) argues for an "integrated communicator" – the generalist specialist who has an understanding and respect for all communication disciplines, a mastery of basic research skills, and strong personal communication skills. The same person is also conceptualized as a "communication czar" in Schultz and Kitchen (2000).

Model-making, map-making, wiring diagrams, and departmentalization

I have previously suggested a short-hand method for explaining the configuration of organizational arrangements required for corporate communication as a system. A system perspective allows the complexity to be simplified – where sub-systems can be considered as communication functions and related to objectives of the (corporate) system as a whole.

Some academics and practitioners believe that marketing, public relations, and other communication disciplines have differing goals and methods and will not (naturally) become integrated (see, for example, Lauer, 1995, p. 27, for a statement from the Education and Public Affairs Committee of the Public Relations Society of America). Others, on the other hand, urge that taking the view that marketing and public relations are the same function is in the best interests of the corporation (Harris, 1993, cited in Lauer, 1995). The scope of responsibilities assumed and work undertaken does seem to be determined by the existing structure and working arrangements of operating departments. If configured (organized) by public or market (that is by the nature of the relationship with various stakeholders) then greater overlap of interests, assumed purposes and roles, strategies and tactics – even definition of communication – could be expected. The question would then not be concerning who owns particular groupings of tasks, but who can work together to effectively and efficiently manage specific relationships with key stakeholders. Analysis of domain similarity, that is who shares the same goals, skills, and tasks, and resource dependence, helps to identify the scope for re-configuration on the primary basis of goals rather than skills and past history of task execution (that is ownership).

What is required is a conceptual representation of coherent stakeholder relationship management which can provide the basis for organizational review, identification of communication relationships, definition of communication rules, task definition, and task allocation. Various communication objectives of the corporation can then be mapped to the relationships: input to decision-making; participation in public discourse; reputation enhancement; product promotion; and so on.

The "wiring diagram" approach emphasizes *connections* rather than components, in other words, focusing on the communication activities and effectiveness of the various "islands of communication"; this approach considers the "bridges" between specialist groups, and allows, in principle at least, the wiring to be reconfigured around the functions required by the firm.

If we shift the level of analysis from "functions" to "communicative activities" we can imagine the possibility of rewiring communicative relationships and information flows – the communication system. This rewiring consists of: rethinking communication policies, practices and incentives; installing new "pipelines" which support collaboration and participation; and, provides a new definition of communication that unifies communication functions, distribution technologies, and programs. This rewiring is both physical and philosophical – it must be a literal and figurative configuration. In doing this, attention should be paid to processes rather than functions – organizational structure consists of sub-systems of logically connected activities and purposes, whereas a function is a grouping of specialists who are responsible for running the respective business processes.

The departmentalization of communication management

Organization is an economic and an adaptive social structure – a system of relationships which define the availability of scarce resources and which may be manipulated in terms of efficiency and effectiveness. Organization charts map how decisions are supposed to be made – the formal structure is detailed to define the behavior expected from participants in the system, in terms of accountabilities, responsibilities, and affiliations. This issue is simply one of allocation of persons to particular types of activity (in defining a job or role to perform). Senior management must take responsibility for organization design and must choose a suitable "departmentalizing pattern." This pattern, at the level of total system (the corporation) or sub-system (the department or unit) may be activity-based, functional, or may be market-based. Functional departmentalization provides vertical groupings for efficiency, autonomy, and economy due to specialization, and is particularly appropriate for operations within a relatively stable environment. Over-specialization (professions, crafts) may lead to inflexibility and internal tribal warfare over power, control, and resources. Departmentalization by horizontal market-linked groupings gives more emphasis in jobs on cooperation and interdependence with related functions. The result may be faster response and greater sensitivity to needs as decision-making is shifted nearer the point of marketing, and requires a variety of skills. We can think of a department as a group of people who share an identity based upon the notion of a common task. Table 4.1 compares organization by function with organization by market or public.

Each sub-system is linked with a stakeholder group and these stakeholder satisfaction centers become the focal point for performance measurement. Each operates semi-autonomously, although internally they may display a process/functional profile. Key positions are held by a small central staff whose main responsibility is planning, and there are formal analytical procedures for assessing divisional performance. Each is decentralized, differentiated from one another, and internally interactive.

Table 4.1 Bases of departmentalization compared

	The process-oriented organization	The public-oriented organization
Structure	Departmentalized by skills and resources – control by costs and budgets, formal, centralized	Divisions match up with publics – formal, analytic, differentiated, individualistic, decentralised
Context	Clear, stable, homogeneous – small and medium-sized organizations	Heterogeneous, open – large organizations
Ideology	Instrumental – based on technical specialization, efficiency, singular	Plural, "product" development, customer satisfaction
Strengths	Economies of scale, skill development	Concentration on customers and products, adaptation to local conditions, economical on top management decision-making, risk reduction
Failures	Top managers' decision-making overloaded, excessive meetings, slow to change, professionally-oriented rather than customer-oriented, bureaucracy of procedures and planning systems may develop, may be excessive conflict and politicking	Duplication of resources is possible, difficult to standardize products, innovations may not be diffused, loyalty to division rather than to company?, loss of in-depth skill development, may compete for limited resources instead of cooperating

Source: Adapted from Duncan, 1979; see also Butler, 1991.

Marketing, advertising, public relations, and employee relations are closely related in terms of their functions and methods but are often considered to be separate areas of corporate activity. The distinctions made are usually based on precedent of organization design and inter-divisional competition than on any major differences in their corporate functions. These specialist groups have often felt that they are competing for resources and influence. This competitive stance is not productive since these groups of specialists have complementary and interdependent functions. Reassuringly, reports Lightcap (1984), the artificial barriers that have traditionally separated groups of managers of communicating are fading away and cooperation and collaboration are becoming more common. Nonetheless, integration of communication goes a long way beyond simple bundling of communication activities so as to speak with one voice. Thus, from a truly corporate standpoint, the concern of responsive and responsible managers is not encroachment, but how to remove barriers to real cooperative working so that communication effort really can add value to business enterprise. The mental model does not mean promoting the engagement of non-specialists in competition to manage traditional communication departments. Rather the aim is to foster greater recognition of corporate dependencies and shared corporate (business) goals, and to make stronger, direct linkages between those who need to communicate and those who are charged with enabling and facilitating such interactions. A value-creation perspective on the departmentalization issue is required if the power-control assumptions and desires of the traditionalist manager are to be overcome for the benefit of the corporate community. This will require that managers recognize corporate communication as central to the work of the (their own) enterprise community.

Perhaps one reason why turf wars arise is the absence of clarity about the purpose of managing communication. In my view, the problem seems straightforward. Promotion and persuasion are often the communication purposes. Most public relations practice is about the creation of a preferred or favorable climate of opinion or image. This is impression management where image may not be congruent with identity. Public relations can be managed communication to create understanding through knowledge, often requiring and effecting change.

Marketing communication practice is primarily promotional – essentially persuasive – but marketing in itself *is* communication. Society needs both the marketing concept and the promotion concept (Shimp, 2000) if value is to be created and exchanged. The marketing concept requires the adoption of the corporate offering to customers' needs and wants. Promotion cements the exchange relationship by attempting to adapt the customer to the corporation's needs and wants. Without both, any such behavior is not marketing.

Figure 4.2 is an attempt to illustrate the mapping of traditional functional departments onto a motive–orientation diagram.

The inner/outer distinction refers to the community of people who produce value and those who consume. Understand and exchange are distinct motives for communicating. A provider can be seen as a responsive responsible value-production system. The outer element of the total environment, termed here the enterprise community, is the stakeholder network within which the producer responsibly and responsively participates. When marketing and public relations enactors compete, only one motive is served. In this, I am simplifying the corporation's necessary communication functions as public relations and marketing, and imagine such activity domains as employee relations and planning as adopting either, or both, of the basic motives for communicating. For example, market research and performance measurement seek to understand, whereas contract negotiation and selling seek to exchange. My choice of the term "community" is a recognition of the trend from market towards community as the basic operating environment for the business enterprise corporation (see Halal, 1996, for extensive evidence of this shift towards economic democracy). Perhaps surprisingly, the connection between

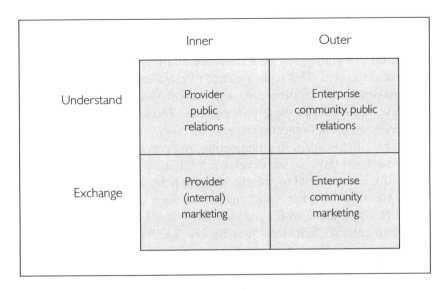

Figure 4.2 Motive–orientation mapping

internal marketing and internal public relations has been little recognized – mostly because the two perspectives have been "owned" by two largely discrete disciplines (an exception is my own work – see Varey, 1996a, and Varey and Lewis, 2000, Ch. 17). If an overarching motive of establishing, maintaining, and enhancing relationships is adopted, the two fields can become one. Relationships are the necessary focus of contemporary management (Fulop and Linstead, 1999, for example, bring together a number of writers that support this view).

Conclusion

I always challenge my students to answer the necessary "so what?" question in concluding their essays on the management of corporate communication. This is an attempt to ensure rigorous and critical thinking in addressing relevant practical issues of managing communication for business management purposes.

So here goes. So what has this discussion revealed?

Is the emergence of corporate communication as a management system no more than a highly visible manifestation of a take-over strategy for empire building? It does not have to be so. Competition for a dominant voice in communication is destructive and counterproductive when it undermines alternative voices in intra-corporate power struggles.

Implications for organization design are clearly that managerialistic assumptions of control and ownership are counter to the notion of responsive and responsible management through participation and stewardship. Inherent differentiation has be recognized and responded to through integrative management. This is the essence of conciliation of conflicts around the management of relationships with stakeholders and the underlying reputation that mediates these relationships. Today, managing is relationship management, not object management.

Mintzberg helps again in commenting that corporations become highly politicized when they cannot develop a harmonious distribution of power. He sees this as beneficial to society, because politics kills corporations that are not well suited to their environments. So do you have to swim with the sharks? If you choose to do so, you had better become a bigger shark. Recall two central characters from Steven Speilberg's 1975 classic film *Jaws*. The macho fisherman and the rather peckish great shark certainly had a relationship. Do you believe that anything good can come from any relationship of dominance and victimization? Adversarial interactions usually result in lose–lose outcomes as the film graphically portrays.

As I have argued elsewhere (Varey, 2000), unless we broaden our ways of conceiving human communication as a phenomenon of the social world beyond that of a tool for objective informing, we will not get the real point of this issue. Our Western mental models of relating are fundamentally oppositional and adversarial and this is reinforced and modeled in our sender–mediator–receiver notion of communicating. Corporate communication can help facilitate and underpin a framework for integrated communication systems.

Reconfiguring and Organizing for Strategic Communication Management: the BP Oil Experience

In 1992 BP – the British Petroleum Company – made a loss and cut the shareholders' dividend. BP Oil, the company's refining and marketing part of the business, dealt with the shock by shifting internal communication from being a soft option to a strategic imperative to help turn the business round. The aim was to make communication a line management responsibility, recognizing that communication is a two-way relational process among staff and management. Quite simply, communication and leadership are fundamental to the business.

For BP Oil the challenge was to retain and mobilize commitment and motivation while transforming the way the business operates. The company had to change from one where employees were protected from the hard facts of commercial life and a job with BP was a job for life, to a company where knowledge and understanding of business performance provide the stimulus for motivation, and where returns and the need to manage costs were accepted as the day-to-day way of working everywhere in the organization, from the chief executive's office to the forecourt.

BP Oil took a big step away from the functional model of "communication management," towards a recognition that managers are responsible for their own communication competence and that of the corporation as a whole. This required them to think about how they could help their team workers to communicate effectively as a work group and with other work groups, and for them to act as representative between teams. Leadership and communication competence *became recognized* as inseparable.

The next stage for BP was to take the organization design a stage further to create the coincident domain model of corporate communication. Then communication management becomes a core competence and corporate communication provides the system for good management – coherence, direction, leadership, and better business results. In order to achieve this paradigm shift, managers have to be convinced of what Drucker (1973) observed – that communication is the *mode of management* and not the means. Communication for business effectiveness and efficiency is far too important to be left to professional communicators. The holy grail is to convince more of them.

The results speak for themselves. In four years BP's share price trebled. Former Group Chief Executive David Simon's original financial targets of cutting debt by a $1 billion a year, making $2 billion a year profit and holding capital spending to $5 billion a year were achieved a year early. BP Oil moved from almost bottom of the industry league table to the top in terms of return on assets and in two years more than doubled its operating profit, largely through self-help measures.

BP Oil are among a growing number of corporations who have moved to become more democratic in their decision-making by creating a participative culture and exploiting technology-enabled cost-free information flows. Not only is communication more important, it is also a different kind of communication that reflects a shift in power relations. Technical communication – packaging and disseminating information – is necessary, but not sufficient. Managers have to become managers of systems for communicating – communication management is a strategic competence. Specialized communication groups cannot be left to simply operate as autonomous service providers, who compete to win contracts to peddle other people's ideas. When "tribal warfare" persists, everyone loses out – unless you take Mintzberg's point of view, and see the slaughter as a cleansing process for society! Forget the idea that "knowledge (information) is power." In contemporary society it is participation in systems of communication that brings influence and its benefits and rewards. Communication certainly is too important to be left to "communicators," but let us not ignore that communicators are too important to be only communicating. Managing and communicating cannot be divorced – both are relational phenomena.

Competent management requires *a project of integrating business* enterprise in the face of natural differentiation. Centralization tools, motivated by desire for control, such as strategic plans, corporate identity programs, staff newsletters, and Vision-Mission-Values statements, will not deal with this differentiation productively. Integration of business functions is about co-ordination that recognizes interdependence. The effect is incorporation and

ILLUSTRATION (cont'd)

transcendence, rather than stultifying unification and consolidation. Emergent properties result – innovation that enables response and responsibility. Corporate communication, then, is a transcendent management strategy, not a battle for ownership of turf. The term and concept of integrated marketing communication has become a strong currency in business and management schools, but of course it can be seen as evidence of an attempt by marketing specialists to subsume public relations within a stronger discipline wherein they retain ownership. Needless to say, Schultz and Kitchen (2000) have not slipped into this potentially adversarial trap. Communication is studied, generally, outside the business and management schools. Divisive and counter-productive turf wars are rife among academics too! Casting integration as imperialism is a fatal conceit (Hayek, 1990) in an emerging stakeholder-community form of society.

Source: Based on Varey and Mounter, 1997.

(*Note:* Pamela Mounter was a Communication Counsellor with BP Oil at the time of writing the case study. The original paper won a Research Foundation Best Paper award at the 1997 Conference of the International Association of Business Communicators in Los Angeles.)

Chapter
The role of integrated communication in the interactive age

philip j. kitchen and don e. schultz

ILLUSTRATION

"The Transformation of British Airways World Cargo"

British Airways World Cargo (BAWC), which for a long time had been seen as the "other part" of BA, faced some significant challenges in the changing airfreight market of the early to mid-1990s. BA even considered pulling out of the airfreight business altogether. But a change program, spearheaded by integrated communication, implemented with a clear engagement strategy, helped transform the organization into a profitable global business.

In the mid-1980s, BAWC, the freight carrying arm of British Airways, was a strategic business unit in crisis. Not only was it the poor relative of a passenger focused business, it was located in an increasingly hostile fiercely competitive business environment. And, a happy resolution was not in sight.

But like all good stories, there is a beginning, a middle and an end. This is the story of how that beginning and middle were shaped and how BAWC transformed itself from an ugly duckling into a swan. In testament to this story stands a new building at Heathrow, the length of three soccer pitches. More importantly, integral to that building and the business it personifies is a world-compatible workforce, committed to a business of which they can be justifiably proud.

BAWC has always been a key part of British Airways and is currently the fifth largest cargo carrier in the world. It started operating as a separate business within British Airways in 1983. Despite its traditional "little brother" image within the airline, in 1998 BAWC generated $947 million worth of revenue.

Over the past twenty years, the cargo market worldwide has been undergoing major changes. The competition has reinvented itself and continues to do so (echoing a theme throughout this text). Integrators (such as FedEx)

82

have expanded into the traditional cargo market, and freight forwarders accelerated from small, local operators into international companies. Customers are ever more demanding: the requirement is for a time definite product. There has also been increasing commoditization of general freight. Last, but by no means least, there has been the opportunity to increase global network coverage through airline alliances – and that opportunity has been quickly grasped by other airlines around the world. In addition to this changing environment, by the mid-1990s, BAWC was facing its biggest [marketing] challenge ever. Despite being a revenue generator for BA, it was perceived within the broader business as a company which regularly over-promised and under-delivered, which had high unit costs, whose processes were not consistent worldwide, and whose employees paid little heed to laid down standards – if such standards existed at all. Quality of service was poor and getting worse, working practices were out of date, productivity was low, and ineffective operations at the Heathrow hub were preventing the capture of a larger share in the expanding world market. Certainly not a pretty sight. Coinciding with a review of whether BAWC's businesses were core or non core, BA was starting to question whether it should be in the air cargo business at all.

But the final decision made by the BA board was a resounding "yes." It did want to maintain its stake in the cargo industry. With that strategic decision came a $40 million investment to cover the construction and fitting of a state of the art New World Cargo Centre at Heathrow plus investment in new technology in the form of bar coding equipment and track and trace technology. The company needed change to become a profitable, global business and to make that shift, it needed a comprehensive change program which would deliver:

- clear direction within a flexible business strategy
- new processes and working practices to become more effective and customer oriented
- new IT systems that would enable operational effectiveness
- skilled and motivated people
- improved working relationships within the business
- visible and strong leadership

Working with consultancy PricewaterhouseCoopers, a logical structure to the change program was achieved. This included a strategic map, which outlined clear goals for the period 1997–2001, and a "route map" which showed the steps required to achieve each of the goals, accountabilities, and measurement criteria. A balanced business scorecard was also introduced to manage business and change performance. But, if all this structure was being put in place around the hard side of change management, what was being developed on the "soft" side?

(See also illustration at end of chapter "Managing the Soft Side of Change.")

Source: Originally a corporate brochure developed by Smythe Dorward Lambert and cited with the kind permission of Smythe Dorward Lambert, 55 Drury Lane, London WC2B 5SQ. Internet: www.smythedorward.com.

Introduction

The case of BAWC illustrates several elements necessary for success in the global economy:

- the business was a large strategically viable business unit within a global company
- it constituted a major player in a global industry in its own right
- it faced the challenge of an increasingly competitive and hostile global environment
- there was a significant need for internal change to become more flexible and accommodate the needs of an expansive but increasingly discerning group of global customers and critical stakeholders
- competitors had either adjusted or were adjusting or flexing to new marketplace realities
- the organization needed to deliver what was being promised through marketing communication programs
- an integrated communication program underpinning the internal need to change minds, hearts, and behaviors needed to *precede and run alongside the structural changes* (see end illustration).

During this time, the corporate parent – British Airways – was facing its own problems of addressing the needs of globally discerning customers and publics. The jury is still out on this ...

Today, "raising the corporate umbrella" means approaching integrated communication not just from a local or national but from a global perspective. Given the speed, span and reach of electronic communication today, we argue there are technically no local or national firms, only global ones. Even the pizza parlor on the corner is involved in global communication through their website and Internet connection. And the truth is, organizations no longer have any choice. Once they decide to enter the electronic arena, they become global almost instantaneously as witness the growth of Amazon.com, PriceLine, Charles Schwab and other "new economy" brands. This "global without choice" situation creates a twofold scenario for executives, that is: (a) integrated communication that is created and related primarily at the corporate level; and (b) integrated marketing communication that takes place primarily at the level of the individual brand or brands.

Today, we often see the corporation or firm as a brand in its own right. Thus, the communication decision is not just traditional product branding directed by the mid-level managers but corporate and organizational brand and communication as well which generally is the purview of senior corporate managers. The issue of corporate branding is discussed in this chapter and expanded upon by Jim Garritty in Chapter 6 and by Marilyn Roberts in Chapter 7. The important point, of course, is that both areas of communication are interactive, synergistic, and generally global. This duality in communications at varying levels of management in the firm has caused much of the disruption in traditional communication planning.

We start by considering the contextual global environment in which integrated communication (corporate) and/or integrated marketing communication (product or service) will be deployed. We then consider the move to a global/brand oriented approach. This is followed by definitions of the two approaches. We then justify the need for the two types of communication, one taking place at the corporate level, the other at the operating marketing level. Obviously for business-to-business firms, or those with unitary product or service lines, this distinction may require more analysis, and in some cases, may not even be relevant. But, for those firms with multiple product lines, diverse brands, and brand architectures that rely on the corporate name for support and relevance, the issue is clear and the discussion below appropriate. More importantly, the principles discussed, and the processes as outlined here and in subsequent chapters can, we believe, be used in many other organizational scenarios. The argument that follows is based on that in our earlier book, *Global Communications: An Integrated Marketing Approach*, published last year (Schultz and Kitchen, 2000). Our views, at least on this topic, have not changed markedly in the intervening period.

The contextual global environment

Clearly, we cannot consider all types of global marketing activity in this text (see Dunning, 1993, for an excellent explanation). Since the period from the mid-1980s to the present day has defined the contemporary *global economy*, this is where we focus our attention. It is in this economy and related marketplaces that corporations are engaged in the battles for market and mind share, competitive positioning, and global dominance. Today, the world is still progressing through a series of environmental upheavals that are impacting business activity around the world. This has been created by an exponential advance in information technology that potentially is universally accessible; by the dislocation of labor away from the country of origin mainly toward the Asian, Indian, and now Eastern European economies; and by the rise of informed streetwise, savvy, and sophisticated consumers at least in the triad regions (that is in the U.S.A./Canada, Pacific Rim, and the European Community). These factors are all influenced and impacted by the fluid nature of capital that can flow from one side of the world to the other at the flick of a computer button. And, all this is compounded by the rising social issues and the growing unrest over globalization not just in underdeveloped countries but in the U.S.A., Australia, and other apparently globally connected countries.

Extending the earlier quotation from Chapter 1, Dunning (1993), with marked insight, states:

> The decision-making nexus of the MNE [global firm] in the early 1990s has come to resemble the central nervous system of a much larger group of inter-dependent, but less formally governed activities, *aimed primarily at advancing the globally competitive strategy and position of the core organization.* This it does, – first by efficiently combining its organizational specific resources with those it acquires from other firms: – second by its technology, product and *marketing* strategies: and, – third, by the nature of alliances it concludes with other firms. (italics added)

Dunning then cites Bartlett and Ghoshal (1989) (see Chapter 1) who suggest that achieving corporate success in today's highly competitive environment requires development and management of a cross-border network of separate but interrelated activities including:

(a) taking full advantage of scale economies;

(b) understanding the differences in supply capabilities and consumer needs on a country by country basis; and

(c) seeking to use the experience gained nationally and internationally to strengthen the resource base of the organization.

To these we might add, a full understanding of the development and implementation of information technology. For example, North America is primarily focused on the development of broad-brand communication while China, India, and South America are focusing on wireless. While the two are compatible in a market, they are also extremely competitive in terms of development, usage, and customer acquisition.

These four activities involve a continuous sensitive interaction in terms of communication and necessary balance between globalization and localization.

But, all firms are not at the stage where global decisions need to be made on a continuing basis. Each firm is located at some or various points on the developmental continuum from domestic to global in terms of traditional marketing evolution. In spite of the fact that global communication is available, albeit sometimes uncontrollable, each firm may, at its choosing, be using what they believe to be singular or plural approaches to communicate with those publics/customers/consumers/users who could either impact corporate performance or constitute a target market. Further, each firm may also range from a clear focus on one element of the promotional mix (that is selling or direct marketing), to an integration of all communication and promotional elements combined. And those can be implemented in either a corporate or product marketing communication format. The goal of integrated communication, therefore, is to enhance the competitive strategy, position, and capability of the core organization to ensure success – in the competitive marketplace while recognizing that product-level branding and communication are still critically important to most firms.

Competitive performance, we believe, is the major function of marketing effort since marketing is basically about creating exchanges. From a global external perspective, market share – or put another way – satisfaction of consumer needs and thus greater shares of customer requirements, is the desirable outcome. From the same perspective, consumers and publics need to be communicated with, effectively, efficiently, and in an integrated manner. Following Shimp (2000), it is evident that in the highly competitive global marketplace, whatever is marketed (product, service, corporation, political party, idea) also has to be *communicated*. The most meaningful physical metaphor for what is to be communicated is the *concept of brand*.

The movement of communication toward a global brand oriented approach

Marketing is perhaps the *major* business development of the twentieth century. It affects almost every aspect of a consumer's daily life. But, from a business or even an academic perspective, it is only recently that marketing has become a legitimate and recognized corporate activity with attention now being devoted to the subject at the boardroom level. But not all organizations have this belief in marketing. In some corporate suites, marketing is still suspect and often considered a suspect art, not a real science.

It has been argued by Sheth et al. (1988) that marketing rests inexorably on two pillars: (a) thorough understanding of consumer needs and behavior; and, (b) critical analysis of opportunities for competitive advantage. To these, we would add a third pillar, (c) creating, and maintaining positive relationships with publics or stakeholders who could impact or influence corporate performance.

In this text, we view marketing as being about creating satisfactory exchanges with consumers and customers as a result of integrated marketing communication programs. We believe communication must be superimposed on the marketing discipline because of the necessity of building and maintaining positive two-way relationships with other publics who could impact organizational performance. Those might include such firms or persons as suppliers of material, labor, and capital, the stock market(s), business analysts, employees, and other influential publics or stakeholders, all of whom can be impacted through effective corporate communication programs. Conversely, such publics also impact corporate performance.

Businesses today must be consumer, profit, and publicly oriented. Only a few years ago, the first two would have sufficed. But, in support of our dualistic argument regarding the marketing concept, that is – creating exchanges that satisfy individual and organizational objectives more effectively and efficiently than the competition – Philip Kotler (2000) has labeled marketing as *inappropriate* in a world of environmental deterioration, population expansion, worldwide hunger and poverty, and neglected, under-funded, and business-like social services. Thus, marketing as exchange has been augmented by the need to preserve or enhance consumer and societal well being, too. Increasingly, this extends beyond the sound-bite rhetoric of "seeming" rather than the needed "substance" of corporate performance; the former being the empty rain-coat of corporate values.

This new type of societal marketing, when coupled with rapid and irreversible change in the international environment, means that business has to engage in a three-pronged balancing act between company prof-itability, consumer need fulfillment and satisfactions, and as we suggested above, public interest. Each of the three elements can be delivered by inte-grated communication and integrated marketing communication. From a pure marketing perspective, profits and consumer want satisfactions are delivered by means of appropriate products/brands, conveniently available, priced appropriately, and communicated in various ways. Whether one uses McCarthy's Four P's – Product, Price, Promotion, Place – or the Six P's (Kotler, 2000) – the Four P's plus Power and Public Relations – they are the fundamental basis for many effective marketing strategies and tactics. They are focused on target markets. They are inter-active and synergistic. They have a role to play in communication terms. But are they enough?

One recent example from a major global corporation illustrates the point. Following nearly a century of textbook marketing development, the supposedly premier-brand marketer – Procter & Gamble (P&G) – would be expected to get things right. But they discovered they had forgotten someone. Who? The very consumers they were intended and intending to serve. In the years 1995 to 1997, P&G was reportedly making over 55 price changes a day across 110 brands, offering over 400 sales promotion each year, and tinkering continually with package design, color, and contents. In an article in the *The Wall Street Journal* Europe (Narisetti, 1997) Durk Jager, at that time P&G's President and CEO, admitted "we were confusing them" – the customers. But it was not just the customers who were being confused, investors seemed to be confused as well. Thus, the stock market also took a jaundiced view of P&G value and the stock market valuation plummeted. Since that time, P&G has changed to a more concentrated, less ambiguous, approach towards both customers and consumers and the finan-cial marketplace. They have changed CEOs too.

It is clear that "marketing" has moved from its national environmental moorings to a more global scale. From the U.S.A. to the U.K., from Japan to Johannesburg, marketing is now not a corporate choice but a global necessity. Competitive rivalry is no longer company versus company in a domestic setting, but global powerhouse versus global powerhouse in a worldwide arena. Witness, for example, the sustained rush of mergers and acquisitions by firms jockeying for global position, that is to be players in the global marketplace. In oil, British Petroleum has taken over Amoco. In automobiles, Daimler has merged with Chrysler (Martin, 1998). But not all globally-focused take-overs, such as BMW and Rover in the U.K., have been successful. That marriage did not create the anticipated production economies of scale, nor was BMW able to take advantage of learning and experience curve effects as had been hoped. There were significant image problems in that liaison as well. Following a multi-million investment, BMW – having hived off the parts considered to be of value to it – was delighted to offload Rover Cars for the nominal sum of just £1. Meanwhile, Daimler-Benz' reputation for engineering excellence does not seem to square well with Chrysler's overt focus on finance and marketing (see Schultz and Kitchen, 2000). So, while marketing is believed to be magic by some managers, it cannot compensate for inherent corporate or idiosyncratic executive problems.

Undoubtedly, the drive for global competitive geocentric position impacts on consumer behavior as well. It has been argued by Davidson (1998) that consumers don't really care about who owns the various brands they purchase and consume so long as desired benefits are forthcoming. We disagree. In our experience, more and more consumers are becoming concerned about which firms make and market which brands. And they also care about what those firms *do* in areas other than the specific product or service.

Meanwhile Schultz (1998) has argued that the *brand* is the very key to integrated marketing. The brand is increasingly the central core or hub of what consumers want, need, and consider to be of value. And, it is the brand with which customers and consumers have ongoing relationships. But, in this text, we will be using the brand concept in a two-dimensional way. The brand can be a functional product wrapped in appropriate packaging, or it can be the corporation itself as brand. Obviously, the yin and yang of those combinations are what really challenge the communication manager.

So, the brand is key! Or, is it? In the wake of the new media revolution and expansion, in the revitalized appearance of narrow-casting, in the focus on brand/consumer dialogues, in the jockeying for global market share position, in the rising exponential curve of information technology, and with the worldwide accelerant for marketing to *prove* its contribution, there is pressure on all firms not only to consolidate but to integrate as well. But what needs to be integrated?

In our view, integration needs to take place dualistically, in order to be of value. In an age of increasing commonality among competing brands, in an age where price strategies are fairly uniform, in an age where distribution channels have all the differentiation of a row of detergent packets on supermarket shelves, *communication is becoming the sine qua non of marketing.* As a result many theoretical and practical arguments have focused on the need for *all* organizational communication to be integrated, But, these arguments depend not just on organizational fiat, but also corporate culture, strategies, and brand life cycles, none of which is easily manipulated or changed.

So, what needs to be integrated? Undoubtedly, the brand has become, or is becoming the dynamic hub around which the entire organization revolves. So brand is king, at least for the moment. But, in our view, although firms "create" brands, consumers "own" those brands. Firms strive to create brand identities but consumers give those brands their imagery. Brands can be modern or old fashioned depending on how customers and consumers view them. Brand images can change but generally not without the approval of the customer base. Fashions and life cycles change, or put another way, consumers' ways of satisfying their needs change and, thus, brands must change. But, in all these instances, the consumer or customer or buyer has control of the brand for he or she or the business-to-business firm can decide to continue to buy or not to buy. This is the life of the brand.

Five years ago, Levi Strauss was galloping down the highway of global expansion, with a pair of 501s fixed firmly in the saddle. Today, Levi's sales and profits are declining significantly. The ambitious goals of this privatized company are being supplanted by lay-offs and factory closures across the U.S.A. and around the world. In this case, and despite the spin-off toward work day clothes in the form of the Dockers brand, Levi Strauss, as a jeans company, has encountered the downside of the fashion/casual clothing life cycle that has impacted its brand in unexpected ways, that is being supplanted (maybe temporarily) by newer and more fashionable products driven by more attractive (at least to the consumer) icons and more desirable to the retailer and consumer brands. Levi are fighting back with new brands and new offerings more appropriate to 21st century customer tastes. Whether it can succeed or not is still in the balance.

To take the Levi Strauss example a bit further, Figure 5.1 indicates how and in what ways a brand can be fulcrum or hub for profitable growth.

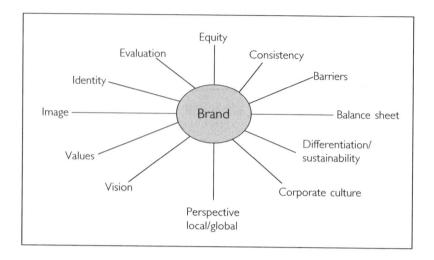

Figure 5.1 Brand structure

For many firms the brand is a twofold entity. The first entity is the brand consumers encounter, learn about, consider, value, purchase, and finally, use. From jeans to jetskis, from razor blades to roller-blades, consumers the world over know these brands. But, the individual brands no longer suffice. Consumers are increasingly wanting to know more about the company behind the well known brands. What does the parent company do? What values does it personify? Which personalities are running the company? These are key questions in many markets and among many consumers today. For an example, look at the major social issues Nike, one of the world's premier brands, faces on a continuing basis as a result of its wage scale in factories in underdeveloped countries.

If we are to talk brands, then companies have the usual choices concerning alternative branding strategies, that is product line branding, specific product branding, corporate branding, combination branding, private label branding, no brand identity and so on. From a communication perspective, and from an integrated marketing approach, specific product brands, that is Crest, Pampers, Snickers and so on, come to mind. These could be integrated under the heading of what has been described as the promotional mix. But the corporation, behind these brands, stands for an identity, often deliberately planned by corporate communication specialists, and an image possessed by those publics impacted by the corporation. This is conceptualized in Figure 5.2.

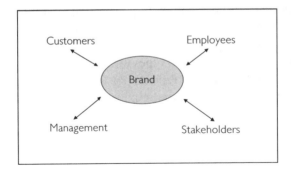

Figure 5.2 The brand ties together the four
key organizational elements

From this figure, the corporate brand can be seen as the central meaning that provides the basis for identity programs, strategy and competitive thrust to the basketful of individual brands within its portfolio. Meanwhile, individual brands, powerful corporate assets in their own right, promote exchanges that build brand loyalty, provide brand equity, and immeasurably enhance and empower corporations that ostensibly "own" them. But these individual brands can be affected by consumer likes, dislikes, tastes and perceptions. Hence the somewhat arbitrary movement away from the Levi Strauss name by marketing and, one would assume, corporate communication managers in the late 1990s. But equally, perceptions of the corporation can influence individual brand performances. For example, the Nestlé imprimatur is known the world over as a symbol of quality and value and it continues to expand and grow with acquisitions and organic growth of the firm. So the corporate brand can add value to the product if properly managed.

The model proposed, however, is imperfect. It does not show the interactions between brands within the brand puzzle, nor does it show the interactions between individual brands and the corporation in terms of reflecting overall values associated with both. That is what creates the puzzle for communication managers or executives. How much of what? What mix of what? What inputs will result in the best returns for the marketing organization and for the corporate entity?

So, there is indeed a brand puzzle to be solved. From an individual brand perspective, communication needs to be integrated, not just at the tactical level, but ultimately in terms of finance and corporate strategy as well. A strategy of communication, underpinned by a sound ongoing analysis of consumer behaviors, in terms of returns on investment by behavioral segment is needed. From a corporate perspective, a similar strategy needs to be deployed. But, that strategy must be against internal organizational members, channels, suppliers, retailers, influencers, and analysts. Interactions between the two different types of brand, that is the corporate brand and individual product brand within its portfolio, are still being analyzed in boardrooms around the world (see Schultz and Kitchen, 2000).

Integrated communication

To many managers, executives, and leading-edge managerial and marketing thinkers (Keegan, 1999) globalization is already a reality. But, as we have indicated in our previous book (Schultz and Kitchen, 2000), the driving force of marketing, and branding products, services, and corporations is the marketplace. The "marketplace" whether local, national, international or global, does not stand alone. It is a direct consequence of market economies bound up in those who "buy" or "sell" in it. Sellers, according to Ted Levitt "marshall materials, technologies, people, sentiment, wits, and money to their intended ends, *meeting head-on in an amalgamating and unforgiving crucible*" (Levitt, 1983, italics added).

Levitt also stated:

> The purpose of business is to get and keep a customer. Without solvent customers in some reasonable proportion, there is no business. Customers are constantly presented with lots of options to help them solve their problems. They don't buy things, they buy solutions to problems. *The surviving and thriving business is a business that constantly seeks better ways to help people solve their problems.* To create betterness requires knowledge of what customers think betterness to be. *This precedes all else in business.* The imagination that figures out what that is, imaginatively figures out what should be done, and does it with imagination and high spirits will drive the enterprise forward. (Levitt, 1983, italics added)

Admittedly, much of this discussion concerns *marketing* and exchanges. Marketing and managerial imagination commonly drive initial marketing impetus. And that marketing impetus has to be customer-focused or consumer-oriented. But eventually, consumers start to ask questions and to hold attitudes toward the companies behind the products and services they buy. Note, at this stage, they do not just buy or not buy brands (that is usable, functional, or symbolically representative products). They also buy or do not buy, support or do not support, and carry images (positive or negative) toward companies which they themselves have often created or often have had created for them by various media vehicles. The company or corporation now has meaning and resonance for consumers and other publics. The question, of course, is whether or not that meaning or resonance or image is beneficial to the firm.

Corporate performance is not just a function of how well its brands are doing, but also of how well the company *as brand* is doing. In our view it is insufficient to integrate all communication activities at brand level only. All communication activities at the level of the business or corporation must be integrated as well. And, this – together with the principles given in this text – is one of the ribs of raising the corporate umbrella.

Moreover, there must also be interaction between the two forms of communication in an ongoing, interactive, interdependent, and synergistic manner. There should be no walls or barriers, despite their often different functions, between these types of communication, for both ultimately are needed to drive the business forward.

A. The corporate brand perspective

Around the world, many individual product or service brands are in trouble. They are being impacted by lack of innovation, excessive trade dealing, confused or non-rationalized brand portfolios, inconsistent brand extensions, all of which create customer ambivalence toward the brand. Include then, inadequate services and inconsistency in terms of communication and it is clear that firms are being challenged (Figure 5.3). All these problems are generated – *not by customers or stakeholders* – but by the organization. This raises the important question of the value of the corporate brand in relation to the individual product brands and whether or not the corporate brand should impose structural relevance on what the individual brands could or should do. Thus, by definition we are implying an interrelationship and interaction between corporate and marketing communication in terms of totally integrated communication.

But, just what is the corporate brand supposed to do? Does it help create sales for the product line or is it something that creates value for customers, shareholders and employees?

We would argue that trying to measure marketplace sales results from a corporate communication program, at least at the corporate brand level, is generally the wrong approach. The aim of the corporate brand is or should be to supplement, underpin, and reinforce the various product and service marketing activities being used by the product brand(s). Corporate

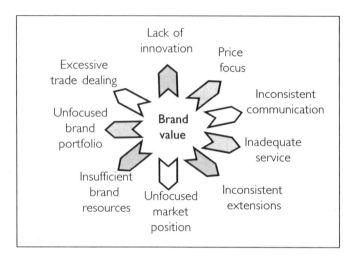

Figure 5.3 Factors impacting the declining value of brands

communication should thus provide value to customers, publics, stakeholders, shareholders and the like, in addition to customers and prospects for the product brand(s). But, it should be noted that those values may not be immediately measurable in terms of increased exchanges. And, that is the measurement challenge for corporate branding. What value? Over what time? With what return on investment? We deal with this issue in the final chapter of the text for it is a critical one for senior managers.

The purposes of corporate branding have been illustrated by de Chernatony and McDonald (1998) and are adapted by us below to indicate what a corporate brand is and what it can potentially accomplish:

■ make the company name known, distinct, and credible in the minds of existent and potential customers, consumers, and stakeholders

■ facilitate the building of relationships with existing and potential customers, consumers, and stakeholders

■ portray, if possible, the benefits offered to buyers and stakeholders that embody the value system of the corporation.

To these criteria, we would add the corporate brand also provides value to employees, shareholders, market analysts, community leaders, and on and on. We focus first, however, on the value the corporate brand can provide to consumers, customers, and other more closely aligned stakeholders.

Trademarks –	These are the symbols, names, icons and the like the firm owns and can protect. Corporate communication is generally responsible for this through the legal department.
Brands –	These are the relationships with customers and consumers and stakeholders that products and services create for the firm through the promises they make and the experiences these stakeholders have.
Trustmarks –	These are the quality and experience that are the result of brand activities promised and delivered through the various brands and trademarks. For the most part, these are reliability, trust, consistent dealings and the like that reside within the corporate organization. The corporate communication group is responsible for seeing that the brands and trademarks provide the trust that the organization owns or wants to own.

Figure 5.4 Three levels of branding

Many major organizations have done a great deal of work in this area. Electrolux, for example – a multinational manufacturer of consumer electrical goods – has divided the corporate brand into three levels as shown in Figure 5.4.

Our theme "raising the corporate umbrella" could be metaphorically seen in this light where the umbrella becomes the "trustmark" and "trademarks" and "brands" become the ribs supporting the corporate umbrella. One cannot survive without the other.

B. Building brand identities

As shown in Figure 5.5, Electrolux management believes corporate brand identity is composed of familiarity which comes from the marketplace – that is from customers, consumers, stakeholders, and the like through their knowledge and experience with the firm's products and services. That's what corporate communication is supposed to do, build familiarity for the trustmark. That is critical. If stakeholders don't know or aren't familiar with the name or brand or the firm, little else matters.

In addition, brand identity is also influenced by two other major elements. One is specialization, that is, what the organization does best, what it is known for, its place in the market. This can be separated into

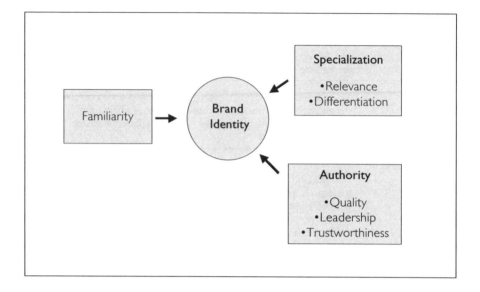

Figure 5.5 Building corporate brand identity

relevance and differentiation. In other words what does the firm do that is *relevant* to the stakeholders and what makes the organization *different* from its competitors? These two areas are vital at the market and individual customer level.

The second element is authority, that is, what is the basis for or the support for the corporate identity? Electrolux believes there are three factors. Quality, which is straightforward, that is, workmanship, ingredients, construction, distribution, service, and so on. Leadership, defined as where and how the organization rates in the world or in certain attributes or activities. For example, are they leaders in various areas such as technology, pricing, intellectual capital, value, and so on? The third factor is trustworthiness. That is, can the stakeholders trust the company and its management? Has it been honest and fair in its dealings with various publics over time?

Using this approach Electrolux management is then able to construct its brand architecture approach, that is, how the various units can or should use the corporate brand in all forms of communication (Figure 5.6).

Electrolux has created a corporate brand architecture that ranges from *solo*, where the brand is on its own with little or no corporate identification, to *hallmark*. Hallmark equates to instances where the corporate brand means authority and a reason why the expertise of the corporate

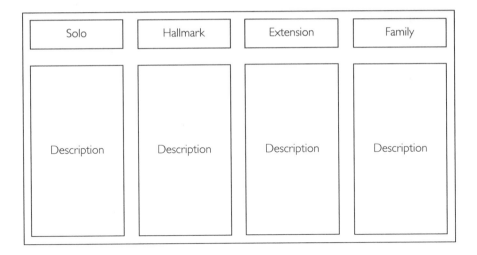

Figure 5.6 Corporate brand architecture

parent enhances or supports the promises of the individual brands. *Extension* indicates how or in what ways the corporate or individually supported brands can be extended and expanded into other product and service areas. Finally, there is *family*, that is, the firm creates a family of brands under the corporate name as organizations such as Virgin or Nestlé have done. All these structures are, of course, dependent on how corporate brand value is created and what it means to customers and prospects.

C. Creating corporate brand value

The corporate brand can then be valued based on power, quality, price, and loyalty. Electrolux uses a graphic that helps it define the value of the corporate brand (Figure 5.7).

As shown, corporate brand value comes from four things. Quality that is maintained throughout the firm. Power, which means the authority and capability that the firm is able to generate through internal and external resources such as R&D, manufacturing capability and so on. Price, which means the value they deliver to stakeholders in all areas. And, Loyalty, that is how much support and advocacy the firm has been able to develop over time in the marketplace from customers, employees, channels, and so on.

Loyalty has been a major problem for the new economy dot.com firms. Because of their lack of time in the market, level and quality of customer

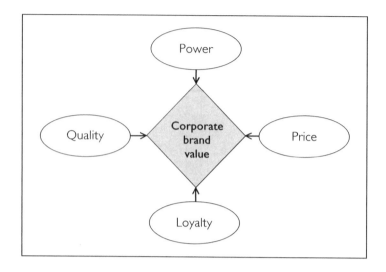

Figure 5.7   Corporate brand value creators

experience, and their resulting questionable profitability, it has been extremely difficult for these and other start-up firms to build either a product or corporate brand.

D. Surrounding stakeholders with corporate communication

The goal of corporate communication is to surround the various stakeholders with communication that inoculates or at least helps insulate them from other external influences. Charles Handy (1995) taught the principle of the American doughnut in *The Empty Raincoat*. He stated that the principle of the doughnut requires it to be "inside-out" with the hole on the outside and the dough in the middle. It is therefore, as with most useful metaphors, an *imaginary doughnut*, a conceptual doughnut, one for thinking about, not for eating, but the concept holds great relevance for our discussion (Figure 5.8).

    In this figure, we are using Handy's metaphor in a different way. The core of any organization are the corporate values it represents. This we personify as the corporate brand. And corporate brands exist irrespective of the communication policies advocated by senior management. In the 21st century, corporate communication must be the core element in all organizational communications for it is the basis for all organizational

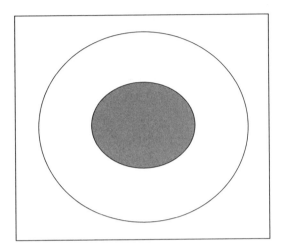

Figure 5.8 The doughnut principle

direction and purpose. This core of corporate values is then surrounded by the various forms of product branding and the associated integrated brand and marketing communication programs that might be developed and delivered. Thus, the corporate brand should form the core of the communication program and all other forms of communication must be allied to and integrated with the core. Likewise, at the marketing level, individual brands become the core for communication associated therewith. In Figure 5.9, we illustrate how the organizational core must closely correspond with the need to interface with stakeholders who could impact corporate activity and performance levels.

To us, stakeholders are the main focal point of any integrated communication activity. The diagram shows major stakeholders as customers rather than consumers. The stakeholders are surrounded with the actual things the organization does and the resulting experiences the stakeholders have or might have. For example, that could include products, pricing, channel contacts, customer services, perceived value compared to competition and the like.

The outside ring is what the corporate communication does or tactics the communication manager employs. As shown, it includes crisis management, vision and leadership from the top management, globalization, corporate advertising, marketing public relations, and so on. All topics covered in this text.

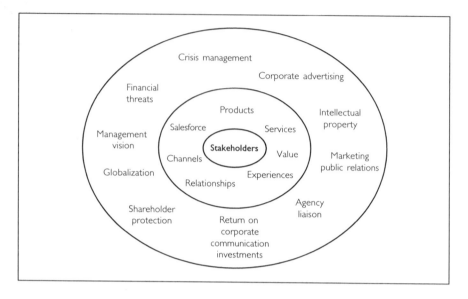

Figure 5.9 Surrounding stakeholders with corporate experience and corporate communication

Corporate communication is aimed at *publics* via a variety of interactive deployable tools. These include corporate advertising, corporate publicity, public affairs, government relations and lobbying activities, issues management, financial and analyst relations, and corporate sponsorship. These are conceptualized and explained in Kitchen (1997) and Cutlip et al. (1994). The aim of such activities is to support and underpin both the *image* and *identity* of the firm.

E. Corporate image

Corporate image has been described by van Riel (1995) as the picture people have of a company. In other words, corporate image is "owned" by people without any conscious effort going on by the company concerned. Dowling (1986) described image as:

> the set of meanings by which an object is known and through which people describe, remember and relate to it. That is, the net result of the interaction of a person's beliefs, ideas, feelings, and impressions about an object [company]. (brackets added)

Table 5.1   Integrated communication – the corporate global approach

1.   Integrated communication, like marketing, needs to be *managed*. It is preceded by a sound understanding of the dynamic(s) of each public. Relationships have to be *planned*, then *implemented, monitored* and adjustments made when and wherever necessary. This implies that different marketplaces may require different approaches and different strategic alliances and relationships while not losing sight of the strategic imperative for a globalized approach. Integrated communication is driven by the long term and the strategic. The process is not short term, or ad hoc. It is not unplanned. Reactive fire-fighting may occasionally occur, but must always be balanced by the strategic imperative.

2.   Integrated communication is not about one activity. It is diverse in nature and may involve singular or multiple deployment of elements of the corporate communication arsenal.

3.   It is not one-way communication, but is two-way, interactive, aimed at creating mutual benefits. Thus, it is concerned with identifying, establishing, and maintaining relationships with various publics *nationally, regionally, internationally, and most of all, globally*. These relationships presuppose regular monitoring of awareness, attitudes, and behavior inside and outside an organization. *The Economist*, as early as 1989, suggested that this means that big companies (multinationals, international, global and so on) have to change the way they talk to and listen to people both inside and outside the organization.

4.   Publics who could impact organizational performance are not singular (that is consumers) but *plural*. This means analyzing and potentially adjusting corporate and marketing policies in line with the public's interests, and with the concomitant focus on organizational survival and growth in a globalized market scenario.

Source: Adapted from Kitchen (1997), p. 27.

This definition corresponds with the idea of fields of experience and memory organization packets (see Schultz and Kitchen, 2000). People can be employees; consumers; suppliers of material, parts, labor, or capital; customers; distributors; agents; joint venture partners; business analysts; share dealers; newspaper editors; business journalists; or pressure groups. Each has a view, an opinion, an image, which consciously or unconsciously sway expectations and direct steps toward or against the brand or firm. Integrated communication at the corporate level implies that relationships with publics, groups, or stakeholders need to be managed in a pluralistic interactive manner and with a long-term relationship marketing perspective in mind (expanded in Table 5.1).

Image is too important a subject to be left to chance. Relationships need to be built and managed over time. Image can be strengthened, reinforced, or altered positively by organizational efforts to create and manage the corporate identity.

F. Corporate identity

The corporate image can, to a degree, be seen as representative of the identity of an organization. Undoubtedly, such identity is conveyed by the messages (signs, signals, symbols) that an organization communicates about itself. Thus, we argue that images are the internal criteria which people have of an organization, while identity is the planned or managed effort by an organization to communicate with its target groups. At best, image will be a microcosm of the attempts an organization makes to communicate its identity. Firms and businesses approach identity, or the ways in which they attempt to communicate with publics, in different

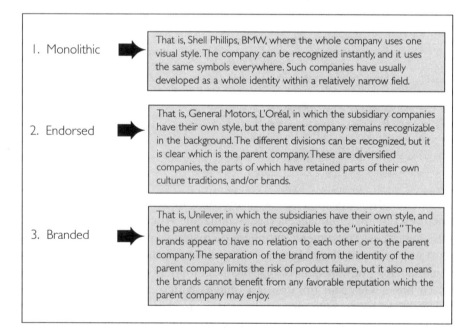

Figure 5.10 Corporate identity approaches
Source: Adapted from Olins (1989), cited in van Riel (1995).

ways. Not all are at the same level, nor do they communicate in the same ways. Olins (1989) discussed at least three different strategies to approach corporate identity (Figure 5.10).

Ultimately, these identity structures (which are not mutually exclusive) are related to different types of overarching strategy (see Kammerer, 1988, cited in van Riel, 1995). While it is not necessary to review all types of strategy here, plainly companies are not only at different stages in terms of their international, multinational, or global development, but they also adopt different strategies based upon the overarching organizational strategy, which itself is a function of historical development. However, it is our view that corporations are becoming more visible, more accountable, and less able to hide inside empty corporate raincoats. Corporations have to play a role, become global citizens, be seen to contribute in some way to the quality of life on this planet. In other words they must go beyond quid pro quo exchanges. For example, what a company does in Pacific Asia in terms of employment policy impacts on corporate image around the world.

Global insight

In December 1984, an explosion in Bhopal, India killed more than 2500 people. Union Carbide, the USA firm that owned majority shares in the company, started to receive more than 5000 media calls a day. Bhopal Union Carbide was lambasted by the media. The result (in 1984) was the formation of a public relations team. It was estimated (*The Economist*, 1989) that 75% of the chairman's time was then taken up with communications. Following the Bhopal disaster and a resultant out-of-court settlement, Union Carbide found itself on the receiving end of a take-over bid (Kitchen, 1997).

Texas Instruments now maintains a major software development in Bangalore, India, connected via satellite to a global network. American Express has consolidated much of its back-office work in Europe from 16 regional centers in major and expensive cities to one suburban town in Southern England. In the most extreme case of global specialization, Nike does not own any factories, but subcontracts all production to partners in Southeast Asian countries. Kodak,

> IBM, Hewlett-Packard, and Texas Instruments all conduct research in Japan to tap into that country's technical innovation. Conversely, Japanese companies such as Nissan and Mazda maintain design facilities in California (Yip, 1996).

Corporate communication at its simplest is primarily a mechanism for developing and managing a set of relationships with publics or stakeholders who could affect overall performance. These relationships must be viewed in a long-term strategic fashion. For monolithic or branded or endorsed companies all the tools of corporate communication will need to be deployed. Even for those firms which maintain a branded approach, many publics (including consumers) are becoming more and more interested in what a company is, where it is coming from, who is managing it, whether there are problems created of an environmental nature because of business processes, and how and in what ways the organization as a whole is acting as a solid corporate citizen.

Moreover, each type of firm is involved in the process of analysis, planning, implementation and control of corporate identity programs in various markets around the world. Images are, to a very significant degree, dependent on the meanings inherent in the identity programs deployed. And, it is relatively straightforward these days via the Internet to not only access positive information (via a company website), but also to gather criticisms of firms, products, and brands, – at least some negative aspects of corporate and brand behaviors which most firms would probably like to see ignored. Organizational image, in our view, can act as a powerful and protective force field in containing and nurturing the basketful of brands within corporate portfolios. Expenditures, however, in the corporate domain, are *dwarfed* by the expenditures taking place at the level of individual brands and it is to that area that we now turn.

Integrated marketing communication

Integrated marketing communication (IMC) is the *major* communication development in the last decade of the 20th century. Most of the history of IMC approaches, theory, and contribution, however, are very recent in nature. Just as businesses do not spring, full-blown, into the arena as

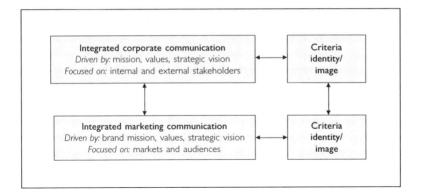

Figure 5.11 Corporate and marketing communication: an integrated approach

global forces, so businesses do not suddenly decide to become "integrated." It is clear, though, more and more firms are considering communication as the key competitive advantage of marketing per se. We agree with them. Figure 5.11 outlines the relationship between integrated communication at the corporate level and integrated marketing communication at the individual brand level.

Most firms are starting to raise, or have raised, the corporate umbrella over the basketful of brands within their portfolios. These brands are powerful strategic assets. They need to be protected, nurtured, and developed into international, and in some cases global, brands. But to consumers, the only real brand equity they possess is their knowledge organization packets about the brands they buy, are persuaded to use, or in some cases reject. What do consumers believe about a company, product, service, or their relationship with the brand? Put another way, what really creates and sustains brand loyalty? It is communication and customer experience! Product design, packaging, brand name, pricing strategy, location and ambience of accessibility (or distribution) are all (following Shimp, 2000) forms of *communication*. And, indeed, we argue that communication is essentially the experience the customer has with the brand over time. Quality is a form of communication. Customer service is another form of communication as is availability, price, and so on.

From our perspective, all forms of communication over which the company can exercise control or influence can be *integrated*. Firms obviously do not arrive at integration overnight either. Instead they progress through at least four stages as shown in Figure 5.12.

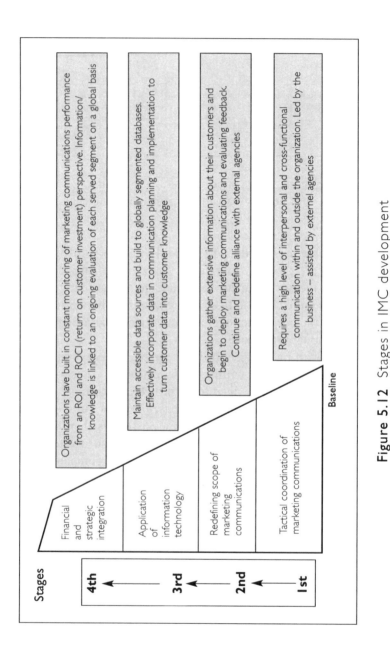

Stages

4th Financial and strategic integration

Organizations have built in constant monitoring of marketing communications performance from an ROI and ROCI (return on customer investment) perspective. Information/knowledge is linked to an ongoing evaluation of each served segment on a global basis

3rd Application of information technology

Maintain accessible data sources and build to globally segmented databases. Effectively incorporate data in communication planning and implementation to turn customer data into customer knowledge

2nd Redefining scope of marketing communications

Organizations gather extensive information about their customers and begin to deploy marketing communications and evaluating feedback. Continue and redefine alliance with external agencies

1st Tactical coordination of marketing communications

Requires a high level of interpersonal and cross-functional communication within and outside the organization. Led by the business – assisted by external agencies

Baseline

Figure 5.12 Stages in IMC development

A. Tactical coordination

Firms in this first stage of tactical coordination focus on the idea of *one sight, one sound*; that is, they attempt to integrate promotional elements such as advertising, sales promotion, marketing public relations, direct marketing, and/or the Internet firms also strive to maximize consistency and synergy among all promotional mix elements. They may typically instruct advertising agencies to maximize all potential exposures to the brand through a multiplicity of different media. Typically, and in accord with marketing communication theory, messages will vary in content but the same core values will be depicted repeatedly. Repetition of the same promotional campaigns, however, that have been successful in, for example, the U.S.A., often mean problems if adopted and implemented wholesale overseas. Typically, consumers may respond in different ways simply because their fields of experience differ.

B. Redefining the scope of marketing communication

In the second stage, the firm starts to adopt an outside-in, as opposed to inside-out, perspective. Typically, the focus here is on the customer's or consumer's reception, perception, and perspective. Rather than simply integrating from a tactical Stage 1 perspective – businesses look at *all potential contacts* a customer or consumer may have with a product, service, brand, or company. For the first time, firms start to consider integrated communication – from the dual perspective of both internal and external communication activities. Thus, they begin to attempt the alignment of all communication to fit the needs of corporate publics, including consumers, and exchange partners, customers or consumers.

C. Application of information technology

The third stage does not constitute the arrival and incorporation of consumer and customer data as the driving force for marketing activity. Usually, this empirical data is already available inside the organization. Instead, the firm starts to *understand*, *aggregate*, and *apply* the data to *identify*, *value*, and *monitor* the impact of integrated communication programs to key customer target markets or segments over time. It is generally here that communication clearly becomes a strategic corporate tool and not just a departmental tactical activity.

D. Financial and strategic integration

The fourth stage constitutes the highest level of integration at this time. Here, the emphasis moves to deploying both the marketing database(s) identified in Stage 3, with the previous abilities developed from Stages 1 and 2 to drive corporate and marketing strategic planning using customer information and insight. Firms in this stage tend to re-evaluate financial information and infrastructures to aid in the development of "closed-loop" planning and evaluation. Thus, firms at this stage are able to evaluate marketing expenditures based on some type of return-on-investment in customers or in marketing communication activities.

Contextual overview

The majority of firms, whether international or global in scope or scale, are moving through these stages, though relatively few (possibly a handful) have now arrived at Stage 4. Most multinationals and global marketers, in our experience, will be working at Stages 1 or 2. Initially, their goal is to find ways to integrate the broad variety of brands they have created over time. They also struggle with the integration of the large number of individual marketing databases and with the customer segments or niches they are serving and relating all these to the to-be targeted marketing communication plans they hope to deploy. However, overlaid on this ideal template will be the firm's position in its historical, cultural, managerial and contextual situation. Likewise, each brand within the corporate portfolio may be positioned nationally, internationally, regionally or globally which, of course, compounds the communication management problem.

While a specific study of corporate communication has not, to our knowledge, been conducted such as the one on IMC cited above, we strongly believe the same type and structure of integration development would likely be found. Thus, we believe the four stages of integration are applicable to corporate activities, not just to product communication. Further, we believe the framework outlined can be used by corporate communication managers as a guideline for integration development in all types of firms.

Summary and conclusion

This chapter has considered the global marketplace in which integrated communication or integrated marketing communication will need to be deployed. The key word is *contextual*. Contextual in the sense of firm and environmental dissimilarities. Contextual in the sense of differential approaches by firms over time. Contextual in the sense of brand positioning either from a corporate or marketing perspective.

We then considered the move to a global approach in which brand dimensionality (external image versus internal identity) drives firms to consider more socially oriented approaches. We cannot back away from this. In the early 21st century, the process of businesses and consumer exchanging brands and monies will undoubtedly continue. But the corporate brand, what the firm is, what it stands for, will be of major interest to consumers, customers, and stakeholders around the world. Information, not just from a partisan company perspective, will also be available from anywhere in the world. For example, the many reports about the Apple iMAC (some positive, some not so) are freely available on the World Wide Web.

Consumers, customers, and stakeholders are no longer dependent on company-generated information. This will, we believe, necessitate two types of integrated communication – namely corporate and marketing. For some firms, this distinction will be irrelevant. For others it will be crucial. Businesses must decide for themselves. Even those pursuing a branded stance will, however, need to take note that the days of empty corporate raincoats are starting to fade into the sedimentary strata of the corporatist past. Stakeholders want to know who the firm is and what it stands for and how it operates. Today, there is no escaping, and "stonewalling" is certainly not the solution as firms such as Monsanto, Coca-Cola and others have learned to their chagrin.

We then defined and justified integrated communication and integrated marketing communication and attempted to draw distinctions between the two. For most organizations it is not a case of either/or, but one of realignment, combination, and integration. This is likely the greatest challenge facing global organizations today.

Starting with Chapter 6 we offer suggestions and solutions from a wide range of communications experts. Their experience and practical suggestions will provide a fuller platter of alternatives for practicing corporate communication leaders, and their CEOs. Indeed, the contributions made by these experts will help readers understand and place the ribs and cloth of the corporate umbrella in a taut protective position for the global corporation and its portfolio of individual brands. How corporate branding and advertising can be used as an effective rib to help raise the corporate umbrella is next. So, read on.

ILLUSTRATION

"Managing the Soft Side of Change"

The cultural and communication objectives of the BAWC change program were developed with consultancy Smythe Dorward Lambert. They included:

- to articulate the promise of a compelling vision for the business

- to connect all parts of the jigsaw of change

- to engage everyone in the change

- to humanize the change process

- to put soul, passion, and conviction into the change

A set of communication principles were developed with the leadership team to govern all communication around the change process. From 1996 onwards, two-way communication channels were set up, including a weekly worldwide news bulletin, monthly face-to-face cascades, discussion groups, discussions down the line and the takeover of an already existing senior management face-to-face forum.

A communication coordinator was established for each workstream of the change program and a monthly survey on attitudes to the change process was carried out with a sample of employees worldwide. A communication planning discipline was put in place through a weekly schedule of meetings and actions. Senior managers and members of the Cargo Executive Team (CET) received coaching in communication and change management skills to help them lead the change process forward in a visible and effective manner.

But this was just the "hygiene" communication infrastructure – it kept people informed about the change, it provided mechanisms to listen to their views and concerns and it shaped a clear sense of leadership. Something more was needed to achieve in full the objectives of truly engaging hearts and minds in the change process, gaining commitment rather than compliance to the shifts required and improving relationships between managers and other staff across the business.

The following interventions were all developed to achieve exactly those aims. They were entirely different to the traditional style of communication within BAWC. All were designed to bring the change experience to life for people through a different style of leadership around the business and by creating real two-way dialogue between the management of the business and the staff.

Work was carried out with the Cargo Executive Team to challenge them to articulate an agreed and compelling vision for the future of the business. As a by-product, this work forced decision-making in the change process to accelerate, particularly around the people involvement issues. This vision was then shared with all staff at Heathrow through a series of half-day sessions where a mixed group of 20 people from across the business participated in a series of facilitated discussions with two senior managers. Rather than a strapline, the vision took the form of an extended conversation around the different elements that made up the big picture of the future BAWC.

Using a mixture of video, posters, and interactive debate, these low-tech events were designed to give people a real and compelling understanding of the future, warts and all. The half-day sessions covered why the business had to change (using a video of a bad freight journey to make the point), what the new business might look like and what impact the change would have on people and their jobs. The sessions also delivered the hardest message of all in an open and honest way – that the Heathrow-based workforce would be reduced from 1500 to 1100.

The senior managers leading the sessions received coaching in how to engage people in meaningful discussion, how to deliver difficult messages and how to make the experience of the sessions symbolic of the vision and values for the new business. In feedback after the events, both managers and staff commented on the change in relationships the exercise had brought about. For the first time, it was felt that honest dialogue was taking place as opposed to mere information exchange.

In measurement carried out after the events, 96 percent of people inside the business agreed that the business needed to change. This shared understanding was responsible for the result of a critical ballot in 1996, where the workforce agreed to let the change process proceed, despite its impact on jobs.

So what does the future hold in terms of achieving the soft objectives of change? Moving into 1999, a new combined strategy had been developed by the Communication team, HR and Marketing functions to ensure that people's ongoing experience of change is managed in a consistent and meaningful way. The new building at Heathrow was opened in May 1999 by John Prescott, the Deputy Prime Minister, and the rollout of new technology and processes around the world is almost complete. The ugly duckling is well on the way to transforming itself into a swan.

The next challenge will be to articulate clearly the new commercial promise of BAWC for its customers, and to internalize that alongside the new values.

ILLUSTRATION (cont'd)

This will mean that the whole organization can truly "live with the brand" with people behaving in a way which is totally aligned with that promise. Work has already begun with the CET in terms of focusing on their own behavioral change ... but that's another story.

Acknowledgement

We gratefully acknowledge the kind permission of John Smythe of Smythe Dorward Lambert, 55 Drury Lane, London WC2B 5SQ. Internet: www.smythedorward.com for the use of the illustrations in this chapter.

Chapter

Corporate branding and advertising

jim garrity

ILLUSTRATION

From Nowhere to No. 1 – Launching the Compaq Consumer Division

Selling to the uninformed

Personal computers (PCs) have not always been "cool." A case in point: in the early 1990s, manufacturers in the PC category spent considerable energy boasting about faster processors and larger capacity hard drives. Further, the "Intel Inside" program was in its early years, implying – at the expense of the actual PC manufacturer – that computers were the same as long as they had the all-important "ingredient": an Intel processor. Finally, in this consumer landscape, Compaq Computers – headquartered in Houston, Texas – was not even a blip on the brand radar screen. The company had built its reputation as a high quality, innovative business computer company without a presence in the consumer market. Business-to-business was what Compaq did and did well.

Identifying the product as the extension of the brand

But, in 1992, Compaq made the decision to step into the burgeoning consumer market. The challenge: take a non-consumer-player into a market dominated by IBM, Apple and a few others, and grab a piece of the ever-growing personal computer sales pie.

The first strategic move at Compaq was to look inside the organization. That took the form of an inventory of the assets that could be brought to this market, and then determining how to differentiate Compaq from the more-established competitors. (Does anyone still remember the brand "Packard Bell," a major player at that time?)

Reviewing the assets Compaq had developed over its 10 years as a leading manufacturer of PCs for the business-to-business market, it became clear that there was opportunity for differentiation in the consumer space. Computer companies, since their inception, had been greatly influenced by the technologists (engineers) who were often enamored with the technology itself (technology for technology's sake, the well known "feeds and speeds" approach) rather than with providing clear, end-user benefits. That approach had worked well when the computer companies were selling primarily to other technologists, that is, the information technology group in the client companies. Compaq management realized that its success in the commercial market was the result of a cult-like employee commitment to what would ultimately be described as "useful innovation," something that went beyond just the technology.

The insights provided by extensive consumer research led the Compaq management team to conclude that consumer PC marketers were all pretty much falling into the same positioning trap, the technological view of the engineers. Compaq management concluded that the company could bring a product line to the consumer market that would represent true "useful innovation" in terms consumers would understand and appreciate.

Expressing the brand through advertising

Resisting the temptation to gloat over their technology, the Compaq consumer team chose to focus on the aspect of their computer that was readily understandable to non-computer-savvy consumers: the practical, end-user benefits. The message was developed into a dynamic launch campaign that included a wide range of TV and print advertising, and point-of-sale (POS) merchandising directed at the relatively unsophisticated consumer end-user.

To capture the "useful innovation" positioning, Compaq's agency, Ammirati & Puris, recommended an inquisitive tag line ("Has it changed your life yet?") and developed advertising that demonstrated the PC's usefulness *one benefit at a time*. For example, in one TV spot, a young man asked a woman for her telephone number. She gave him an e-mail address instead which, following a quick fade, the commercial resumes by showing him using that address to reach her. (Note, amazing though it seems now, e-mail was an attention-getting innovation at the time. AOL only had a few million subscribers in the early 1990s, and this television commercial clearly demonstrated a true lifestyle benefit.)

In another commercial, an elderly woman offered to share her brownie recipe with a friend by printing it from her kitchen computer. The other elderly woman responded with, "Just fax it to me." Without using any tech-nological terms, in fifteen seconds Compaq was able to communicate a lifestyle benefit from having a computer comfortably located at home in the kitchen. The reference to faxing the recipe was a subtle hint at the innovative fax capability, a standard feature on the early models of the Compaq machines. A number of other fifteen-second commercials showed the Compaq PC (sub-branded the "Presario") demonstrating further usefulness in the daily personal lives of ordinary people.

The consumer launch also included print advertising in an unusual medium for that time: lifestyle magazines. In the early days of the home computer category, manufacturers placed print advertising almost exclusively in tech-nology and computer magazines. With their sights set on an audience that wasn't quite comfortable with the mind-numbing jargon of the PC industry (MS-DOS, ROM, BIOS, WYSIWYG, and so on), the Compaq brand team knew it had to show that the Compaq Presario line was user-friendly and potentially a big part of everybody's ordinary life. Advertising a PC in *Rolling Stone* and *Men's Health* (two lifestyle consumer publications, that is, music and health) was groundbreaking, demonstrating how communicable the benefits of the Compaq PC really were to ordinary people. Furthermore, it signaled that computers, like jeans and vodka and component stereo systems, were indeed "cool."

What changed?

Did Compaq's consumer launch change lives? Without a doubt. It introduced the computer as a lifestyle product. It also tremendously increased the company's fortunes. Compaq's marketing focus on end-user benefits, show-casing innovations like all-in-one design, built-in fax capability, audio CD player, voice mail, and so on, paid off handsomely. The Presario campaign was launched in 1993. Within three years, Compaq was the No.1 brand and the No.1 selling PC in the world.

Source: Author.

Introduction and overview

In this chapter, we demonstrate many of the concepts discussed in Chapter 5, that is: the increasing need to relate and in some cases, combine corporate and product brand advertising. As shown in the preceding case vignette, we illustrate how an organization, Compaq

Computer, which was a business-to-business marketer, focusing almost entirely on the use of corporate advertising and corporate branding, transitioned into the consumer or product market and moved the brand along as well. Later in this chapter, we use another case example, that of First Union Corporation of Charlotte, North Carolina, one of the leading financial institutions in the United States, to illustrate how an organization moved in the other direction, that is, from historically using product advertising and branding to the construction of one of the leading corporate brands in the country. In this chapter, we will cover:

■ Branding versus advertising
  ■ from branding to integrated marketing communication
  ■ what is a brand?
  ■ brands are not just advertising
  ■ the importance of the customer experience
  ■ the importance of corporate advertising

■ Stage one: branding from square one

■ Stage two: going to the next level
  ■ being too successful
  ■ too many "moving parts"

■ Stage three: extending the brand
  ■ developing new advertising
  ■ building an integrated program
  ■ the First Union process

■ Stage four: benchmarking best practices
  ■ take stock of identity
  ■ nurture teamwork
  ■ develop employee brand evangelism
  ■ keep it consistent

■ Stage five: cohesiveness

The chapter will then conclude by providing some lessons learned about sports and event marketing, and summarize what is meant by brand building success strategies.

The Compaq illustration is the sort of case vignette you often find in college textbooks, the kind that exemplifies business success through a few brief strokes. Of course, reducing Compaq's PC consumer launch to a few paragraphs significantly understates the organizational effort required to bring about success. Compaq's success, as with many other corporate examples, was not simply the effort of a handful of creative advertising people, nor even a few "breakthrough" advertising campaigns. Instead, Compaq's success was the result of an entire corporation, from CEO on down, recognizing their company's ability and worth, and dedicating themselves to supporting their marketing initiatives company-wide and then translating those into clearly stated, easily comprehended, and most of all, attention-getting advertising and marketing communication. One thing that comes through loud and clear in the opening vignette is the importance of internal, that is management and employee, agreement and support for the branding initiative and the marketing communication. Indeed, it is increasingly clear that brands, such as Compaq and First Union as described in this chapter – and advertising as well as marketing campaigns – *are reliant* on the support and backing of the entire organization, not just clever creative concepts, memorable icons, or cute slogans.

Nonetheless, the advertising Ammirati & Puris devised for Compaq's consumer launch *was* remarkably astute, and its creative execution spoke directly to the target segment research had shown was most likely to respond. The success of the Presario was virtually unqualified. But sometimes, when reviewing unqualified marketplace successes, not as much is learned as when following the development of a work-in-progress example.

Companies like Coca-Cola, General Electric and Disney own thriving brands built and maintained with effective advertising and promotion over decades. But, to some degree, their stories are too far advanced over time to demonstrate relevant and topical lessons for companies launching *new* brands or trying to find ways to combine product and corporate brands which increasingly seems to be the case today.

In this chapter, we will use an ongoing, still work-in-progress case example, that of First Union Corporation of Charlotte, North Carolina. This provides an opportunity to follow the development of a brand and the corporate advertising and promotional lessons that were learned by this organization. This helps illuminate clearly the challenges faced by many organizations as they attempt to combine existing product branding with an increasing emphasis on the corporate brand. Just as Compaq moved from a corporate brand directed to business-to-business to a consumer brand, First Union shows how a product brand can be leveraged into a strong corporate brand. Both these directions are very real requirements faced by most corporate and marketing communication directors in today's rapidly changing global environment.

Branding versus advertising

Before working through the First Union example, a brief primer on the differences between branding and advertising will be helpful. Several key differences are significant:

■ *What helped make the Compaq Presario so successful was not just advertising. It was a fully integrated marketing and communication campaign that built the Presario brand from the ground up.* First, the company defined its core competencies. Those core competencies were then translated into a brand message. Then, the brand message was expanded into advertising, merchandising, PR, and so on – all the parts of an integrated marketing communication campaign at the tactical juxtaposition level (Schultz and Kitchen, 2000).

Many communication people may confuse branding with advertising. Advertising is one of many vehicles – albeit a major one – for building or maintaining a brand but it is not the only element necessary to build a brand in and of itself. Too many dot.com companies found that out in 2000 when all the media expenditures and all the "edgy" creative couldn't overcome the basic problems of a poor business plan.

Most successful companies change their advertising from year to year to keep it exciting and to make sure the message is sharp and relevant but, they don't change the basic values of the company or the brand. New creative approaches to advertising can help keep a brand alive and interesting. "Did somebody say 'McDonald's?'" has been one of that restaurant chain's many creative advertising executions. But the company's brand attributes remain the same over time: "Great-tasting food, superior service, everyday value and convenience." Those are what have made McDonald's one of the leading brands in the world. And, those base elements do not change although the advertising may. The key to successful brand advertising therefore is finding new ways to continue the development of the brand essence or value.

■ *People define brands in many ways. A brand, very simply, is a collection of perceptions in the mind of the consumer.* The definition by Aldo Papone of American Express is appropriate here:

A brand is a *covenant* between a marketer and a consumer. A covenant in this context is an unspoken contract, a package of associations and stipulations that are understood and honored by both marketer and consumer. The product is a *thing*, but the brand is a *promise*.

Compaq promises useful innovation. Volvo and Michelin promise safety. Coke promises refreshment. Nike promises athletic performance. It is important to note that each of these promises focuses on the customer's experience, not on product attributes. The product attributes are necessary but they aren't the theme or focus of the advertising nor the other forms of communication, just as a CEO communicator would be ignored if he/she constantly beat on the single key of the corporation he/she represented (see Chapter 2).

With the proliferation of products and services in today's society, consumers are turning increasingly to brands to simplify their purchase decisions. Importantly, they are also interested in the corporation ostensibly owning and managing these brands (see Figure 6.1).

As shown in the figure, consumers and customers alike go through a process on their way to adopting a brand and becoming loyal to it.

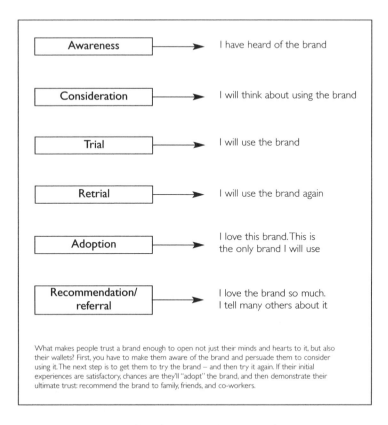

Awareness	→	I have heard of the brand
Consideration	→	I will think about using the brand
Trial	→	I will use the brand
Retrial	→	I will use the brand again
Adoption	→	I love this brand. This is the only brand I will use
Recommendation/ referral	→	I love the brand so much. I tell many others about it

What makes people trust a brand enough to open not just their minds and hearts to it, but also their wallets? First, you have to make them aware of the brand and persuade them to consider using it. The next step is to get them to try the brand – and then try it again. If their initial experiences are satisfactory, chances are they'll "adopt" the brand, and then demonstrate their ultimate trust: recommend the brand to family, friends, and co-workers.

Figure 6.1 Brand adoption model

Awareness is required. That is then followed by Consideration, then Trial, and so on. The final step is, of course, Recommendation or Referral, in other words, buyers and users who have become advocates and tell others about their experiences. In the interactive marketplace of the 21st century, this advocacy or referral model has and will become important to almost any brand, whether product or corporate.

To reinforce this model, consider this research from the 1997 Yankelovich Monitor:

A known/trusted brand is a strong influence on [my] purchase decisions:
  – 1994   51%
  – 1997   63%

69% of consumers polled also agreed strongly with the statement that "once I find a brand I like, it is very difficult to get me to change brands."

As shown, while brand loyalty and brand importance are increasing, there is little question that advertising and other forms of marketing communication have much to do with reinforcing opinions and attitudes.

■ *Advertising is just one of the elements in building a brand. Today, brands are built with customer experiences and that includes much more than just advertising or even marketing communication.* It involves the entire company, and not only its agents and partners, but most of all its employees.

Today, brands can be built with relatively little traditional advertising. Just look at the success of The Body Shop, Dell Computer, Amazon.com and others. While advertising has a place, brands today are generally built with a full range of marketing communication and customer experiences. For instance, some people are raving fans of Starbucks – as both a customer *and* a marketer. People love drinking coffee early in the morning. Some have even said:

If I'm travelling and find a Starbucks near my hotel, it's a huge plus for the overall experience of the trip – and even impacts my view on how much I like that city or location. If the hotel actually serves Starbucks coffee, it's a must-stay location whenever I'm in that city. (Garrity, 1999)

To these kinds of people, it is obvious that the quality of Starbucks' product is very important – the taste, the smell, and consistency. But there's so much more to the experience than the coffee itself. It's a combination of the product, the eclectic decor, merchandising, music, and their lively people, or "baristas." The service is always excellent –

even during those rare times when the coffee was "on the house" because the customer had to wait while the requested blend was brewing.

Starbucks demonstrates best marketing and communication practices in everything they do. Note that the company's founders didn't set out just to sell a hot beverage. Their goal was "to become a daily ritual in many different cultures." "We've always known that our brand must stand for something – it must be authentic, reliable and aspirational," says Chairman Howard Schultz in the company's 1999 annual report. "Every day, the passion and enthusiasm of our people and the quality of our coffee enable us to build a rewarding relationship with our customers. This connection has given us the chance to do things no one thought possible ... ." The "impossible" was to build a global brand with an age-old commodity, coffee – in a product area that was admittedly already crowded. Today, only eight years after taking the company public, Starbucks has 2500 stores in 13 countries around the world and the growth is still continuing.

■ *A brand is built with consistent consumer experiences delivered by the organization, not just promises in the marketing communication or the advertising.* So, just how did Starbucks, Dell, The Body Shop and others build their brands? By ... *consistent customer experience.* In a videotaped interview about branding, Nestlé U.S.A.'s SVP of Communications Al Stefl observed:

A consumer builds a brand impression like a bird that collects bits and pieces to build a nest. So, if they are picking up disparate pieces all around, they are not building a very sound nest. *It all has to look the same.* And as consumers travel through their day, they are exposed to many impressions, be it on site, ... on a package, ... in a communication over TV, ... on a poster, ... on a bus or whatever. To create a cohesive brand, those impressions always have to reinforce each other.

Simply put:

■ consistency builds trust
■ trust builds loyalty
■ customer loyalty builds a brand.

■ *Corporate advertising can help build brands and increase shareholder value.* Of course, now that we've established that advertising isn't the be-all and end-all of corporate brand building, we do, however, confirm its power. Consistent brand building through advertising can help a company reach important goals, including boosting its stock price. A

1988 study by the Strategic Planning Institute and the Ogilvy Center for Research & Development showed a positive correlation between advertising expenditures and a company's profitability. The brands that had the highest return on investment were also the brands with the highest relative advertising-to-sales ratios. The study showed corporate advertising on average accounted for 4% of the variance in the price of a stock (Ogilvy and Mather/Houston, November 1988).

In another 1988 study, the stock of consistent advertisers rose 28%, while the stock of inconsistent and non-advertisers rose only 13% (Ogilvy and Mather/Houston, July 1988). More recently, a 1995 study showed that extensions of brands that rate very high on both positive brand attitude and brand awareness create a positive stock return of between 2 and 9% (Pettis, 1995). But, with all these successes from brands, there are still many unanswered questions. The main question for readers will be: how can an organization build a strong corporate brand? The First Union case study that follows provides a solid example.

Stage one: branding from square one

For a company to identify its brand is no small task. First Union offers an excellent case study of advertising and branding in the new 21st century marketplace. After a series of some 70 acquisitions from 1985 to 1996, the 88-year-old company had become one of the largest financial service providers in North America. Yet, the First Union name was virtually unknown by customers in the newly acquired markets. Even long-time customers in the company's traditional markets knew the company only as a bank and were unaware of the breadth of services First Union offered, such as brokerage, insurance, mutual funds and annuities. In other words, First Union was known for its product brands but not for its much broader corporate capabilities that were bound up in those brands. The only memorable attribute that distinguished the company in the eyes of many customers was its logo (Figure 6.2).

In 1996, First Union senior management made the strategic commitment to define and promote its corporate brand. With the help of its advertising agency, Hal Riney & Partners, the corporate marketing team conducted 50 interviews with First Union managers and a dozen customer focus groups up and down the East Coast of the United States, its traditional marketing area. With the insights from this research, the company defined its brand as "smart, straightforward financial solutions in the

Figure 6.2 The First Union logo

customer's best interest." Like any good brand positioning, the message leveraged proven strengths that historically had enabled First Union to prevail in head-to-head competitive situations with other banks and financial institutions. And it was closely linked to the company's vision and business strategy: "To meet *all* of the customer's financial needs by building a relationship, not just competing for isolated transactions (that is, making a loan or opening a checking account)." (Note the focus here of moving from a group of product brands to a single, all encompassing corporate brand.) Thus, First Union's key attributes were defined as "personal, objective, proactive, innovative, easy and expert." See Figure 6.3 for the core promises First Union developed.

Note the similarity in the approach shown above with the focus of this text as described in Chapter 5. Here, the brand promise is at the core of the organization, that is, this is what First Union promises to customers and prospects. Surrounding that core promise are the people, products, services and channels through which that core promise can and will be delivered. Much the same as Compaq differentiated itself by focusing on the lifestyle benefits of its technology (recall the illustration at the start of this chapter), First Union chose to focus on consumer benefits at a time when most competitors were focused on product features. Again experience shows that brands are built by customer experiences delivered by employees, management, channels and the like, that is, things that comprise the total customer relationship with the brand. Advertising and other forms of marketing communication provide the definition and enhancement of the brand but do not create the brand itself.

First Union launched its first major TV advertising campaign across the East Coast of the U.S. in 1997. It evoked historic images of the Wright Brothers' first flight and the tumbling of the Berlin Wall to symbolize another first: the *first union* between a bank and a brokerage (recognizing First Union as the first bank to acquire a mutual fund company). The

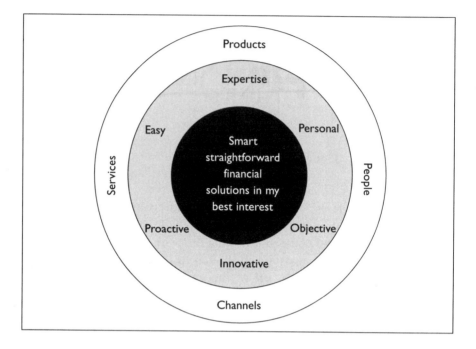

Figure 6.3 First Union core promises

campaign netted substantial gains in brand awareness among consumers in all First Union markets.

But the First Union Chairman and CEO, Ed Crutchfield, was not satisfied with this early success. He wanted advertising and marketing communication that was bolder and more breakaway; that would get the attention of wealthy investors and decision-makers in Fortune 1000 companies. Marketing First Union's sophisticated Wall Street-style investment banking capabilities was defined as the key objective of the new advertising program. Crutchfield became actively engaged with the Corporate Marketing team and the advertising agency in developing a new advertising campaign to promote the First Union brand and to carry the message of change. On a personal note: in the author's 25-plus years in the advertising world, I have found this to be key to any advertising and brand building effort – you must have the personal buy-in and commitment of the CEO as the ultimate brand champion. Without leadership from the top, few will take the program seriously. When leaders fail to lead, everything goes one-way – downhill.

In the financial industry, the typical approach to reach target audiences of wealthy investors and decision-makers in Fortune 1000 companies is to place advertising in traditional media vehicles such as *Forbes* or *The Atlantic Monthly*. But to make the First Union message more compelling, the decision was made to use the medium with the greatest impact: television. One of the main drivers of the new campaign was to break through the clutter of look-alike financial advertising and set First Union apart. The advertising agency, now called Publicis & Hal Riney, made a convincing case for the need to be different. They did this by compiling numerous financial services TV commercials into one composite video. With the names concealed, when shown to First Union management, it was impossible to tell one spot from the next or one company from another. In short: there was literally no brand differentiation in any of the financial advertising that had been gathered and was currently running in the marketplace. This example brought home the fact that no matter how entertaining a television commercial was at the time of exposure, if it left no lasting impression or was counterbalanced by "me-too" similarities, it had failed in its objective.

The new First Union TV advertising campaign, launched nationwide in September 1998, created a virtual "Financial World." It was brought to life by the Hollywood visual effects wizards at George Lucas' company, Industrial Light & Magic. In fact, many of the special effects used in the commercials were engineered by the same people who developed the special effects for the movies *Star Wars* and *Men in Black*. Each 60-second spot opened in outer space, overlooking the "Financial World," and a continent shaped like a dollar sign (Figure 6.4).

Zooming from space into the "Financial World," the viewer encountered a fast-paced, chaotic street scene full of risk and uncertainty. The scene then dissolved to a tranquil setting where buildings rose from the skyline, appearing more or less as mountains. The First Union "mountain" towered above the rest as the voice-over read the closing statement, "Come to the mountain called First Union. Or if you prefer, the mountain will come to you."

The goal of the communication was to acknowledge that navigating the financial world of today can be unsettling – even scary – unless the customer or prospect has an expert like First Union to help. Each 60-second spot was virtually a mini feature film, bringing together the talent of model makers, actors, animal trainers, computer programmers and a host of other artists to clearly establish the message and deliver appropriate core values.

Figure 6.4 The Financial World

Stage two: going to the next level

Success

Within six months, the brand tracking study used by First Union showed that unaided awareness of the brand among the target audience – corporate CEOs and CFOs, as well as wealthy investors – was two and a half times what it had been before the start of the advertising program as shown in Figure 6.5.

As can be seen in the figure, the First Union program consisted of an integrated marketing communication approach. That is, it began with the television advertising and was followed in a few months with a print campaign. The two, combined with other internal marketing and communication programs, enabled First Union to increase unaided awareness of the firm by 33 percent over a 22 month time period.

In addition to the change in advertising awareness, on average over one hundred customers and prospects were calling First Union on 1-800-MOUNTAIN through a unique phone number introduced with the campaign where they could get additional information. First Union management was

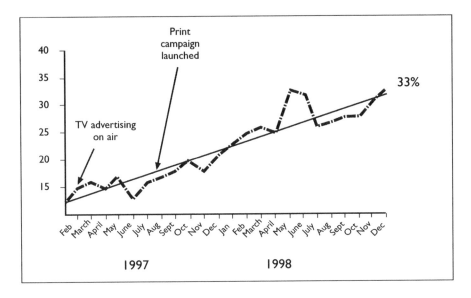

Figure 6.5 Unaided awareness (share of mind)

particularly pleased with this level of customer response since they were trying to reach a fairly narrow audience and more especially since the campaign was designed to build name recognition but was not specifically designed as a direct response approach. In other words, there was no specific product or service offered with an urgent message to "Call now!" in either the print or television advertising. In addition, the tracking study also showed that the number of customers who would consider buying a mutual fund from First Union virtually doubled during the advertising period.

Although the specific target for the advertising campaign was corporate decision-makers and high-end investors, the brand management team at First Union also hoped the campaign would appeal to the much larger mass market of investors at all levels. After the campaign started, First Union marketing communication management asked a third-party research firm, McCollum Spielman Worldwide (MSW), to test the effectiveness of the campaign among this mass market and to compare those results with other financial services advertising. By several important measures – clutter breakthrough, recall of the main idea, and likeability of the commercials – the campaign scored 53–60 percent higher than MSW's financial services advertising norms, as shown in Figures 6.6, 6.7, and 6.8.

In Figures 6.6 and 6.7, the two commercials "Launch" and "Sharks" scored almost 1.5 times as high as the MSW norm.

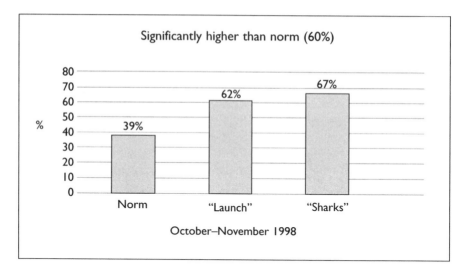

Figure 6.6 Likeability

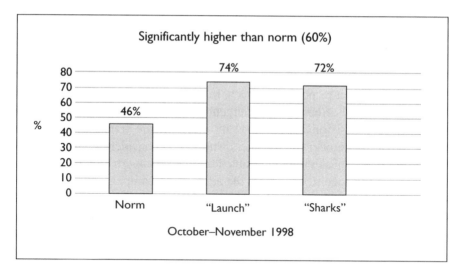

Figure 6.7 Clutter breakthrough (unaided awareness)

The same was true for the two commercials in terms of Main Idea Recall (Figure 6.8). As shown above, both commercials scored 1.5 times higher than other commercials MSW had tested over the years. But, while First Union appeared to be successful in its marketing communication

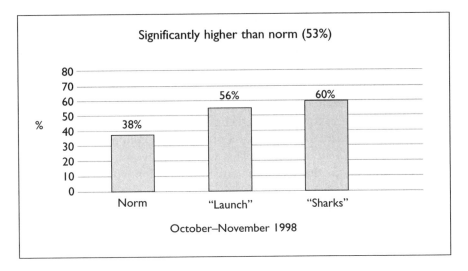

Figure 6.8 Main idea recall

program to introduce the new corporate brand, all was not well. Here, there may be more learning than in only those campaigns that are termed a "success" by traditional measures.

Too many "moving parts"

While the campaign itself was a great success, something began to happen that altered the way some customers and prospects perceived the organization. Six weeks after the campaign began, the company had completed a major systems conversion for a recent business acquisition. At the same time, they were working to assimilate another merger partner into existing First Union operations. And, at the same time, the company was introducing a major program to reinvent the traditional retail bank branches as full-service financial centers equipped to offer a wider range of services and products. New delivery channels were also being introduced through telephone and online banking. In short, it was a time of great change both internally and externally at First Union. These internal changes, and not just external tinkering with promotion, often are the hallmark of companies developing integrated approaches to communication (see Gould, 2000; Schultz and Kitchen, 2000). Usually, they spell a period of organizational readjustment in terms of developing greater customer focus. First Union was no exception to this.

Making all of these changes at once proved to be too much not just for customers and prospects but for the First Union employees as well. Customer service levels started to slip. Managers began hearing feedback that customers believed the company was having service problems. That First Union had "grown too big, too fast" was a common complaint. The fast-paced, high-tech advertising campaign – that was initially well received by the mass consumer market even though they weren't the target audience – now seemed to reinforce a growing perception that First Union was now "too big *and* uncaring." This was certainly not the type of feedback one would hope that a new advertising campaign would generate.

One of the most basic tenets of advertising came to the forefront: no matter how good the advertising, there can be no success if there is dissonance between what the advertising promises and what customers are actually experiencing. First Union found that while its advertising messages might be heard by customers and prospects, they could not and would not be believed or effective until the company could consistently deliver good customer service. Thus the lesson: while advertising and other forms of marketing communication have a role, it is limited by what the organization can actually deliver. A further lesson here is that internal stakeholders need to walk down the road of agreement toward a greater marketing and communicative relationship with the rest of the management team and with key external stakeholders. Put another way, the marketing and communication team cannot march to one beat, while the rest of the internal team are marching to another. Thus, there was a need for reassessment.

And, indeed, after airing the "Financial World" commercials for 12 months, the brand communication team stepped back to reassess its advertising message. But more importantly, in the fall of 1999 the company took immediate action to fix its customer service problems. Within a year, customer satisfaction scores were back on track. Having fixed the most immediate service problems, the corporate objective was then revised to develop and deliver service excellence that would ultimately provide a sustainable competitive advantage in the marketplace.

Stage three: extending the brand

New advertising

After new service policies were put in place, the timing seemed appropriate for a new advertising campaign. The mass market, that is, those customers and prospects who were peripheral but vital to First Union's ultimate success, had lost confidence in the company's ability to serve them well, and in spite of the fact that the firm's service levels had been restored, even reaching historically high levels, the perception persisted. The brand team felt it needed to send the message to customers, "We care about you." Therefore, a new marketing communication campaign was developed with the recurring question, "What kind of a company are we?" Through a series of vignettes showing everyday people and businesses, the campaign said that First Union was a company made up of people "not all that different than you." "We are here to help you make the right financial choices," the ads said, and "to make your life better, easier, more prosperous and secure."

At this point, First Union proved another important advertising and branding truth. Just as McDonald's brand position has always remained "great-tasting food, superior service, everyday value and convenience" – regardless of the current creative execution – the First Union brand had to remain the same even though the creative approach was dramatically different. Even today, the First Union brand positioning continues to be "smart, straightforward financial solutions in the customer's best interest." The key branding attributes of "personal, objective, proactive, innovative, easy and expert" also remain the same, with a particular emphasis on "personal, easy and expert." But, as shown, over the years, the advertising executions have changed and sometimes dramatically. Thus, the important point: the brand value or essence is ongoing while the advertising is often different. This is an important point and one that often gets lost in the excitement of the marketplace. Yet, it is the duty of the communication group to make sure that the advertising fills its brand responsibility and doesn't overwhelm or stray from the basic values of the brand.

Building an integrated program

The formula for consistent customer experiences is integrated marketing communication. Undoubtedly, creative executions come and go, as do people and management. That's why marketing communication groups need processes and an infrastructure in place to ensure consistency in the overall brand experience over time. The ability to speak consistently with one voice in every customer interaction is something every company wants to achieve but often has difficulty in making happen on a regular basis.

Consistent customer experience is tough to manage in an organization as complex as First Union. For example, typical customer interactions are manifold. They may include experiences in one or more of the 2300 financial centers, or through the network of 3500 ATMs, or interaction with the over 5000 First Union Direct associates located in various call centers. Other interactions may occur through television, radio and print advertisements; financial center merchandising; direct marketing; promotions; sponsorships; media coverage; and at firstunion.com, the Internet site where customers can track finances and/or transact online. How can a communication group integrate all these interactions from a communication perspective in a company whose 70,000 employees serve 16 million customers across the country and around the world? Yet, that was the challenge at First Union and it is not unlike the challenge communication directors face in similar scenarios globally.

First Union began wrestling with that challenge in the late 1990s. As we have seen, through mergers and acquisitions, First Union had grown exponentially, reaching into numerous parts of the U.S.A. In many instances the company, its heritage and even its operations were virtually unknown. At the same time, the company was branching out into new business areas, such as investment banking, brokerage and insurance. The goal was to create a new national brand in the financial arena, promoting the new identity as a financial services provider with capabilities far beyond those of an ordinary bank. The challenge was: how could First Union ensure that the new brand identity was consistent in every interaction with every customer?

The process First Union used is instructive

The first step was to review the structure of the marketing department. The goal was to make integrated marketing communication a living, breathing and ongoing process at First Union, not one that was developed and then put aside to rest on a marketing manager's bookshelf. After much consideration, First Union executive managers restructured the way the marketing division did business. And that is generally the key to a successful integrated marketing and corporate communication system, re-thinking and restructuring the form and responsibilities of the group.

Under the new structure First Union created, the foundation of the brand communication programs was placed with a staff of dedicated personnel known as Communications Integration Managers (CIMs). They became the brand experts. The CIMs provide a one-stop shop for developing marketing communication and strategies, and they serve as liaisons between internal clients and external agencies. The CIMs' central role in the communications process ensured that everything from product names to photography to merchandising copy was consistent with the First Union brand. And because the CIMs were assigned to several internal clients, they were able to promote partnership and consistency across the various business units. First Union learned, as so many other organizations have, that integration starts internally, not externally.

With the CIMs successfully in place, the next step was to create a Senior Executive Communications Forum focused on the overall customer experience. This group took a proactive, segment-based view of who the company reached, how often, and with what messages. With representatives from all channels (financial centers, online, ATM, call centers) and all product areas, this group was charged with responsibility to ensure that customers had consistent and positive experiences across all channels every day. Channel integration is key in developing an effective and integrated program.

Stage four: benchmarking best practices

Once the First Union marketing group had been restructured, the group felt a need to have an outside evaluation of what had been done. Calling on an external consultant, the group requested a review of all of the processes that had been put in place. Based on the suggestions made by the consultant, First Union embarked on a "best of breed" benchmarking study. This entailed turning to some great brand companies to see how they maintained the integrity of their brands through integrated communications. Through various association memberships, the marketing team was able to gain access to companies known for their brand-building prowess and their communication capabilities. The companies benchmarked included Sears, Roebuck, MasterCard, Lucent Technologies, General Electric and Federal Express. All well known for their success in developing relevant, successful, integrated marketing communication programs.

In Fall 1998, core teams from the First Union marketing group conducted site visits and met with the senior marketing executives of these companies. Prior to the meetings, the group analyzed the core competencies of the various companies. Functional specialists within First Union who were already skilled in those competencies were selected to conduct the research. For example, the First Union sports and events marketing team visited MasterCard, which has a reputation for developing strategically successful sports and events marketing. The company's merchandising team interviewed the executives at Sears; and First Union's brand managers spent time with the executives at General Electric and Lucent.

In some cases, the research with other companies reinforced the current or existing integrated marketing communication practices already in place; in others, it suggested new ways of doing things. At every stop along the way, the First Union managers asked the executives at the companies being benchmarked:

- Do you have an integrated marketing communication process?

- How have you achieved acceptance of this process internally?

- How is your marketing team organized?

- How do you foster cross-functional teamwork?

- Who manages the integration and communication of your marketing communications plan with business units?

- How are public relations and investor relations integrated into your marketing communications plan?

- How do you instill the brand promise in all employees?

Following are some of the key findings from the First Union best practices research. They can be very helpful to other communication managers who want to develop and implement an integrated marketing communication program in their company.

- *Take stock of your identity* – General Electric, one of the companies visited in the benchmarking process, is known for its consistent creative standards. They carefully weave all of their business unit strategies into the overall brand. Based on some of the key findings from companies like GE, one of the first steps the First Union communication team took was to formally review the organization's corporate identity. With so many different internal partners and agencies responsible for creative work, it was found that consistent standards needed to be set to ensure the brand was leveraged throughout all marketing efforts. Upon review, it was found that, like many other organizations, the most immediate need was for a graphic standards manual. That was required to ensure that the brand always was conveyed in the same, instantly recognizable way. The First Union team also created a system for selectively developing product names that could add value to the First Union brand (while rejecting those that did not). Finally, the team developed a set of copy guidelines that were distributed throughout the organization. Those were needed to make sure that the company was speaking with one voice in all advertising, collateral and merchandising materials.

■ *Nurture teamwork* – at First Union, the Communication Integration Managers (CIMs) are responsible for ensuring that the graphic and copy standards are understood and used by all internal clients. That helps keep the brand message consistent. To reinforce this consistency drive, the group organized regular "Creative Summits" with other divisions within First Union that were responsible for marketing communications. These "Summits" included the creative services groups of business units out in the field as well. In addition, there were a number of agency relationships that needed to be organized and included in this process. In order to promote consistency in the work agencies created for First Union, a quarterly "Agency Summit" was established. This "Summit" was used to help build bridges among the various agency partners, and to make sure that all involved were using the same script when it came to the brand and brand messaging.

■ *Develop employee brand evangelism* – at companies like Coca-Cola and Disney, the First Union benchmarking team found that employees have a fervor for their brands. That was believed to be a key element in their success. Therefore, the First Union communication managers actively began working to develop that same sense of investment in the brand among all First Union employees. The reason: employees are the direct face of First Union to its customers. It is crucial that their interactions with customers reflect the agreed upon brand promise of simple, straightforward financial solutions in the customer's best interest.

To ensure that this employee-driven brand relationship was developed, a new process was installed. Even before new employees are hired at First Union, standardized and focused recruitment information – both printed and on the Internet – are made available. These are designed to reflect the true meaning of the brand. In the orientation of new employees (through internal satellite broadcasts and on the "Discover First Union" CD-ROM), the brand message is continually reinforced. Training of frontline employees has included discussions of what it means to internalize and live the First Union brand attributes, such as being proactive and innovative. And the brand was continually promoted internally by the integration of brand themes and messages through such things as satellite broadcasts, employee newsletters, the Intranet and employee training programs.

After seeing what other top brand companies (Coca-Cola was felt to be a particularly good example) were doing with employees, the team also developed a two-day "brand boot camp" for all marketing employees. A shorter version of that program was then developed that will eventually involve all employees. The basic idea is to immerse new hires in the brand and teach them both strategic and tactical ways to incorporate the brand into their day-to-day work. The goal of the brand team has been to make the "boot camp" convey the corporate belief that managing the brand is every bit as important as managing balance sheets.

■ *Keep it consistent* – First Union found that the greatest increases in unaided brand awareness generally came when the entire marketing division worked closely with the customer-facing employees as well as the Corporate Communications and Investor Relations teams. This is based on the learning that advertising commonly goes hand-in-hand with daily customer experiences, as well as with the messages that were being sent to the media, analysts and investors.

An excellent example of this new integrated approach was the launch of the first national television advertising campaign in 1998. The internal rollout of the campaign included the CIMs introducing the campaign at divisional meetings of corporate marketing heads, satellite broadcasts by Ed Crutchfield (CEO) discussing the objectives of the campaign, and an Intranet preview of the ads with a Q&A session afterward. At the same time, the new campaign was developed and implemented externally on a number of fronts as well. For example, the communication strategy was coordinated with the public relations department, and *working together*, these groups then developed core messages to be communicated to the press. Finally, print and video press releases were developed that were sent to traditional financial editors as well as to other editors in advertising, communication, and those covering consumer trends. This coordinated combined effort created a news media buzz around the ads, leveraging their uniqueness and their advanced cinematic effects. There is little question that the basic consumer awareness of First Union occurred as a result of this synergy between people, teams and departments. Notice here the absence of turf wars, as communication groups work together to achieve overarching objectives.

Stage five: cohesiveness

First Union has now put into practice many of the brand-building techniques practiced by leading brand companies. Of course, print and television ads are the most visible, exciting elements of most brand building activities. But it is the less glamorous work of integrated communication that generally determines the long-term strength of any brand. Investing employees in the brand, structuring marketing functions to keep the brand consistent, and fostering teamwork among all communication partners are all part of the formula. And, they work, as the First Union example illustrates.

One of the key elements of a successful brand building program is to think of the various advertising and other agencies as integral members of the team. For instance, the quarterly "Creative Summits" have proven to be a very important tool in team-building. Ensuring that all of the brand's agencies and internal creative partners speak with one voice is essential. And, that requires time, effort, direction, trust, and planning. It is not a chance phenomenon. For example, if there is a lack of cohesiveness among all the players doing marketing, advertising, and other communication under the same brand, the results are often fragmented. A worst case scenario is when disparate communication efforts actually conflict with each other with the customer the ultimate loser, as was the case with world-class car-maker Mercedes-Benz and the introduction of the A-class. Again, the point is reinforced that promises made via advertising, and reinforced by corporate statements, need to be backed by appropriate performance. Hiding behind reputation may work short-time, but repeated product "accidents" can rapidly dent a well-earned corporate image (Gronstedt, 2000). All the communications must work as one in delivering and reinforcing brand values.

The need for consistency also extends into event marketing partnerships and other types of cooperative ventures. If the firm's marketing partner's brand messages don't demonstrate some symmetry with the company's brand, similar conflict often results. (See the First Union case illustration at the end of this chapter on how this approach has been applied in the sports and event marketing area.) Furthermore, inconsistent brand messages projected by individuals anywhere on a company's frontline can have significant impact. Integration means integration of all the pieces and parts, people and groups, not just some or a few of them. A quick glimpse at the recent Firestone debacle shows how weakness in just one or two aspects of brand maintenance (product quality and public relations, in that particular case) can sabotage a company's hard-earned reputation and imperil its stock value. In our view, had the company swiftly accepted responsibility and made clear their intention to compensate victims and rectify safety problems, they may well have risen above the controversy with brand integrity intact. Dodging responsibility for weeks was disastrous because "safety" is an integral part of automobile tire branding. By comparison, Johnson & Johnson handled the Tylenol drug-tampering controversy years ago with such sure-handedness that it remains the leading brand in the pain-killer category. Tylenol's employees had so thoroughly adopted product safety as a core value that there was no question but they would pull all their product from the shelves until it was safe. (See Chapter 9 for discussion of the proper handling of crisis communication programs.) Examples like these demonstrate that brand building is about more than just advertising. It is a unified effort from every element of the company to maintain the integrity of commonly held corporate values.

Conclusion

Today, fly-by-night brands appear to be numerous and growing. New technology companies bombard the airwaves and their print campaigns dominate the media with quirky messages designed to make them stand out from the crowd. A few, and only a few it seems, will survive. Amazon.com and eBay seem like genuine brands, whereas a stunningly long list of others pop up on TV or in magazines with expensive marketing and advertising campaigns only to vanish after ill-conceived business plans fail to succeed. Most often, in our view, they fail because they completely underestimate the necessary steps required to build a brand – especially customer service, consistent customer experiences and a total commitment by the employees and management to focus on the customer and prospects that make brands possible at all. Those companies that build lasting brands place brand-building efforts on virtually the same level as that of product development and service. That emphasis is necessary. The communication age has created more experienced and knowledgeable consumers than ever before; at the same time, it has inundated them with a morass of information to sort through. It is even harder to build a brand in this cluttered environment. The failure rate of marketing deliveries is not wasted on ordinary consumers. Everyone with something to market is making promises, more loudly, and through more invasive means than ever before, via telemarketers, the Internet, event marketing, and even public schools. To become or remain a solid brand in the dawning era of global marketing and increasingly sophisticated, well-informed consumers, companies must recognize that the promises they make must be fulfilled from the frontline service level all the way up to the CEO. It would be a mistake to say all the way down from the CEO.

It is worth it! The efforts of communication at creating instant name recognition, perceived quality, and unquestioned customer loyalty, once accepted and taken to heart, do offer powerful rewards. There is an undoubted and proven link between brand strength and company profitability. But the link needs to be continually reinforced by integrated approaches to brand communication which not only promise consistent delivery of core values, but actually deliver those values. And that is the responsibility of everyone in an organization, not just those with the word "communication" inserted in a job title.

Summary of brand-building success strategies

So, what has been learned? What lessons can be taken that can be applied to other types of organization by the corporate marketing communication group? We believe there are several.

First, the CEO is also the brand steward. That does not mean that the CEO is the brand manager on a daily basis, but, he/she must provide the vision, the resources, and most of all the patience in the development and implementation of all the various marketing communication activities necessary to grow and build the brand both internally and externally.

Second, the organization must view brand building as an investment and the brand as an important strategic element. While it is true that brand-building investments must be taken as short-term expenses, the longer view must prevail. This requires a long-term view of the organization and the results, not a quarter-to-quarter review of sales records.

Third, employee branding is an essential foundation for a strong brand. There is little question, brands start inside and move out. They don't start outside and then involve employees, channels, affiliates and the like. Thus, the brand is what the employees believe it is, not just what customers want it to be. Where do your employees stand on this issue?

Fourth, consistent customer experience is essential. While advertising and other forms of marketing communication are essential in bringing together all the various stakeholders into a common view of the brand, it is the ongoing, day-after-day experience that customers and prospects have with the brand that really determines success or failure over time.

Fifth, consistency is delivered by all channels (note, not just outward-bound advertising). Too often in our experience, brand activities are assumed to be only those that emanate from the firm, in other words, only external communication is counted. Brand communication comes in many forms and in many ways, most of which are totally dependent on the employees and management of the firm.

Sixth, consistency is delivered via all touchpoints. However, whenever and in whatever form, every time the customer touches the firm or the firm touches the customer, the brand is either built or destroyed. All touchpoints must not only be understood but also managed.

Seventh, consistency is delivered via every interaction. Again, it is customer experiences that are important. Interactions either build or destroy the brand and once a poor interaction occurs, the challenge of renewing the original brand essence becomes difficult if not impossible.

We emphasize: there must be a single brand "voice." All touchpoints, all interactions, all customer experiences must combine and coordinate to provide the single brand essence.

Managers and executives must resist the desire to change the creative approach too frequently. The old saying "The company tires of the advertising before its customers see or understand it" is true. Keep the communication fresh and relevant but don't expect customers and prospects to work at keeping track of what you are doing. Why? Because internal wear-out factors long precede external wear-out. And, remember, employees are to be considered as external audiences when it comes to communication. It takes them time to absorb, understand and act on the external marketing communication programs.

There must be clarity among the individual communication ingredients and integration between them. There is little question that all elements must be clear, concise and relevant. But, they must also be coordinated and they must all fit together to achieve the goals of the communication program. That means the brand, the advertising, the public relations, and the product or service must all work together to create the brand essence. In total, it means that the brand, the advertising, and the product must all work together to build the brand and the organization.

Lessons Learned: Extending and Expanding the Brand Through Sports and Event Marketing

The development of an integrated marketing communication program at First Union highlighted many new areas of advertising and promotion ranging from in-bank merchandising to branding. The development of the integrated concept brought home more than ever, the need to have clear, concise goals for all communication investments but most of all to have a solid approach to using the various techniques increasingly available. All must contribute to the overall value of the brand and all must build and enhance the essence of the brand.

As First Union built its communication program, it became clear that various marketing and communication techniques had developed their own set of planning tools. While these were useful in developing and maximizing the individual activities, they did not always contribute to the overall program that was being developed or to corporate brand enhancement. Sports and event marketing was one of those areas. A review of this area provides a good view of how individual programs and activities, often under the guidance of different, specialized managers need to be coordinated and focused to help support and build a strong brand presence.

The first step in the First Union sports and event marketing appraisal was a review of what was being done across the organization. The review proved that First Union sports and event marketing strategies for the year 2000, were made up of a diverse portfolio of properties that had grown organically and by decentralized acquisition through 1998. Sports properties included Major League Baseball teams, National Football League (NFL) teams, National Basketball Associations (NBA) teams, and National Hockey League (NHL) teams. Moreover, college sports teams and a wide variety of other sponsorships existed as well. However, the review showed that the marketing efforts relative to the properties owned were mostly about building brand awareness, and had a questionable business building effectiveness. For example, Figure 6.9 shows the range and locus of the wide range of marketing communication programs that existed at First Union.

As shown, First Union divided its sports and events communication programs into those termed "Broad-Based," in other words those that were designed to reach a broad range of customers and prospects commonly in a non-personal manner; and those that were more personalized, that is "One-to-One." In truth, what First Union had done was not uncommon. Many

Broad-based	Advertising
	■ Television
	■ Print
	■ Radio
	■ Outdoor
	■ Internet
	Public relations
	Sponsorships
	Merchandising
	Collateral
	Direct mail
	Investor relations
	Commercial proposals/bids
One-to-One	Daily customer contact
	■ Financial centers
	■ First Union Direct
	■ First Union Online
	■ ATMS

Despite what you may think, advertising is not the only form of brand communication. There are many other ways that a customer gains a perception of us and what we do. And that's where teamwork really comes in. Each and every one of us has to fulfill our promise to the customer. If our advertising promises a key attribute, we must live up to that promise when we open an account for a customer, introduce a new product, even when we answer the phone. And don't forget that our customers are everywhere, even within our own organization. So it's just as important to keep our promise when we're registering a fellow employee for training or when the warehouse fulfills an order. Everything we do must make each customer think smart, straightforward financial solutions in my best interest.

Figure 6.9 Integrated marketing communication
(*Source:* Author)

companies do acquire affiliations for a wide variety of reasons, then retrofit them on occasion to meet business objectives. And more often than not, companies are investing in rights fees rather than marketing relationships in a meaningful way. In other words, First Union was attaching its name to teams and events but not developing targeted programs that would achieve specific, measurable business goals. Plus, First Union's transformation from a traditional, product-focused consumer bank to a financial services provider including brokerage services, capital markets capabilities and other corporate services was not evident from the mass market approach that was being taken with all the various sponsorships. Interestingly, First Union Securities (the retail brokerage unit) wasn't fully engaged as a partner in sports and event marketing despite its relationships with the company's high value and high priority customers. Simply put, very few integrated marketing programs were in place when the new brand-building program was initiated.

The new First Union sports and event marketing team created an interim plan to activate those programs that were felt to be capable of producing measurable business results, and to begin paring down the list of sponsorships that were of questionable value to the company. The first step was to redefine the company's sponsorship strategy with strong emphasis on several factors:

- Development of specific business and marketing objectives
- Identification and targeting of customer acquisition and retention potential among various groups
- Selective rights acquisition of sports and events
- Brand-building synergy across the spectrum and within the organization
- Corporate and local business unit buy-in, both financial and strategic
- Disciplined activation of the programs once they were in place
- Rigorous accountability to measure the actual returns on investment
- Shrewd deal making.

Reassessing all of current sponsorships, the sports and event team decided on a rigorous evaluation process to assure that the above factors became part of every deal; otherwise, no commitment would be made. Figure 6.10 shows graphically how the rationales for sports and event marketing programs were matched with the various audiences.

As shown, it was important for the various sports and events to match up with the various audiences of First Union. And, equally, the rationales used

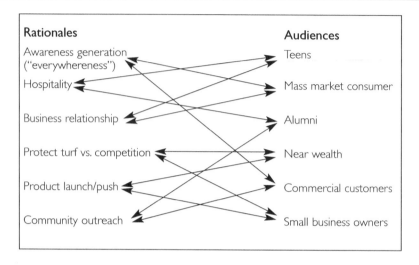

Figure 6.10 Divergent goals and audiences

had to fit multiple audiences. The result was a more focused and comprehensive approach to identifying and agreeing upon sponsorships. That meant
negotiating more closely with potential partners, determining brand synergies ahead of time, and agreeing on program specifics before signing
contracts. It also meant building measurable goals into each program, with
the understanding that First Union was only participating in the partnership
because it offered true potential for brand building and business results.

The team's sharper focus on active partnerships with synergistic brand
messages drastically changed First Union's corporate sponsorship roster in a
single year. In 1999, some 53 corporate sponsorships – many of them merely
rights fees investments – were in place. For 2001, the number of corporate
sponsorships – tailored to be more effective in achieving business goals –
was down to 21. The programs generated by the roster have also been
remarkably successful. For example, in Philadelphia, the First Union Center
All Access Program – a promotion to raise the number of online services
customers for First Union – offered the chance to win a year's worth of
tickets to every event at the First Union Center. The promotion succeeded
in reaching its goals in the first four weeks of a six-week campaign. Furthermore, it eventually surpassed that goal by 168 percent.

Much of this refocused activity came as a result of a formalized method of
evaluating sponsorships, that is, the various sports and events that were being
offered to First Union. The evaluation process is illustrated as Figure 6.11.

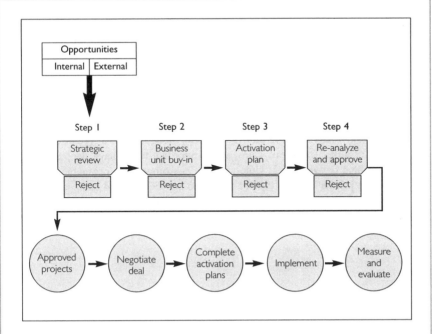

Figure 6.11 Sponsorship evaluation process

As shown, the Sponsorship Evaluation Process at First Union involves four steps and four decision points. Step 1 is a Strategic Review of the various opportunities that either are being offered to the First Union sports and events team or those the team may develop on their own. Step 2 calls for a Business Unit Buy-In. That simply means that the business unit, that is, consumer banking, securities or whoever, must agree to the goals for the program, the funding and the commitment to be made. Following that, Step 3 is the Activation Plan where the various parts of the program are put into place. Step 4 is the Re-analyze and Approve stage where any adjustments to the program are made, the business unit reviews the program and it is finally approved. As shown in the illustration, the proposed sponsorship can be rejected at any of the four stages in the process.

Once approved, the various steps in the development of the sponsorship start to occur. As shown, those range from negotiating the deal to measurement and evaluation. It is this final step, Measure and Evaluate, that First Union has found to be the most valuable. Knowing what the sponsorship was supposed to achieve gives both the team and the business unit a basis for determining what programs should be renewed and which ones should be dropped. Most important, however, is the structured process that assures the sponsorship fits with the overall goals of the organization for the brand and for the customer experience with the brand.

Using the approach described above, in just a month's time, two other promotions also accomplished considerable business increases. One with the Miami Dolphins football team accomplished a 34 percent increase in new online accounts; and, in metro-Atlanta, the Atlanta Braves (baseball team) Double Play Program generated 12 percent more new CAP (asset management) Accounts. These programs, and others like them, have deepened the relationships between First Union and its customers in a profitable way for both. And, just as importantly, in addition to achieving sound business results, the communication team has been able to create a more cohesive articulation of the brand message throughout all the various sports and event marketing venues.

Global issues in branding, communication and corporate structure

marilyn roberts

Coca-Cola Shifts to New Globalism

On October 2, 2000 a feature story by Andy Beckett in the *Guardian* (London) focused on the global soft-drink giant Coca-Cola. The article contained quotes from Tom Long, the newly appointed head of operations for Britain and Ireland. Long had spent most of his decade-long career in the Atlanta headquarters in market research and as global director for strategic marketing. Long stated:

> We [Coca-Cola] need a good examination every now and again … Our response to last summer's (Belgian) product crisis should have been a heck of a lot faster. We haven't been good marketers some years. We've found out that a centralised (sic) structure didn't let our people experiment. The company had gone for efficiency and scale … the way to be big is by being small. (Beckett, 2000)

Only two months later, on December 2, 2000, Coca-Cola's hometown newspaper, *The Atlanta Journal and Constitution*, Business section front-page headline announced, "One agency gets Coke Classic ads …" (Unger and Leither, 2000). The lead sentence began:

> In a significant shift in advertising strategy, Coca-Cola Co. said Friday it will use just one ad company, the Interpublic Group, to develop a global message for its flagship Coke Classic brand.

The announcement was obviously great news for the Interpublic Group (IPG) as Coca-Cola was estimated to spend close to one billion dollars worldwide on its flagship brand. IPG President, John Dooner, stated:

> Our team's mission is to reassert the essence of brand Coca-Cola and determine how it can be best communicated across the full spectrum of media, including online, experiential, in-store and traditional advertising.

To accomplish these lofty goals, IPG will form "a marketing communications advisory council" with Coke marketers. The IPG advisory council will include a range of agencies and other resources including: McCann Erickson World-Group, The Lowe Group, DraftWorldwide, Initiative Media Worldwide, Octagon Sports Marketing and the Allied Communications Group – in effect mirroring corporate requirements at Coca-Cola to move either globally or locally as circumstances and corporate policy dictate and to provide a wide range of communication approaches and delivery systems. Stephen Jones, Coke's chief marketing officer commented:

> Coke's strategic alliance with New York-based Interpublic ... will replace the company's relationship with about 10 ad agencies that had been working on brand Coke's strategy around the world.

While the changes apparently reflect the mantra of Doug Daft, current chairman and chief executive officer of the world's biggest brand: "Go local," the corporate giant has assured their various stakeholders that IPG's work will not interfere with the recent "think local, act local" strategy it has been trying to develop over the past several months. Nonetheless:

> Some observers this week found it strange that the company has been promising a local approach, but is now establishing a global think-tank. (Brabbs, 2000)

Still, Andrew Coker, Director for Coca-Cola Great Britain, appeared comfortable with the proposed change. Coker stated:

> Each country can still appoint local agencies to implement the brand message devised by Interpublic. This is not a return to the control days of Atlanta. (Brabbs, 2000)

The interplay between globalization and localization promises interesting reading in the next few months insofar as Coca-Cola is concerned. And, interesting challenges both inside and outside the organization are likely to be found as well. Communication specialists would do well to "watch this space" for it may be a pre-cursor as to how major global brands will attempt to solve and resolve the problems all are facing.

Source: Author.

Introduction and overview

Inherent in the challenges Coca-Cola faces in trying to develop a global strategy are the questions of corporate brand and product brand. As noted in the initial comments by Beckett, Coca-Cola, its employees, bottlers, stockholders and other interested parties took a real "hit" both in reputation and actual financial value as a result of the "troubles" in Belgium and the Benelux during the peak selling months a few years ago. From the view of the corporate communication director, the contamination problem could have been considered an "operations" or a "marketing" problem. In truth, it was and continues to be a "corporate" problem with a number of management groups and issues all involved. Thus, the newly announced Coca-Cola plan to centralize brand strategy through the Interpublic Group signals one organization's attempt to deal with the complex issues of modern business. And, it returns us once again to the question of the interplay between the corporate and the various product brands in the firm's portfolio.

From our point of view, the decisions of Coca-Cola management in terms of marketing, advertising and ultimately other forms of communication raise some major issues for the corporate communication director. For example, how much a part of the "marketing team" should the corporate communication director be? What type of organizational structure should the firm consider in trying to move to this new order of globalization? And, since the product brand at Coke is also the corporate brand, what type of interaction should there be among and between the various managers and the various communication programs?

This chapter has been developed to address the three major issues that impact on corporate global communication. We develop those themes by exploring current best practices employed by the widest range of global advertisers, agencies and the media; discussing how an advertiser's organizational structures affect various agencies' global branding and communication efforts; and providing an illustration of how recent changes in the organizational structure of one of the strongest global brands are indicative of these trends and challenges. One might argue here that "what we do and how we organize at the corporate level has little to do with our relationships and our work with our external suppliers, agencies and the like." Yet, how the corporate organization structures itself has much to do with the service and the type of communication capability it receives from its agencies of all types. Thus, we believe it is critical for the corporate communication director or manager to understand the views of the various agencies he or she employs or has dealings with. That is part of the basis for this chapter.

We will explore these issues by presenting the findings of the Global Best Practices study coordinated by the International Advertising Association (IAA) in conjunction with its corporate members, particularly VISA International, and the University of Florida's Department of Advertising, a certified IAA institute.

The overarching purpose of the chapter, therefore, is to examine the Global Best Practices' findings to determine those approaches and methodologies that are presently employed by the widest range of international advertisers, agencies, and media. This will help in understanding the type of "corporate umbrellas" that are being raised around the world. It provides further support for the concept that all the "ribs" of the corporate umbrella must be the same and must work together. One cannot successfully "raise the corporate umbrella" if one rib is more developed than the others or if one lacks strength to withstand the challenges of the marketplace.

It is worth noting that a number of other IAA corporate members shared valuable information about their global structures, trends and case studies for this project. Among those who participated were: BBDO Worldwide, Bozell Worldwide, Grey International, J Walter Thompson, McCann-Erickson Worldwide, Saatchi & Saatchi, TBWA, and Young & Rubicam Advertising. These global agencies generously provided 30 case studies that form a major backdrop for the approaches and concepts presented in this chapter (see Acknowledgements).

The global challenge and some glimmers of hope

Today, organizations are attempting to build global brands in the midst of a changing global environment, an ongoing almost exponential technological revolution, and the accelerating strategic complexity of culturally sensitized consumer segments. By examining the structures and strategies of multinational marketers, advertising agencies and the media, we can describe the current trends and share the global branding and communication lessons learned by those on the firing line of these transitions.

In order to facilitate the analysis of the Global Best Practices' study, this chapter examines several factors that contribute to the best practice of advertising in the rapidly changing global environment. The first section provides a brief historical view of the sources of global advertising and a perspective on how it now fits in the overall structure of the multinational firm. The second section examines the areas of organization structure, staffing, creativity, and information transfer to determine what best practices actually are and to identify specific trends. Here, we look extensively at the advertising agency for that is the organization that is commonly used or resourced to help build the corporate brand, and is almost always a key player in the development of product brands. The final portion of this chapter revisits the initial illustration of Coca-Cola to underscore how the reorganization of the Coca-Cola's flagship brand and the newly consolidated relationship between the advertiser and its agency are indicative of current trends in global brand building and communication.

Genesis

The development of modern global advertising can be traced back to the 1950s. Following World War II, international trade began to increase with the majority of the activities being concentrated between the United States and Europe. By the 1960s some organizations expanded their foci to include specific Latin American countries, such as Chile, Argentina and Brazil. That time period was further driven by a general trend of internationalization in the marketplace. Cost and control considerations during the era brought forth highly centralized and standardized structures and various forms of international marketing.

Early encounters and movements toward global marketing, especially in the communication arena, proved that marketing across borders was a formidable challenge where mistakes were costly and poorly designed strategies could quickly damage brand images and corporate reputations and values. Thus, the history of international marketing and those exploratory companies' early attempts to globalize is littered with examples of managerial gaffes, embarrassments, and outright miserable failures.

Nonetheless, with the growth of international trade and the internationalization of the marketplace, many local organizations wanted to bring with them those groups that had helped develop and maintain their brand images and corporate reputations in their major home markets. The concomitant emergence of multinational advertising agencies was, therefore, simply a natural evolution and progression of those local market successes (see Chapter 12).

Domestic media also began experimenting with international editions to provide new cross-border advertising venues. A "Brand Revolution" emerged from a shift in focus from building corporate name awareness to developing specific product-focused brand names. Later this shift gave way to a "Creative Revolution" among multinational agencies who assisted in building global brand images (IAA, 1998). The latest phase is seeing individual and corporate brands allied together in the desire to build effective communication with all relevant markets, publics, and stakeholders (see Chapter 8).

Historically, therefore, corporate communication was an entity to itself as was product brand advertising. Today, however, we are witnessing the alliance and amalgamation of the two. That's what many questions and concerns seem to revolve around today.

By the 1970s other non-U.S.-based multinationals, observing the expansion success of the U.S. corporations in the 1960s, had embarked on their own expansion endeavors. The concept of globalization received a boost in the 1980s when Harvard Business School Professor Theodore Levitt strongly argued that the same products and services could be sold the same way, everywhere. Levitt's (1983) article provided organizations with valuable, albeit questionable, ammunition to argue that standardized communication approaches and centralized organization structures were the optimal and most cost-efficient mechanisms for international success. In effect he urged corporations to "go global." Those who took his advice, sometimes without considering the ramifications of culture and consumer sensitivity via careful analysis, often reaped the rewards of international failure. Parker Pen is an illustrative example of this type of slavish focus on globalization without considering the local issues. (This case is cited elsewhere in this text.) Nonetheless, Levitt's article did serve to ignite an ongoing academic and professional debate about the various advantages of standardized versus adapted (localized) approaches, just as his 'marketing myopia' article had provided the touch-paper for marketing accelerated expansion around the world (see Levitt, 1960).

Simultaneously, in almost every market, agencies were "re-positioning" themselves to better serve their clients with new revitalized emphasis on international expansion and global brand building. The collapse of the Berlin Wall at the end of the 1980s, and the collapse of the Soviet Union in 1991 have provided new, yet challenging, consumer markets in central and eastern Europe all seemingly eager for new products and services. In Latin America, the progress toward more democratic forms of government and economic stability has brought about the significant development of middle-class consumerism in many parts of that region. Likewise, the economic awakening of the sleeping Chinese dragon heralds further market expansion opportunities for both marketers, their agencies and the media as well.

Since the 1990s, advertisers, their agencies and the media have become increasingly globalized and have continually undergone major changes and faced new challenges. For example, the Pacific Rim has seen multinational investment boosted dramatically in spite of the "meltdown" of the middle 1990s. As evidence, Asian advertising volume and revenues have surged.

Multinational agencies have responded to the movements of their clients by adding personnel, creating new business lines, and layering their account management structures, while simultaneously offering full line promotional development in-house.

Looking back to 1960, international billings constituted only six percent of the gross revenues of the top ten U.S. advertising agencies. By 1991, this percentage had climbed to almost 60 percent (Ducoffe and Grein, 1998). And the percentage continues to grow. Advertisers increasingly want their brands and marketing communication managed by multinational agencies for they believe that can help create and maintain a consistent unified brand image in the global marketplace, assuming that is what markets and stakeholders want.

One of the greatest challenges to future brand building and communication is how the use of the Internet, the proliferation of erstwhile dot.com organizations, and e-commerce endeavors, will be integrated into current communication efforts. Many multinational and global corporations and their agencies are in flux as to how to address that dimension of their businesses. Therefore, this chapter cannot address how global marketers and their agencies think about and conduct their business in the virtual world. While the Internet might seem to form a separate area of communication in its own right, one must always remember that for the most part, the firm's customers and prospects now move effortlessly among all forms of communication. Thus, the customer who goes online is the same one who sees the latest television commercial and the same person who may order all their Christmas gifts on the Internet and through various websites is also the same one who visits the "bricks and mortar" retail outlets the firm may operate. So, while we agree that the Internet and electronic commerce will likely expand, we would not go as far as Molenaar (1996) whose early claims for Internet marketing must now be viewed askance (see Hamill and Kitchen, 2000).

With this historical view of why and how internationalization and globalization developed, we are now ready to see what organizations are doing about it.

Organizational structures

An *Advertising Age* international survey (see Figure 7.1) of 38 U.S.-based multinational marketing organizations revealed three different approaches to global advertising decision-making and these approaches have and are having a major impact on the marketing controls that are being put in place. The study found those are: centralized strategy, decentralized strategy, and a hybrid strategy (Dietrich, 1999). But, under ongoing pres-

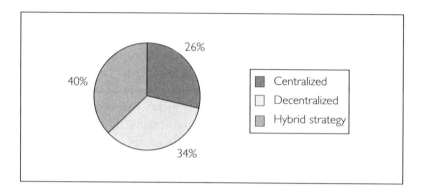

Figure 7.1 Global ad decision controls

sure to perform better, it appears few marketers stay faithful to a single model. For these corporations the hybrid strategy represents a strong central strategic direction coupled with local execution (or the activities appear to be local, thus fulfilling the "glocalization" approach).

For most managers, it will come as no surprise that multinational companies are moving toward various forms of matrix organizations with business responsibilities sited in one location. Strategy, brand, and value decisions are centralized with local units having higher degrees of authority or influence on execution. Efficiency in local execution and adaptation is growing more important. Other multinationals, however, are opting for a pan-regionalism approach by establishing regional "centers of excellence" and then employing innovative and creative regional shops. It all seems to depend on the view of the managers as to what works or should work best for the firm. And, there seems to be no common agreement as shown by the almost even split among the three alternatives.

New globalism: fewer are better

From the study, multinational companies, especially for their top 5–10 markets, appear to be centralizing brand management by working with a limited number of agencies. Agencies in other markets, therefore, are working on locally tailoring the global strategy to their local markets that has been developed from the centralized core. Multinational agency networks, with their ability to offer uniform resources, services, and talent around the world appear to be in a much better position to add more multinational clients to their portfolios than are strictly locals. A prevailing

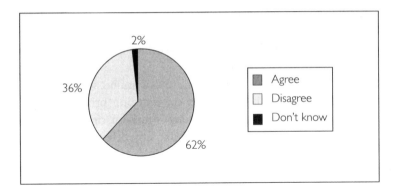

Figure 7.2 Advertisers increasingly want a single agency network to handle all advertising

organizational principle is to meet the needs of global accounts and to standardize as much as possible the service delivery around the world.

A 1999 survey of 201 major international advertisers conducted by *M&M Europe*, a trade publication for marketing and advertising professionals, revealed that, increasingly, advertisers prefer to work with a single agency network. For example, almost two-thirds of those responding preferred a single agency network (see Figure 7.2).

Alternatively, an *Advertising Age International* survey (see Figure 7.3) of U.S.-based multinationals shows that less than four agencies are used worldwide by two-thirds of the marketers surveyed. Among those, the majority prefer to work with one or two advertising networks (Dietrich, 1999). While the argument seems clear, that fewer agencies are better, there still appears to be a need among client organizations to structure their

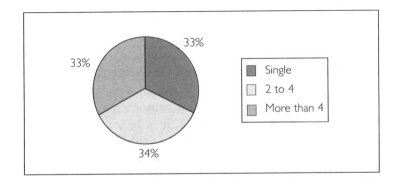

Figure 7.3 Number of agencies used worldwide

agency affiliations based on their specific businesses and their perceived global and local needs. However, a consolidation of big global ad budgets with one or two worldwide agency networks is apparently becoming a predominant trend in the business.

One of the challenges of the corporate communication manager is, of course, can the agency that develops outstanding product brand advertising do the same for corporate communication or brand advertising programs given the differences in goals, objectives and strategies, as mentioned in other chapters of this text? Thus, this idea of centralization and consolidation can have an impact on the decisions of the corporate communication director and on the product brand managers as well. Increasingly, in our view, the coordination of corporate and product branding becomes one of the most important issues in the firm. Thus, the corporate communication director must be alert to the trends and changes in the product brand area for that can have great impact on senior management's views of agency arrangements and affiliations.

Agencies as business partners

To better understand the opposing forces at play within international advertising agencies, both those favoring global integration and those favoring national responsiveness such as ethnocentrism, it is helpful to examine the organizational structures of the agency sample (Ducoffe and Grein, 1998).

Advertising agencies appear to mirror the structures of their clients; some changing their structures to become more client-driven. However, this approach, in which ad agencies were perceived to reflect their client's views rather than alter them as trendsetters, has come under severe criticism. The *M&M* Advertiser Survey also showed that advertisers increasingly want their agencies to adopt the role of a business partner, that is, someone who enhances overall marketing strategy rather than just tactical developers of "on–off" promotional campaigns.

As a result of this change, advertisers are raising their expectations for agencies to develop innovative ways of meeting global needs and developing highly integrated marketing communication programs. If these higher expectations cannot be fulfilled, it is believed that management consulting and global media firms will likely fill the gap. This question of who will provide the communication management function is quite important to corporate communication managers. On the one hand, control of external resources is important to building a solid communication strategy, while at the same time, striving for corporate consistency is important as well. This question of who will supply the external communication strategy, not just the creative product, is, we believe, one of the key choices corporate communication directors must make.

Creative alone is not enough

In view of the increasingly complex and highly competitive market environments around the world, creative alone often does not fulfill the needs of both local and multinational companies. What is increasingly expected of advertising and all other types of agencies is to prove the effectiveness of the advertising and marketing communication programs they create via some form of measurable and integrated approach (see Schultz and Kitchen, 2000). Even though creative is still the agency's main task, a solid balance of capability insight as well as local creative inputs are becoming increasingly important. Being effective and locally competent at each step means more than being big in terms of size. Consumer insight, market planning, creativity, and media execution have become equally important elements of the agency value chain. Thus, fully integrated brand management and communication services are increasingly relevant client requirements.

Today, international advertising agencies are increasingly being held accountable for a brand's global performance. Multinational advertisers' rising expectations for a return on investment (ROI) demand greater insights into each specific country's or region's target consumers. Clearly, all elements of the marketing and communication mix must be calibrated precisely, regardless of whether the structure is centralized, decentralized, or hybrid.

Unbundling

Another trend is the unbundling of agency products. Media, direct marketing, and specialist support services are increasingly separated as are the more service-oriented areas such as account planning, strategic development and the like. More and more agencies are separating creativity from media and other specialized tasks, and establishing different entities to handle these functions, some of which are directly related to the existing agency structure and others are being spun out as stand-alone firms. While as many as 60 percent of the respondents to the *M&M* survey found this trend to be a good one for their business, 36 percent disagreed.

Globalization, marketing, creativity, and organizational structure

When entering new markets one of the primary challenges of multinational companies is to decide to what extent they will adapt their product, their marketing mix and their advertising and marketing communication campaigns. A survey conducted by J Walter Thompson (cited in the *M&M* report) showed that companies have the greatest resistance to adapting their brand name and/or logo, their product specifications and/or their product positioning and strategy. They are most amenable to changing or adapting their consumer promotions, specific media choices and public relations programs. For example, 32 percent of the respondents said that they would resist changes in the advertising strategy. However, for the advertising execution, the opponents to adaptation decrease to only 14 percent.

The JWT study also revealed that a company's structure is the underlying factor in the respondents' response on the standardization versus adaptation issues. Similarly, the case studies we analyzed also revealed that the organizational structure of the multinational companies generally shapes the way agencies handle the creative strategies for the products or service. Therefore, one of the most important areas to consider among multinational companies which are attempting to manage their global selling strategies and how they structure their decision-making methods is to uncover the trends in development, execution and production of the creative product. Not something that many market or financial analysts have considered in the past.

In our analysis, we found multinational company structures are located on a continuum ranging from centralized to decentralized. Few can be found operating at the extremes on either side. Thus, the majority are clustered near the center, which can be best described as a hybrid solution that combines the better of two worlds (see Figure 7.4). Another term coined for this center-oriented approach is "glocalization." Companies with a hybrid perspective reach consumers with a global message that fully supports local programs. This permits multinational companies to build global brands while simultaneously appealing to local or regional tastes. As the study's *M&M* report author states:

> Local market development can be integrated with global brand development when promotion strategies designed for a local market are linked to a broader worldwide theme.

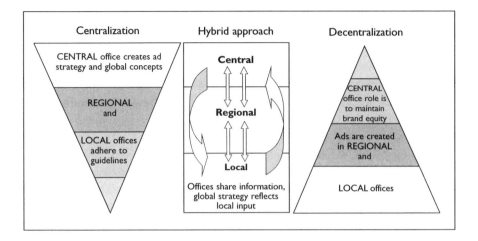

Figure 7.4 Structural alternatives

There appear to be some commonalities among organizations pursuing each of these strategies. A review of what those are will help put the issue in perspective.

Centralization approach

Companies favoring centralization focus on achieving economies of scale, synergies and brand consistency. Both the M&M and the AAI surveys reveal that more companies prefer to make global marketing decisions on a global or regional level. These companies interpret the technological developments of the 20th century as the force behind the global consumer and the global marketplace. Developing advertising campaigns and strategies for these clients is the responsibility of the central agency. A recent example is Ford's decision to run the same commercial all around the world welcoming the new millennium. The commercial began on the Internet and first appeared in New Zealand. It then headed west "following the sun just like the millennium" as it was described by Jim Schroer, Ford Vice President for global marketing (Elliott, 1999).

For centralized companies, the common practice is for agency and client headquarter executives to interface to set global objectives. Once the global guidelines are set, they are then sent to the local agencies to execute. Regional or global Internet systems or servers are increasingly useful in distributing finished ads, concepts and artwork to the local offices. Local and regional markets implement from the headquarters lead, taking into account the competition and other local conditions.

Creativity guidelines are strictly followed by the local agencies. In certain cases a degree of flexibility is permitted to accommodate local mores or values. An example: for the first time in its history, Shell Oil Company decided to run double-page ads in 25 different local editions of the *Reader's Digest* around the world. A company was hired to work closely with Shell's global agency and Shell's local offices to resolve translation problems. According to Tom Henderson of Shell International, as much "trans-creation" was involved in the process as was the translation. He also said "they made sure that the control is there from the center without losing local nuances" (*Advertising Age*, June 1999, p. 21).

Among the cases analyzed in the current study, there were very distinct examples of this approach. A leading multinational agency reported that one of its clients in the fashion industry preferred the agency headquarters to handle the strategic planning of the global brand. Then, once the print and television ads were produced, they were distributed globally with creative guidelines to which all the regions were required to adhere. In another case, the lead agency, which happened to be the agency headquarters, created and administered the development of all the client brand image and service strategies, as well as the creative concepts. Regional offices took strategic direction on media and message priorities from the headquarters. Then, acting in concert with the client's regional offices, global strategies were translated into country programs. One other leading agency notes that in the case of a very centralized client there are few opportunities for local client managers to take national initiatives. Unfortunately, they also believe that the strictness of the client's approach has negatively affected the agency's capability for pushing for new and innovative ideas.

Decentralized approach

Companies favoring decentralization base their argument on four factors: proximity to the market in order to reach even the narrowest segments, flexibility, cultural sensitivity, and faster response time. These multinational companies, most of whom are consumer product companies, have long felt there is no such thing as a multinational consumer. Consumers respond best to ideas that fully match and relate to their needs and values.

According to a Deloitte and Touche report (1999): "decentralization supports the process of globalization and drives strategic decision-making down through the organization." Sometimes the nature of the product or product line requires that the creative designs be tailored to the market. As one of the worldwide advertising agencies suggested, analyzing the strategy and legal requirements is vital within the "over the counter" category of medicine sales. This particular category also requires local production with country-specific insights. Another trend in top advertising agencies handling global megabrands is a more focused role from the lead agency and the agency headquarters on global brand equity development.

A third reason given to choose the decentralized approach is that in many cases, the product variations throughout the world are so great that global executions become almost impossible. That is why the local agencies of the leading multinational agencies produce creativity according to their interpretation of the centrally agreed strategy. It also appears to be a common practice for some agencies to run a campaign originally developed by another agency but re-direct it to a different market or a different audience.

Our study also revealed that clients may sometimes ask their agencies to create different campaigns, that is some developed centrally to run in the international market and some local productions to meet the requirements of specific markets. The choice of course is driven by the local market conditions, in other words, a decentralized approach.

Hybrid strategy

Companies opting for a hybrid strategy mix strong central coordination with local input. As Schumacher (1973) argued in his book, *Small is Beautiful, Economics as if People Mattered*:

> Once a large organization comes into being, it normally goes through alternating phases of centralizing and decentralizing like swings of a pendulum. Whenever one encounters such opposites, each of them with persuasive arguments in its favor, it is worth looking into the depth of the problem for something more than compromise, more than a half-and-half solution. Maybe what we really need is not either-or but the one-and-the-other-at-the-same-time.

Gary Schmitz of Motorola believes that for companies who wish to be "both global and yet to be local," this is the best approach (Dietrich, 1999).

The overall brand positioning, as well as the creative strategy developed for these companies reflects the inputs of local regional markets. Charles Frenette, a previous chief marketing officer of Coca-Cola, believes that the fundamental marketing challenge of the corporation is to reconnect with consumers on a daily basis. He claims that "though globalization is [about] knocking down borders ... we [still] can't treat them as a homogenous set" (see *Advertising Age*, October 25 1999, p. 32). Frenette's statement indirectly acknowledges the need for "not either-or but the one-and-the-other-at-the-same time." According to Jan Soderstrom (1999), at that time Executive Vice President of Visa International, "glocalization" can be achieved when:

- there is a general agreement about how the brand is to be positioned globally and how that positioning should be translated into each geographic area; and,

- there is a well-balanced power structure between the headquarters and regional offices, including an equal share of the marketing responsibilities.

One of the best courses for an agency is to work with the client in developing a brand positioning that reflects the inputs of all the local and regional markets. Through this, brand and product strategies can then move to more closely reflect the personality of specific products within each market. During this process, other markets can be analyzed to see if there are any ideas that can be used later.

According to another major multinational agency, global brand awareness is built through consistent messages developed during the creative process. Consistency can be achieved through central development strategy guidelines and then by executing them locally. Thus, by establishing synergy between regions on common products and similar creative executions like tagline, logo and art direction, consistency can be achieved.

Another agency develops its messages and incentives by following in the footsteps of the overall brand positioning concepts and then developing final executions within the local market. A search for available materials from around the world is undertaken in order to determine what materials can be shared. Generally, what is shared is the art direction of the brand campaign. The copy platform is usually adjusted to accommodate the regional or local market differences.

Overall issues in globalization, brand marketing, creativity, and organizational structure

Our case studies revealed that to be able to understand the trends in advertising creative and how it is conceived, developed and executed, one must look at the client's corporate structure and the product positioning. While a campaign's creative genesis can come from any source (headquarters, region, or local market), some multinational advertisers appear to opt for standardized campaigns as they move toward more centralized structures. If this is the case, the advertiser empowers the agency headquarters to develop the overall campaigns and then the local markets adhere to them. The common denominator, though, is the search for an overall brand consistency that can then be reflected in the global marketing and advertising campaigns.

Increasingly, multinational advertisers want ideas that will travel across geographic and psychographic borders of the areas in which they operate, and among the customers they wish to serve. At the same time they want their agencies to pay more attention to the local needs of the market. Reaching narrow segments within a market has become more important as opposed to pursuing efficient communication to reach the masses.

The reality is that there are very few totally standardized global campaigns. Even those campaigns that at first glance may appear identical contain subtle adaptations in their creative executions. More and more, multinational advertisers and their agencies are laying out the "footprints" of the global campaigns rather than overseeing the global implementation of centrally developed strategies. They therefore assume the role of an "integrator" whose priorities are to maintain the global brand consistency and facilitate the sharing of creative concepts and approaches among the different markets. Through the use of local Intranets and servers, local agencies can therefore take advantage of the large reservoir of finished ads, artwork, and other creative material that can be further tailored to meet the local needs.

Importantly, advertising agencies are beginning to realize that they cannot "cookie cut" ideas that worked for one client and pass them on to another. Marketing a product around the world using the same information is now seen as an idea that has proven to be ineffective. Trying to export commercials other than ideas to different cultures and different parts of the world is being replaced with new approaches to globalization. Today, the focus must be on finding ideas that will work around the world and then adapting them to meet culture-specific requirements.

Advertising agencies that have demonstrated a capability in compelling brand positioning and in driving those messages in an integrated way throughout the global market are considered to be very successful. It appears that those agencies also work very hard to be a team player with the clients' other agencies to ensure that a truly integrated marketing communication program is realized around the globe.

Undoubtedly, integration spells another problem for agencies serving clients' needs, and that problem is staffing, the topic of the next section.

Staffing

At the 1996 15th IAA World Advertising Congress that met in Korea, WPP Group Chief Executive Martin Sorrel (1996) spoke about the urgent need of the advertising industry to modify:

> its organizational structure [in order] to offer clients more strategic thinking if it is to adapt to an increasingly competitive global marketplace.

With the dawning of the new millennium, several leading U.S. multinational advertising firms are attempting to meet this challenge by becoming more diversified and by thinking globally and acting locally. This strategic way of handling their accounts is well reflected in the organizational structures of the top U.S. advertising agencies that operate worldwide. Their global success has often been contingent on their ability to adapt by learning more about the various target cultures they hope to serve. This goal has been accomplished by integrating global marketing strategies with local variations.

Organization of agencies

The current trend in today's top international advertising agencies is a mixture of centralized and decentralized matrices. Of all the companies in the IAA study, only one had a purely centralized structure. The remaining agencies mirrored their client's organizational systems since that allowed them to provide a competitive and efficient standard of service. One major U.S. advertising agency analyzed for this study is using a diverse staffing distribution to achieve their client's global marketing goals. Their commitment to providing the best customer service is reflected in their organization of the Brand Management Team and in their assembling of client teams. For example, if their client has more than one marketing center, they mirror that in their organization of the Brand Management team. In addition, their client teams are usually located nearest to their client's headquarters. Although their account service team is centralized, creative execution is up to the discretion of local management. Creative messages are created at the local level to provide the most appropriate fit. Production of the message is managed both centrally and locally depending on the needs of the clients and the distribution of the message in the region.

Some agencies that create and execute the marketing mix for multinationals with extensive product lines organize their staff according to the marketing demands. Two agencies in particular use a combination of central, regional and local personnel to target their client's customers worldwide. Depending on the scope of the brand and the regions to be targeted, these agencies distribute the creation, production and execution of the message to their local operations. The goal in this case is to produce the most effective message for each market.

In some cases, the headquarters and the regional offices will work in tandem. In others, the brand is considered the CEO's brand. For this reason, the CEO makes all the decisions from top to bottom. While in others, the global strategy is handled by the regional market heads. In this case, the regional division heads are free to interpret and adapt the global strategy to fit their local markets.

Yet, not all companies believe in a decentralized staffing system for a global brand. One particular company examined in the current study is highly centralized. For the most part, they oversee the implementation of global strategies. A degree of flexibility is allowed in local execution as long as they have a successful record in advertising to that particular market. Brand Managers of common brands have regular meetings to discuss and resolve strategic refinements.

Two companies in particular that participated in this study were highly decentralized. The first company set up client teams in the same country as the client's head office. In some cases, national teams were recruited by local offices to service the client's local offices. Local teams worked with the client's local market to develop and adapt centrally produced campaigns to local requirements. Creativity was both centrally and regionally produced and was either produced by each local market or adapted and translated from the home market strategy.

An international firm that services different industries presented another good example of decentralized staffing. Account teams were assembled according to the product. These teams were located all around the world. Brands were therefore either managed by regional directors, a lead agency, or the agency's corporate headquarters. Strategic planning was handled through regional planners in the U.S.; or by regional offices located in several different continents. Depending on the specific needs of the brand, creativity was handled on a local level, or regionally.

Trends in staffing

The biggest trend to emerge from the analysis of staffing was "mirroring," that is, replicating the structure and staff of the client company. Most, if not all the international advertising agencies studied, mirrored their client in one way or another.

The need to communicate effectively, not just efficiently, was evident in this research as well. International advertising firms have usually structured their client teams close to their client's headquarters and/or in the local market being targeted. In addition, the message was, by and large, adapted to the local market. This was true even if the message was crafted outside the local market. Thus, the degree of local involvement had a direct correlation to the degree of decentralization. The greater the degree of decentralization in the agency, the greater the local involvement and input.

Decision-making

As noted above, the degree of centralization and decentralization of the agency dictated its decision-making processes. If the marketing mix was handled at the regional or local level, the degree of adaptation and customization of the message was greater than at the centralized level. Firms that were centralized were structurally more complicated. These firms usually had central, regional and local managers who controlled the creation, distribution and production of the advertising message at different levels. In some cases, this led to conflict. Overall, the execution and/or production of creativity were more decentralized than the other aspects of staffing.

In 1998, the world's fourth largest advertising agency, Japan's Dentsu, began an intensive restructuring of its head office in Tokyo. To speed decision-making and to meet client needs more effectively and efficiently, power is being pushed down the management lines. Dentsu claimed that it was "aiming for a structure that allows it not only to carry out all stages of advertising activities on a global scale, but also to anticipate client needs."

Information technology

The transfer of knowledge from one person to the next can be the life or death of a multinational corporation. The efficiency of the flow of information is essential in educating everyone working on a brand and to keep them abreast of the new developments in client markets. Most agencies are willing to adapt their structure to match the organization of the client.

It is also common practice between advertising agencies to have their organization divided into two to four categories, based upon whether the client is centralized or decentralized. In the centralized areas, the focus is to maintain the brand's strategic integrity, which usually includes its positioning and sometimes its packaging. Global client/agency meetings are useful but not more than bimonthly appears to be required and there is common agreement that those should occur no less than annually.

Many companies are beginning to incorporate future-oriented technology in their client capabilities in order to create a "pseudo" meeting of brand managers through the use of teleconferencing. This allows companies to mentally meet together, toss around new ideas even though they are not physically meeting. Teleconferencing is a cost-effective piece of technology, and today more and more companies are familiarizing themselves with it in order to cut down on costs and traveling.

Many companies are also taking full advantage of the wealth of resources and knowledge available on the Internet. They are setting up their own private servers to distribute creative materials to others in the company. This technique allows the people within the agency to comment on ideas that would otherwise be impossible to discuss or even review.

The growing use of new media is a good example of cost-efficiency. One agency commented that global meetings were not seen as beneficial because they often became a "show-and-tell" conference instead of a "learn-from-others" conference. Many brands do not overlap and managers were not gaining information that was useful for their particular areas. Although this was not the mainstream of comments, we feel that this could become a more prevalent problem as markets become more intricate and products more specialized.

The creative review processes of most companies were not thoroughly discussed by each agency, but most accomplished this by annually reviewing and studying their goals and how they met them. One ingenious idea shared in the study was a creative review board. This would theoretically allow a global creative director access to a panel of ideas from an ongoing company-wide discussion. The board would have a listserv among them that allowed ideas to be spread and tested for enthusiasm by others. This sort of communication is exactly what will help save the company money as they move from one product to the next and from one client to the next.

Staffing issues

Integration is a major key to the effective functioning of an organization at the global level. It is a growing trend for decentralized organizations to shift to "more closely integrated marketing programs" by weaving the headquarter's strategies with local and regional marketing programs to form one coherent framework (Jones, 2000).

For such a level of functioning to be viable, responsibilities must be shared between headquarters and the regional offices. Communication is essential in such a level of operation to effectively work out problems that may arise. The idea here rests not in "becoming agencies with global coverage," but rather in "becoming globally integrated agencies" to keep up with the demands of clients. The criteria used for agency selection, after all, is dependent upon "how the firm is organized for international marketing and the type of assistance it needs to meet its goals and objectives in foreign markets" (Jones, 2000). International companies are encouraged by experts to use international agencies with global reach equivalent to that of the client, especially in the case of firms that are globalizing and striving to create and/or maintain a consistent corporate (or brand) image worldwide.

> The trend toward mergers and acquisitions and the formation of mega-agencies with global marketing and advertising capabilities suggests the international agency approach will become the preferred arrangement among large companies. (Cited in Jones, 2000)

Our case study research has also shown that clients are becoming more reliant on their agencies to help in "keeping their global organization in line." Advertising agencies must meet this expectation if they wish to keep their clients, and therefore must provide some level of strategic guidance of value. This can only be possible through a genuine integrated effort of management worldwide.

The importance of recruitment and training efforts in this arena cannot be stressed too much. Training must be oriented to turn out personnel more understanding of the global implications that their jobs entail. As Belch and Belch (1997, p. 636) advised: "Train your people as global brand builders, not just advertising people." In recruitment, look more for people with global brand experience and hire those specialists who can aid in gaining insight from foreign markets. These are the ones who will provide valuable information as far as trends, positioning and targeting are concerned. Staff must therefore be "re-engineered" to keep up with trends and be able to better serve clients.

Consolidation of agencies: the trend

There is a consolidation occurring among advertising agencies as clients begin to narrow down their dealings to one global agency. This trend to develop a close, "long-term partner" with only one global agency instead of multiple regional and local agencies means an increase in expectation of what the ad agencies have or will have to offer. While some agencies are meeting this challenge head on, others are struggling to keep the clients that they already have.

Summary and conclusions

When examining the types of "corporate umbrellas" that are being raised in the international marketplace, the findings of the Global Best Practices study revealed that there is no single one best practice employed. Instead, global communication organizations are taking their cues directly from their clients. That is, clients are the drivers of change in global communication firms' organizational structures. It is possible that a single organization's portfolio of accounts may call for more than one brand communication structure within the same organization. Historically we witnessed communication organizations following their clients into the global marketplace. Just as it has been in the past, achieving successful long-term client–agency relationships tests the dedication of agencies to meet their clients' corporate and brand communication needs. What the Global Best Practices study's finding provides is insight into what some of the most successful global communication organizations are doing to meet their clients' needs.

Fewer advertisers and their agencies are choosing one specific approach. Instead the majority are choosing to raise their "corporate umbrellas" via a hybrid organizational structure that is neither purely centralized nor decentralized. Brand and corporate communications may be centrally strategized by the corporate headquarters, but decisions regarding local adaptation of creative and tactical decisions appear to be made closer to the global consumer than was the case in either the 1980s or the 1990s.

Perhaps the most essential development that has driven the propensity to use the hybrid organizational structure has been the emergence of the Internet, the digitalization of creative content, and real time communication opportunities. The "ribs" of the corporate umbrella have now become the Intranet structures connecting worldwide personnel with brand-building ideas and concepts that are borderless. Solutions can come from anywhere. Corporate and brand management teams can exchange information. Ad hoc global teams can form in cyberspace to work on specific projects. Gone are the yearly global brand manager meetings that usually turned out to be a glorified show and tell. Today's technology now allows for information transfer that connects the "ribs" of headquarters, pan-regional, and local offices working on a particular brand.

If one were to think of the top point of the corporate umbrella as a lightning rod, certainly information transfer provides its electricity, taking messages, images, strategies, and ideas effortlessly across borders. The English language dominance and quick response time help to keep brand and corporate consistency in the forefront of worldwide promotions.

Organizations are expecting more from their agencies. More in terms of long range planning, and accountability. In return, major global clients are consolidating and reducing the number working on any one global brand account. Increasing strategic complexities and intensified local competition have slowed the more dramatic pendulum swings from centralized to decentralized approaches. Today, it appears that there is a more defined range of motion that strikes a balance: "glocalization." Centralized aspects of the structure would develop the central corporate and brand communication or strategic "footprint." More decentralized approaches would be employed once the "footprint" is established. Next, regional offices or country-specific affiliated subsidiaries would be empowered to work out the specific creative and media placement details in the areas that they know best.

While organizations may have hoped to gain from maximizing economies of scale as in the past, the Global Best Practices findings suggest that the emphasis has shifted to maximizing efficiency and effectiveness. Corporate and brand communication directors want a long-term partner in this endeavor. As more corporate organizations seek partnerships with a smaller list of agencies, the challenges and opportunities for those select few will be great.

ILLUSTRATION

Assessing Coca-Cola's Structural Change

Returning to the Coca-Cola illustration that began the chapter, let us walk through it again and assess the issues surrounding the corporation's significant shift in advertising strategy and organizational structure changes. Look again at Tom Long's quote:

We've found out that a centralised (sic) structure didn't let our people experiment. The company had gone for efficiency and scale ... the way to be big is by being small. (Beckett, 2000)

What Long appears to be saying is that the purely centralized approach that built one of the world's most powerful name brands is no longer the most appropriate strategic and organizational structural model for today's competitive global marketplace. As one determines the differences in a purely headquarter-driven centralized approach, it is often the communication managers in the trenches that truly know better the market conditions, what effective messages and culturally-resonant concepts would be for their particular market situation. "[It] didn't let our people experiment." In other words, regional and country-specific approaches and input are limited under a highly centralized approach. "The company had gone for efficiency and scale." As was underscored in the findings of the Global Best Practices study, the achievement of economies of scale, if not effective communication, is simply not efficient communication either.

What organizational communication structure has the Coca-Cola pendulum swung towards? "Glocalization." The Interpublic Group (IPG) will develop the global message for the flagship brand. The IPG team's mission is "to reassert the essence of brand Coca-Cola." Thus, Coca-Cola is asking IPG to reassert the value of the brand worldwide by creating a global "footprint" to ensure brand and corporate consistency. At the same time, Coca-Cola is allowing a much greater degree of flexibility in exactly how specific integrated marketing communication programs are executed and the tactical decisions are made. Thus, allowing Coca-Cola with its long-term partner IPG and its holdings to determine how the brand essence can best be communicated across the full spectrum of traditional and non-traditional media, via sporting events and via cyberspace. As Andrew Coker commented, "Each country can still appoint local agencies to implement the brand message devised by Interpublic. This is not a return to the control days of Atlanta." Is Coca-Cola going against the trends found in the Global Practices study? Absolutely not. In reality Coca-Cola's shift in strategic and organizational structure typifies and underscores the movement toward a more hybrid strategic approach. The consolidation trend is also apparent. The cola giant appears willing to "glocalize" its decision-making in order to not only survive, but thrive, in today's fiercely competitive global marketplace.

Source: Author.

Acknowledgments

The author gratefully acknowledges the following University of Florida graduate students: Elif Adali, Alina Diaz, Paisley Page, Govind Shanadi, Chong Moo Woo and Hadi Zabad. They helped analyze secondary research and carried out a detailed examination of the 30 case studies to identify the findings offered in this chapter.

The author also wishes to acknowledge others directly involved in the project. They were: Caroline McNally, Senior Vice President, Global Brand Management, VISA International; Norman Vale, Director-General of the International Advertising Association; and Dr. Joseph Pisani, Chair, Department of Advertising at the University of Florida.

The findings were first presented at the American Academy of Advertising's 2000 International Advertising Pre-Conference: The Global Best Practices Roundtable and later displayed on the IAA website iaaglobal.org. Updates of the Global Best Practices research and the forthcoming e-commerce component of the research will be placed on the site.

Marketing public relations: where the twain shall meet 8

tom harris

iMac Rescues the Corporate Brand

The future of Apple Computer was very much in doubt in 1997 when Steve Jobs was persuaded to return to the company he co-founded. Apple market share, customer confidence, employee morale and consequently its share price had plummeted. The company's chief financial officer said the company "was in a death spiral." Jobs who had been forced out of the company a decade earlier was enjoying great financial rewards from his new company Pixar's production of the computer-generated Disney hit film *Toy Story*. He was initially reluctant to return but when he took charge, he streamlined the company, its commercial product line and its retail channels and in the process tripled the value of the stock. Jobs rehired Chiat/Day, the ad agency that made Apple famous and the agency produced the "Think Different" campaign that identified the company with the great thinkers of the century. But what made Apple's comeback complete was its triumphant return to the consumer market.

Jobs electrified the industry with iMac. The cool new computer had been a closely-guarded secret until, as *The Wall Street Journal* reported, Jobs "blind-sided reporters with the new machine." The symbolic setting for the unveiling was the Cupertino, California site where the Macintosh was launched 14 years earlier. Unveiling the translucent teal box, the likes of which had never been seen before in the industry, Jobs declared that "iMac does for Internet computing what the original Macintosh did for personal computing."

The press launch ignited massive media coverage. Apple gave its public relations firm, Edelman Public Relations Worldwide its marching orders: "Get iMac everywhere." Rave reviews in the tech books were only the beginning.

Major stories appeared in all of the U.S. newsweeklies and TV networks and online media before iMac appeared in the stores and iMac advertising in the media. Steve Jobs himself conducted television interviews by satellite from company headquarters.

Apple partnered with Macintosh retailers like the CompUSA chain to maximize the impact of the introduction. Midnight madness sales attracted not only hordes of customers but media headlines in major markets.

The publicity for iMac was so pervasive that when the full-page ads and billboards appeared it was unnecessary to identify iMac. The distinctively designed box was by now so well recognized that the "Think Different" tag line was enough.

The integrated program included a major product placement push that found iMacs on many top rated TV sitcoms and Hollywood films.

By the end of its first full month on the market, iMac had become the best selling computer in the U.S.A.; a position which it retained through the introduction of models in five delicious "flavors," a laptop version dubbed in one outdoor board "Road Scholar" and a DVD model that enables users to direct and edit their own movies.

The astonishing success of Apple's iMac demonstrated the convergence of a product that answers a real consumer need, easy access to the Internet, spectacular design, a successful targeting of Mac lovers and first time computer owners, a legendary executive spokesperson, marketing partnerships with retailers, a memorable print advertising campaign and an all-inclusive publicity and product placement.

Source: Author.

Introduction and overview

This chapter aims to illustrate how marketing public relations fits under the corporate umbrella. Recent marketing success stories demonstrate how brand reputation impacts corporate reputation and conversely how corporate reputation impacts brand reputation, all of which can be driven by marketing public relations.

Over the past several years, there has been a smoldering conflict between marketing and public relations academicians and practitioners. Marketing has aggressively tried to include various types of public relations under the Integrated Marketing Communication (IMC) banner. Public relations practitioners have resisted the inclusion citing "marketing imperialism" and the invasion of their traditional corporate communications turf (Chapters 4 and 6 inevitably mention this subject also). Out of the fray has emerged marketing public relations, now defined as:

> Marketing Public Relations (MPR) is the use of public relations strategies and techniques to achieve marketing objectives. The purpose of MPR is to gain awareness, stimulate sales, facilitate consumption, and build relationships between consumers and companies and brands ....
>
> The principal functions of MPR are the communication of credible information, the sponsorship of relevant events and the support of causes that benefit society. (Harris, 1998)

An earlier definition was provided by Kotler (1991) who stated that:

> MPR is the offspring of two parents: marketing and PR. MPR represents an opportunity for companies to regain a share of voice in a message-satiated society. MPR not only delivers a strong share of voice to win share of mind and heart; it also delivers a better, more effective voice in many cases.

MPR attempts to bridge the gap between the two functional communication activities and groups for the benefit of both the organization and the consumer and to more closely tie the corporate brand and the various product brands together. To us, there is little question but that in the interactive and converging marketplaces and communication systems of the 21st century, it is to the benefit of all that marketing and public relations find common ground for there is indeed synergy among and between them. This chapter attempts to identify where those strategies, programs and activities might most effectively be combined and illustrates some of the major successes of MPR in the recent past.

In this chapter, we will illustrate all three of the primary functions of MPR:

- delivery of credible information about products and services to both targeted audiences and the broad general marketplace including constituencies and stakeholders
- sponsorship of relevant events, and
- support of various social causes.

In all three functional areas we provide both examples and case histories. We also include an MPR planning process that can be used to develop effective and measurable programs. Of particular interest to readers of this text, we review an ongoing MPR success story that demonstrates how brand reputation can impact corporate reputation and vice versa, thus reinforcing the interaction between individual and corporate brand. Overall, the objective of this chapter is to show how MPR can make these connections under the corporate umbrella.

MPR in perspective

From the opening case vignette, it is clear that all of the tools, skills, talents, and capabilities of the organization will be needed – not just to survive in the 21st century marketplace – but also to thrive. The iMac illustration provides an excellent example of how Marketing Public Relations activities, *at both the corporate and brand level*, can be brought together to the benefit of both. Indeed, today, there is little question, as was discussed in Chapters 2 through 6, that the organization must consider and find ways to build both the corporate and the product brands because, in many cases now, the two are inextricably intertwined and increasingly inseparable. Thus, the somewhat fictitious separation of the corporate and brand communication, while it may be useful from a marketing and public relations managerial discipline perspective, makes little sense in the world of real consumers, real employees, real investors, and other savvy sophisticated, and streetwise stakeholders (see Kitchen and Papasolomou, 1997).

The interdependence of corporate brands and product brands

The interdependence of corporate brands and branded products was defined this way by the late Thomas Mosser, former chief executive of Burson-Marsteller, the world's largest public relations firm. Mosser said, "Every institution has two assets upon which success and survival are based – its Brand (capital 'B' – the image, reputation of the corporation or institution itself including its financial assets, performance and people) and its brands (lower case 'b' – the products or services it sells or provides). More than ever, the interrelationship between these two assets is critical to survival and success. The efforts against each must be considered relative to the impact of the other. And at different phases of recovery or success, the emphasis will move from one to the other" (Mosser, 1993).

The Apple experience is a prime illustration of the impact of the inter-relationship between a breakthrough (small b) brand can have on the corporate (big B) Brand. The success of iMac dramatically reversed Apple's decline in market share and the value of Apple stock. Marketing public relations played a critical role in connecting product success with corporate well-being.

Burson-Marsteller has been measuring the impact of the CEO on reputation since 1997. It found that in 1999 the CEO was held responsible for 45 percent of a company's reputation, an increase of 14 percent over three years. The survey concluded that the CEO's reputation is now a powerful tool with clear payoffs, particularly impacting stock price but also in recommending the company as a good joint venture partner, as a good place to work, and in terms of paying attention and space to the company in the media – and also believing the company if it is under pressure.

Ellen Ryan Mardiks, worldwide director of brand strategies for Golin/Harris International believes that the time is fast approaching when brand strategy will finally equal corporate strategy. She states:

> With the customer so firmly in charge of everything from communication to transactions, the boardroom will catch up with the idea that everything done or said in a company that markets products is about the brand. Today, brand strategy is something controlled by and cared about by the marketing department. Tomorrow, brand strategy will be what the CEO talks about first. Every CEO of every consumer brand company will respect the intellectual connection between people and brands. (Mardiks, 1999)

We agree with Mardiks. Increasingly, it is not just the individual brands that CEOs need to be talking about, it is also the corporate entity that ostensibly owns them. We would, however, indicate that the connection between people and brands may not just be intellectual, it can also be emotional and psychological. Perception is not just a function of intellect. Thus, we may need to continually consider the connection between brand reputation and the management of that reputation.

Brand reputation or reputation management?

The value of public relations extends throughout the brand's life cycle but its role in generating awareness of new products is most universally under-

stood by marketers and public relations personnel. A major product introduction offers a unique window of opportunity to make headlines, an
opportunity that comes just once in a brand's lifetime.

In their book *The 22 Immutable Laws of Branding*, marketing consultants Al and Laura Reis declared that the birth of a brand is achieved with
publicity, not advertising. They believe that a new brand must be capable
of generating favorable publicity in the media or it won't have a chance in
the marketplace (Reis and Reis, 1998).

The Reises say that in today's world brands are built with publicity and
maintained with advertising. Citing brands like Compaq, Dell, Oracle,
Cisco, Microsoft, Starbucks and Wal-Mart, all of which were born in a
blaze of publicity, they observe that as the publicity dies out, brands like
these have to shift to massive advertising to defend their position.

Public relations has also taken the lead in integrated brand programs for
some of the most successful product launches in recent years. Brand visibility in the media and online built awareness, receptivity to the advertising, and anticipation for brands as diverse as iMac, the new Volkswagen
Beetle, Gillette's Mach3 shaving system, along with Pfizer's Viagra, plus
blockbuster entertainment events such as the latest *Star Wars* episode
which is described in this chapter. All employed public relations to attain
unprecedented high levels of brand awareness before mass advertising
broke. All had major impact on the corporate bottom line and share value.

Conversely a strong corporate brand can not only help a company
compete effectively in the marketplace for goods and services but for equity
capital, ideas and employees, according to Harlan Teller who manages the
worldwide corporate practice for Hill & Knowlton, a leading global PR
firm. He says that consumers, investors and employees all want to feel good
about the company behind the brand. His view is supported by a 1997 Lou
Harris poll that demonstrates that when you link a product brand to a well
known and trusted corporate brand in the mind of a consumer, there is an
increase in intent to purchase. Teller says that the "silent partner" brand, a
brand that means something to the financial community and nowhere else, is
virtually dead. He states that "clients are looking for programs that will
increase corporate equity and create a halo effect on product brand preference, as well as help them in the marketplace for ideas, equity capital and
employees" (Teller, cited in Reis and Reis, 1998).

There is currently a debate within the public relations industry on
whether the goal of corporate public relations should be managing the
corporate brand or managing the company's reputation. Paul Holmes,
editor of *Reputation Management*, believes that brand and reputation are
not the same. He says that:

Brand is all the things a company wants you to think and feel when you hear its name, the sum total of its communications while reputation is all the things you really do think and feel, the result of communications plus behavior. Brand is something you build: reputation is something you earn. Brand is a promise; reputation is the result of keeping that promise. (Holmes, 2000)

Others believe that the distinction is a matter of semantics. Bob Druckenmiller, President of Porter-Novelli, another leading international PR firm, believes that corporations have brands and these brands have real and perceived value – at the functional level, at the personal or emotional level and at the core of a company's character. He says that marketing-based perspective is critical to successfully building long-term value in any corporate brand by enabling it to better understand and meet the needs of its audiences (Druckenmiller, 1999).

The Yankelovich Company, a leader in market research, recently designed a new methodology for Hill & Knowlton called Corporate Equity Performance System that measures the value of corporate reputation. It provides corporations with a benchmark of how they are perceived by such key audiences as employees and recruits, customers and prospects, financial analysts and portfolio managers, opinion leaders, business peers, suppliers and the trade, regulators and other government audiences, activists and advocacy groups, academics, the news media, and the general public. The CEPS process begins with a senior management audit that provides an "inside-out" look at the company and is followed by an "outside-in" survey of key stakeholder groups. An analysis of this input defines the attributes that drive the company's behavior. Further analysis combines attribute and behavioral analysis with evaluation of the company versus its competitors.

The system is designed to identify key attributes that have the greatest potential for motivating key audiences to support the company in several key ways: to buy its products or its stock, recommend it as a trade partner or place to work, believe in it at a time of crisis, or support it in the public policy arena.

An overview of MPR: what it is and can be

Too often, marketing public relations has been considered a sub-segment of the more general area of corporate public relations or, as discussed above, corporation reputation. Therefore it has often been viewed as crass or commercial or just plain trashy when compared to the supposed loftier goals of business and financial management communication. Yet, there is

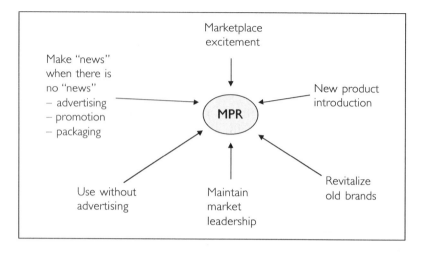

Figure 8.1 Effective roles for MPR

increasing evidence that public relations strategies and tactics, when used to increase and enhance sales, or distribution and satisfaction of product brands with consumers and customers, does much to increase and enhance the total corporate well-being as well. Whether MPR is used to increase the impact of product brand activities, reduce the investment level costs of new product introductions, revitalize existing product lines, or to tie the organization to useful social causes or something else, the primary goal is almost always to extend and enhance the relationships of various stakeholders with the parent organization or firm and its products and services. Over the past 15 years, we have found MPR to be particularly effective in the areas shown in Figure 8.1 and discussed in the following segments:

Creating marketplace excitement
Because of MPR's unique ability to dominate various news agendas, it has been used to drive some of the most successful marketing campaigns in recent years, that is, the introduction of the Volkswagen Beetle, the initial acceptance of the prescription drug Viagra and the global introduction of the Gillette Mach3 shaving system.

Introduce new products before the advertising breaks
MPR is most effective in generating awareness and building up anticipation of new products. Examples of recent successful MPR programs include the Eastman Kodak Advanced Photo Systems (ASP) launch, Nintendo 64 and the McDonald's "Arch Deluxe."

Bringing new high-tech and health-care products to market
Because of their naturally high consumer interest, MPR has been particularly effective in introducing and explaining various high-tech and health-
care products. Some recent examples have been Windows 95 from
Microsoft and Tagamet MB from SmithKline Beecham.

Introducing new products when there is no advertising
New and improved products have often been successfully introduced
when MPR is used in place of heavy advertising spending. Examples
include the Breath Rite nasal strip and the new line of Crayolas from
Binney & Smith. An earlier example was the success associated with
Cabbage Patch Dolls.

Revitalize old brands
MPR can be used to revitalize, reinvigorate, relaunch and reposition
existing brands. Look what MPR did for Hush Puppies and the general
product category of Aspirin.

Maintain market leadership
MPR has the power to help successful brands maintain their marketing
leadership. For example, MPR strategies and tactics have been employed
by Chrysler Corporation to maintain their sales lead in minivans, by
Purina Dog Chow to reduce customer brand switching, and by Pampers
disposable diapers to maintain its historic category leadership and product
development position.

Make advertising news when there is no news
Today, customer and consumer attention is critical for all types of products. There are two ways to maintain that attention: one, have great advertising and invest heavily in it; and two, use MPR to build anticipation for
and maintain interest in the advertising that is available. The Super Bowl
is one of the premier venues for building interest in forthcoming advertising. Other organizations such as Taster's Choice, the product category
Milk and Taco Bell, all have used MPR to create enhanced and expanded
interest in their advertising programs through the skilful use of MPR.

Make promotion news when there is no promotion news
Like the promotion of advertising, MPR can be used to build additional
interest, excitement and involvement in various types of sales promotion
programs. Prime examples include Gillette's activities in major league
baseball and Miller Beer's activities in connection with the Super Bowl.

Make packaging news when there is no product news
When there is no product news, marketing organizations often use a packaging innovation to give new life and excitement to an existing and well known product. Heinz Ketchup, Doritos, Sucrets and Swanson TV Dinners have all used MPR in this way (Harris, 1998, pp. 33–115).

Of course, there are many other uses of MPR, all of which involve generating additional interest and excitement for products or services through the use of traditional public relations activities. All these successful uses of MPR are based on a solid, well developed and carefully implemented foundation. We discuss a proven MPR planning approach in the next section.

Writing an integrated marketing public relations plan

The following format is most commonly used for writing the MPR plan. It consists of five steps and an executive summary. We provide only a skeleton outline in this chapter. A more complete description of the entire plan can be found in *Value-Added Public Relations* (Harris, 1998). The planning process is conceptualized in Figure 8.2.

Step 1: Reviewing the situation
Traditional marketing and public relations planning begins with the situation analysis, which answers the question "What's happening?" It involves the collecting of all relevant facts and important information needed to understand the marketing problems and opportunities. This includes infor-

Step 1:	Situational review
Step 2:	Set objectives
Step 3:	Develop strategy
Step 4:	Develop tactics
Step 5:	Measure and evaluate

Figure 8.2 The integrated MPR plan

mation about the product and business environment; that is, the market-place and the consumer. MPR programs begin, concentrate on, and end with, information about the consumer. That is the primary difference in MPR planning and traditional marketing or public relations planning ... the focus is on the consumer or customer.

Step 2: Setting MPR objectives
MPR plans should always be considered as a part of the master integrated marketing plan. They must relate specifically to the achievement of marketing objectives. Marketing objectives differ from traditional public relations goals in that they describe what needs to be done to reach sales goals. They are specific and measurable and address what will or is to be accomplished. Both trade and consumer audiences figure importantly in the development of marketing objectives therefore both are often targets of MPR programs.

Step 3: Developing an MPR strategy
Strategies are different from objectives. They define and explain how quantifiable objectives will be reached. They should take into considera-tion target primary and/or secondary markets; national, regional and local emphases; specific competitive situations; seasonal considerations; and timing. Specifically, MPR strategies should include:

■ Design of the marketing timetable so that opinion leaders, including professionals, industry analysts, trade publications and influential media are reached well in advance of the public

■ Maximize the news value of new product introductions, new advertising campaigns, and event sponsorships

■ Time public relations events to reinforce advertising/promotion campaigns and/or maintain high visibility between campaigns

■ Reach important secondary markets, defined demographically and/or psychographically, geographically, and ethnically, that might not be targeted by advertising or promotion.

There are three distinct kinds of MPR strategy:

1. *Supplementary/complementary strategies*: MPR deals with information and education. Therefore, product and service claims must be substant-iated with factual information. As a result, MPR strategies commonly

are used to supplement or complement the claims being made in advertising and promotion programs.

2. *News/borrowed-interest strategies*: these are commonly used in publicity-centered MPR programs. MPR is uniquely capable of dramatizing product news. When there is really nothing new to say, borrowed-interest can often be used.

3. *Push–pull–pass strategies*: "push" simply means "pushing" the product or service into the channels through salesforces, promotions and the like. "Pull" calls for investing in consumer advertising, promotion or MPR to build consumer demand that "pulls" the product or service through the distribution channels. "Pass" is a strategy that overcomes marketplace resistance from groups such as consumer watchdogs, environmentalists, government regulatory, religious-interest groups and the like to the successful introduction, distribution or sale of the product or service.

Any or all of these strategies may be appropriate in the development of a successful MPR campaign.

Step 4: Marketing public relations tactics
Tactics are methods, actions and activities used to achieve objectives. They translate the directives of strategies into specific programs. Tactics should relate specifically to each strategy and should specify what activities will take place, who will do them, when they will be done and at what cost. Tactics can range from awards to hot lines to media tours to product placement to stunts and all activities in between.

Step 5: Measuring and evaluating MPR programs
The evaluation must measure how well the MPR plan did in meeting its objectives. Three levels of measurement of MPR are:

- *Outputs*: these measure transmission, that is, the amount of exposure in the media, the number of placements and audience impressions, and the likelihood of having reached specific target audiences

- *Outgrowths*: these measure the message reception. It measures whether or not a target audience actually receives the messages directed at them, and whether they paid attention to, understood and retained those messages

■ *Outcomes*: these measure attitude and behavioral change, that is, whether anyone changed his or her mind or went out and did something as a result of what was said or done through the MPR program.

The key, of course, in any measurement system is to select the right measurement approach or tool, whether that be outputs, outgrowths or outcomes to measure the impact and effect of the MPR program. Again, that goes back to the objectives that were set in Step 2 of the process. Thus, we see the circular nature of the MPR planning process.

Executive summary

The final step in any MPR plan is the summarization of the entire program into a one- or two-page document that quickly and easily explains the entire program. This generally is the key element in getting senior management approval for the MPR program (Harris, 1998, pp. 229–80).

In the following sections, we outline several case histories of successful MPR programs. All demonstrate the planning elements just described in more detail and illustrate how successful MPR programs are being used to build both corporate and product brand value around the world. In these cases, we illustrate how one of the three MPR functions, that is, the communication of credible information, the sponsorship of relevant events and the support of causes that benefit society, has been used. We start with event marketing.

Building the corporate brand through event marketing

With more than $600 billion in assets, Bank of America is the largest bank in the United States. The bank took full advantage of its position as the first national bank sponsor of the 2000 Summer Olympics in Sydney, Australia to make an impression on all of its key stakeholders – customers, employees/associates and communities where it does business across America. The goal was to enhance the world-class brand image of Bank of America.

Olympic sponsorship is a long-term brand-building commitment for Bank of America. It has signed up a multi-year contract as the official bank of the U.S. Olympic Committee.

Unlike many Olympic sponsors who break the bank on sponsorship fees, entertaining big customers and buying TV advertising, Bank of

America created an event that generated consumer participation and media attention throughout its marketing region for an entire year before the games began.

In the process it pre-empted other Olympic sponsors in capturing attention nationwide and within its key markets.

Bank of America's "Down Under Tour" kicked off a year to the day before the opening of the 2000 Olympic Summer Games on NBC's *Today Show*. A 60 by 70 foot inflatable facsimile of the Sydney Opera House was erected in New York's Rockefeller Center that was the backdrop for three hours of interviews, lead-in, fade-outs and weather reports on the network featuring U.S. Olympic champions gymnast Mary Lou Retton and track and field star Jackie Joyner-Kersee, a team of painted Aboriginal dancers, a famous animal handler with a trio of Australian marsupials, a wallaby, a tiny sugar glider and a kangaroo.

America's biggest bank made no small plans. "Bank of America's Down Under Tour" covered 18,000 miles and 48 cities in 21 states for a year, beginning with the launch in New York and concluding in San Francisco on September 15, 2000 – the day of the opening ceremonies of the Olympics in Sydney. The tour was designed to help customers, employees and communities who wouldn't make it to Australia to experience the Olympics.

A team of public relations officers from every region advanced the tour and built media excitement in news, sports and business media in tour cities.

The traveling exhibit was itself an interactive, multi-sensory experience that took visitors on a virtual journey of Australia. In addition to the inflatable opera house, a five story Olympic Flame, an Outback Airlines simulator ride and an Aboriginal art exhibit were set up in tour cities.

"Tour ambassadors" from each of the ten Australian states were on hand at every tour stop to greet visitors, answer their questions and demonstrate authentic Australian activities.

Other "Down Under" exhibits included an exciting four-minute interactive adventure incorporating a journey through the Outback and white water rafting. An Aboriginal art exhibit featured authentic dot paintings, wood carvings, musical instruments and live demonstrations by Aboriginal artists and musicians. There was also a mechanical rock climbing experience that enabled visitors to experience the challenge of the climb without leaving the ground.

U.S. Olympic team merchandise, items indigenous to Australia and original Aboriginal works of art were sold at "The Down Under Tour" Outpost with all proceeds going to the U.S. Olympic Team and the Aboriginal Arts Council.

When Bank of America asked for volunteers, it was overwhelmed by the response of several thousand associates (what it calls its employees) who wanted to lend a hand in their communities.

On each stop on the tour, a special preview was held for school children before the event was opened to the public. These visits were tied to an education program that reached 600,000 children in 20,000 classrooms in tour markets.

One of the main goals of the entire Olympic program was to inspire Bank of America associates. Mary Lou and Jackie were members of a five person team of Olympic champions enlisted by Bank of America as "associate coaches." They met with Bank of America associates wherever the tour appeared to talk about how the ideals of the Olympic movement mirror Bank of America's core values. Each of the Olympians chosen represented one of the core values that the bank seeks to instill in its associates: winning, leadership, trusting, and teamwork, doing the right thing and inclusive meritocracy. The Olympians were also introduced to bank customers. In addition to the five Olympic medallist "associate coaches," the bank also assembled a team of Olympic coaches and athletes to speak at various customer and associate functions. They worked with associates on community service projects in Bank of America markets.

The bank believes that its community outreach component will build consideration for Bank of America among prospective customers and loyalty among long-term customers.

Creating an MPR program in the new interactive marketplace

Electronic communication has radically changed how we think about communication in all its forms. The World Wide Web, the Internet and other forms of interactivity have opened up a huge new venue for the use of MPR programs. While the availability of the electronic forms has gotten much of the attention of marketers and communicators around the world, it is, in fact, the change in the basic approach to communication and marketing that has been most impacted. Two of those concepts, interactivity and total customer experience, both of which involve the customer or prospect in the act and activity of interacting with and in some cases actually consuming the product or service during the course of the communication contact, have radically changed the way we think about constructing communication programs. Thus, we have moved from a view of the communication recipient as a passive absorber of messages directed toward him or her to being an active participant in the communication process. The following case example of Legoland illustrates the point of this new interactive participation in the marketing and communication of a product.

Building a world brand interactively: Legoland

Marketing authorities David Aaker of the University of California, Berkeley and Erich Joachimsthaler (1997) of the University of Virginia say that U.S. companies would do well to study their counterparts in Europe who "have found that communication through traditional mass media has been ineffective, inefficient and costly." These European companies have discovered "alternative communication channels to create product awareness, convey brand associations and develop loyal customer bases."

There's no better evidence of the European marketing model than the success of Legoland.

Back in 1934, toymaker Ole Kirk combined the Danish words for "play well" and came up with the word Lego to describe the wooden vehicles, animals and yo-yos he was making. After the war, Kirk bought his first plastic molding machine and began producing those colorful "automatic binding bricks" now known the world over as Lego toys.

Today more than 200 billion Lego elements and 11 billion Lego and Duplo (those big blocks for little kids) bricks have been created and played with by 300 million people.

Seeing the effect Lego toys had on children and adults, the company decided to extend this play experience by building the first Legoland. Opened in 1968 in Billund, Denmark, the company's home town, it quickly became the country's most popular tourist attraction outside of Copenhagen. The second Legoland park, opened in Windsor, Great Britain, is that country's most popular new attraction.

The newest Legoland opened in the United States at Carlsbad, California in 1999. The 128-acre park is unlike any other theme park. There's no mistaking the Lego-ness of its 40 rides and attractions. There's even an automated Lego factory tour where Lego bricks are molded, decorated, assembled and packaged. And before they leave, visitors can stop at a shop that's stocked with more Lego merchandise than any toy store. Somehow all that brand exposure enhances the fun rather than detracts from it. That is the genius of Legoland and why Legoland has become such a great marketing showcase.

After visiting the park James Sterngold (1999) of the *New York Times* reported that "Legoland seems to be based on a different premise from that of many other theme parks, where the focus is frequently on thrills. Here, the emphasis is on comforting, childlike pleasures. It is based on the premise that if kids love Lego blocks, they will love the amusement park built around them and literally, out of them."

Visitors to Legoland parks spend the better part of a day being exposed to, excited by, and interacting with, all manner of attractions built entirely of Lego plastic.

The park is conceived to attract kids from toddlers through pre-teens. More than 1.5 million kids and their parents and grandparents visited the California park in the first year.

Among the most popular attractions is a driving school where kids are instructed on how to drive safely before wheeling around a track in their Lego plastic electric cars. Those who stop at stop signs and traffic lights are awarded a Legoland driver's license.

Legoland California is composed of six major themed areas – called "blocks" surrounding a 1.7 acre man-made lake offering cruise boats for the foot weary. The cruise takes tourists through Miniland, described by its makers as "the ultimate expression of Lego art form." Miniland meticulously replicates great American sights from the California coast to a New England harbor and the monuments of Washington, D.C. to the New York City skyline and the Statue of Liberty. All of them are reproduced in Lego bricks at 1.20 and 1.40 scale and animated with cars, trains, people movement and sound. It took 20 million Lego bricks to build Miniland, an attraction that appeals as much to adults as to kids.

Legoland is designed to be an interactive experience. The little kids can play and build with big Duplo bricks while the older kids can create things with a new "intelligent" Lego brick that has a computer chip imbedded in the brick and build robots with computer-controlled Lego Technic models.

Legoland has an ad campaign in California but it relies largely on its website, publicity and word of mouth from satisfied visitors to carry its message across the U.S.A. The website, engagingly done up in primary colors and Lego brick designs tells adults all they need to know about the park, what's there, what it costs, how to get there and how to skip the real lines by buying tickets online. For teachers, there is information about educational programs for their students. For prospective employees, there is a list of job opportunities at the park that is updated weekly. For the kids, there are matching games, coloring pages and puzzles and an e-shop for exclusive Legoland California stuff. For everybody there is a virtual tour where you can visit the attraction of your choice by clicking on a

Legoland map. Kids can choose a picture postcard of their favorite attraction and e-mail it to tell their friends they've been to Legoland.

The success of Legoland California has been driven by savvy media relations. Legoland began inviting key reporters to the park when it was little more than a few barren hills, issuing them hard hats and helping them visualize what was coming. Now insiders, these reporters were brought back every few months for a look-see at what was going on.

The same challenge was issued to reporters that human resources was giving to applicants for "model citizen" jobs – to build a Lego animal in twenty minutes. The media went for it and stories ran on network affiliates in 50 markets.

With a cadre of enthusiast media boosters on board, Legoland set up a "Media Village" in the parking lot for the press three days before the gates opened to the public. The grand opening was covered live by more than 400 journalists and TV stations. Across the country in New York City, the Legoland story was brought to the network program with the largest morning audience, NBC's *Today*. Lego model makers recreated the New York skyline. *Today*'s cameras zoomed in on a reproduction of the show's outdoor venue complete with the show's hosts made up in bricks and live fans cheering.

In the first nine months, Legoland California generated more than one billion media impressions, gaining TV and print exposure in all 50 top U.S. markets. With all that coverage, Legoland California began packing in visitors from the state, the country and the world.

Building new product acceptance without an advertising campaign

As outlined in the section on what MPR can do, is the critically important task of building public awareness and acceptance of a new product without the use of a large-scale, generally very expensive, media advertising campaign. While the brand name "Star Wars" was broadly known and wildly successful a number of years ago, the development and distribution of the Lucasfilms' *Star Wars: Episode I – The Phantom Menace*, a sequel to the original, sought to use MPR to trade off the brand name recognition and to build consumer interest without a major advertising investment. The following case history describes the MPR program that was assembled and executed on behalf of this new production, which, in a traditional marketing sense, was primarily a product-line extension. Of particular interest is the manner in which the MPR planners took advantage of the new forms of media that had been developed since the original *Star Wars* had been released some 16 years earlier.

Lucasfilms wins Star Wars in cyberspace

A meticulously-crafted marketing public relations campaign, including publicity in selected key media worldwide and management of news on the internet ensured that *Star Wars: Episode I – The Phantom Menace* would capitalize on the *Star Wars* brand to become one of the top grossing motion pictures of all time – despite mixed reviews and without a saturation advertising campaign.

A year-long interactive and media relations campaign was so effective, in fact, that advertising was virtually unnecessary. The campaign effectively replayed the *Star Wars* saga to build extraordinary interest in the "prequel" among the army of *Star Wars* cultists and an entirely new market of consumers that didn't exist when the last *Star Wars* episode was released 16 years earlier. Bits and bytes of information were carefully parceled out to every conceivable print and broadcast media outlet, tailored to the specific editorial interests of each. Key messages were delivered about the movie, the man behind the movie, George Lucas and his company Lucasfilms.

The publicity machine was in full-gear six months before the premier when a two-minute trailer of the film was released. The news attracted hordes of fans who lined up and paid full price to see the preview, skipping the Brad Pitt feature film that it accompanied.

In every city where *The Phantom Menace* premiered, newspapers, radio and TV interviewed die-hard fans who camped out days before the first midnight screening. *Newsweek* ran an 11-page cover story and sponsored a live online discussion with the writers. The media coverage was so pervasive that the publication did its own content analyses showing how key messages appeared in major stories in other magazines, newspapers and TV programs (Ansen, 1999).

Rival newsweekly *Time* included a three-page pullout "Galactic Guide" to the characters, creatures, aliens and droids that populate the picture and an exclusive interview by social pundit Bill Moyers with George Lucas. "Exclusive" interviews with Lucas were granted to the *New York Times*, CBS's *Sixty Minutes* and NBC's *Today Show*, respectively the most influential newspaper and prime time and daytime television programs in the U.S. These major stories and much of the media relations effort focused not only on the product *Phantom Menace* but the man George Lucas and the corporate umbrella Lucasfilms.

New media that did not exist when earlier *Star Wars* films were released played a critical role in the success of the new episode. In addition to the official *Star Wars* website, more than 1000 other sites were devoted to *The Phantom Menace*, each carefully cultivated by the film maker's publicists. The most popular of these were getting as many as 20,000 hits a day when the film opened. Apple Computer's website, host of a file containing the trailer, had been downloaded more than eight million times.

National Research Group surveys determined awareness levels of 94 percent. Those unprecedented scores translated into box-office bonanza. *The Phantom Menace* passed the $200 million mark faster than any other film in history, a figure that was more than doubled by the end of its first run in the U.S. and prior to international distribution. As financier as well as writer-producer-director of the film, Lucas reportedly earned $2 billion from the film.

The third leg – accepting social responsibility

Of the three MPR strategies, the most difficult to execute is the support of causes that benefit society. Many organizations have tied themselves to various social and charitable activities and events ranging from heart and cancer research to various forms of charity. Some have been successful but many have failed because the stretch of social good to corporate returns never quite worked for either. One of the most successful of all uses of MPR to build social responsibility and connect it to the corporate brand has been conducted by McDonald's and the Ronald McDonald House Charities. This example is described in more detail below.

Social responsibility and the corporate brand

Corporate brand and product brand are one and the same at one of the world's best known companies McDonald's Corporation. McDonald's is dedicated to earning the customer's trust. A recognized leader in social responsibility, McDonald's community involvement programs span the country and the globe. The company supports Ronald McDonald House Charities, one of the world's premier philanthropic organizations. RMHC provides care to children and their families by awarding grants to organizations through chapters in 31 countries and supporting more than 200 Ronald McDonald Houses in 19 countries.

The company's 1999 annual reports states "The McDonald's brand lives and grows where it counts the most – in the hearts of customers worldwide. We, in turn, hold our customers close to our heart, striving to do the right thing and giving back to the communities where we do business. At McDonald's, social responsibility is part of our heritage and we are committed to building on it worldwide. Being an active, responsible leader in our communities instills pride among McDonald's people – the people who are ultimately responsible for providing customers with a positive McDonald's experience" (see Alsop, 1999).

Other ways MPR impacts corporate public relations (CPR)

Breakthrough product introductions and social responsibility programs are just two of the ways in which marketing public relations impacts the corporate brand.

Among the other ways discussed in this chapter are using event marketing to enhance the corporate brand, involving people with products and using databases to cultivate a core consumer base and communicate product news to shareholders, employees and trade audiences.

Perhaps most important is the role of public relations in defending products at risk and giving consumers permission to buy. Effective crisis communication restores confidence in the brand and the corporate brand behind it. See Chapter 9 for a discussion of crisis management.

Summary and conclusion

We have seen how companies are using public relations to effectively build their corporate brand not only through attention grabbing product introductions but by sponsoring educational, recreational and cultural events, by involving people with products live and online and by participation in programs that benefit their communities and the larger society.

We have seen why managing the corporate brand is a critical factor in building product brand success. And why public relations is particularly effective in building brand equity. MPR has the power to positively enhance the assets that add value to both the corporate brand and the product brand: corporate brand assets like vision and leadership, social responsibility and workplace environment and product brand assets such as brand awareness, brand quality and brand loyalty that identify and differentiate the brand.

Don Schultz, co-author of this book, views branding as one of the few things that binds the organization together and creates shared value. He says that the brand provides value to all four key organizational groups: consumers, employees, management and shareholders.

Marketing public relations has the responsibility to communicate with, indeed relate to all of these corporate stakeholders. The brand is the embodiment of the relationship between the company and *all* of its constituents.

We now face a bewildering array of brand choices and in the future those choices will continue to proliferate. As these choices outstrip our ability to cope, consumers' perceptions of the company behind the brand will become an ever greater influence in our purchasing behavior. That is why brand communication and corporate communications must be clear, consistent and coordinated. And why consumers will continue to buy brands of companies that have earned their trust.

ILLUSTRATION

Corporate Reputation in Crisis Situations – The Corporate Brand Behind the Brand: Johnson & Johnson and Tylenol

While in this chapter we have discussed Marketing Public Relations primarily in terms of its ability to build and grow the sales and value of the product brands and therefore the value of the corporate brand, the greater true value of MPR may well be in its ability to help build corporate reputation for both the brand and the firm. In our view, this corporate reputation may well be the most important element of MPR for it can often allow the brand and the corporation to survive unanticipated situations that could easily destroy the value of both. Johnson & Johnson and its brand Tylenol has become a classic case in how MPR was used to offset major marketplace crises faced by the organization. The lessons are so clear, the issues so relevant and the example so powerful, the story bears repeating here as a lesson to all marketing, communication and public relations managers. In truth, the story of Tylenol is timeless.

A 1999 nationwide online survey of 10,830 Americans conducted by Harris Interactive and the Reputation Institute, a private research and advisory organization dedicated to advancing knowledge about corporate reputations, identified the companies that enjoyed the best corporate reputations with American consumers at the end of the century.

The survey found that the company most admired by Americans was Johnson & Johnson, a 112-year-old company best known for its baby powder and shampoo.

Johnson & Johnson is a company that lives by its credo, written in 1943, that puts customers first, even ahead of shareholders. The credo begins "We believe our first responsibility is to the doctors, nurses and patients, to mothers and fathers, and all others who use our products and services." It is no coincidence that Johnson & Johnson is still widely remembered for putting that credo into action in handling the Tylenol crises in the 1980s. The Tylenol case has become the public relations' text book example of what to do right when the consumer – and the brand – are at risk. What Johnson & Johnson did is precisely what you would expect it to do: to protect the consumer and to protect the brand. Tylenol survived two crises that might well have destroyed the brand. The first was in 1982 when an unknown murderer contaminated Tylenol capsules with cyanide and seven people died. The second when it was reported that a woman died after taking a capsule of Tylenol. The actions taken by Tylenol were to immediately pull its products off the shelves, suspend its advertising, reintroduce the product in tamper-resistant packaging and offer to replace capsules with solid-form caplets. The company communicated openly, honestly and frequently to all of its major stakeholders – consumers, trade customers, doctors, hospitals and employees – directly and through the media. By leveraging the equity and reputation of its parent company Johnson & Johnson with all of its internal and external audiences, Tylenol was able to regain trust in its brand and retain its leadership in a highly competitive product category.

The effectiveness of corporate branding can be best measured by how the company is perceived by its publics. The Harris/Reputation Institute survey took into account six building blocks in assessing the corporate brand. They are products and services, workplace environment, financial performance, emotional appeal, social responsibility, vision and leadership. Effective corporate public relations can enhance perceptions of all of these building blocks.

People want to do business with companies they know and trust. James Burke, Johnson & Johnson's CEO at the time of the Tylenol crisis, has defined a brand as "the capitalized value of the trust between a company and its customer." In explaining the high esteem in which the company is held today,

ILLUSTRATION (cont'd)

Ralph S. Larsen, Johnson & Johnson's present CEO says "Johnson & Johnson is more than a trademark. It is a "trustmark" (Alsop, 1999); (see also Chapter 5).

The "trustmark" concept is defined by Kevin Roberts, chief executive worldwide of Saatchi & Saatchi plc as "a distinctive name or symbol that emotionally binds a company with the desires and aspirations of its customers." He says that "we live in an economy where people are bombarded with messages day in, day out and brands don't cut it. First we had products — which were the equivalent of management. Next we added trademarks and developed brands — which were the equivalent of leadership. Now we've got to move beyond brands to trustmarks. A trademark plays defense. It's the way that you protect what you've already built up. It's your copyright, your patents, your table stakes. But a trustmark plays offense. It's the emotional connection that lets you go out and conquer the world!" (Roberts, 2000).

Chapter

Crisis communication management: protecting and enhancing corporate reputation and identity

james e. lukaszewski

BurgerMax

To illustrate the principles and strategies of crisis management, a hypothetical U.S.-based global company, BurgerMax, has been created. BurgerMax's problems are based on composites of real events from a variety of companies around the world. We have chosen to use a hypothetical model so that it can be applied to a wider array of problems and circumstances to create more interesting and complex issues companies in trouble can experience. This case illustration will run throughout this chapter.

Initially, BurgerMax's problems become public knowledge through the illness and death of several children who ate its pre-prepared hamburger patties. The company's first response is to deny that a problem exists. If there is a problem, its position is that responsibility rests with its suppliers, along with government negligence in inspection and failure of the industry itself to establish standards, which could have prevented such a situation from occurring.

Meanwhile, victims and the families of the sick, dying, and dead are left on their own for medical and burial expenses. Their psychological and social needs are not addressed. Yet the company announces a $100,000 gift to create a new foundation for the study of food-borne illnesses to be established in London "to prevent similar events from happening again."

As government investigations are announced in various countries, the company begins its response by running a series of advertisements designed to remind the public of the quality of its product and the contributions it has made to local organizations in the communities in which it operates. Current and past employees are enlisted to verify the company's good local behaviors and attest to how well the company treats its employees and retirees.

Trial lawyers are busy organizing victims' families into large groups for the purpose of suing the company, its suppliers, and any one connected with the delivery of the tainted product.

60 Minutes in the United States and *The Fifth Estate* in Canada along with a number of broadcast and print outlets in Europe have announced major investigations of the company's operations and promise devastating reports critical of the company, the government, and the industry as a whole.

At present, five children are dead in the United States, three in Europe. Hundreds have gone to the hospital in various countries, and the company has announced that it will no longer purchase meat from the suppliers it feels are responsible for providing defective, contaminated product.

Source: Author.

Introduction and overview

This chapter is targeted toward practitioners in the global marketplace and their senior managers, who must be able to recognize and proactively prevent or respond to the risks that arise from corporate and employee interaction with customers and significant publics locally and globally. It is also targeted to legal professionals charged with managing the damage to reputation caused by the litigation surrounding negative events. Corporate managers who supervise employee conduct, managers of human resources, and corporate counsel will find the ideas, concepts, and issues addressed useful in carrying out their daily responsibilities to recognize, mitigate, and be prepared to respond to adverse events, and to regain, even enhance reputation, credibility, and brand share following damaging situations.

The chapter contains four major sections:

Part I   *The Nature of Corporate Crisis and Management's Response*
In this section we define crises in a very useful, management oriented way. We introduce the dimensions of crisis that require strategic management thinking and response planning. The types of crises management can face are clarified, and a case is made for the most effective ways to trigger prompt management action.

Part II   *How Value and Belief Systems Affect Crisis Response*
There should be a linkage between what an organization says it

believes in, the rules that guide its behavior in day-to-day business operations, and how it actually behaves in a crisis situation. This section explains why this is almost always the case and lays out several management strategies, including a model communications policy, response priorities, and an accountability framework to guide management action in concert with corporate values and principles when responding to crises.

Part III   *The Dimensions of Crisis Response Strategy*
Acceptable response behaviors are driven by community expectations. There are predictable management behaviors that perpetuate trouble, cause additional embarrassment, humiliation, and victims; and, if allowed to occur, are responsible for unnecessary damage and litigation issues. An intriguing contrast between the community's expectations and typical corporate priorities helps explain why so many people in so many organizations can become angry so rapidly when crisis response is mishandled.

The heart of this section deals with the seven dimensions of crisis communication management, which have been structured as a contrast chart to illustrate principles and values against damaging behaviors with examples of appropriate correct approaches. The intent is to show a strategic matrix of management behaviors that are expected by the community, typical behaviors management may be considering, and the approaches that will meet community expectations.

Part IV   *Crisis Communications Standards and Principles*
In this section we return to concepts that establish management crisis communication and operational principles. As in the previous sections, each of these basic communication principles is easily understood, unassailable, fundamentally sound, and teachable. These guiding principles and standards present other tools to offset the typical institutional behaviors that break the trust between a business and its constituencies. Specific behaviors and language to avoid in trust-busting situations are also presented and described.

   As this book proceeds to publication, two major world brands are in crisis together, the American owned Ford Motor Company and the Japanese owned Firestone Tire and Rubber Company. A worldwide recall of certain models of Firestone tires is underway following the deaths of more than 50 people in Ford vehicles equipped with Firestone's tires. This real-life scenario is unfolding in a manner quite similar to our hypothetical model. The existence of the problem was exposed on the Internet and through the news media, triggered by calls from victims and their families. Firestone at first minimized the problem and suggested that there should be no particular worry. What began as an American news story soon expanded into a worldwide, country-by-country surprise disclosure of recalls already in progress outside the United States.

Enormous collateral damage is occurring to the reputation of one of America's largest auto manufacturers, the Ford Motor Company. There is a growing question about the survivability of the Firestone brand. While some important things are being done correctly, the clash of cultures of the two giant companies and how this inhibits effective response is an emerging lesson in global crisis management.

The ideas, standards, principles, and analysis presented in this chapter work in a global environment. There are variations in culture, country-to-country. But, the ultimate reality is that community expectations are the same in virtually every culture. Human beings everywhere expect protection of their health and safety, of property they own, of the possessions they have accumulated, and of the environment, peace of mind, freedom from fear, and fundamental pride in themselves and their community. And on top of all this, there is Internet communication that has made many kinds of "local" crises multinational, and of global concern. Welcome to the 21st century.

PART I

THE NATURE OF CORPORATE CRISIS AND MANAGEMENT'S RESPONSE

The most challenging part of crisis communication management is action – with the right response – quickly. A credible response requires that behavior always precede communication. Non-behavior or inappropriate behavior leads to spin, not communication. In emergencies, it's explaining the non-action or half-hearted response and the resulting spin that cause embarrassment, humiliation, prolonged visibility, and unnecessary litigation.

Defining corporate crisis is extremely important. Too often the public relations practitioner, as well as other staff functions in the organization, presents laundry lists of adverse events, which – from a management perspective – are simply part of the everyday life of an organization, and call them crises. This leads to a severe loss of staff credibility by management, who generally do understand what a crisis is: something that adversely affects their goals, the organization's goals, or their careers in an extreme way. Here is a useful definition that will set the bar high enough so that management's attention and support can be gained for prevention, detection, and response, and so that truly productive strategic management issues can be anticipated:

Crisis is defined as a people-stopping, show-stopping, product-stopping, reputationally defining event, which creates victims and/or explosive visibility.

Many adverse events can befall an organization or company, but to be truly a crisis, there must be victims and/or explosive visibility. Victims can be people, animals, or living systems. If there are no victims, chances are there will be no crisis.

Helping management understand the impact of inappropriate or poorly thought out crisis response is one of the most important strategic services the public relations practitioner can provide. Carefully done, the public relations practitioner can momentarily become a member of the operations team. Useful strategic discussions about crisis communication require an approach that has value without insulting the executive's intelligence, has impact without belaboring the obvious, inspires action without oversimp-lification, and suggests options and choices without teaching unnecessary, ill-advised lessons in public relations. The strategic discussion revolves around key dimensions each crisis exhibits.

Examining the management dimensions of a crisis, which executives can clearly recognize and relate to, helps the public relations counselor provide truly meaningful, strategic advice. This is an analytical approach that helps senior management avoid what can be career-defining moments, unless those moments are deserved.

True crises have several critical dimensions in common, any one of which, if handled poorly, can disrupt, derail, or perhaps destroy even the best efforts at managing any remaining opportunities to resolve the situation and recover, rehabilitate, or retain reputation. Failure to respond and communicate in ways that meet community standards and expectations will result in a series of negative outcomes, despite the best of intentions. Later in this chapter we will focus on seven critical dimensions of crisis communication management:

■ Operations

■ Victims

■ Trust/credibility

■ Behavior

■ Professional expectation

■ Ethics

■ Lessons learned.

Convincing management to act promptly is the most challenging aspect of crisis management. Perhaps the single most serious mistake crisis communication managers make is assuming that operating executives will immediately see, understand, and act upon the obvious moral, ethical, potentially legal, and reputational damage being caused by a crisis situation.

Prompt corporate action is extremely rare. Even in the legendary U.S. Tylenol tampering crisis in the early 1980s, it took Johnson & Johnson nine days to decide to remove the product from store shelves nationwide. Prompt action is found mostly in corporations that have already made serious crisis response mistakes and have attempted to learn from those experiences. Yet time and again, we see that institutional memory is no guarantee of prompt action when subsequent crises occur.

Understanding management's mentality is essential. When it comes to developing crisis response strategies, some advance understanding of management's approach to problems is necessary to literally stay in the game and at the table where important decisions ultimately get made.

Management rarely plans for crises unless required to by law, rule, or regulation. Most management teams consider themselves competent enough to deal with virtually any situation in a manner that will suit even the most discriminating critic or regulator. Those experienced in this arena understand the fallacy of this type of thinking. But it persists and governs corporate behavior when crises occur.

In some respects management is correct when it assumes competence in handling problems. That's because, in general, there are three kinds of crises that can affect organization:

■ *Operating situations*, those that are a part of the operation of the business – hauling, shipping, loading, manufacturing, people handling, logistics, deliveries. The vast majority of all corporate crises are the result of day-to-day operating situations.

■ *Non-operating problems*, those situations and events that are outside the scope of the organization's daily activities and management's training and experience – sexual harassment, kidnapping, extortion, workplace violence, job actions, angry neighbors, adverse public policy, Internet attacks, product tampering, disgruntled employees, rumors.

■ *Combination ops/non-ops scenarios* – takeovers, acquisitions, divestitures, sudden changes in stock price, labor organizing, disgruntled employees.

It is the non-operating problems that require intensive analysis, understanding, and preparation. While management may be very rightly confident that it can manage operating problems, it is unlikely that management has any experience in dealing with the non-operating situation or the combination event with very significant non-operating components. A further difficulty is that management is often resistant to even seriously considering preparation for events it views as unlikely to occur. Yet, it is these non-operating situations that ultimately define a corporation's reputation, an executive's career, and the future of an organization or brand.

From a crisis management perspective, these anticipateable management behavior patterns must be part of the contingency planning process, designed to minimize their damage and maximize whatever actions can be taken until a full-blown response is clearly authorized.

We call this strategy pre-authorization. And, frankly, if we could define crisis preparation in a single word, it would be the word pre-authorization: the intentional pre-decision-making necessary to act with immediacy once specific scenarios or event patterns occur. Lack of pre-authorization – in fact, the inability to find people to authorize decisions and actions in real time – is often the most critical deterrent to effective response. If the goal for crisis planning and prevention were the simple scenario-driven pre-authorization of the commitment of fundamental corporate assets and actions, those few items that do fit the definition of potential corporate crises could be reduced further; and certainly, they could be managed more effectively.

One crucial goal for crisis planning and preparation is the elimination of at least the most obvious threats before anything happens. In simplest terms, this means why would one develop a crisis response plan in case a decrepit boiler blows up? Doesn't it make more sense to install a new replacement boiler, one that will eliminate the threat altogether?

Effective crisis planning reduces threats to organizations.

PART II
VALUE AND BELIEF SYSTEMS AFFECT CRISIS RESPONSE

Time and time again, despite the existence of widely publicized corporate organizational value systems, when we analyze how poor, delayed, or unnecessary manipulative communication has damaged or destroyed the reputation, credibility, or the future of an individual, organization, brand, or product, it often seems that then, and only then, does the search begin for the rules, tests, and standards needed to achieve effective, problem-anticipating, ethically sound communication in crisis.

Too many times organizations have difficulty translating their stated value systems into specific actionable responses when crises occur. Three fundamental strategies are required to make the organization's values systems actionable during crises:

- An effective communication policy model

- A method for immediate prioritization of actions and communication during urgent situations

- An accountability process, which can move the entire response to conclusion while simultaneously regaining credibility and re-establishing reputation.

Crisis communication policy model
The responding organization interested in having an effective, consistent, positive relationship with its victims as well as with its constituencies must work within the framework of those constituencies' expectations. These expectations become the strategic communication standards that produce the behaviors constituencies and victims anticipate. These standards are shown in Table 9.1.

Communication priorities
Although actual communication response steps can vary based on specific crisis scenarios, successful short- and long-term communication is the result of sound communication priority setting, from the start. Table 9.2 forms a hierarchy of priorities.

True emergencies require virtually simultaneous communication activity in all five priority areas, but the order is important. Effective execution is a primary concern precisely because time is at a premium and crisis resources are limited and stretched. This order of priority is effective for containing, controlling, and reducing the visibility impact of emergent situations and the resulting reputational damage.

This approach also tends to reduce the ability of media and critics to alter the outcomes of situations because those affected hear from and deal directly with the source of their problem without the filtration, inaccuracy, or emotionalism reporters and critics bring to high-profile situations. This approach is principled, ethical, and productive because it puts the highest priority on the most important aspects of crisis response. Besides, is this

Table 9.1 Strategic communication standards

1.	*Openness, accessibility* – availability and willingness to respond. "We will talk."
2.	*Truthfulness* – unconditional honesty. "We will tell the truth, from our perspective, promptly."
3.	*Responsiveness* – recognition that any constituent or victim concern is by definition legitimate and must be addressed. "We will answer all questions, no matter who asks them."
4.	*Transparency* – behavior, attitudes, plans, even strategic discussions must be unchallengeable, unassailable, and positive. "There will be no secrets."

Table 9.2 Hierarchy of priorities in crisis scenarios
Priorities

1.	Address the fundamental cause of the situation. Resolve, mitigate, contain, or eradicate it.
2.	Assist and care for those most directly affected (victims, intended and unintended).
3.	Inform and involve employees (sometimes they are victims, too).
4.	Alert those indirectly affected (neighbors, friends, families, relatives, customers, suppliers, government, regulators, and third parties that are involuntarily a part of the crisis situation). Get and benefit from their input.
5.	Manage the news media, other channels of external communication, the self-appointed and self-anointed – those people and organizations who hop into the situation for their own reasons and agendas.

not the way our mothers, neighbors, victims, and employees would want us to do it anyway?

Accountability
Making an organization's values and standards work, especially during crisis situations, requires an identifiable process approach, which is aggressive, conclusive, and unassailable. An approach, such as that suggested here, contains the seven essential steps required to resolve true crisis situations (Table 9.3). In fact, each of these steps must be executed before a crisis will be successfully mitigated or reduced to a longer term, low or no visibility resolution.

Make no mistake about it, the lesson of accountability is that each of these steps, if executed promptly and in the order illustrated here, will significantly reduce the impact of crises on the organization and substantially respond to the concerns of victims and those adversely affected.

Table 9.3 Resolving crisis situations: the 7-step approach	
Steps	
1. Candor	Outward recognition, through promptly verbalized public acknowledgement (or outright apology), that a problem exists; that people or groups of people, the environment, or the public trust is affected; and that something will be done to remedy the situation.
2. Explanation	(No matter how silly, stupid, or embarrassing the problem-causing error was.) Promptly and briefly explain why the problem occurred and the known underlying reasons or behaviors that led to the situation (even if we have only partial early information). Also talk about what you learned from the situation and how it will influence your future behavior. Unconditionally commit to regularly report additional information until it is all out, or until no public interest remains.
3. Declaration	A public commitment and discussion of specific, positive steps that will be taken to conclusively address the issues and resolve the situation.
4. Contrition	The verbalization of regret, empathy, sympathy, and even embarrassment. Take appropriate responsibility for having allowed the situation to occur in the first place, whether by omission, commission, accident, or negligence.
5. Consultation	Ask for help and counsel from victims, government, and from the community of origin – even from your opponents. Directly involve and request the participation of those most directly affected to help develop more permanent solutions, more acceptable behaviors, and to design principles and approaches that will preclude similar problems from re-occurring.
6. Commitment	Publicly set your goals at zero – zero errors, zero defects, zero dumb decisions, zero problems. Publicly promise unconditionally that to the best of your ability situations like this will never occur again.
7. Restitution	Find a way to quickly pay the price. Make or require restitution. Go beyond community and victim expectations and what would be required under normal circumstances to remediate the problem. Adverse situations remediated quickly cost a lot less and are controversial for much shorter periods of time.

Negative visibility will be reduced and liability made more manageable while successful litigation becomes more difficult.

Each of these seven steps conclusively and unassailably addresses critical concerns often raised by the media, litigators, victims, government, and the public. Failing to respond to these areas of inquiry promptly will raise suspicion, prolong inquiries, and drag out negative, often devastating media coverage.

The larger the organization involved, the more likely it is that other negative circumstances are occurring at the same time the crisis situation is happening. Prolonging response time often drags these collateral issues and problems into the spotlight and into the public's mind. They are all muddled together, making things look even worse. The media strive to make connections between one negative behavior or outcome and another, and the ever-present global litigator begins to hunt for a pattern of litigate-able vulnerability.

The patterns of crises can be identified. The behavior of victims, employees, government, the media, and critics is well understood. The poor behavior of corporations and large organizations is assumed. A values-driven approach is achievable and is the most effective counter-action strategy to protect and preserve reputation.

PART III

THE DIMENSIONS OF CRISIS RESPONSE STRATEGY: SOME COMMUNICATION STRATEGIES ARE GUARANTEED TO PERPETUATE TROUBLE

All too often when large companies and organizations fix mistakes and cope with disaster, embarrassment, and difficulty, a familiar pattern of initial behaviors occurs that actually generates more adverse results.

Typically there are few acts of corporate courage early on, especially at the highest levels. It's more often confusion, contradiction, and avoidance: denial, victim confusion, testosterosis, arrogance, search for the guilty, fear of the media, and management by whining around.

Organizations do have vulnerabilities and show-stopping problems – the landfill to be sited or closed; the labor agreement that's getting tougher to negotiate; the sudden appearance of a new tax provision in an otherwise benign piece of legislation; a product recall; a kick-back scandal; saying too much; buying too much; selling too much; blowing something up; burning something down; allowing something to leak, seep, smoke, or stink – and critics who grow stronger with every newly revealed mistake. The bigger the enterprise, the greater the potential for large-scale problems or collections of scattered negative events being gathered into a pattern of negative behavior.

There are seven early management behaviors that crisis management strategies must plan against. If these behaviors are allowed to occur unad-dressed, management will quickly multitask itself into long-term difficulty (Figure 9.1).

Behavior 1: Denial

Refusal to accept that something bad has happened; that there may be victims or other direct effects that require prompt public acknowledgement. There's denial that it's really serious; denial that the media or public have any real stake or interest in whatever the problem happens to be; denial that it should take anyone's time in the organization except those in top management specifically tasked to deal with it; denial that the problem is of any particular consequence to the organization provided no one talks about it except those directly involved. "Let's not over-react." "Let's keep it to ourselves." "We don't need to tell the people in public affairs and public relations just yet. They'll just blab it all over." "If we don't talk, no one will know."

Behavior 2: Victim confusion

Irritable reaction to reporters, employees, angry neighbors, and victims' families when they ask for help, information, explanation, or apology. "Hey! We're victims too," says management. Symptoms include time-wasting explanations of what a good corporate citizen we've been, how we've contributed to the opera, the community, and the schools. "We don't deserve to be treated this badly." "Mistakes can happen, even to the best of companies." "We're only human." "People make mistakes." When these behaviors don't pass the community, media, or victim straight face test, or are criticized or laughed at, a stream of defensive threats follows such as:

- "There is risk in everything humans do."
- "We've only known about this problem for the last two years." "There aren't even any government standards to cover it. Until there are standards, how can we be expected to comply?"

Behavior 5: Search for the guilty

Shifts blame away while digging into the organization to look for traitors, turncoats, troublemakers, those who push back or make mistakes, and the unconvinceables. The news media and employees probably would be shocked to learn how much energy is diverted to the search for "guilty" individuals and to finding others to blame.

Behavior 6: Fear of the media

As it becomes clear that the problem is at least partly real, the media and victims begin asking, "What did you know, and when did you know it?" "What have you done, and when did you do it?" along with other humiliating, embarrassing, and damaging questions such as, "What have you done and why?" "What do you refuse to do and why?" and "How many victims will it take to get action?" There are no really good, comfortable answers because the organization's leaders have stalled for so long.

Those in public affairs and media relations know this phase has begun when they hear comments like, "There they go again, just attacking business like always," or when the communications department manager or director is asked why his/her "friends" in the media once again intentionally misunderstand business. Orders are issued to "stop the story," "ban reporters," "keep employees from talking to the press," "call the publisher," and to "reconsider the advertising policy" (yes, some executives still think this way).

■ "If the government enforces this regulation, it will destroy our competitiveness."

■ "If we have to close this plant, it's their fault." "It's the only decision we can make."

■ "If we are forced to address this problem to this level, many more will suffer needlessly."

Behavior 3: Testosterosis

Looks for ways to hit back rather than to deal with the problem. Refuses to give in; refuses to respect those who may have a difference of opinion or a legitimate issue. Shows disrespect for critics, victims, families, angry employees, and neighbors. Because there is so much at stake, there is extraordinary negative energy inside the executive circle. That's what testosterosis really is … an attack of negative adrenaline. Another definitive testosterosis indicator; the use of military terminology – "enemy," "beachhead," "attack," "counterattack," "retreat," "truce" – builds a macho atmosphere. This emotional mentality sets the stage for predictable errors, omissions, and mistakes.

Behavior 4: Arrogance

Reluctance to apologize, express concern or empathy, or to take appropriate responsibility because, "If we do that, we'll be liable," or, "We'll look like sissies," or, "We'll set bad precedents," or, "There'll be copycats," or, "We'll legitimize the bad actions of people who don't like us anyway." It's contempt for adversaries, sometimes even for victims, and almost always for the news media. It's corrosive. It shows. It causes even more powerful negative responses.

Behavior 7: Management by whining around

Shuffling around, head down, finger stuck in bellybutton, whining and complaining about bad luck, people we don't respect who have power, being misunderstood by the media, and why we "aren't getting credit" for what we've already contributed to society. Self-talk prevails. When the decision is made to finally move ahead, the corporation talks only about its own pain, which makes victims, employees, neighbors, government, and the media even angrier. Here are some of my favorite whiney management phrases:

■ "Who appointed the media to deal with this?"

■ "We can't be competitive if the media gives away our secrets."

■ "This is our business and no one else's."

■ "How can reporters do a story without all the facts?"

■ "It's just harassment and personal media attacks."

■ "Aren't reporters interested in the truth?"

■ "The media are a bunch of liberal zealots … "

■ "It's the only way these creeps can raise money for their cause."

Figure 9.1 Early management behaviors crisis management must avoid

Community versus corporate priorities: a powerful paradox

The key to understanding why corporate reputation is so easily threatened is understanding the different priorities communities and individuals set versus the corporation. On a day-to-day basis, companies and organizations tend to operate around what is in their economic and operational best interest. So long as the community and/or individuals are unaffected, there is little difficulty. However, when a crisis situation occurs, it is the community's value system that predominates. The corporate or organization that refuses to acknowledge, abide by, accept, and operate in response to the community's value system is the corporation or organization whose reputation, ability to operate, and, perhaps, future is threatened. Remember the community's definition of a value:

> *A community value is a personal protective belief. It is about something that cannot be changed without the participation and permission of the community or the individuals directly involved.*

Figure 9.2 simply but dramatically illustrates the community's priorities versus corporate priorities. When a crisis occurs, to successfully resolve the issues and preserve, even enhance, reputation the corporation or organization must immediately adopt the community's value priorities until such time as the community gives its permission to allow the company or organization to resume its normal method of operations. Companies wishing to maintain

Figure 9.2 Corporate versus community priority timeline

good relationships with constituents will recognize the power of these community values and expectations, and build corporate operational values and behaviors around community *and* constituent expectations.

Case Example: BurgerMax and the Dimensions of Crisis Response Strategy

The Timeline

Day One: Customers and the media call to ask about those who are getting sick. BurgerMax denies any responsibility and refuses to talk with the families except through an attorney. Intense media speculation forces the company to make public statements and to issue a news release. Company officials did call in the department of health.

Day Two: Continued media speculation forces BurgerMax to acknowledge that something might have happened and that it might have been the cause. "If it was our burgers," more than likely, the company said, "it was the fault of the supplier who provided contaminated meat." The company cautioned the media to be responsible and not to start a panic. The U.S. Department of Agriculture (USDA) was already examining the supplier's facilities. Other countries have made similar announcements.

Day Three: The first deaths are reported. Many departments of health suggest shut down of all BurgerMax restaurants for inspection and sanitizing. The company agrees to shut down the three restaurants where victims had eaten. Families of the victims hold news conferences demanding that BurgerMax take responsibility. BurgerMax runs ads saying, "It's just an isolated incident," "We follow the law," "Come on down and enjoy a MammothMax." BurgerMax releases a statement condemning meat inspection programs. "This might not have happened had there been more qualified inspectors." "It's an industry-wide problem."

Day Four: Two more children die. The department of health reports that cooking temperatures were probably too low to kill the bacteria. BurgerMax says, "We followed all approved procedures," "Food safety is our number one concern," "If the meat had not been contaminated by our suppliers, there would not have been problems in our restaurants."

Day Five: Another death. BurgerMax announces it will sponsor an international study of food safety. It contributes $100,000, declaring that meat inspection is a "government problem that needs to be promptly addressed." Two former employees, speaking anonymously, suggest that they may have, "cut a corner or two," especially during busy times. "Managers just looked the other way."

Day Six: Two more deaths. The families of the first victims announce litigation against BurgerMax and demand criminal investigations. The company announces a plan to help victim families obtain assistance more easily and suggests that they come to the company rather than to government agencies or the news media.

Applying the dimensions of crisis communication management response

Using the BurgerMax scenario and all its implications, let's analyze this problem for the significance of the seven critical dimensions. Each requires affirmative management decision-making as a part of the process of surviving the situation. There is some duplication in recommendations and observations, mostly because bad news is repeated in different ways and in different places unless it is dealt with conclusively, promptly.

1. The operations dimension

Regaining public confidence following a damaging situation first requires operating decisions that alleviate the community's anguish; restore confidence in the brand, organization, individual, or activity; and rebuild relationships – especially with the victims – while at the same time reducing media coverage of the story because the organization, which created the situation, is actually *doing* what the community expects.

Over the years I've developed a series of standard operating behaviors (see Table 9.4) that seem to meet the criteria for re-establishing community support. The reality is that for truly serious situations, the perpetrators will need to take action in each of the seven areas as a condition of re-establishing public confidence. The optimum order in which these actions need to be taken is shown here. It is not possible to skip a step. In fact, the

Table 9.4 Standard operating behaviors to re-establish community support

Urgent crisis management operating responses	BurgerMax damaging behaviors	Correct approaches
I. Candor: ■ Outward recognition through promptly verbalized public acknowledgement that a problem exists; that people or groups of people, the environment, or the public trust is affected; and that something will be done to remediate the situation.	■ Released self-serving messages and communication. ■ Made assumptions about the truth without really knowing what the truth was. ■ Failed to accept responsibility. ■ Shifted the blame to others in an attempt to deflect criticism. ■ Disparaged the media and government agencies. ■ Viewed the outbreak as a "PR" problem. ■ Issued news releases that were self-serving. ■ Hid behind weak arguments, for example "We used recommended average temperatures" and "complied with government standards," and gave the appearance of minimizing its role in the harm that was done.	■ "It's our fault." ■ "It shouldn't have happened." ■ "We are helping the families through these terrible times." ■ "We will relentlessly examine every aspect of our business to find out what happened, to fix it, talk about it, and see that it won't happen again." ■ Use appropriate spokespeople with statements. Avoid news releases. ■ Stand up and answer the questions. ■ Act to find the cause.

cont'd

Table 9.4 cont'd

Urgent crisis management operating responses	BurgerMax damaging behaviors	Correct approaches
2. Explanation (no matter how silly, stupid, or embarrassing the problem causing error was): ■ Promptly and briefly explain why the problem occurred and the known underlying reasons or behaviors that led to the situation (even if there is only partial early information). ■ Talk about what was learned from the situation and how it will influence the organization's future behavior. ■ Unconditionally commit to regularly report additional information until it is all out, or until no public interest remains.	■ Created conflict ("We don't know what the cause is, but eat here anyway") around the source of the problem, which led to public confusion. ■ The company perceived itself as a victim, its suppliers as the perpetrators, the government and media as persecutors. ■ Shifted blame and responsibility to a failed government inspection system. ■ Refused to admit that it wasn't prepared for what could easily be recognized as a critical vulnerability to the public health. ■ "We can't act until we have all the facts." ■ "You can't prepare for everything"	■ Find the truth. ■ Take conclusive action: close the stores. ■ Talk to and about the victims and their families' suffering. ■ Act like a neighbor. ■ Commit to the obvious, for example we weren't ready for this. ■ Keep focused on solving the local problem. ■ Release information incrementally, constantly. ■ Immediately correct erroneous information with more current, more accurate information.
3. Declaration: ■ A public commitment and discussion of specific, positive steps to be taken. Conclusively address the issues and resolve the situation.	■ Stonewalled with a scripted, insensitive, overly technical, and irrelevant operational response. ■ Failed to bring in truly independent resources or independent expertise to the situation. ■ Waffled about helping others. Saying, "We'll do the right thing," while not doing anything. ■ Conducted no serious, credible, independent external investigation.	■ Talk from the victims' point of view. ■ Minimize the technical "stuff." ■ Be explicit about doing whatever it takes for the victims. ■ Avoid disingenuous phrases: "if we could turn the clock back" "if we had only known."

Table 9.4 cont'd

Urgent crisis management operating responses	BurgerMax damaging behaviors	Correct approaches
	▪ Inadequate implementation of very late recall (lost hundreds of cases of potentially contaminated hamburgers). ▪ No commitment to fix recall plan deficiencies.	"these things happen, unfortunately." "we'll set new standards, for everyone." "we didn't want to cause panic." "the media sensationalize everything."
4. Contrition: ▪ The continuing verbalization of regret, empathy, sympathy, even embarrassment. Take appropriate responsibility for having allowed the situation to occur in the first place, whether by omission, commission, accident, or negligence.	▪ Took only conditional responsibility. ▪ Selfish focus on shareholder concerns and customer retention. ▪ Used a news release to announce its sympathy. ▪ Expressed only conditional regret: "We're sorry, but . . . it was the supplier." "We're sorry, but . . . we didn't want to create a panic." "We're sorry, but . . . we didn't know about the new regulations because the government didn't do a good job of telling us." "We're sorry, but . . . the government didn't diligently inform us." "Nothing was wrong but . . . we will change our quality testing procedures anyway."	▪ Talk and act like someone that you care about has been hurt. ▪ Meet with families. ▪ Take the families of victims to church. ▪ Let employees speak for the company. ▪ Involve employees with each victim family. ▪ Use empathetic language. ▪ Express unconditional sympathy.

cont'd

Table 9.4 cont'd

Urgent crisis management operating responses	BurgerMax damaging behaviors	Correct approaches
5. Consultation: ■ Promptly ask for help and counsel from victims, government, and the community of origin – even from opponents. ■ Directly involve and request the participation of those most directly affected to help develop more permanent solutions, more acceptable behaviors, and to design principles and approaches that will preclude similar problems from occurring.	■ Never asked for input from the victims. ■ Initially blamed the government. ■ Used a "voluntary" internal investigation as a cover to avoid scrutiny. ■ Never asked suppliers to participate or contribute to the resolution of the problem. ■ Kept its distance from government inspectors; viewed regulators as an enemy.	■ Announce an unassailable panel of independent experts to study, recommend, and report publicly. ■ Let government agencies do the talking, while the company concentrates on solving the problem. ■ Establish a vendor advisory group. ■ Help victims speak out and make suggestions.
6. Commitment: ■ Publicly set organizational goals at zero. Zero errors. Zero defects. Zero dumb decisions. Zero problems. ■ Publicly promise that to the best of the organization's ability similar situations will never occur or re-occur.	■ Made absolutely no attempt to commit to zero. ■ Completely ignored the concept of zero: "Zero isn't possible." "We can't promise no future mistakes." "There is risk in everything people do."	■ Establish a permanent, broadly representative advisory group to assure the public of the company's intentions on an ongoing basis.

Table 9.4 cont'd

Urgent crisis management operating responses	BurgerMax damaging behaviors	Correct approaches

7. Restitution:
■ Find a way to quickly pay the price.
■ Make or require restitution.
■ Go beyond community and victim expectations and what would be required under normal circumstances to remediate the problem.
■ Adverse situations remediated quickly cost far less and are controversial for much shorter periods of time.
	■ Stalled and delayed victim compensation yet gave $100,000 to a trade association for research.
	■ Only did the absolute minimum required.
	■ Limited contact with victim families.
	■ Required receipts and a validation process for all reimbursements.
		■ Exceed community expectations:
		  – Close all restaurants the night they learned of the possible problem.
		  – Take direct, immediate, quiet action to address and alleviate victims' concerns and fears.
		  – Immediately establish an independently administered fund to cover short- and long-term medical, related, and follow-up costs for victims and their families.
		
		Note: The check written today will be the smallest check written. *Checks will be written.*

faster these actions are taken, in the correct order, the more quickly victim anger will be lessened. Employees will have fewer bad feelings, and there will be less media coverage and litigation. Companies that behave appropriately and solve problems promptly are neither newsworthy nor easily sued.

2. The victim management dimension

When organizational action creates involuntary adverse circumstances for people or institutions, victims are created. Victims have a special mentality and their perception and behavior is altered in fundamentally predictable ways. Victims designate themselves. They also determine when they are no longer victims.

The perpetrator needs to recognize victim expectations and respond affirmatively. Otherwise there may be very negative consequences. For example, victims may resist reasonable solutions, use the media to communicate heart-wrenching stories, or begin high-profile litigation. Closure becomes very difficult. Disgruntled former employees and well-meaning current employees often come forward to verify victim allegations. Victims don't usually hear much beyond their own pain.

Victims move through recognizable cycles as they work to resolve the situation in which they have involuntarily become a part (Table 9.5).

3. The trust and credibility dimension

Credibility is conferred by others based on an organization's past behavior. When bad things happen, past behavior is used to predict future actions. When past behaviors have been good and helpful, and current and future behaviors don't match those expectations, there's a loss of credibility.

Trust is the absence of fear. Fear results from unexpected injury caused by circumstances or by someone or something that was previously trusted. Fear is the most powerful human emotion to remediate. When there is physical injury or death, it may be impossible to do more than attempt to reduce the fear. Left unattended, fear turns to frustration, anger, then to retribution. There are seven trust-building, fear-reducing, credibility-fixing behaviors:

■ Provide advance information

Table 9.5 Recognizable victim cycles and communications strategy

Cycles	Victims need	BurgerMax
I: Recognition of impact	▪ Assistance with grief.	▪ Considered victims a part of the government inspection/supplier problem.
▪ Agony, search for the "reason this happened."	▪ Expression of regret.	▪ Made participation difficult.
▪ Anger.	▪ Involvement.	▪ Patronized families.
▪ Concern over lack of response.	▪ Information.	▪ Reduced death to a press release.
▪ Disbelief, dread.	▪ Recognition.	▪ Was embarrassed into taking more empathic action.
▪ Expectation of help.		
▪ Frustration at "intentional delays."		
II: Seeking retribution	▪ Life rebuilding assistance.	▪ Delayed payment.
▪ Seek or attempt to implement their own solutions.	▪ Ongoing counsel.	▪ Made victims guess about help.
▪ Feel that help received is inadequate, late, and insincere.	▪ Outcome-focused action.	▪ Gave $100,000 to a trade association for research.
▪ Hit back.	▪ Understanding.	▪ Trivialized victim suffering.
▪ Search for the obviously guilty.	▪ Contact with accident/death site.	▪ Made victims provide receipts.
▪ Turn to the plaintiff's bar to get retribution.		▪ Used low-level PR people to spin.
III: Severely distorted recollection		▪ No ongoing relationship with victims to provide closure and healing.
▪ "No one understands what I'm going through."		
▪ "They could have done more, faster."		
▪ Growing sense of helplessness.		
▪ A permanent sense of anger with endless analysis.		
▪ Fearful worrying about the future.		

- Ask for input
- Listen carefully
- Demonstrate that you've heard, that is, change your plans
- Stay in touch
- Speak in plain language
- Bring victims/involuntary participants into the decision-making process.

Note the BurgerMax behaviors did not match the above. Its actual behaviors are shown in Table 9.6, compared to what they should have done in Table 9.7.

Table 9.6 BurgerMax behaviors

1. Stalled and delayed in getting information to the victims and to the public.

2. Never had a good grasp on exactly what information would be useful to the victims:
   - What to do if you're experiencing symptoms
   - How to get more information about E. coli
   - Exactly what BurgerMax was going to do to make the situation right.

3. Only looked internally for expertise. Didn't seek help from external resources.

4. Rejected recommendations for an advisory board.

5. Blamed consultants, government, and suppliers for what was ultimately its own responsibility.

6. Listened with a corporate ear; heard only the financial markets.

7. Responded financially first, "This will cost a lot of money." Promised to help but then delayed payments.

8. Had little or no follow-up with victims. Concentrated follow-up efforts with the government, but only because the company was required to do so.

9. Relied on technical language to support its position that suppliers contaminated the meat and also to explain why it wasn't adequately prepared to manage this crisis. Seemed to have no understanding of risks associated with this bacterial strain; maintained that the problem was not its fault. Appeared to be testing its legal defense strategy through the news media.

10. Never considered the victims as BurgerMax victims, but rather as victims of faulty government inspection systems and non-compliant suppliers. Ignored the fact that its employees felt like victims as well.

11. Probably lied about what it knew and when it had crucial information. At the very least, it hid behind legal definitions rather than be forthcoming early in the scenario.

Table 9.7 Credible versus actual behaviors

Behaviors that illustrate credibility	BurgerMax actuals
1. Talk openly.	1. Hid from the truth from the beginning. "Millions and millions of burgers safely served."
2. Reveal what the public should know, even if they don't ask.	2. Never acknowledged its role and responsibility for the outbreak, even though it subsequently raised cooking temperatures. Only provided information when forced to do so, then only a minimal amount.
3. Explain problems, delays, and changes quickly.	3. Avoided discussing problems. Never admitted there was a question about its food handling processes. Even though it made changes to its cooking procedures, the company maintained that it had a commitment to quality all along.
4. Answer all questions, even those that victims wouldn't think to ask.	4. Ducked and stalled. Never answered any questions not directly asked.
5. Cooperate with the media.	5. Priorities were reversed. It was concerned mainly about business, operations, finances, and keeping customers coming through the door.
6. Demonstrate that victims and employees have a higher priority.	6. Ignored victims, at first.
7. Respect and seek to work with victims and opponents.	7. Disparaged those who criticized its actions.

4. The behavior dimension

Post-crisis analysis involving hundreds of companies, industries, and negative circumstances reveals a pattern of unhelpful behaviors that work against rebuilding or preserving reputation, trust, and credibility. The greater the negative nature of the incident and the greater the number of victims, the more opportunities there are for trust-busting behaviors to occur. Good crisis plans are structured to work directly against, anticipate, and eliminate negative behavior patterns. Negative behaviors to plan against are illustrated in Table 9.8.

5. The professional expectation dimension

What is often omitted in analyses of crisis situations is a comparison of the behaviors and actions of public relations professionals against the standards set by their industry. Increasingly in litigation, juries look to industry standards and practices to help determine a factual basis for damages and compensation. Community expectations, as reflected in codes of conduct and codes of ethics, are useful analytical and response tools. This section looks at the BurgerMax situation from the perspective of the Public Relations Society of America's (PRSA) Code of Professional Standards and the International Association of Business Communicators (IABC) Code of Ethics for Professional Communicators (see Table 9.9).

6. The ethical dimension

There is always a moral and ethical dimension to crisis management. Management's greatest difficulty in crisis response is how to handle the moral and ethical aspects of crisis management.

- What do we say, and when to we say it?
- Who do we tell, and how much do we disclose?
- Who do we really have to tell, and can we avoid disclosing some things forever?
- If we do anything, are we admitting there is a problem and that we are responsible?

Table 9.8 Negative behaviors to plan against, mirrored to BurgerMax behaviors

Negative behaviors to plan against	BurgerMax behaviors
1. Arrogance, no concern.	1. Was concerned mostly about the financial impact.
2. Minimize victim needs.	2. Actively made situation difficult for victims. Failed to acknowledge victims.
3. Blame shifting.	3. Aggressively blamed suppliers, government departments of health, and government inspection systems. Maintained an "anybody but us" mentality.
4. Broaden situation unnecessarily (or for PR reasons).	4. Encouraged industry initiatives to intercede. "We are the victims of the government's lax approach to regulating the meat industry." Gave $100,000 for "research" rather than to compensate victims. Note: The most common truly damaging PR tactic is to create or drag in third parties.
5. Inappropriate language.	5. Was careless and inhumane. Was consistently stupid and self-serving.
6. Inconsistency.	6. Attacked suppliers, the government, and the media.
7. Inflammatory statements.	7. Had no recall plan in place to deal with the problem despite many stories in the news and in trade publications.
8. Little or no preparation.	8. Had no crisis plan. Failed to anticipate crisis.
9. Minimize the impact.	9. Did not communicate until overwhelmed by negative events. Then it used a completely defensive approach, "It's isolated to just three of our 31 stores."
10. Missed opportunities to communicate with government, the public, and victims.	10. Waited to communicate until forced to do so. Should have proactively communicated with the victims and others directly affected by the problem.
11. No admission of responsibility.	11. No admission to this day.
12. Victim confusion.	12. Senior management was embarrassed and felt it was the real victim.

Table 9.9 PRSA Code of Professional Standards and IABC Code of Ethics

Public Relations Society of America (PRSA)	BurgerMax

Code of Professional Standards*
 	
■ Shall conduct his/her professional life in accord with the public interest.
 	
■ Shall exemplify high standards of honesty and integrity.
 	
■ Shall deal fairly with the public, giving due respect to the ideal of free inquiry and to the opinions of others.
 	
■ Shall adhere to the highest standards of accuracy and truth, avoiding extravagant claims or unfair comparisons.
 	
■ Shall not knowingly disseminate false or misleading information and shall act promptly to correct erroneous communications for which he or she is responsible.
	"Apparent" standards
	
	■ Priorities:
	  – Shareholder value.
	  – Customer retention.
	  – Reputational salvage.
	
	■ Approach:
	  – Blameshifting to others (government, vendors, department of health).
	  – Conditional responsibility.
	  – Creation of conflict to deflect criticism.
	  – Escalation of outbreak to a "national problem."
	  – Arrogance and selfishness.
	
	■ Outcomes:
	  – Damage to brand and vendors.
	  – Unnecessary, prolonged media coverage.
	  – No substantive change in government meat inspection system.
	  – Unnecessary victims.

Table 9.9 cont'd

International Association of Business Communicators (IABC)	BurgerMax
Code of Ethics for Professional Communicators	■ Viewed outbreak as a "PR" problem.
	– Used self-serving language.
■ Practice honest, candid, and timely communication and foster the free flow of essential information in accord with the public interest.	– Attempted to raise issue to the national level.
	■ Was media driven.
■ Disseminate accurate information and promptly correct any erroneous communication for which they may be responsible.	– Used news releases to communicate information that was important only to it.
■ Sensitive to cultural values and beliefs and engage in fair and balanced communication activities that foster and encourage mutual understanding.	– Used press conferences to shift the blame to others.
	■ Misdirected emphasis to company constituents.
■ Refrain from taking part in any undertaking that the communicator considers to be unethical.	– Shareholders: Were assured that the impact of the outbreak was minimal.
■ Obey the laws and public policies governing their professional activities and are sensitive to the spirit of all laws and regulations and should any law or public policy be violated, for whatever reasons, act promptly to correct the situation.	– Financial analysts: Were the first audience to be communicated with directly (through an analyst teleconference).
	– Customers: Were told via ads and press statements that it was safe to eat at BurgerMax.
■ Protect confidential information and, at the same time, comply with all legal requirements for the disclosure of information affecting the welfare of others.	■ Attempted to minimize the damage.
	■ Failed to recognize the true victims.
■ Honest not only with others but also, and most importantly, with themselves as individuals; seeking the truth and speaking that truth first to the self.	– BurgerMax viewed itself as the victim.
	– Customers who became ill were the victims of a failed government inspection system.

* As this book goes to press, the Public Relations Society of America is completing a rather dramatic revision of its Code of Professional Standards.

Business organizations and institutions are expected to have consciences and to act in ways that reinforce this public expectation. That's why someone will be held accountable whenever there are victims.

When there are victims, moral and ethical assessments are essential. This assessment process consists of answers to a series of questions, or at least being prepared to answer these questions publicly and promptly.

When an issue involves integrity and moral or ethical dilemmas, get to the moral reasoning and questioning quickly. When the public's deepest values are offended, extraordinarily fast action is required. Ethical issues demand the moral courage to ask difficult, tough, direct questions immediately, and a commitment – the strength of heart – powerful enough to take the most appropriate action promptly. Acting on matters of principle will counter the negative impact of a situation the public, employees, and other audiences find morally troublesome. Moral issues require individuals to illustrate their personal belief systems through their behavior (Table 9.10).

7. The lessons-learned dimension

In situations similar to the BurgerMax episode, it's ideal for the organization to plan to learn from its successes and mistakes as it executes its crisis response and remedial actions. Institutional memories are short or non-existent. Besides, managers detest dealing with crises, especially once the urgent issues have been identified. It's a critical part of any crisis response process that a lessons-learned approach be in place so that the institution can learn to remember the mistakes, the miscues, the successes, and the victories in real time – meaning contemporaneously with problem resolution. The public, especially the American public, expects organizations to talk about and describe the lessons they learned from mistakes, errors, accidents, or negligent acts. Speaking publicly about lessons learned is a major corporate step toward obtaining public and employee forgiveness.

The potential for successfully managing future crises can depend on the deliberately created institutional memory the public relations counselor brings to management's attention. Since most crises result from operational activity as opposed to random events or bad luck, the lessons-learned approach teaches the organization how to forecast, mitigate, and perhaps even significantly reduce the likelihood of a similar situation occurring or re-occurring. Successful military organizations habitually analyze how their strategies succeeded or failed in various scenarios. War is by definition crisis and chaos. The corporation or organization in crisis

Table 9.10 Moral and ethical issues and community expectations

Moral and ethical questions	BurgerMax assumptions	Community expectation realities
1. What did they know and when did they know it?	1. Quality was fine.	1. When did Quality Assurance know about the regulatory change? Why was it not acted upon?
2. What are the relevant facts of the situation? ■ What decisions were made? ■ Who was involved/affected? ■ What was sacrificed to benefit the victims?	2. Victims were caused by someone else's negligence. Shareholders became the victims along with company management.	2. The decision to only partially recall product was totally unacceptable.
3. Was there a firsthand attempt to find the truth?	3. We always deal in the truth.	3. Concealed by company for "fear of releasing proprietary information."
4. What alternative actions are available?	4. We'll do whatever we're forced to do to get this situation under control.	4. Take immediate action. Make public acknowledgement and take responsibility. Raise cooking temperatures. Move to the aid of victims. Explain what to do if ill.
5. Who would be affected?	5. Predominantly our shareholders, employees, and customers.	5. The need to clear all stores of possible contamination potential.
6. What ethical principles or standards of conduct are involved or at issue?	6. Our standards are fine. Our ethics are okay. Leave us alone so that we can fix the problem.	6. Behaved badly and in doing so, prolonged/expanded the problem. Slandered suppliers. No protection of the public interest.

cont'd

Table 9.10 cont'd

Moral and ethical questions	BurgerMax assumptions	Community expectation realities
7. How would these principles be advanced or violated by each alternative action?	7. It's not necessary that these be considered.	7. We expect the company to do what's right, promptly.
8. Is it really the company's problem?	8. It's a problem only because someone else screwed up.	8. It's the company's problem until it proves to us that there is no further reason to worry.
9. What is the duty to update and inform?	9. Answer only the questions that we are asked directly.	9. Tell us as much as you can, when you can, and keep telling us until we tell you we no longer need information.
10. Who should be advised or consulted?	10. Let's stay focused on those we know are directly affected.	10. First, the victims, then those who feel they may be affected – employees and those of us who may have purchased food at BurgerMax.
11. What was the fundamental cause – omission, commission, negligence, neglect, accident, arrogance, other?	11. It's someone else's problem, which we're obliged to fix and take the blame for.	11. All of the above.
12. How could this have been avoided?	12. Need better inspectors; select a higher quality supplier.	12. Failed to take immediate dramatic action.
13. Are all the crucial ethical questions being asked and answered?	13. This really isn't an ethical situation; it's a business problem that we've resolved by changing suppliers.	13. Temporary but significant loss of credibility and public trust until it can be re-established by the company.
14. Are the actions open, honest, and truthful?	14. We'll tell as much of the truth as our attorneys will allow.	14. Actions were closed, conditional, and beneficial only to the company.

Table 9.10 cont'd

Moral and ethical questions	BurgerMax assumptions	Community expectation realities
15. What affirmative action is being taken now to remedy or remediate the situation?	15. We'll do whatever we're told to do.	15. Do whatever it takes to make us feel comfortable to dine at your stores again.
16. Is there an institutional "code of silence" when morally questionable decisions or actions come to light?	16. Probably not, we only spend as much time on this as is necessary. Besides, the public only has a limited right to know anyway.	16. As more and more disgruntled employees speak out about BurgerMax's food handling practices, clearly the company isn't telling us everything we need to know.
17. How will future unethical behavior be disclosed? To whom? How fast?	17. We may tighten some things up, but it's not really our problem.	17. We want a process in place that company management doesn't control.
18. What lessons can the organization learn as this dilemma is resolved?	18. Mainly operational information and procedural changes.	18. Ethical behavior is a leadership responsibility. Failing to act ethically is a failure to lead honorably.
19. As an organization, are we prepared to combat the behaviors that lead to ethical compromises?	19. We could be criminally prosecuted.	19. Should BurgerMax be criminally prosecuted, which is possible, it will most likely be forced to establish very rigid compliance and integrity processes. This will eradicate ethical compromises.

cont'd

Table 9.10 cont'd

Moral and ethical questions	BurgerMax assumptions	Community expectation realities
20. How many "typical behaviors" do we know go on that can potentially cause trouble:	20. These can't happen here.	20. If one thing turns out to be wrong, there are most likely a lot of other things that are also wrong and need to be looked into thoroughly.
▪ Lax control;		
▪ No tough, appropriate, centralized compliance;		
▪ Underreporting of infractions;		
▪ Leadership that allows supervisors to overlook bad behavior;		
▪ Allowing employees to experiment with "unapproved methods";		
▪ Encouraging a "do whatever it takes" mentality;		
▪ Minimizing oversight and compliance processes;		
▪ Structuring incentives in such a way that they compromise safety, public health, or product integrity;		
▪ Overlooking shortcuts;		
▪ Avoiding confrontation with managers;		
▪ Operating "on the edge";		
▪ Ignoring signs of rogue behavior;		
▪ Tolerating inappropriate behavior or management by individuals who are "critical to the organization's mission";		
▪ Belittling or humiliating those who suggest or seek ethical standards;		
▪ Dismissing employees who report bad or outright wrong behavior; and/or		
▪ Demeaning the internal credibility of internal whistleblowers.		

Table 9.11 Lessons learned/case study outline
■ Collateral damage
■ Ethics/compliance/standards of conduct
■ Events timeline
■ Impact of variations from approved procedures
■ Lessons learned
■ Open questions
■ Operations issues
■ Recommendations for similar future events
■ Recovery issues
■ Relevant patterns from similar previous events
■ Response timeline
■ Special action(s)
■ Strategic facts
■ Strategy gaps/failures
■ Surprises: negative/positive
■ Unintended positive/negative consequences
■ Victim management/mismanagement
■ Visibility timeline/profile

can feel as though they are in a war. Use the situation to prevent or mitigate the next crisis.

The "Lessons learned/case study outline" in Table 9.11 lists important
elements in the critical study of a crisis situation. While most of the information contained in a case study will also be in the public domain, corporate
counsel may want to supervise case study contemporaneous development.
The organization's legal position could be affected should the information
and its interpretation go to litigants through the discovery process.

Decide quickly, act fast, use uncommon sense

The repeated use of the word "promptly" in the BurgerMax analysis
should clearly convey the strategic importance of acting quickly. It is often
better to act quickly and make mistakes than to fail to act until it's too late
or the action becomes a meaningless gesture. In fact, solving problems and

"winning" in crisis situations is a function of speed, of decision-making, of action, of reaction, of collaboration, of swiftly applied uncommon sense. Timidity, hesitation, and decision resistance are the parents of defeat, humiliation, and embarrassing litigation.

Now, a few words about uncommon sense in crisis management communications. Uncommon sense in crisis management has five critical components detailed in Table 9.12.

Above all, avoid the infamous excuses that are dead giveaways that more serious questions lie below the surface of the crisis at hand, excuses like:

- "It's too soon to act." Why?

- "It's only competitor criticism." Do they have a point?

Table 9.12 Five critical components of uncommon sense in crisis communication management

- **Pre-authorization:** The single most important aspect of crisis planning and crisis strategy development is making decisions ahead of time so that speed of implementation is the only issue facing managers on the scene when a crisis occurs. And, implementation speed will not become an issue if there has been adequate preparation and simulation.

- **Conclusive action:** Most crises occur with incredible speed and leave enormous problems behind to resolve. Good crisis planning involves recognizing that no action an organization can take will have the response magnitude of the crisis itself. Therefore, effective responses to crisis are incremental in nature. Plan to emphasize positive, conclusive increments in the response process. Each of these increments ends with certainty a portion of the crisis has been resolved and limits its collateral damage.

- **Unassailable behavior:** Too often surprise begets embarrassment, which begets fear, which begets foolish behaviors, denial, and stalling. Executives who do or say foolish, challengeable things before, during, or after a crisis slow reputation rehabilitation. What is done should be done promptly and carefully. What is said should be brief, important, and worth being heard and repeated. There are no secrets in crisis situations. Everything comes out eventually.

- **Humane words and deeds from the start:** One of the great shortcomings in most managers is that they first appear cold, arrogant, unfeeling, and corporately driven when bad things happen and there are victims. These behavior perceptions are the source of employee anger and frustration; litigation; shareholder action; angry neighbors; and bad, embarrassing media coverage. Say you are sorry. Apologize continually. Help the victims no matter what. Treat everyone as though they were a member of your family. If you make them victims, or it appears that you did, they will be your problem to resolve until they no longer feel victimized.

- **Personalization:** Deal directly with victims and with those indirectly affected – customers, vendors, and employees. This approach reduces the power of opponents, the self-appointed outsiders, and the media. Control your own destiny. Act personally at the highest appropriate level. This puts responsibility for a solution and the opportunity for reputational rehabilitation where it belongs – with the organization that caused the problem.

- "It's caving into people or ideas we don't respect." But aren't you responsible anyway?

- "Our peers expect us to fight this." Do they really care?

- "It's just an isolated incident." Says who?

- "The standards are unreasonable or unachievable." By what standard?

- "We need more time." Haven't you had enough already?

- "Let's not over-react." Why don't you just act?

- "If we say something, people will find out." Are you afraid they'll discover the truth?

- "We obey the law." Why are you now in this jam?

- "We can't take responsibility; we'll be sued." Won't you be sued anyway?

- "Fast action will trigger copycats." Where's the evidence for this?

Using this approach will, to some degree, box in executives and attorneys who have never dealt with crisis before or who are stumbling over the conflict between what they know they should do and what they think the boss or shareholders expect. Disallowing these excuses closes off some of their verbal escape routes and prevents making critical, strategic, ethical, or untimely crisis management errors.

Understand the difference between crisis communication management and crisis management. Help management understand that bad news never improves with age. Fix it now.

Ultimately, management needs a competent, conclusive, straightforward, grand strategy that makes sense in a management context while addressing the various critical dimensions any crisis causes. The elements of such a grand strategy were referred to earlier in this chapter:

- Deal with the problem causing the crisis

- Assist the victims and those directly affected

- Communicate with and enlist the support of employees

- Inform those indirectly affected

- Affirmatively manage the media and other self-appointed outsiders.

PART IV
CRISIS COMMUNICATIONS STANDARDS AND PRINCIPLES

A *standard* is an authoritative set of rules and procedures for the measure of quantity, weight, extent, value, or quality. For crisis communication, the source authority for the standard is constituent expectation – usually the expectations of those most directly affected by the problem your organization has caused or is causing.

Principles are comprehensive, yet fundamental rules, laws, doctrines, or assumptions that guide behavior. Here again, in the matter of crisis communication management, the explanations that will be necessary and the understanding that must be achieved rapidly must be based on solid thinking, fundamentally sound approaches, and predetermined standards of conduct that are publicly acceptable. Standard-setting fundamental crisis communication principles are illustrated in Table 9.13.

Standard-setting crisis communication protocols

Further analysis of communication breakdowns between constituencies and businesses, employees and businesses, and neighbors and businesses reflects a lack of fundamental thinking about what recipients of corporate and organizational communications expect. It is really a combination of attitude, behaviors, and specific language. The protocols in Table 9.14 are designed to respond to constituents' expectations of effective communications.

Trust-busting behaviors and language to avoid

It is relatively easy to tell when an organization, or its leadership, is behaving in ways that will reduce credibility and cause additional reputational damage. The media and those who oppose tend to focus on corporate trust-busting behaviors and language, often killing any immediate hope of negotiation, mediation, or solution. While the media or the opposition are often blamed, the failing lies with those who use this approach in the mistaken belief that it is effective or will somehow avoid having to deal with issues and questions. The price is too high. Avoid it. Since there is a relatively limited range of these unwanted behaviors and language, it seems appropriate to place them here as protocols to avoid (Table 9.15). There are

Table 9.13 Standard-setting fundamental crisis management principles

Principle
1. **Communicate with those most directly affected first.** Our organization's first obligation is to the health, welfare, and safety of the people most directly affected, our employees, and the protection, restoration, and recovery of company operations. When events are unanticipated we will: ■ Respond quickly ■ Act conclusively ■ Take appropriate responsibility ■ Ask for help and understanding ■ Inform company employees immediately ■ Show concern ■ Strive for transparent decision-making, behavior, and results ■ Be open to suggestion ■ Explain to the community as soon as possible ■ Invite local officials to help with explanations, where appropriate ■ Seek out and talk to affected groups ■ Seek out and talk to affected agencies ■ Use simple, direct, positive messages ■ Stick to the facts and company policy ■ Use common sense ■ Be unassailable, unchallengeable
2. **Remember that local communication is best.** Communication should be handled as close to the site of impact or emergency as possible. Field operations and facility managers, rather than the public affairs staff at headquarters, should speak, unless company-wide effects are anticipated.
3. **Speak with one voice,** but not necessarily with a single spokesperson. Consistency, accuracy, and promptness are important goals in communication with the media, employees, local officials, and others. Although the spokesperson can be flexible in the way information is presented to different audiences, messages should be consistent. In field and plant emergencies, headquarters should remain in frequent contact to ensure that everyone has the same information and that spokespersons are saying the same things at each location.
4. **Act quickly in communicating news of any adverse incident.** The first hour or two are critical in getting the word out and setting the record. The media can broadcast a story across the country within seconds. If the coverage is based on facts our company has confirmed rather than on speculation by reporters, the news is likely to be more accurate and balanced. The first hour of emergency response is critical to establishing the perception of our ability to manage a crisis.
5. **Cooperate with the media.** Make every effort to respond promptly to press inquiries and provide appropriate assistance, after having dealt first with those most directly affected.

cont'd

Table 9.13 cont'd

Principle
6. **Make fundamentally sound decisions.** This involves simple but subjective criteria:
∎ How many raised eyebrows and shoulder shrugs does a decision cause among base audiences (and employees)?
∎ Does the decision fly in the face of questions that can be anticipated? Such questions might be:
– Why didn't you act sooner?
– What did you know about this?
– When did you know about this?
– How long have you known about this?
– Why didn't you tell us sooner?
– Why do you have to do it that way?
– Why did you wait until now to act?
– Why now?
– Is there no other way?
– How many alternatives have you looked at?
– Why do you have to make us fearful?
– How can we trust you now when we couldn't trust you before?
– What do you plan to do about it?
– What if your approach doesn't work?
∎ Is our approach merely based on love of our own technology, site, data, and habits rather than on community or specific constituent expectations?
7. **When the issue involves integrity or moral or ethical dilemmas, do the moral questioning quickly.** When the public's deepest values are offended, extraordinarily fast action is required. It demands the moral courage to ask tough questions immediately and a commitment (the strength of heart) powerful enough to take the most appropriate action promptly. It may be necessary to go to extremes as a matter of principle to counteract the negative impact of situations the public, employees, and other audiences find morally troublesome. Use a reasoning process based on moral questioning to move toward solution options. See Part II of this chapter.

Table 9.14 Responsive management protocols

1. **Responsiveness:** When problems occur we will be prepared to talk about them internally and externally as aggressively as we respond to them operationally.

2. **Openness:** If the public should know about a problem we have or are about to have, which could affect them or our credibility, we will voluntarily talk about it as quickly and as completely as we can, especially to those most directly affected.

3. **Concern:** When business problems occur, we will keep the communities and constituencies most directly affected posted on a schedule they set until the problem is thoroughly explained or resolved.

4. **Respect:** We will answer any question any constituent may have and suggest and volunteer additional information in the event they do not ask enough, or the right, questions. We will respect and seek to work with those who oppose us.

5. **Cooperation:** We will cooperate with the news media as far as possible, but our major responsibility is to communicate compassionately, completely, and directly with those most directly affected by our problems, as soon as possible.

6. **Responsibility:** Unless incapacitated or inappropriate, the senior operating executive on-site will be the spokesperson during emergencies and other significant events.

7. **Sensitivity:** At the earliest possible moment we will step back and analyze the impact of the problems we are having or causing. Our intention is to inform and/or alert all appropriate audiences.

8. **Integrity:** If we are at fault or there is the perception that we are, we will acknowledge the situation promptly, be empathetic, and explain our mistakes, if any, or the misperceptions as quickly as possible. We will be true to our corporate and personal consciences. Our conduct will be morally correct.

9. **Compassion:** We will always exhibit concern, empathy, sympathy, remorse, or contrition – whatever the case may require. We will use such words as: Alarmed; Appalled; Ashamed; Concerned; Disappointed; Embarrassed; Empathize; Failed/failure: Humiliated; Let you down; Mortified; Regret/regrettable; Sad/saddened; Shocked/surprised; Sorrowful/sorry; Sympathize/sympathetic: Tragic: Unfortunate; Unhappy; Unintended/unintentional; Unnecessary; Unsatisfactory.

cont'd

Table 9.14 cont'd

10. **Consent:** We will achieve consent based on viewing the issues from the perspective of our constituents. The process involves seven steps designed to alleviate community or constituency anguish, restore confidence, rebuild relationships, and reduce media coverage:
    - *Identify* constituent issues, questions, vulnerabilities, including those they may not recognize.
    - *Analyze/prioritize/link* issues to stakeholder segments including:
      - Voluntary impact; and
      - Involuntary impact.
    - Create a timeline of events and look for patterns.
    - *Build* stakeholders' opinions, attitudes, and misconceptions into the timeline.
    - Revise the timeline to realistically reflect stakeholder impact and concerns.
    - *Develop* a positive counteractive action/message strategy.
    - *Decide* to postpone or abandon efforts based on whether they are acceptable to stakeholders.

11. **Generosity:** We will find a way to go beyond what is expected or required, even to "do penance" where appropriate.

12. **Honesty:** We will learn from our mistakes, talk publicly about what we've learned, and renew our commitment to keeping errors, mistakes, and problems from re-occurring. Our goal is zero errors, zero defects, zero mistakes, zero crises.

Table 9.15 Trust-busting behaviors and language

1. **Aloofness:**
   - Wait to respond: "Maybe no one will notice."
   - Develop our own story: "They are uneducated and unsophisticated."
   - "It's only one or two hotheads."

2. **No Commitment:**
   - Refuse to talk; volunteer nothing. "Let them figure it out for themselves, like we had to."
   - Answer only if they get the question right.

3. **Delay:**
   - Stall responses.
   - Hire a big-time outside expert to do a study; report something next year (maybe).
   - "We can't talk until we know all the facts."

4. **Disdain:**
   - Avoid opponents; disparage them.
   - Belittle uneducated questions and people.

5. **Irritation:**
   - "They have no business being involved in this."
   - "Let's get the emotion out of it …; just stick to the facts."
   - "There is no news here, why do they care?"
   - "Be careful not to take responsibility."
   - "It's only an activist fund-raising technique."
   - "It's political."

6. **Stonewall:**
   - Have the lawyers convey our "no comment."
   - "Not to my knowledge."
   - "Talk to the lawyers."

7. **Hunker down:**
   - "Anything we learn will be saved for litigation."

   - "We'll talk only as a litigation prevention strategy."
   - "If they can't get it right, we don't and won't have to talk to them."

8. **Arrogance:**
   - No apology; no admission; no empathy.
   - "Up yours."
   - "Butt-out."

9. **Reticence:**
   - "We must not set a precedent."
   - "Let's not get all emotional about this. Stick to the facts." "It will probably go away by itself."

10. **Avoidance:**
    - "Offer them 10 percent less than they need; that way they'll have to turn it down."
    - Let them sue. We'll investigate, stall, and pay as little as possible much later on, if ever."
    - "They don't deserve this much attention."

11. **Abstention:**
    - "Our mistakes are our business. Accidents happen; everything in life carries some risk."
    - "Zero is impossible."
    - "We'll do the best we can and that will just have to do."

12. **Defensive threats:**
    - "There aren't even any standards to cover this, so how can you expect us to comply?"
    - "We can't make a decision until the data is complete."
    - "You don't understand why this process is important."
    - "This is the only way this can be done!"
    - "If you don't leave us alone, we'll take our jobs, industry, and payroll elsewhere."

12 categories of trust-busting behaviors and language. They are almost exact opposites of the standards and protocols shown in Table 9.14.

Summary and conclusions

The vast majority of all true crises are the result of day-to-day operations of businesses and organizations. This means that with appropriate attention, analysis, and action, the vast majority of crises that occur can be recognized and prevented. First, there has to be operational interest in prevention. Then, there has to be competent staff assistance to capitalize on the opportunity to prevent crisis situations when the management interest is present or can be generated.

There is a far smaller but much more devastating potential for crises from non-operating situations. These, by and large, are not preventable. In our experience, the most crucial part of crisis planning and prevention comes in identifying and preparing to mitigate those events that are non-operational in nature and, therefore, where management and employees are likely to have the lowest level of preparation, knowledge, and information.

As businesses and large organizations continue to globalize, preparation for managing crises and adverse situations must increasingly take on an international context.

Because worldwide news coverage has become American-style news coverage, organizations operating outside the United States, which suffer incidents and situations that gain substantial negative visibility, will be subjected to responding as though the incident occurred in the United States.

The Firestone recall is global. The collateral damage caused will be calculated for a long time:

■ The Ford Motor Company has closed several plants to free up tires for replacement

■ Disposing of millions of used tires, now hazardous waste

■ Anger and frustration by customers who are having difficulty getting replacement tires

■ The potential for more tire-related deaths as the recalls drag out

■ Overcoming revelations of recalls preceding action in the United States

■ The deaths of dozens of people in many countries

■ Inability to overcome inter-company cultures to act appropriately, promptly.

As you follow this story and its litigation in the months ahead, or look back on it from some time in the future, outline the events of the product problem in timeline fashion as illustrated in this chapter. This approach will yield a fascinating and powerful series of management communication lessons, which can then help other organizations avoid or minimize the damage done by a similar future circumstance.

As this situation unfolds, matures, and then concludes, analyze it against the dimensions of strategic crisis response. What are the operational issues and questions? What are the moral and ethical dilemmas? What do victims and those indirectly affected expect? Is there stalling, blameshifting, management by whining around? Who is taking positive, affirmative, prompt action to resolve the situation with those most directly affected?

Companies, large organizations, and governments will continue to make mistakes as they always have. What is changing are the level, speed, scope, and duration of exposure when these problems occur.

Virtually every aspect of crisis management is predictable and can be prepared for. There are no surprise questions in crisis, only inadequately prepared organizations and companies.

Successful crisis communication management depends on adequate visibility analysis and crucial vulnerability identification; aggressive hypothesizing and scenario development; pre-authorization of appropriate decisions and actions; empathy; and prompt, decisive, conclusive action.

Editor's note: Readers may leave comments, discuss or question information in this chapter directly with the author via e-mail at jel@e911.com. To read related articles, monographs, and newsletters by the author, please visit his website at www.e911.com.

Take-over and merger: the jaws mentality

richard j. varey

ILLUSTRATION

Stakeholders Communicate

In November 1999 Vodafone AirTouch (the largest FTSE 100 corporation by market capitalization following a merger of Vodafone and Airtouch in January 1999, and a partnership agreement with Bell Atlantic in the U.S.) announced its intention to make a "friendly" $106 billion take-over bid for Mannesmann AG to make them "natural partners." This was to be the largest unsolicited take-over offer made in the European Union to date. The corporations had already been in "synergy discussions" since Summer 1999. They had an agreement not to compete in Germany and a mobile phone partnership in Germany, France, and Italy. As Mannesmann had provocatively acquired Orange plc in October for $36 billion, the take-over was inevitable. When the Mannesmann executive managers refused to consider the bid, claiming that it was "extremely unattractive" to their shareholders because the price was too low and their respective strategic plans were incompatible, Vodafone directed its offer to Mannesmann shareholders.

Vodafone CEO Chris Gent published an "open letter" to the Mannesmann workforce in all of the leading German daily newspapers assuring them that a merger would not result in job losses and that all rights of employees and trade unions would be fully recognized, despite the fact that Vodafone did not recognize any trade union to represent its staff in the U.K. He then met with employee representatives, resulting in full acceptance of their principle of co-determination through a joint supervisory board. Meanwhile, French telecom group Vivendi was approached by Mannesmann as a potential "white knight" to ward off Vodafone. The proposed merger fell through. Then Vodafone announced a deal with Vivendi for an Internet joint venture that was conditional upon success of the proposed Mannesmann take-over.

Telephone calls to shareholders by Mannesmann managers indicated that at least 45 percent planned to accept the Vodafone offer. As it became clear that the hostile take-over might succeed, Mannesmann senior managers changed

---

ILLUSTRATION (cont'd)

their strategy and agreed to negotiate the terms of a "friendly" or "polite" take-over. Finally, in January 2000, a deal was agreed that provided an improved share exchange value (at almost twice the price originally offered – $204 billion) and defined terms for integration and future strategic development. The take-over produced a combined $350 billion market valuation.

The corporate culture of Mannesmann is not very international. How will post-acquisition integration proceed? Vodafone AirTouch is now the 25th largest corporation in the world!

Source: Author.

Introduction

The business of merging or acquiring businesses has at least a 120-year history and notably provides rich pickings for lawyers, accountants, and public relations specialists. *The Wall Street Journal*, the *Financial Times* and other business and financial journals feature merger and acquisition stories almost on a daily basis. Yet, there remains great ambiguity in terms of the usefulness, cost, and justification for such business reorganization.

In recent years, we have entered an era of "mega-mergers" that provide a further spurt of growth even for mature businesses. Witness BP–Amoco, Compaq–Digital, Bell Atlantic–GTE, Zeneca–Astra, Ford–Volvo, for example. Big business merger and take-over is a burgeoning big business. In 1989, the Kohlberg Kravis & Roberts acquisition of RJR Nabisco Inc. for $25.1 billion was the biggest deal in corporate history. By 1998, the BP-Amoco deal was finalized as the largest EU acquisition at $48.2 billion, and Exxon-Mobil became the largest U.S. deal at $86.3 billion.

Why do so many mergers and take-over attempts take place when the evidence from several significant studies is that the outcomes are disappointing, if not disastrous? In terms of shareholder value (often the primary motivator), for example, to date no merger of drug producers has produced a real increase in productivity (Cookson, 2000). Maybe it is simply a macho manager thing! If competitors grow, managers sense a loss of weight in scope and scale that may result in encroachment. The financial markets fuel these restructuring moves by reacting positively to dramatic action. For example, Wall Street raised the combined market value of Travelers and Citicorp by $30 billion in a single day. Local disruptions in trading performance are felt less by large companies. Of course, we should not forget that managers get increased share options and bigger salaries when their responsibilities increase following a merger or acquisition.

Mergers strengthen competitiveness by building larger and stronger units, driven by a desire for size, or a belief in diversification, or for internationalization and the pursuit of global brands. Intended outcomes may be consolidation (cost saving), or increased market access (for example, in the food and drink industry, Guinness bought Bell's, Argyll bought Distillers, and Elders bought Allied-Lyons in the mid 1980s). Acquisition provides an opportunity for corporate regeneration through escape from a mature business. Such competitive moves benefit the shareholders of the acquiring company, but are an easy way of avoiding the necessity for foresight and of finding alternative ways to deploy existing capabilities. There are, obvious to even the casual observer, problems of cultural integration and policy harmonization. The acquirer pays for the critical skills and resources wanted, as well as for those already possessed or less strategically valuable. Acquisitions may help managers to cover up poor growth in the core business, however studies show that acquisitions destroy shareholder wealth more often than they create it (Hamel and Prahalad, 1994). The U.K. chemical industry is increasingly adopting merger and acquisition as a strategy for restructuring to counter the prevailing poor public image of the industry and companies.

Several theories have been posited to explain merger and acquisition forces. These are summarized in Table 10.1.

From these explanations, at least two major stances can be identified. The Predator seeks "to merge" (imposed M&A) in the seduction of shareholders in picking off weak, badly managed business units – as the superordinate party, this corporation has a strong share price while the subordinate party has a weak share price and is thus clearly vulnerable to a hostile purchase bid. Corporate predators buy big businesses and make them smaller! Hanson Group has, for many years, been a good example of an asset stripper who buys enfeebled businesses to sell off property and machinery for cash, and reduce top layers of management and the labor force to make cost savings. The Partner, on the other hand, enters courtship (negotiated M&A) to build larger and stronger business units through a merger of equals. Acquisition can bring survival or protection. In the globalized pharmaceuticals industry, for example, size matters for both marketing and R&D capabilities.

Clearly, there are some interesting stories to tell, especially for those being merged! Yet, surprisingly, there is no huge body of literature giving

Table 10.1 Theoretical explanations for merger and acquisition	
Managerial efficiency differential	Efficiency improvement is gained from related mergers
Managerial failure	Inefficient and ineffective management is replaced
Operating synergy	Economies of scale and scope – complementary capabilities
Financial synergy	Availability of investment and complementarity of internal cash flows, with lower cost of capital and lower risk
Pure diversification	Investment risks are reduced – knowledge and reputation are transferred
Strategic alignment to changing environment	Size and capabilities for faster adaptation
Under-valuation	Market value does not reflect true or potential value
Signaling	The offer causes the market to revalue share stock, or managers to implement a more effective strategy
Agency and managerialism	The last resort in gaining control over opportunistic or over-optimistic businesses – assumes conflict of interest between shareholders and senior managers
Market power	Increased concentration and monopoly effects
Redistribution of wealth	Some stockholders gain from the loss of others

specific advice and evidence of the impact of managed communication – although a number of roles can be identified for corporate communication management and the professional manager of communication in preventative and active measures. These will be examined following a discussion of culture and communication.

Issues of culture in mergers and acquisitions

Culture is a complex phenomenon built on many dimensions. Within one single organization there exist many different cultures due to differences in ethnicity, gender or nationality of members. Shared values, shared beliefs, shared meaning, shared understanding, and shared sense-making are all different ways of describing culture, according to Morgan (1997). Corporate culture can be a powerful determinant of behavior when employees share a common belief of how to do certain things around the company.

Organizational cultures can be very different. This dissimilarity can lead to conflicts manifest in different work legislation, language, working practices, company procedures, management styles, and employee attitudes. The greater the cultural differences and the higher the degree of socio-cultural integration desired by the acquirers, the more people will be affected by the cultural changes and therefore, the greater the potential for problems (Hubbard, 1999). Haspelagh and Jemison (1991) identify absorption (unitary), preservation (dual), and symbiosis (interdependent autonomy) as degrees of post-merger integration.

On a political level, culture relates to the distribution of power throughout the organization and the dominant managerial styles of decision-making. From this point of view, corporate cultures locate on a continuum from dictatorial at one extreme, to one of total employee empowerment on the other. The likelihood of true cultural compatibility depends on where each company's culture is located on the cultural control continuum.

On an emotional level, corporate culture is defined as the collective thoughts, habits, attitudes and patterns of behavior from the employee's individual perspective. Managers try to establish the framework of corporate culture by laying down the parameters of employee behavior, preparing cultural guidelines that dictate the employee's day-to-day activities and behavior. Yet, the defining traits of corporate culture are established over a period of time, as a result of the synthesis of personalities and environmental influences.

Organizational identity derives from subcultures. Albert and Whetten (1985) claim that organizational identity is important "when an organization is formed or when there is a major change to the continuity of the goals of the organization or when the means of accomplishment are hindered or broken." Organizational identity is a subset of the collective beliefs that establish an organization's culture. Dutton et al. (1994) claim that the individual aspect of organizational identity is concerned with what individual members think and feel about the organization to which they belong. From the collective viewpoint, organizational identity refers to the degree to which feelings and thoughts about the distinctive characteristics are shared among the members (Dutton and Dukerich, 1991). Chatman et al. (1986) make a similar point:

> When we look at individual behavior in organizations, we are actually seeing two entities: the individual as himself and the individual as representative of his collectivity ... Thus, the individual not only acts on behalf of the organization in the usual agency sense, but he also acts, more subtly, "as the organization" when he embodies the values, beliefs and goals of the collectivity.

	Integration	Differentiation	Ambiguity
Consensus	Organization-wide consensus	Subcultural consensus	No consensus (Multiple views)
Consistency	Consistency	Inconsistency	Complexity (Not clearly consistent or inconsistent)
Clarity	Exclude ambiguity	Channel ambiguity outside subcultures	Focus on ambiguity
Metaphors	Clearing in jungle	Islands of clarity in sea of ambiguity	Web, jungle

Table 10.2 Three perspectives on organizational culture

Source: Martin and Meyerson (1991) cited in Choo, 1998.

Brown and Starkey (1994) observe that a collective cultural identity founded on shared understandings may co-exist with cleavage, tension and disagreement. While some beliefs and values may be pervasive within the organization, others may be held only by certain subcultural groups. These subcultures may be radically different from each other and they may also compete with each other for status, power and resources, thereby increasing political tension in an organization. An organizational culture rarely has values and assumptions that are shared by all organizational members. Instead it may consist of different subcultures that may have quite conflicting assumptions about reality.

Martin and Meyerson (1991) suggest three perspectives for the study of corporate culture: the integration perspective, the differentiation perspective, and the ambiguity perspective. Table 10.2 summarizes the main features.

The integration perspective assumes that to reach the best outcome from an acquisition, the two companies should be forced into one homogeneous culture. The acquired company is usually forced into the acquiring company's culture. Both firms are viewed as being very similar in culture, and thus it is believed that the merger will work without friction when the differing cultures are integrated into a mutual corporate culture (Risberg, 1997). This perspective is illustrated in Figure 10.1.

However, in spite of perceived similarities, there are always differences between two cultures, but these are often denied and may subsequently cause obstructions in the cooperation between the two companies. Such denial of differences and ambiguities will probably lead to unsolved difficulties. It is usually the top management group that force the two companies to

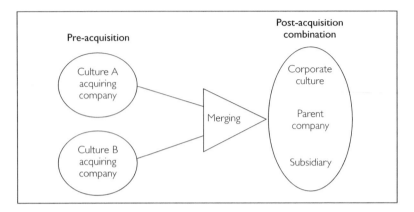

Figure 10.1 Acquisitions viewed from the integration perspective
Source: Risberg, 1997.

become one with an (apparently) homogeneous culture. They deny the cultural differences because they do not want to face the ambiguities that may occur because of these differences. However, overcoming problems during an acquisition requires that cultural differences are acknowledged.

From the differentiation perspective, the underlying assumption is that organizations consist of subcultures based on differences in power, interest areas, and work or professional practices. The defining features of this view are that consensus exists only within subcultures and clarity is maintained within subcultures while ambiguity is channeled outward (Choo, 1998). Note here that ambiguity is not denied. This approach stresses subcultures and the differences between them, for instance the difference between marketing culture and engineering culture. Each of the merging companies represents one homogeneous culture. This perspective emphasizes the inconsistency and lack of consensus in the corporate culture and views culture as either harmonious or conflicting (Martin and Meyerson, 1991). Figure 10.2 depicts the differentiation perspective.

The ambiguity perspective considers that there is no organization-wide or subcultural consensus and that any local consensus is temporary and limited to particular issues (Choo, 1998). Cultural manifestations are not clearly consistent or clearly inconsistent with each other. The corporate culture is viewed as fragmented, consisting of many subcultures with both different and shared values. When the two corporate cultures meet, the ambiguity is acknowledged and it is sometimes even made the focus of attention. The culture is neither in harmony nor in conflict. Instead, members share some views, disagree about some, and are ignorant of others. Figure 10.3 illustrates the ambiguity perspective.

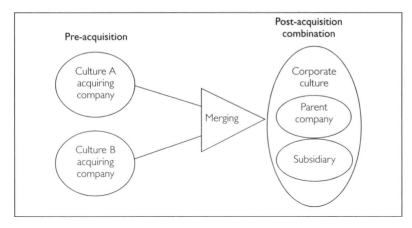

Figure 10.2 Aquisitions viewed from the
differentiation perspective
Source: Risberg, 1997.

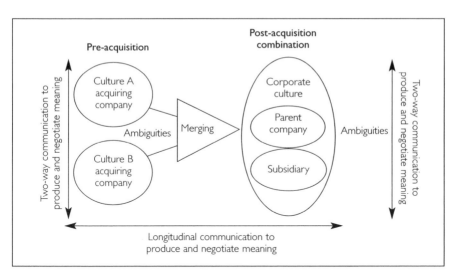

Figure 10.3 Acquisitions viewed from the ambiguity perspective

Note that in this third example the acquired company is not forced to
adapt fully to the parent company. It is, instead, allowed to maintain its
differences within the framework of an overall corporate culture (Risberg,
1997). Cultural differences must not always be seen as something negative
to the acquisition. To make two cultures work together, the solution should
not always be to try and homogenize them, but to acknowledge the ambiguity in values and assumptions.

Bridging cultural gaps

"Ensuring cultural fit is central to a successful corporate combination. In fact the proverbial 'culture clash' has marked the demise of countless mergers and acquisitions. Unfortunately, many people do not know how to identify the characteristics that make up a company's culture – and what factors may ultimately lead to culture clash" (Clemente and Greenspan, 1999). It is necessary to achieve cultural fit if the organization wants to follow a strategy that is not compatible with its current mindset. As Johnson and Scholes (1989) state, one of the difficulties in blending two corporate cultures is that each sees the world through its own cultural filter. They refer to this as "familiarity blindness." For instance, if everyone in a group seems averse to risk, then it will appear to the group that the entire world shares their perspective.

Raynaud and Teasdale (1992) observe that the combination of the distinct cultures is a frustrating task, and is further complicated if the merging companies have been hostile competitors prior to the acquisition. According to Rankine (1998), the wider the cultural gap between the two organizations, the more difficult and challenging the implementation of change and integration. Bicultural audits can be used as a means of bridging the corporate culture gaps. The bicultural audit examines the compatibility of the organizational philosophy, structure, communication and information networks, and management approach of the merged company with its objectives. It is a three-phase process used to neutralize post-alliance culture shock. The stages of the bicultural audit are as follows (Raynaud and Teasdale, 1992):

Culture gap identification – gaps in perception of vision, values, structure, management practices and behaviors are identified using questionnaires and interviews.

Culture gap analysis – data obtained through the culture gap identification process are analyzed to highlight the inconsistencies that might weaken the alliance.

Culture bridging – work teams are built to negotiate ways of bridging the gaps. They formulate proposals for corporate restructuring, choose the appropriate management techniques, strengthen internal communication links, and get agreement on a shared list of values, expected behaviors, and performance criteria that will serve as the basis for performance evaluation.

The issue of culture in mergers and acquisitions is one that has extensive ramifications. There is no one right way of bringing together or bridging the gap between cultures. Irrespective, however, of senior management wishes in relation to integration, differentiation, or ambiguity (and living with these variants), there are numerous communication issues to be considered. We address these in the next section.

Communicating change

"To be acquired by another company is often a frightening experience for staff members involved. Both, the present, and the future become risky, uncertain, and ambiguous" (Risberg, 1997). Communication has a vital role in the transformations brought on by the change process as well as in just managing the day-to-day business. Communication, according to Hubbard (1999), is a crucial element of the merger or acquisition process.

Organizational members need to understand what is happening for themselves. The main medium of sense-making is communication. In the turmoil caused by the merger or acquisition, employees often display resistance to change. Managed communication can support employees in becoming less resistant to change. Further, in the absence of information, members engage in rumor, gossip, and storytelling.

But, care is needed. More communication is not always better communication. Communication is interpreted differently by different people. The hedron communication triangle is a simple model of communication that considers communication in its broader sense (Figure 10.4). The hierarchy builds up from a base of the most common view of communication, that is information. The middle of the hierarchy is inter-personal communication, used as a means of affecting people's behavior and attitudes. The top of the triangle is symbolic communication using decisions, policies and procedures (Shepherd, 1997).

As Varey (2000a) states, communication is usually understood as "getting your message across," "sharing ideas," or "informing." It is taken to be the transmission of information and the reproduction of intended meaning (Varey, 2000b). Most writers consider communication as infor-mational. Brown and Starkey (1994) view the organization as a "meanings system" and "information processor." Following the same tradition, Daft and Weick (1984) view organizations as complex interpretive systems that use environmental information to make strategic business decisions. Thayer (1997), on the other hand, suggests that the issue in communi-cation is not information but something like minding. Similarly, Weick

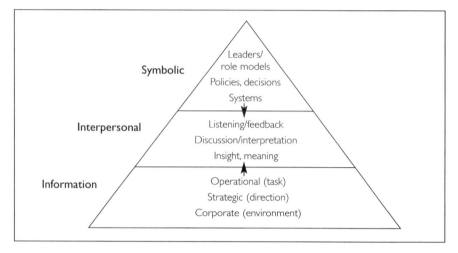

Figure 10.4 The hedron communication triangle – a
hierarchy of internal communication
Source: Shepherd, 1997.

(1995) identifies the alternative conception of communication as a
common construction of meaning.

However Daymon (2000) has stated that:

> The notion that communication is a series of informative messages transferred
> from senders through channels or networks of relationships to receivers over-
> looks the fact that communication exists within a cultural context. It is this
> context which provides meaning to messages.

In other words, cultural norms act as a lens, distorting how communicators
perceive, interpret, and judge all forms of communication. This view is
explained in the ladder of inference illustrated in Figure 10.5.

The ladder starts from the observation of an event. As people observe,
they start to select data to think about. Although the same event is
observed, data selected by each person are dissimilar. It is culture that
determines how observers select what to notice. As progress is made up
the ladder, the divergence increases as the effect of culture builds. Then
observers add meaning to the data selected. This meaning is determined by
how the data selected fit into the context of the observer's world. Based on
the meanings added, the observer makes assumptions about the situation,
the people involved and the words spoken. Finally, conclusions are drawn.
The result is that a new belief is formed, an old belief is reinforced or an
existing belief is changed. Certain actions are taken based on the belief.

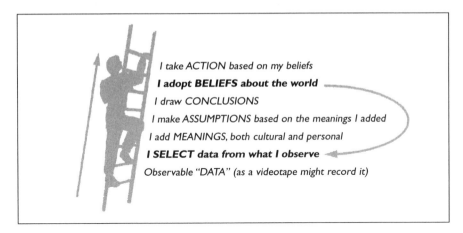

I take ACTION based on my beliefs

I adopt BELIEFS about the world

I draw CONCLUSIONS

I make ASSUMPTIONS based on the meanings I added

I add MEANINGS, both cultural and personal

I SELECT data from what I observe

Observable "DATA" (as a videotape might record it)

Figure 10.5 The ladder of inference
Source: Shepherd, 1997, based on Argyris, 1982.

Beliefs also affect the filters through which data are selected, in a reflexive loop (Shepherd, 1997).

Daymon (2000) further stresses the link between culture and communication stating that culture acts as a guide and a filter for how individuals understand the utterances they hear and speak. Organization members use the shared language, beliefs, and values of their organizational culture in trying to make sense of new events or ongoing experiences and they act according to their understandings. Their former understandings and assumptions are confirmed or adjusted as they gain new knowledge and understanding about their work realities and as they introduce insights from their experiences outside the organization. Communication activities, which are shaped by the cultural patterns, balance the possibilities of culture with the desires of the members. In this perspective, communication is not merely a transmission of information, but is a dynamic process of meaning-making, which shapes the contexts in which people work. Communication and culture are thus interlinked, the cultural context giving meaning to communication.

Given that groups and members have different beliefs, values and histories, developing a set of shared meanings usually requires resolving the tension between wishing to follow one's beliefs on the one hand and building consensus by including other points of view on the other. Feelings of doubt and stress are induced when the available information does not harmonize with the individual's expectations. Communication behaviors can help relieve tension between self-values and shared consensus (Choo, 1998).

The different cultures in the acquisition must understand each other. Schein (1993) advocates that communication over cultural boundaries may facilitate the understanding of each other's culture. If the other culture is understood, it can more easily be accepted. Therefore, communication can help the acknowledgement of multiple cultures within an organization and facilitate cooperation among the cultures (Risberg, 1997).

When the acquiring and target company managers enter into negotiations, they have certain expectations about the purpose of the acquisition, future performance levels, and the timing of particular actions. During the negotiations, the possibility of disagreement is high and managers often agree to disagree until later. Through this, they manage to keep the deal on track. However, as time passes, the ambiguity that was essential to reaching an agreement previously causes conflict and difficulty. The parties must eventually clarify the parts of the agreement left ambiguous before (Haspeslagh and Jemison, 1991).

Ambiguity and uncertainty can easily occur in cross-cultural acquisitions because of difficulties in communication (Risberg, 1997). As Choo (1998) points out, when ambiguity is excessively high, organizational members lack a clear and stable frame of reference within which their work and behavior have meaning and purpose. Managers and others should use rich information channels such as face-to-face discussions when they are dealing with ambiguous, complex, or conflict-laden situations. In other words, they should employ rich media to talk about the environment and to negotiate an understanding.

Ambiguity occurs in an organization when there is no clear interpretation of a phenomenon (Feldman, 1991). People can experience different types of ambiguity at different times. Many researchers define ambiguity as the lack of information (Risberg, 1997). Frost et al. (1991) claim that ambiguity can be decreased by providing more information, in other words, communicated information can be used as a way to produce and negotiate meaning for the individuals involved and to reduce the uncertainties and ambiguities. However, Risberg (1997) suggests that if communication is used to homogenize the different cultures with no consideration of multiculturalism, then this may give rise to uncertainty and ambiguity.

Communication management

Hubbard (1999) advocates that communication management as part of the overall acquisition strategy is important for four basic reasons: to maximize the likelihood of successful communication on the day of announcement; to cope with the necessity of increased information; to coordinate internal and external messages; and, to allow for contingency planning if leaks of negotiations or the deal occur.

As Rankine (1998) states, the communication strategy should be designed around a careful consideration of three factors:

- The audiences who will receive the message, taking their style, expectations and fears into account

- The message to be delivered, promoting the core values of the acquiring company and the position of the acquired company under new ownership

- How the message will be delivered (the media that will be used).

Mergers and acquisitions often cause the employees of both companies to feel uncertain, anxious, and worried about their futures. If the companies do not recognize what the business implications of these emotions are, the results can be rampant rumors, low morale, loss of valued employees and decreasing profits; signals for failure. However, many of the problems can be dealt with in advance if management creates and implements an effective plan for communicating the facts to all affected audiences, which are mainly the employees, labor unions, customers, vendors, and the business and general press (Berk, 1996).

An effective merger communication plan begins by identifying all the major audiences to be reached, focusing on the concerns of each audience, and drafting position statements to address these concerns. "Each audience has its own interests, and in the absence of information communicated by the companies, people will suspect the worst" (Berk, 1996, p. 31). Employees usually tend to attend to information which reinforces their worst fears, without considering the validity of the source (Cartwright and Cooper, 1992).

In the confusion caused by the acquisition, workers' anxieties produce many unanswered questions. If management neglects communicating with employees about the acquisition, or the communication is ambiguous, instead of getting information from informed parties, workers will try to reduce the ambiguity by providing answers themselves and will listen to rumors, which often have the effect of adding fuel to the workers' anxiety rather than reducing it. Rumors will most probably provide the employees with "worst scenario" answers (Risberg, 1997). If the questions and the concerns of employees are not acknowledged, they will jump to extreme and inaccurate conclusions, observed Berk (1996):

> Once the rumor mill gains control, speculation rather than rational management defines the terms and dictates the agenda. The management that defensively denies something that everybody knows is in trouble.

The sense of chaos and the ill will that result when employees learn about their company's actions from the mass media rather than from management must not be underestimated. The communication plan must be put into action as soon as the deal is signed to ensure that employees and other important stakeholders hear the news from the acquirer before they hear it on the radio, see it on television, or read about it in their newspapers (Rankine, 1998).

Communicating with the employees as soon as possible is the only way to deal with their anxiety. Cartwright and Cooper (1992) state that in order to dispel rumors and reduce uncertainty, organizations should not use ambiguous language and jargon particular to their own organization. A specific group of individuals should be assigned to handle merger or acquisition related communication. As Hubbard (1999) states, timely and accurate communication during times of change helps to keep negative rumor spreading to a minimum. The earlier the managers communicate about the change, the more successful they will be in reducing uncertainty.

Dialogue is a way to tackle the misunderstandings in the new organization. Focus groups can be set up to give feedback to senior executives on the implementation and acceptance of change. Survey techniques can be used to check the extent to which change processes are being followed, understood, or welcomed.

Hunger and Wheelan (1993) consider good communication throughout the organization as a prerequisite for successful cultural change. Gordon (1985) suggests that to achieve a successful change the following should be communicated to all organizational members:

- the current performance and position of the organization in comparison with its competitors
- the objectives of the organization
- the progress the organization has made in achieving the elements identified previously as important
- the outlook for the future.

The focus of this communication is internal and is managed through training and development programs. However, this level of communication activity should also occur throughout the stakeholder network, especially when the network may be de-stabilized because of environmental turbulence.

The allocation of sufficient time is a prerequisite for effective communication. The person in charge of communication should not be brought in the day before the announcement. Since there are several tasks to be accomplished, weeks or months are needed to prepare an effective program. The corporate communication person representing the acquiring company should have enough time – at a minimum at least 10 days to two weeks – to develop plans, draft statements, letters, announcements, and speeches – in order to be ready to implement the strategy immediately when the deal is announced (Berk, 1996).

A statement explaining the new situation should be given to the media. This statement should be used as a benchmark for consistency, being the foundation on which the internal communication program is based. It should contain quotes from the CEOs of both firms, carrying the message that both view the merger positively. It is critical that the stories communicated are consistent with each other. If different stories are being told to different parties and these stories are then being communicated to the media, management provokes controversy and the appearance of misleading people.

Assuming the merger or acquisition does take place, it is vital that internal communication is effective from the moment the contract is signed. For example, after its successful hostile bid for Century Oils, Fuchs, the German oil group, made no satisfactory employee communication for six months. As a result, morale collapsed, key employees left the company, and the target's performance had still not met expectations five years after the acquisition (Rankine, 1998).

Different audiences need to receive distinct messages often by different channels of communication. Using more than one channel of communication for important messages is a way to ensure that the messages get through. For instance, a combination of spoken and written communication, such as team briefings and bulletin board releases, is generally effective. Time and cost considerations also necessitate the use of different kinds of media (Hubbard, 1999).

Choo (1998) suggests that communication transactions that can overcome different frames of reference or clarify ambiguous issues to change understanding in a timely manner are considered "rich." Those transactions that need a long time to enable understanding or that cannot overcome different perspectives are lower in richness. Rich information media use multiple cues, feedback, and language variety. Face-to-face meetings are the richest information medium as they use all of these three elements.

The message to be delivered is a determinant of the complexity of the necessary communication plan (Hubbard, 1999). If there are mixed messages affecting a large number of employees and the information to be delivered is sensitive, the plan will clearly be complicated. The number of the audiences, the number and complexity of the messages, and the amount of time and resources the organization has all affect the extent of the managed communication program. For instance, if time and resources are limited, key customers may receive more information via several media sources than the smaller customers.

Management has a collective responsibility to communicate with the audiences. In other words, responsibility for the communication program cannot be given to only one person. One of the new management teams can be given the specific role of coordinating the design and implementing the communication process. In a merger of equals, the communication directors of the target company and the acquiring company should be involved in the communication management process at the same time. If the communication director of the target company is not involved in the process until the end, then the communication director of the acquiring firm will (try to) second-guess and anticipate the audiences and needs of the target company. This is less effective than having the most knowledgeable person do the job.

Despite being grounded in "principles of excellent communication," communication strategies often lead to misunderstandings and even resistance in the organizations (Daymon, 2000). Problems in communication management arise from the tendency to concentrate solely on the structure of communication. The tacit dimension of communication, that is the cultural context, is not taken into consideration. Employees are considered to be fairly passive receptors of communication. The fact that messages may lead to ambiguity, resistance, or compliance, despite their clarity and appropriate communication channels, is overlooked.

For effective communication management, it is necessary to recognize the complexity of the organizational context through which internally or externally directed communication emerges since this directly relates to how information is conveyed and interpreted. Using more than one perspective simultaneously offers a more comprehensive illustration of the process of communication and managing communication. By this way, attention is directed to both objective and subjective aspects. The objective aspect is the rational dimension such as the types and roles of communication connections between individuals, the methods of communicating, and their subsequent effectiveness. The subjective aspect is how and why events and messages are interpreted individually and collectively, and what this means for the manner in which members communicate. Daymon (2000) makes it clear that if:

> researchers and managers are to both practise and understand communication management in a meaningful way, they need to strive to interpret other points of view, other sets of values different from their own, other ways of making sense of communication activities.

The responsibility of the communication director

The senior communication professionals have a role as part of a merger and acquisition (M&A) core group that specializes in managing acquisitions, mergers, alliances, and partnerships. No single person can be expected to take on the total responsibility, and a collective responsibility of communicating with stakeholders makes far more sense. Perhaps what is required, however, is an overall corporate communication steward or czar who ensures the systematic strategic design of, and coordinates, the special communication program or programs that are essential.

Thus the communication management task is not simply technical in catalyzing and coordinating the design and production of activities and materials. There is also a much more significant strategic imperative for ensuring that members of the M&A group take into account the communication needs of all of the significant stakeholders, and that suitably inclusive and robust systems for communicating are efficiently operating.

The M&A situations in which managed communication is vital

We can identify certain high priority communication objectives that are specific to a particular situation.

In initiating relationships with prospective partners: in protecting against hostile moves, defensive tactics are twofold. Preventative measures may be taken to reduce the likelihood of a successful hostile take-over, while active measures are used after a hostile take-over has been attempted.

In launching a take-over bid: setting the stage in making the vision of the new combined business public, with one person in charge of communication, having decided how much attention is desirable, and planning for that. The acquirers' values have to be made clear by communicating around a core theme with all stakeholders, ensuring that all are reached in a timely fashion to answer the questions "what is going to happen to me?"; and "what are the benefits?" Counseling is needed in the process of courtship, bid preparation, and private talks for the purpose of negotiation. Tendering an offer to executives and/or shareholders. Informing city analysts and dealers before employees, in accordance with local regulations for M&A. Informing and counseling the decision-makers.

In managing partnership and integration in merger: support preparation for take-over through the creation and publication of an integration process. Merger, suggests Coulter (1996) is a "planned crisis." He likens a merger to a crisis because both require an immediate, coordinated corporate communication program under time pressure. Mounting rumors are picked up by journalists and news reporters, quickly focusing (at least potentially) huge media attention on the corporations. Senior executives come under pressure as just at the time that they become heavily committed to intense negotiations and planning, they are called upon to make key communication decisions and, perhaps, to communicate personally with the inside and outside world. The merger, of course, also disrupts normal business operations as employees anxiously await news. In all of this, the risk is that the corporation's message is lost as other interested parties speak out and ask questions about the changes and their underlying reasons and the motivation of the actors. Recognize post-merger stress to facilitate the grieving process (Suss, 1996) in establishing the new culture and managing sensitively for the survivors. Celebrate the change. When altering the corporate identity – BP Amoco, for example – the combination of two different corporate cultures and identities to form a single global business network requires conceiving of corporate identity as the collective self and organization as collective action. Crucially, the management information and communication infrastructure of the acquired corporation has to be matched with that of the acquirer.

In defending against predatory attack: when the corporation becomes subject to a contested bid, there must be clear objectives in a defense plan for resisting seduction or aggression resulting from an offer being spurned. Support must be gained from key stakeholders (such as the local community and legislators, as well as shareholders) for the corporation to retain independence – the value to stakeholders of the proposed restructuring has to be strongly questioned, the bid has to be discredited (but actions may be scrutinized by regulators, so legality must be ensured).

For example, facilitation of the responses during a proxy fight process means clearly focusing on your relationships with investors. Well-managed high performance communication systems strengthen the business and protect against enfeebling – the corporate communication systems have to be responsive and responsible. Antagonist actions present a threat that puts the corporation into the limelight where positive image in the press – through active corporate communication – is critical. Take-over battles have to be treated as a form of crisis that has to be managed within a short timescale – judgment and planning have to be compressed, yet still be effective. Investor Relations is often the responsibility of the chief finance officer, but take-over, when treated as a crisis, requires attention to a much wider range of stakeholder interests, thus justifying the central role of the corporate communication czar in close liaison with CEO(s) in an M&A team. Anticipation is a key strategy – who might become likely attackers and in what circumstances? Today, the corporate website can provide valuable forewarning of a potential take-over bid. So-called "slug trails" are being left by investment bankers (and others) when they visit websites in search of information!

In enhancing share value: adopting the (natural) promoter role in profiling the corporation among stakeholders, for example through corporate advertising.

In pursuing de-merger: pursuit of independence or to shed a liability is corporate divorce. Sell-off wrenches apart sense-making projects – measures have to be taken to recover these in the new organization. Identity changes – BAT, for example, has returned to calling itself British American Tobacco after the de-merger of its insurance business – require careful appreciation of the standing of the corporation, sensitive judgment, and strong decision-making. There is a clear, but often missed, requirement for managed communication to inform and counsel.

In stewarding the corporate reputation: corporate reputation influences merger and post-merger integration through:

- expectations of, and attitudes toward, the merger
- justifying and explaining a merger
- the "track record" of the acquirers' behavior in any previous mergers
- possible distorted enhancement of reputation in the market.

Clashes stem from a mismatch – feelings of inferiority (defensiveness) and superiority (offensiveness) cause blocks to conducting business, affecting customers and other stakeholders. Investigation of the reputation of the acquirers among the acquired, and vice versa, avoids surprises, but also starts on the rocky road to mutual (re)construction of a coherent identity.

The overall lesson is that if communication is treated as merely a delivery mechanism, the fatal conceit is invoked. This is Freidrich Hayek's (1990) principle that social systems die when they fail to take account of others. A dialogical relationship orientation is much more likely to provide responsive and responsible management that can be truly productive. The trend is toward a shifted emphasis from managing communication to managing relationships that are enacted through communication. Communicating is the mode of relating and organizing.

Summary of principles and lessons learned

Management is no longer merely concerned with objects and processes. Today, the focus has to be on managing relationships. Indeed, the real issue facing managers is the integration of diversity in a network of relationships in which meanings are constructed and organization is mediated by communication (Dixon, 1996).

Announcements of merger proposals require prior research, specialist expertise (which may have to be hired-in), targeting of employees before others, and genuine cooperative team-working that avoids ego and turf battles.

The agenda for discussion and debate has to be set by the corporation unless the positive benefits of merger for shareholders, employees, and customers, are to be lost in a free-for-all of claims, rumors and assumption-based assertions.

Effective communication has a number of characteristics:

■ *Honesty and precision*
  Employees scrutinize available information in order to judge its honesty and they like to know all information including bad news rather than know nothing. They want to learn of redundancies, relocations, and changes in status and job performance. The absence of active communication leaves the members with great uncertainty about their future, and the lack of full and honest communication leads to rumors and other informal communication.

▪ *Consistency of information*
Consistency of internal messages and consistency between internal and external communication are key factors in effective communication during acquisitions. If employees are not provided with a consistent answer to their questions, they will then make up their own, which will probably be wrong and negative/defensive.

▪ *Believability*
Believability is closely related to honesty of communication. An example of an unbelievable communication occurs when management states that it is business as usual after the acquisition in spite of knowing that changes (restructuring, downsizing, and so on) are imminent.

▪ *Appropriate content, channel and timing*
Communication content (style, coverage, and source), channel, and timing are integral parts in the dissemination of information surrounding change. Ensuring effective communication during acquisition requires getting these three elements right. Smeltzer's (1991) model of communication during change is shown in Figure 10.6.

Timing is critical during acquisition. The earlier the company communicates about the changes, the more successful it will be in reducing uncertainty by giving an honest and clear communication. The channel element also needs to be considered. The best form of communication

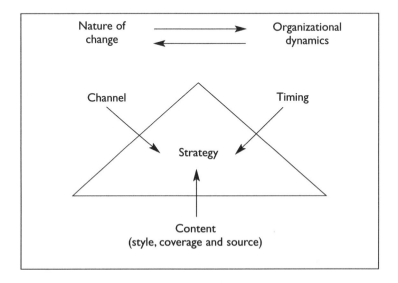

Figure 10.6 A model of communication during change
Source: Author.

differs according to the nature of the changes taking place and the way in which the organization operates. For instance, face-to-face communication is problematic and written communication is more effective in a highly decentralized and geographically dispersed organization whereas in an occasion of wide-scale redundancies, face-to-face discussions are essential to ensure that employees understand the changes and the reasons behind them. Communication content is the other important consideration. Changes to pension arrangements should be communicated to the employees in an appropriate style; the document being in layman's terms so that the employees can understand it. The announcement of the redundancies should come from an appropriate source such as a senior management representative.

Typical communication problems can be identified. Time pressures and work constraints after mergers and acquisitions often hamper effective communication, resulting in anxieties not being surfaced and addressed constructively. The typical communication problems which can arise during implementation are (based on Hubbard, 1999):

- stop–start communication

- rumors and gossip

- inaccurate communication

- distorted messages

- media selection

- difficult communication between the acquiring and target employees.

- *Stop–start communication*
The dual pressures of day-to-day workload and acquisition implementation intervene in efforts to effectively communicate. That information is needed for both running the business and facilitating the acquisition implementation makes informing more complex. New procedures, policies, culture and corporate styles further complicate the information needed to run the company. As a result, managers stop trying to communicate as other issues become a priority. When formal communication stops, informal communication and the rumor mill gain control.

Waiting for information to be communicated is another factor that impedes effective communication. Employees expect communication, yet because of the information void, nothing is communicated. As a result, employees assume that decisions are being made without their knowledge. The right thing to do is to communicate when employees expect it, even if there is nothing concrete to say.

Rumors and gossip

One of the primary truths about corporate communication is that people have a tendency to let their imaginations run wild in the absence of specific information about how something will change their lives. Employees rely on rumors and informal communication when they do not receive adequate formal communication. Rumors are unconfirmed information or fabricated realities that fit the situation (usually assuming the worst possible motives of those in authority), and spring from collective employee concerns and interests. Rumors may be accurate 80–90 percent of the time; yet, the 10–20 percent of inaccurate information is very damaging. Rumors are usually based on a worst-case scenario, thus they are almost always negative and they increase employee anxieties rather than reducing them. In order to control rumors and manage employee suspicions, information should be made available to all staff as soon as possible, and must be frank, requiring open and honest interactions.

Inaccurate communication

Inaccurate communication can be due to changes in the plan or it can simply be not true from the outset. In cases where formal communication is wrong from the beginning and employees discover this, the effect can be quite damaging, even more than the effect of receiving no information at all. The outcomes can be decreased trust in management, increased questioning of the new organization's culture and intention to leave. In cases where the implementation plan changes, and the changes are not communicated, the dichotomy between communication and action can confuse employees, and management credibility can be damaged. However, if management provides adequate explanations, then the staff is more likely to accept the changes.

Distorted messages

Communication messages can become distorted, that is, the message that was intended is not the same as the message received. There are various reasons behind the distortion of messages: misinterpretation of motives, wrong first impressions, hearing influenced by wishing, words having more than one meaning (depending on how the context is understood), missed communication, stereotypical thinking, high emotions, distrust of the sender, defensiveness, and/or unshared assumptions. Further, there is always a tension between commercial sensitivity and the need for reassurance among differing interests. There is evidence to show that during times of uncertainty and stress, attention to congruence and detail of communication is significantly heightened. Actions are often read as communication even though not intended as such, usually with negative effect on morale and trust.

■ *Media selection*
People often express anger, resentment, and discomfort about the way they hear news, although the content may be less difficult and may even be welcomed. Reading for the first time of a merger or take-over in the local or national press can be both shocking and offensive. Problems arise when the external communication systems beat the formal internal communication systems in delivering up news (they rarely beat the rumor mill!). Formal media seem to be preferred over casual communicating, yet check the latest staff survey results!

■ *Difficult communication between the acquiring and target employees*
Communication processes of the two corporations may be inconsistent, creating incoherence and gaps. When employees are competing for the same job or others, or the informer does not trust the recipient, communication becomes difficult. Ambitious people withhold the information that they perceive as strengthening their position. As a result, feelings of power and defensiveness are created and conflict arises. If communication is poor due to low trust between the target and acquiring employees, team-building exercises that promote communication may be advisable.

Conclusion

Consider this option. If, as part of corporate restructuring, marketing were to be brought under the umbrella of public relations, then relationships with all stakeholders could potentially be managed within an all-encompassing business strategy. This is what I mean by the Corporate Communication Managing System (Varey, 1998; Varey and White, 2000). Corporate communication is an umbrella term that I use for the corporate system of relationship management that actively seeks value-creating cooperation through managed interaction and recognizes interdependencies in a corporate community. Thus the corporate communication system of managing is concerned, during merger and acquisition activity, with guarding corporate reputation and maintaining brand consistency and coherence (to foster increased recognition), especially in attempts to create a new common identity, where a fear of loss of identity is to be expected. However, a further concern with (re)constructing systems of communication is evident. Large-scale communication activity to re-emphasize the effects of the changes being brought about, using multiple methods, has to be responsive and responsible – requiring a plan and infrastructure that modify the communication objectives and tone as progress is made.

In a merger, a comprehensive communication plan is necessary for the entire prolonged process of announcement, opponent criticism, regulator investigation, shareholders meeting, vote, and final deal-making. A good merger communication plan identifies all the major audiences to be reached and focuses on their concerns. The planning team also recognizes the misfit and friction in management that stems from cultural differences, while also seeking to identify synergistic emergent characteristics from the restructured businesses. Audience concerns should be addressed openly and each group should be informed about the direct effects of the change on them. If communication with employees is neglected or communication is ambiguous, counter-communication (rumors, gossip, storytelling) will begin and hence anxiety will rise throughout the organization. There exist plenty of prescribed techniques for effective communication in the literature; yet simply following these guidelines is not adequate for success. The cultural context of communication needs to be considered. Contingency planning is necessary – expect the unexpected – and continually evaluate the outcomes from efforts to provide a communication environment within which the changes can be supported.

Communicating with everyone who cares (and some who don't) about the merger or acquisition can be (overly) costly, and has to be strategically managed. During the onset and entrenchment of defensive and fearful "merger syndrome," communication is often stemmed just as an enhancement is needed. The very cultural differences that need treatment through ubiquitous communicating will thwart real communication. Post-merger integration is largely a matter of getting to know each other, learning each others' ways, and coming to work together. The need for dialogical interaction is self-evident. Further, communicating is complicated again by differences of national culture in globalizing markets.

There may well be threats to, and opportunities for, communication specialists in merger and acquisition situations whose outcomes can be likened to love affairs (alliances), marriages (mergers), and shotgun weddings (hostile take-overs). Financial measures of merger and acquisition outcomes take a short-term perspective, whereas a complete settling may take several years. Expectations for immediate results from managed programs may well mitigate against longer-term investment in communication system building. But that is another story. Managers of communication systems have a critical role in the management of the merger/post-merger process, but may be denied the opportunity to make the necessary contribution if that crucial process is neglected.

The communication management process can be summarized in 12 steps as shown in Table 10.3.

Managed communication is the common denominator in explaining how these activities create value during merger or acquisition. Information alone is necessary but not sufficient. How relationships are developed has greater impact. Inevitably, the upheaval of merger or acquisition pushes people into a state of uncertainty over their own position and the identity of the corporation, and frustration as the familiar is disrupted and they are forced to adapt their ways.

When energy isn't expended in communicating, emotional energy is dissipated in facing insecurity and fear of loss in the period of uncertainty. Managing communication as the mode of managing in which collective and individual identities are constructed in stakeholder relationships, rather than

---

Table 10.3 Contact points for the corporate communication system during merger and acquisition

1. Strategic analysis and establishment of the communication management team and a communication plan (including communication needs analysis and a contingency plan to cover the eventuality of leaks)

2. Initiating or responding to, acquisition or merger talks – setting the tone and style

3. Formulating the deal/bid – pre-planning audits of assets: values, management, personnel, marketing, finance, and so on (due diligence) – cultural mapping

4. Tendering the proposal (in accordance with regulations)

5. Presenting the added value of the deal to stakeholders – telling the right deal story and recruiting participation by moving beyond promises and claims to specific details

6. Seeking approvals (from shareholders)

7. Constituency discussions, to diagnose the differing cultures, and to plan transition

8. Negotiating the agreement

9. Merger or acquisition announcement news conference and publications

10. Post-deal planning (including communication infrastructure within the emerging stakeholder network)

11. Post-deal implementation (maintaining the communication management team for integration and promoting merger benefits to key customers)

12. Identity review and re-branding (discovering the "real corporation")

simply as a means of task accomplishment, may just be the key to value-creating merger and acquisition. Successful M&A follows much the same principles as managing any business development project. Communication is critical. Participation produces new certainty. Conceiving of communication as participation, rather than "objective" informing is necessary. Communication management is not merely the means of information management, but crucially also the mode of uncertainty management.

In the end, in the world of merger and acquisition it seems to come down to being hungry or being lunch!

Managing Employee Communication

In June 1998, executives of AstraAB decided to end their joint venture agreement with Merck, raising the challenge of integrating the de-merged Astra Merck and Astra U.S.A. The two organizations had distinct identities and a total of more than 3500 employees, raising the usual dilemma of how quickly to integrate. Executives decided to redesign and staff the new corporation, Astra Pharmaceuticals, in just five months. Only six months after the announcement of the merger, they announced their merger with Zeneca to create AstraZeneca.

Immediately the announcement of the merger was made, a Change and Communication Team was formed, drawing on the experience of both corporations and working in partnership with advisors Smythe Dorward Lambert. The role of SDL consultants in this team was to provide experienced, independent third party support to the members of the team in addressing the overall corporation's change issues and grappling with their own transition issues. The focus of the team was to ensure that the creation of Astra Pharmaceuticals went beyond simply financial, operational, or structural considerations, and that the people aspects of change stayed on the leadership team's agenda. They played a role in defining and shaping communication, rather than being mere messengers. The team was able to bring to the leadership's attention employee concerns and issues, leadership visibility, and change management solutions. SDL people drew on proven merger "best practice" such as regular employee feedback, culture mapping, and the implementation of credible communication vehicles for all employees.

A temporary merger publication was created in both paper and electronic form, and produced for the duration of the pre-merger period and the subsequent integration. This served to distinguish merger news from day-to-day communication, and demonstrated the employer's commitment to employees. In addition, the leaders of each business unit were prompted to provide "town hall" meetings for their people, and were coached in sharing their own experiences of the merger, telling stories, and answering questions.

Managers were helped to focus on the symbolic milestones associated with corporate merger, to communicate around key events: Announcement; "Day One" or Launch; Timelines for staffing processes; Announcement of HQ location; Announcement of the leadership team.

At Astra Pharmaceuticals, and during the subsequent merger with Zeneca, SDL designed a custom-built cultural mapping process to reflect some specific requirements. Leader interviews and employee focus groups, at all levels, were conducted to identify the culture characteristics of the two corporations. This enabled a mapping of the existing cultures and employee aspirations for the type of company they expected and thought necessary for the merged corporation to compete effectively in the marketplace. This was followed by bespoke quantitative research. The results highlighted some valuable insights around management style, desire for accountability, behaviors for dealing with customers, and employee satisfaction and retention. This program worked in partnership with a complementary project team looking at external image and brand, enabling the Astra Pharmaceuticals/AstraZeneca management teams to address the internal and external brand simultaneously.

The findings were used in the decision-making of the integration and leadership teams, to highlight potential integration problem areas to the Integration Team and line managers, to feed into the leadership group for the development of the new vision and values for the new corporation, and to inform decisions about the new company's positioning in the marketplace and its branding.

In order to signal that the new organization would be a "great place to work," SDL also emphasized the need to support people in managing change during the integration period. This was essential because both organizations were experiencing a period of chaos during which values were "felt" to have been suspended, the leadership group initially "disappeared" from sight, and employee feedback indicated that morale was down due to day-to-day ambiguity and the inherent stress of the merger.

Change activity was initiated at three levels. SDL consultants challenged the leadership team to rethink the behaviors they needed to model so as to lead Astra Pharmaceuticals through this tough period. Detailed plans were developed for key leaders that identified and helped capitalize on symbolic and high profile employee events. They were also helped to understand the impact of change on people, and a set of practical tools and techniques were developed to help them manage their experience, thus building organizational change resilience. Managers could call on members of the Change Team, which included both internal and Smythe Dorward Lambert consultants, to conduct change interventions. These included facilitating the close down of teams as well as the start up of new teams, or helping teams plot where they were in the change cycle and what they could do to support people to facilitate their move toward acceptance of the change. In addition, regular articles on coping with change were published in the merger newsletter.

Early in the process, SDL also introduced a single measurement mechanism for employees. Factors that were measured included employee satisfaction with the management of the merger, effectiveness of communication, the degree to which merger principles were adhered to, impact on business as usual and the customer, and leadership effectiveness. The overarching purpose of this was to:

- Identify emerging issues in the merger before they became critical

- Provide an early warning system for potential productivity and/or implementation "hot-spots"

- Involve employees in the creation of solutions to issues raised

- Demonstrate senior management willingness to listen to and respond to employee issues

- Identify the change and communication levers which would have the most impact

- Track the progress of the integration over time.

This was accomplished using both initial qualitative work (interviews with the top team and small focus groups throughout), and then quantitative work (telephone polling of employees) over a period of time to get a feel for widespread issues (positive and negative). Results were then fed back to the entire organization, and action-planning sessions were held with managers to generate solutions to key problems.

Feedback from employees suggested that all of these processes sent a very strong signal to employees and ensured that people felt that their opinions counted and that they were valued. This resulted in the organizations' ability to retain key talent who continued to be productive during this time of major change.

Source: See acknowledgements.

Acknowledgements

The author wishes to acknowledge the contribution of Miss Tatyana Gurciyan MBA, graduate of the School of Management, University of Salford, who provided a substantial basis for this chapter through her Masters dissertation work.

The illustration is based on a case study provided by Smythe Dorward Lambert. The cooperation of Lilian Ing, Consulting Director and M&A communication specialist, is gratefully acknowledged.

Chapter

The corporate entity and agency interaction

11

shekar swamy

General Electric

The television advertisement (see Figure 11.1) opens with beautiful vignettes of well-lit streets of Tokyo. It intercuts with strong and sensitive images of the people of Tokyo – a bunch of school kids, sumo wrestlers, commuters in a train. All the images show the use of electricity, and how intrinsic this is to the quality of life. The viewer notices the jingle is in Japanese. The English translation also appears on the screen.

In the middle of the advertisement, a strong male voice announces the fact that the Tokyo Electric Power Company has awarded the largest order for gas turbines to GE – the General Electric Company. In the process, the people of Japan are assured of good clean electricity, and the American workers are ensured of jobs and security.

The song continues, amidst further visuals of Japanese people and American workers. A line of Japanese workers approaches another line of American workers with the GE logo emblazoned on their backs. The two lines of workers bow to each other, respectfully, Japanese style.

The image moves to the corner of the TV screen. The GE logo appears. The singers in Japanese reach a crescendo. The words appear on the screen – "GE: We bring good things to life."

Figure 11.1 Visual of the TVC in storyboard format

getting electicity

and water

in an economical way.

Together they turn to GE

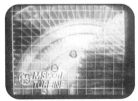

The world leader in gas and
steam turbine technology

SUPER: We bring you closer

to the ones you love

MVO: When Tokyo Electric
Power Company

gave GE one of its largest
export orders ever,

it gave Tokyo

the largest and most efficient
power plant of its kind

in the world.

Which means more jobs

for our people back here

and a better future for
the people of Japan

SUPER: GE. We bring good
things to life

Figure 11.1 cont'd

Introduction

This then is another television commercial (TVC) in a long series that GE has used around the world to build its corporate brand. This particular TVC, called "Daughters Dance," although shot in Japan, was run in the U.S.A. and around the world. The interesting fact is that GE continues to produce their commercials all over the world, and they air them all over the world as well. Thus, they portray a single global corporate voice irrespective of geographies, cultures and nation states.

At GE, the task of waving the corporate flag is a responsibility that is taken very seriously. While the actual program is orchestrated by the headquarters Corporate Communications group, the final approval on the communication is given by none other than *Fortune* magazine's Manager of the Century, the CEO, Jack Welch, himself (*Fortune,* November 22, 2000).

GE – which operates over a dozen distinct business units ranging from power generation to aircraft engines to lighting to consumer appliances to medical equipment to broadcasting to financial services – has been running corporate advertising campaigns consistently for nearly two decades. Supported by an annual investment of several million dollars, it is an outstanding example of a corporate campaign that is proactive, consistent and universally appealing.

Why does the Manager of the Century think this is necessary, and is actually putting money into this year after year? The answer lies in the public nature of the corporation itself, and its relationships with various constituents or stakeholders that never can be taken for granted.

In this chapter we will examine the nature of the corporation, how it serves a great commercial purpose, and how it acts as an engine of prosperity. We will then discuss how in its very origins, the corporation has inherent adversarial relationships with its various constituents, and how communication can assist in aligning these various divergent views. We'll also look at how vulnerable the corporation is and how an external agency can help in reducing that vulnerability.

We'll also review the various situations that encourage senior corporate management to seek outside agency assistance. We'll also discuss the client attitudes and characteristics that will help them get the best out of their agency relationships. Another vexing and common problem is the need to align the corporate brand with the product brands and we cover that as well. We will look at nine important considerations that companies ought to bear in mind while developing their corporate communication programs. Finally, we will delve into a process of integrating the communication so that it delivers the desired impact among the various audiences.

The corporation

The corporation has to be one of the most enduring institutions of commerce. It is a definitive institution in today's global economy, and certainly one that has transformed the very way we live around the world. Of particular interest to us is the large, multinational corporation (MNC). Over the decades, MNCs have proven to be a very flexible vehicle for spreading commercial risk (and reward) and for organizing investment on a grand scale over vast distances, and nowadays on a worldwide basis.

But, managing these huge businesses has become ever more complex, particularly in the case of so many constituents or stakeholders – from customers to shareholders to employees to government – all expecting and in many instances demanding better and better performance from the corporation from their own respective viewpoints. Internal and external communication conducted proactively and consistently, is an important strategic activity that these firms need to undertake, to manage the expectations of their various publics.

The adversarial relationships

The history of these huge businesses, particularly in countries such as the United States, the United Kingdom, and other countries within the European Community, not to mention the burgeoning ASEAN tiger economies, where private enterprise is still on the ascendant, has often been adversarial in terms of relationships with key constituents, and this issue, among others, sparks off the need to communicate or raise the corporate umbrella. Admittedly, the story is somewhat different in countries like Japan and Germany where there has historically been a great deal of partnership between the large corporations and the State.

The corporation versus government

In the United States, for example, the conflict between State and the corporation has been consistent over the years. The latter part of the 1800s and the early part of the 1900s were the high points of freewheeling capitalism, often referred to as "sledgehammer capitalism". During this time, corporations wielded extraordinary clout with little or no apparent countervailing balance of forces from the State.

The U.S. government's attempt to reign in the power of the corporation culminated in the forced dissolution of Standard Oil in 1911 by the U.S. Supreme Court. Such governmental actions, designed to protect the consumer and maintain a competitive balance in the market, continue to this day. Just look at the ongoing anti-monopoly trials faced by Microsoft. It is clear from these that the adversarial relationship between the corporation and government will probably be a continuing fact of corporate enterprise.

One can well ask: Could the judicious use of communication have helped Standard Oil? Or, how can communication help Microsoft? In the case of Standard Oil, the attitude of ownership and management was perhaps one of confrontation, believing in their own strength and sense of power. Standard Oil could potentially have taken the trouble to proactively communicate all the excellent work it was doing in bringing oil to consumers, and what a remarkable role the company was playing in improving the quality of life of all the people. If Standard Oil had taken a more humble position vis-à-vis its constituents, and if it had carefully nurtured harmony through communication, perhaps a breakup could have been avoided. Of course, this is speculative, but a sensible external agency that could have delivered an objective and fearless point of view, of the customers and government of the time, to the management of Standard Oil could have perhaps helped enormously in resolving the matter. In other words, resolution seems to be about balancing organizational, consumer and other important stakeholder perspectives.

Likewise, one can speculate about the current Microsoft debacle. Isn't there too much emphasis on how Microsoft has used its market power and crushed competition? Isn't there a portrayal, by at least some sections of the media, that Microsoft is arrogant and must be brought under control? Isn't it possible that some of these extreme views are most strongly voiced by competitors of Microsoft who have been beaten in the market? And, aren't they the ones who stand to gain the most through a breakup of the organization?

One can argue that in these circumstances, the Microsoft side of the story has not been fully heard. Isn't it possible that consumers have benefited from a single dominant software standard around the world? There will be a high cost to pay if Microsoft is split, but in the debates, this has often been ignored, or poorly communicated to the various audiences. Or, can one say that among all the smoke, dust and drama of the case, the issues have been somewhat obfuscated?

Could Microsoft have avoided this confrontation if the company had been more proactive in its communication over the years? Perhaps solutions would have been found if Microsoft had stressed the benefits that it was obviously bringing to the consumer. Instead of being the whipping boy of the personal computer business, might Microsoft have become the favorite that millions of consumers welcomed and thanked? In the hands of the right external agency at the right time, such a favorable view of Microsoft may have been possible. Just the speculative thought of how things could have been for Microsoft, engineered through careful and strategic and continuous communication, underscores the vital role that well-structured communication can play in the life of a corporation.

The corporation versus employees

Corporate relationships with employees has often been rocky as well. Ever since Frederick Winslow Taylor introduced "Scientific Management" in the late 1800s, the corporation has tended to view "workers" as those whose primary role is to do as they are told. As Taylor himself wrote, "In the past man was first. In the future the system must be first." (cited in *Fortune*, November 22, 2000).

Scientific Management was followed by Henry Ford's mind-numbing assembly line. While production soared, even the pace at which a worker had to move was now predetermined.

With the corporations employing thousands, this naturally led to the organization of labor on a grand scale. Labor unions had a natural adversarial position against corporations, fighting continuously as they did for a better deal. The organization of labor to fight for its rights reached its summit in the U.S. in 1955, when the Congress of Industrial Organizations merged with the American Federation of Labor. While the impact of "big labor" may have declined in recent years, the relationship between labor and big business continues to be more adversarial than cooperative.

Matters have not improved as a result of organizational re-engineering, downsizing, right sizing and restructuring over the past two decades. All of this has only served to confirm a natural suspicion people have generally held about huge profitable businesses. The concept of employee loyalty has been significantly diluted. The recent ASEAN meltdown not only displayed the fragility of the tiger economies, but also meant that the practice of lifetime employment has finally been laid to rest in the sedimentary strata of economic and social history.

A poignant example appeared in a Chicago, IL TV news bulletin in September 2000. Senior management had decided to close the Helène

Curtis toiletries factory on the city's north side, rendering some 400 workers jobless. The factory was apparently old and inefficient, and the production of that factory was being shifted to other locations around the country. The news went on to say that two years previously, Helène Curtis had been bought by the Unilever Corporation. At the time of purchase, Unilever had issued a public statement reassuring the Helène Curtis employees there would be no closure of the Chicago unit, and their jobs were safe. Now, in just a couple of years, the company's decision to close the unit came as a shock to the employees and the community where it operated. Notably, Unilever officials did not comment on the status of Helène Curtis employees who were being let go.

As late as 1998, Levi Strauss Corporation promised its employees one year's equivalent of 1996 base salary as a bonus, if financial targets were met. As a stroke of excellence in internal communications, this was (then) an excellent move. Meanwhile, the intervening of time and tide has seen the fashion cycle turn against Levi and the promised bonus.

Notably many multinationals have abandoned labor forces in high cost countries as the magnet of higher profitability lures them toward Asian, Indian, and east European lower cost employees. Meanwhile, the move toward globalization of markets is facilitated by subdividing the world into tariff free zones such as the European Community, the North American Free Trade Association and the like.

This is not to say that only corporations are to be blamed for the declining levels of confidence between employer and employee. Consider the changes in employee attitude and outlook. When the sometimes unreliable behavior of the corporation is juxtaposed with the emergence of the highly educated, mobile and aspiring employee who does not hesitate to seek better pastures, there emerges a strong version of what is called the "trust gap" (Knapp 1991). On one side is the unfeeling corporation (the "empty raincoat"), with seemingly scant regard for the people it employs. On the other, there is the mercenary employee, who will depart unhesitatingly if he/she feels there is a better opportunity elsewhere.

Communication can play a huge role in bridging the employer–employee gap. This role starts with the recognition that employees are people with feelings and emotions, and that these can be positively influenced by corporations with candid, interactive, and transparent approaches. Companies must first accept the employees' right to know. External agencies can be of great assistance in developing and delivering needed communications programs. Agencies will start with sharing information with employees in a planned manner. Information does lead to insight and understanding. Insight and understanding lead to knowledge.

Knowledge leads to alignment in thinking, outlook and approach. This is the virtuous cycle that consistent internal communication can underpin.

The corporation versus the community

The industrial revolution essentially concerned large businesses exploiting the natural resources of the land, labor, and capital for growth and private profit. In the process, corporations used and oftentimes abused the environment, often with scant respect for nature and with total disregard for the ecological balance. Whether it is a story of dumping of industrial waste in rivers and lakes, or the Three Mile Island or Chernobyl nuclear accidents, the backlash against corporations from various communities has been severe.

Despite all the environmental laws in force in most parts of the world, and the proactive measures taken by many corporations to preserve and protect nature, the suspicion of the corporation as an environmental threat by the community lingers on.

Unfortunately, communication cannot compensate for wanton exploitation of the environment. But communication can certainly place the need for using the natural resources in perspective. Consumers and environmentalists generally understand that the current quality of life can only be sustained by using natural resources properly. These scarce resources should be replenished properly, that is, there needs to be a responsible approach to the entire process. More than any other issue, corporations can build an enormous bridge of goodwill by communicating proactively on this issue and setting to rest all doubts even before they arise. Such communication in the current environment is no longer optional. It has become mandatory.

The corporation versus customers

As someone once said, the art of business is all about "getting someone to part with money without violence." It is hard to think of the corporation as having an adversarial relationship with its consumers/customers, but in a way that is precisely what it has. In reality, the corporation is trying to get someone to pay for something. This requires a mutual willingness on both sides of the selling and buying equation. The proliferation of choice, the spread of the World Wide Web, the free flow of information and the commoditization of many categories of products and services place the consumer in charge of his/her relationship with the corporation (see Schultz and Kitchen, 2000).

Customer loyalty, often taken for granted by many corporations, is at high risk today. Shifting customer loyalties can cause corporations to disappear from the scene or at the very least place them in serious difficulties. Look at what is happening to two icon brand marketers – Levi Strauss and The Kellogg Company. In the case of Levi's, consumers are moving away in droves from the use of their brand of blue jeans, and the company's sales have been eroding in an alarming manner. Kellogg's is facing a softening of demand in its core breakfast cereal category, causing a serious earnings decline for the company. The price of Kellogg stock has declined from its peak of $50 in December 1998 to less than $25 in October 2000 (www.kelloggs.com).

It would be foolish to claim that communication alone could keep customers from deserting a company or brand or service. It is however most certain that customers want to know with whom they are doing business. What is the pedigree of the company? What are the company's values? What is the company culture? Is this an organization worthy of trust? Are these people we can trust? What are their quality standards? Is the company ethical in its dealings? These and other questions can only be answered through an ongoing corporate communication program that can be conducted with the assistance of an external agency. As the customers understand better and better, they can even become opinion leaders for the corporation, and potential adversarial relationships can be turned to something enormously positive.

The corporation versus shareholders

In June 2000, when Procter & Gamble issued a warning that its profit expectations for the quarter would not be met (www.pg.com), the stock price plummeted to $54 from a high of $120 just six months earlier. The stock price recovered to over $70 in October 2000, but it was still 40 percent off its peak. How is it possible that the value of a company with the track record of success like Procter & Gamble can drop so significantly in such a short time? Unfortunately, this is not an isolated case. Several companies that have enjoyed high valuations, have suffered the same fate in the hands of "the market."

Times have changed a bit since the early 1900s. For nearly a half-century before 1914 (when World War I spoilt the party), most of the capital flows could be traced to a few thousand wealthy European families. Today, electronic fund managers, allocating the savings of hundreds of millions of people in pension and mutual funds, drive capital flows. Referred to as the "electronic herd" (Friedman, 1999), the support of these fund managers has been ruthlessly driven on the basis of whether a corporation delivered on its numbers and lived up to their analysts' expectations. Shareholders, one can argue, have become fair-weather friends. They come in when the going is expected to be good, and bail out at the first sign of any difficulty faced by the corporation. Corporate relationships with shareholders have thus become adversarial to the extent that they are unpredictable and, one would argue, even at times capricious (see illustration in Chapter 12).

If there is one group that demands timely and continuous communication from the corporation, it is the shareholder group. It is worth reminding that the pattern of shareholding has dramatically changed in the last two decades. Today, large fund managers play a watchdog role and can and do move tens of millions of dollars at the touch of their electronic buttons. Consider the following characteristics:

- The shareholder of today is well informed, having access to market developments on a real time basis

- The shareholder of today is sophisticated, with access to all sorts of analysis at the click of a button

- The shareholder of today is an activist, and is willing to speak up and be heard, more than at any time in the past

- The shareholder of today has an incredible array of choice, not only within a country, but also often across geographies. It is natural to expect that shareholders will constantly move their investments around to maximize returns.

Given these characteristics, corporations cannot just communicate periodically or sporadically, but have to have open lines of communication operating at all times with these groups. The degree of transparency and the free flow of information have an impact on the degree of support companies receive from their shareholders. Use of external agencies that can assist in meeting the increasing demand for sophisticated communication, can become a very practical way of dealing with this all-important group of stakeholders.

The vulnerability factor

The expectations from the present day corporation are multi-faceted. In countries like Japan, the corporation has been the chosen vehicle to maintain lifetime employment, a practice that is proving to be increasingly burdensome and probably redundant. In many state-directed economies, corporations run townships and schools and medical services, simply as a matter of policy and to direct social benefits. Even in the U.S., corporate America has been made a conduit for health and retirement benefits.

Corporations are strong because of their sheer size and access to large-scale resources. These same factors make the corporations vulnerable as well. As public entities, corporations do not have any latitude to make mistakes. Consumers today tend to punish companies that are perceived to be socially irresponsible. The pounding that Nike Inc. has taken, for its reliance on what critics call "sweatshops" in Asia and elsewhere, is evidence to this. When there is trouble of any kind, the corporation is expected to step in and make amends immediately, irrespective of costs. Just recall the *Valdez* oil spill off the coast of Alaska and the reported $500 million that it cost Exxon to clean it up. Crises are a fact of corporate life and need to be dealt with expeditiously and in a socially responsible manner as is made plain in Chapter 9.

The problem for corporations is that trouble can hit at any time, and it often comes from the most unexpected of quarters. The only way to stay prepared for this is to maintain an open line of communication with all audiences at all times, so that there is ample appreciation among the constituents of what the corporation is all about. If trouble then occurs, the corporation has a ready base of sympathetic audiences to which it can appeal for support, provided there is not a clear case of executive fudge and cover-up (see Chapter 9). Even the highly supportive German trade and business press delivered a barrage of needed criticism to corporate icon Mercedes, when the new A-class continued to veer on two wheels during its test (dare we say "testing") period. The continued trivialization by Mercedes of perceived product weaknesses for the A-class did not endear them either to the German or international media (see Gronstedt, 2000).

The agency additions

From the foregoing, it is clear that corporate image will always be an issue and there will be a need to build and maintain communication bridges with various publics and stakeholders. Companies today are being held to higher ethical standards. Consumers, shareholders, employees, and communities look carefully at all facets of a company's reputation, as well as its performance, when making their judgment calls.

For this reason, corporations commonly employ external communication resources or agencies to help analyze, plan, sometimes strategize, deliver and evaluate their communication programs. External agencies can bring few or many capabilities to bear which are simply not available within the corporation. These capabilities, apart from the special strategic, media, and creative talents to build and deliver corporate communication which are the agency's reason for being, must include the following:

1. A deep understanding of the perspectives of the various constituents from their respective frames of reference is a fundamental contribution that clients must expect from an agency. As the old adage goes, the manufacturer makes the "tangible product," but the customer buys the "brand." While the manufacturer thinks of the physical attributes, the consumers are thinking in terms of what solutions they can find for their problems. Likewise, the company may be thinking of stability and continuity in the employee ranks, but the employees may be thinking of career growth and the desirability of new experiences. The shareholders may be looking for big short-term gains, while the company can be thinking of reinvestments and long-term growth.

   It is an oft-observed truism that the company may become so close to the issues, that it fails to adopt the audience or stakeholder perspective. Here, outside agencies can play a critical role. By using well proven account planning methods, employing simple and/or sophisticated research techniques, or just by applying their experience and common sense, a good agency manager can often diagnose the situation and offer solutions the company had not considered previously or simply overlooked.

2. The outside agency is usually better equipped to determine the kinds of communication tools and techniques that can be employed to achieve a particular task. The company is in whatever business it has chosen to conduct. Both it and the external agencies it employs are in the communication business. However, the agency's sole focus of attention and expertise is in the communication arena. Therefore, the outside agency should be in a much better position to determine the application of the best tools and techniques to help in solving the company's communication problem(s).

Does the situation demand a simple letter from the CEO? Should the problem be addressed through one-to-one meetings with key influencers? Is there a need to go public on a large scale by using mass media? Will corporate communication or public relations provide a ready answer to the question at hand? Should the company mount a focused direct marketing program for best results? Will e-mail provide an adequate and cost-effective solution? How should the Web be used? What is the role of opportunities like the Annual Report? What is the best way to communicate to internal audiences? These, and a host of other questions, are best answered by external agencies or outside experts in communication that have extensive understanding of the tools and techniques that can be applied and which works best in helping solve different problems.

3. Media knowledge and expertise is another area that is best outsourced from experts. As Bruce Crawford, the erstwhile Chairman and CEO of the Omnicom Group (the world's second largest communications group) once said: "Media is where the money is."

    The media world offers a bewildering choice today. For every communication task, a company can look at pursuing multiple options. What is the best course of action to be followed? How should all of these be evaluated? External agencies employ media professionals whose only job is to constantly keep abreast of all developments in the media world, and to interpret these for the benefit of their clients.

    What companies must bear in mind is that on average, over 80 percent of their communication budget is passed on to media owners. The choice of the right media can save vast sums of money and result in improved effectiveness. This is what companies must aim for.

    In a sense, media markets offer huge opportunities for arbitrage, much like the financial markets. This is because the market is quite imperfect in the flow of information and the needs of media owners can often be the opportunities for media buyers. Since the company is not in the media game, this is best left to outside agency experts.

4. The craft of corporation communication is something available only from external communication experts. While companies can be very good in analysis and a logical approach to their problems, they simply do not possess the creative and crafting skills of the agencies.

    Communication in any media will eventually boil down to words and pictures. And both words and pictures have to be crafted to deliver results. Given a parity situation, the superior application of the craft of communication will simply produce better results. This is the creative function provided by outside agencies.

The craft of writing is not a native skill to everyone. It is a special talent. It is shaped and enhanced through experience. It can be constantly improved. The choice of words or the twist of a phrase, the punctuation, the short copy or the long copy, the negative headline or the positive metaphor, the prose or the poetry – all these and many other aspects of the craft of writing can make a huge difference to the quality of communication.

Communication is visual as well. Think of the vast choice in font selection and typography. Think of the myriad ways in which a visual can be rendered – photographs, illustrations, drawings, caricatures and so on. Think of the use of color and what power that can have. Think of the use of symbols in communication. Think of the audio-visual medium of television, and think of the craft that medium involves – the scripting, the direction, the casting, the music, the lighting, the sets, the costumes, the editing, the sound engineering and so on and so on.

Craft persuades. Craft sells. Great craft persuades and sells even more. This specialization is generally available only from external agencies, and companies will do well to demand a high level of craft in the communication work done for them.

5. A strong measure of objectivity and a willingness to speak out is an important characteristic to look for in outside agencies. Outside professionals must have the courage to speak their mind and say what needs to be said, and not merely parrot what clients may want to hear. As the need arises, the agency must challenge clients on their assumptions, and must not hesitate to do the homework that may be required to state and establish a different point of view, if that is needed.

6. A wide range of experience, with different clients, markets and categories can be brought to the table by specialist agencies. Agencies must have the ability to apply their learning from one set of businesses and industries to other scenarios, often seeing the trends and the parallels that are not immediately visible to clients. By doing so, agencies can add substantial value and reduce learning cycles.

7. A sense and a willingness to think differently that can make a big difference is another hallmark of a good professional agency. The business of communication is such that by re-ordering the variables, the impact of

the program can be considerably enhanced for a given investment of resources, or a certain measure of impact can be delivered for a far less investment of resources than perhaps considered necessary. The true measure, and contribution, of an outside agency is in harnessing the potential of communication to solve a client's communication problem as expeditiously and as cost-effectively as possible.

Seeking an agency's support

Over the many years in the business, companies have approached this writer for assistance usually when they are confronted with a "situation," and for which they need immediate solutions. Some of these typical situations, that is, when companies feel the need to enlist outside help, are outlined below.

- The company receives some bad press or is being battered by the media for things it did or did not do. The damage is usually done by the time outside assistance is sought. Under these circumstances, while some damage control may be possible, it is often impossible to undo the damage. The companies fret and fume about the unfairness of it all, and when the situation subsides, they go back to business as usual.

- Companies approach outside agencies when they need to tap the financial markets, and therefore they want some "PR" to get their profile up and gain the attention of portfolio managers and investors. This becomes a purely opportunistic affair, and today's stakeholder audiences they are addressing often see through the game. Still, some sort of profiling gets done, and once the funds are raised or the stock price adjusted to acceptable levels, companies tend to go silent again.

- Senior executives tend to get upset if they perceive the markets, particularly in comparison to other players in the same industry, undervalue their stock price. They blame this on inadequate communication of their company's story, or believe that the markets have not fully understood or appreciated their company's strategies and strengths. They seek a communication program that can correct this and deliver results fast.

- A company that has trouble attracting good talent is one that often thinks that a quick communication program can solve the problem. It brings in the communication experts, and expects them to solve the problem with a wave of their magic communication wands.

- Companies that run into trouble with their labor force, resulting in public strikes and the like, suddenly take a great interest in communication. They feel a great need to tell their side of the story, for often under such circumstances, the media plays up the dispute. The status of labor is an important local community issue, and once the sympathy swings in favor of the workers, many corporations face an uphill battle to get their story heard.

- The comparable situation is when the corporation gets into trouble with the civic authorities over environmental or even public safety issues. Media will invariably blow the story out of proportion. Just see what is happening to the ongoing Bridgestone/Firestone tire recall saga in the United States. There is a strong opinion among leading marketers that the company has seriously mismanaged its communication, and as a result may not be able to survive this crisis.

- Another factor that drives a company crazy is when its competitor walks away with that prize contract or tender or order, over which the company has been laboring for months. The company may feel that its technical bid was superior and commercial terms more than competitive. Yet its chief competitor, who has that better name or image, gets the contract because it is simply safer for the customer to select the company with the better reputation.

  When IBM was at its peak in the 1960s and 70s, more than any other factor, it was its vaunted reputation that ensured that their customers had to think very hard if they were to give the order to any other company. In today's world, Advanced Micro Devices (AMD) makes microprocessors that are supposed to rival Intel in quality. But can any manufacturer of PCs really consider putting anything other than "Intel Inside"? Product quality apart, it is the overwhelming reputation that Intel has built in just the decade of the 1990s that serves as an entry barrier for its competitors.

While there is a real need for effective corporate communication in all the above examples, in many instances companies get into predicaments precisely because they have failed to communicate at all, or rather have made feeble attempts at communication that did not serve its purpose well. Poorly planned or belated attempts at "whitewash" communication that are poorly implemented simply gather no laurels. Instead they receive the brickbats of criticism – especially in today's sensitized dynamic unforgiving marketplaces and marketspaces.

Undoubtedly, the business of corporate communication in its traditional mass media form is expensive and, if the corporation is not directly selling a product and generating direct revenue against the communication investment, it is hard to justify economically. But, in today's crescendo and cacophony of media forms, it is possible to select the right vehicles and the right communication methods, to ensure that they are suitably integrated, in order to deliver cost-effective impactful programs whose results will more than justify the investment.

Being an effective client

So far, we have discussed the need for corporate communication and what value additions a professional external agency can make to the process. In reality, realizing these value additions can be quite a challenge. Managers of corporate communication in companies can cite several examples of how the agencies they have employed have not delivered to their expectations. Likewise, many agency managers can cite examples of how they have had difficulties in dealings with their clients and have not been able to deliver the quality of work desired.

The company employing an outside agency must first and foremost understand the nature of the relationship, and recognize how this is different from most of its other outside relationships. To begin with, the outside agency is a vendor inasmuch as the company pays the agency for its services. But the relationship goes beyond this. The agency is an expert in an area of business that is both intellect and craft based. Often the agency knows more than the client does as far as communication is concerned. The client has to share a great deal of confidential information with the agency and involve the latter in issues that can be highly sensitive. The agency utilizes these inputs and delivers solutions to the client. In the course of all of this, the relationship evolves beyond that of being a mere vendor delivering a product/service for a price. The agency becomes quite central to the manner in which the client conducts business itself.

Clients can gain disproportionate benefit in their dealings with agencies. In order to gain this advantage, client organizations must work with their agency partners by adopting a certain attitude and approach that can produce the desired result. The following is an attempt to lay down certain guidelines in this direction, that clients can follow to get the best from their agencies.

1. Clients should expect agencies to be their "partners," and this can best
    be achieved by offering partnership from their end at the beginning of
    the relationship. The partnership is obviously not financial in terms of
    equity ownership; the partnership is however ownership of the prob-
    lems and opportunities in an emotional sense. Effective communi-
    cation requires deep involvement and even profound thinking from the
    agencies. This is difficult unless there is emotional ownership of both
    the problems and the solutions.

2. Communication is the public face of the corporation. For this reason, it
    is best driven from the top, or at least by senior managers who have the
    required authority and mandate from the most senior management.
    Senior clients can demand involvement from the senior ranks of agen-
    cies that have the authority to command the best of the resources.
    Agencies tend to read the signals coming from client organizations and
    respond accordingly. If top management is involved on both sides,
    more often than not, this can result in that magic and inspired work
    that everyone seeks in communication.

3. Clients should set their expectations clearly and unequivocally at the
    beginning of their relationship with the outside agency. Clients should
    have this in writing if possible and get agreement on this with the
    agency management. The expectation should be in terms of the
    strategic inputs as well as the high standards of the communication
    craft. This is usually reinforced if there is senior management involved
    directly in the process.

4. The briefings from the client to the agency must be clear with respect
    to the issues from the client point of view. Ideally the briefing should
    be in writing, even if there is a great deal of verbal communication
    between the partners. The briefing should be thorough and convey as
    much information as possible. The client should provide all the data
    available with the brief. This way, the agency doesn't waste time
    collecting the same information. The agency's time is best spent inves-
    tigating its hypotheses, developing multiple recommendations and
    testing the alternatives, not just gathering data.

5. The client always has the right to reject the work presented by the
    agency. But when rejecting the work, the client must be reasoned and
    fair. As far as possible, the client should be able to clearly explain
    why a particular piece of work seems inappropriate. A good agency
    will always accept fair criticism and bounce back with more work,

but before it does so it would like to and must understand the objections clearly.

6. Client's should plan their work and prepare well in advance. Developing good communication takes time and effort. There is no such thing as the one best piece of work. There is always the chance to do it better and better, but this will happen only if the agency has a chance to review what has been done and rework the same if necessary. This is not to say that the agency will be unable to respond if there is a crisis or urgency with respect to some projects. The agency can and must respond as the situation warrants. But these should not become the norm, as the signal that is clearly sent is that communication is not important enough to be properly planned.

7. The client should give credit to the agency where it is due and publicly acknowledge its contributions. Agency personnel respond most enthusiastically to such praise, and they tend to redouble their efforts on behalf of such clients. This is a simple gesture, but it is remarkable how often this tends to be overlooked in the normal course of business.

8. Another oft-overlooked aspect of the relationship is market feedback. Did the communication produce the desired result? What sort of a response (formal research-based or even anecdotal) did the communication evoke from the audiences that the communication addressed? Are the people in the client organization pleased with the results? Did senior management notice the work and comment on it?

   Agencies thrive on feedback. They desire recognition for the work they do. They want the work to produce results for clients. If the feedback is negative, they want to know that as well, so that they can go back and correct the work or at least not repeat the mistake in the future. A good professional agency is looking to learn all the time, and this can happen only if there is proper feedback from clients.

9. Clients must recognize and accept that good agencies and good agency people usually have a choice of clients and projects on which they can work. The natural inclination is to work on or devote disproportionate time to those clients whom the agency likes to do business with. Or, even when the agency devotes time, they may not get fully involved. Unless of course the client is a favorite who deserves all support and then even more. These are soft issues that most clients ignore. Clients should set a simple goal for the relationship – to be among the top

three favored clients of the agency. If this becomes a reality, the client will undoubtedly gain support from the agency far beyond its financial commitments.

The various points noted above are just common sense suggestions in getting the most out of the client–agency relationship. But it is amazing how often these are overlooked in the course of the everyday work. Clients should consider these from the point of view of enlightened self-interest. The benefits will surely accrue, and at no extra cost.

Corporate and product brands

Over the years, various corporations have developed many branding approaches based on their type of business. Some companies have adopted monolithic branding like Sony and Philips. Other companies have focused on individual product branding. Typically these companies operate in fast moving consumer goods categories such as Procter & Gamble or Unilever. Then, there are conglomerate brands where a single corporate name is used across a vast array of businesses, like the Japanese brand Mitsubishi (in cars, escalators, heavy equipment, banking and so on) or the Indian brand TATA (covering steel, trucks, computer software, bulk chemicals, hotels, tea, telecom and so on).

Most brand-building approaches have been significantly influenced in the past by (a) companies in consumer goods marketing and (b) their emphasis on the use of television advertising. These companies had learned through experience that the best approach was to focus on a single product attribute or benefit, and then, hammer that message home through repeated television exposures. Concepts like the Unique Selling Proposition or positioning principles advocated the need to be uni-dimensional for effective communication. While this branding approach may still be appropriate for certain types of consumer products, the principle fails to adequately address the needs of corporate brands which are much more complex.

In today's business environment, several categories have emerged that demand a high degree of marketing communication in multi-dimensional forms and messages. This is particularly true in the service categories, many of which have become large-scale communicators. These include financial services, telecommunications, technology, travel, retail and the like. In these categories, the corporate brand often serves as the product brand, or it serves as a strong umbrella overhang for the product brand(s) that are gathered underneath it.

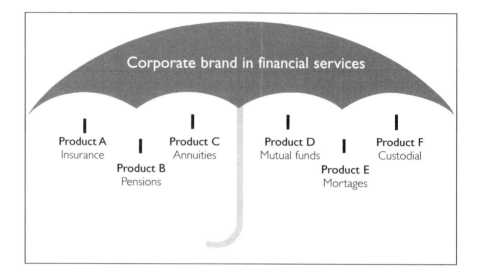

Figure 11.2 A financial services umbrella brand

In these situations, it is important that the corporate brand and the product brands share similar attributes and therefore, reinforce each other. The corporate brand must provide the umbrella cover under which the product brands can thrive and prosper. That concept is illustrated in Figure 11.2 for a financial services brand.

A practical question often arises in these "umbrella" situations. How must the communication be guided and managed to ensure that the corporate and product brand(s) work well together? That comes from the development of a clear and unambiguous written definition of the corporate brand character and tone of voice to be used in all communication. Once this character and tone of voice has been defined, all communication must consistently follow the definition. No communication must be permitted that diverges from this single "brand essence." For example, if the corporate brand character is to be fun and family oriented (as in the case of the Walt Disney company), the individual products marketed cannot be serious and impersonal. If the corporate brand character calls for a serious and intelligent tone of voice (as in the case of Merrill Lynch), the product brand(s) cannot be irreverent and casual in either tone or manner.

A basic requirement is that the corporate and product brand characters be carefully defined and internally consistent. Even as one lamp lights another without diminishing the first, such consistency will result in a larger glow and brightness than is possible individually.

Developing successful corporate communications

Over the years, based on a wide variety of personal experiences and observation of business in many different markets of the world, this writer has evolved a set of guidelines that have served well in creating successful corporate communication programs. These are not meant to be prescriptive. They should be viewed as the distillation of a professional's experiences. While it is possible to deliver successful communication without following these suggestions, chances are that with their adoption, in full or in part, the organization's success rate in a corporate communication program will be much better.

Conviction is key

The first assessment is: how serious is the company about its need and desire to develop a corporate communication program? And, is the company willing to invest the quality time of its top management, and the requisite financial resources necessary for the program to succeed? Without this commitment, any attempt at corporate communication will fail.

One of the most outstanding examples of corporate communication ever came from Mobil Corporation. Mobil ran a consistent corporate communication program for nearly two decades in the 1970s and 80s. Rawleigh Warner, the driving force behind Mobil's groundbreaking corporate identity program said:

> We are convinced that a clear-cut, attractive face to the public will pay off for our company in greater profits.

Based on the recent price Mobil achieved for its shareholders in its merger with Exxon, that would seem to be true.

Another historic example comes from Frank Stanton, the President of CBS from 1946 to 1976, and the driving force behind that company's excellent communication program. Said Stanton:

> I think there are few needs greater for the modern large-scale corporation than the need for a broad scale public awareness of its personality, including a sense of values. (Siegel, 1993)

These words ring even more true today.

Image will happen irrespective

Companies certainly have a choice of whether they want to communicate or not. What many don't seem to understand is that they do not have a choice of whether or not they will have an image among their stakeholders and audiences. For people will form an image irrespective of whether they receive planned corporate communication messages or not (see Chapter 3). For images, owing to managerial inertia, are, in fact, simply formed by default. When businesses fail to communicate, they simply render control of their image to stakeholders. In this context, one is reminded of the old proverb: "One does evil enough when one does nothing good." In a sense then, a company does negative communication when the company does no positive communication.

A classic example comes from the findings of a survey done by the Westinghouse Company in 1991. When the company asked 100 business editors and journalists (people generally considered to be better informed than the average consumer or customer) about its businesses, officials were startled to find that 83 percent of the respondents thought that the company still made appliances. While the strength of the image could have been flattering, the company was horrified because it had exited the appliance business 16 years prior to the study! The problem was not with the respondents. The problem was with the company that had failed to communicate. Key stakeholders and influencers formed their opinion based on their own perceptions which the company had made little or no effort to understand (Massaro, 1991). What was needed here was a corporate identity program.

Be what you want to be

Many corporations mistakenly view communication as yet another activity that needs to "happen" and that this process needs to be "managed" to achieve the best results in the short, medium, and long-term. The simple truth is: Communication is a Commitment. Corporate entities have an ethical responsibility to communicate with (not just to) its audiences and stakeholders. It is worth remembering the Greek philosopher Aristotle who wrote: "If you want to appear to be something, then you must first be what you want to appear to be."

One of the best-known advertising slogans ever is the Hallmark line, "When you care enough to send the very best." This slogan was born in the 1940s. In his autobiography, J.C. Hall the founder of Hallmark wrote:

While we thought we had only established a good advertising slogan, we soon found out we had made a business commitment as well. (Hucker, 1991)

Corporate communication works best when it can simply hold a mirror to what is happening in the business, and what appears in the mirror is a pleasing picture. Credibility is automatically enhanced when this happens. Communication then serves as a really binding force internally as well. But, the mirror needs to be two-way, as in addition to looking internally, it also considers market dynamics externally. Many firms have foundered by gazing fondly (and myopically) at the pleasant internal view, a view not shared by external stakeholders. Too many organizations have been caught napping, when with the aid of internal and external characters, they could have been sharpening their perception of the outside world and acting accordingly.

Ralph Larsen, the CEO of Johnson & Johnson, a company that has nearly 100,000 employees and operates 190 decentralized operating units in 51 countries, says this of the J & J credo:

The only thing that holds us together is our credo, a set of operating principles that outlines our responsibility to customers, employees, managers, share-holders and the communities in which we live. It provides us with a compass for our management and our employees.

ILLUSTRATION

The Johnson & Johnson Credo

General Robert Wood Johnson, the son of the founder of Johson & Johnson who carried his father's name, wrote and first published the J & J Credo in 1943, defining the corporation's responsibility to its various constituents. Over the years, this Credo has been refined to incorporate thoughts like the environment and family welfare. But the spirit of the document remains the same today as when it was first written as exemplified by the Tylenol affair. In 2000, Johnson & Johnson was voted the most trusted brand name in the U.S.A.

We believe our first responsibility is to the doctors, nurses and patients, to mothers and fathers and all others who use our products and services. In meeting their needs, everything we do must be of high quality. We must constantly strive to reduce our costs in order to maintain reasonable prices. Customers' orders must be serviced promptly and accurately. Our suppliers and distributors must have an opportunity to make a fair profit.

ILLUSTRATION (cont'd)

We are responsible to our employees, the men and women who work with us throughout the world. Everyone must be considered as an individual. We must respect their dignity and recognize their merit. They must have a sense of security in their jobs. Compensation must be fair and adequate, and working conditions clean, orderly and safe. We must be mindful of ways to help our employees fulfil their family responsibilities. Employees must feel free to make suggestions and complaints. There must be equal opportunity for employment, development and advancement for those qualified. We must provide competent management, and their actions must be just and ethical.

We are responsible to the communities in which we live and work and to the world community as well. We must be good citizens – support good works and charities and bear our fair share of taxes. We must encourage civic improvements and better health and education. We must maintain in good order the property we are privileged to use, protecting the environment and natural resources.

Our final responsibility is to our stockholders. Business must make a sound profit. We must experiment with new ideas. Research must be carried on, innovative programs developed and mistakes paid for. New equipment must be purchased, new facilities provided and new products launched. Reserves must be created to provide for adverse times. When we operate according to these principles, the stockholders should realize a fair return.

Source: www.johnsonandjohnson.com.

Understand the need

External agencies must understand at a deep level why a corporation is seeking to implement a corporate communication program. Sparked by new technologies, businesses of all sizes are undergoing a radical transformation. The old hierarchical ways are yielding ground to flatter structures and networks. Vendors are getting integrated in seamless supply chains and becoming partners. Reverse auctions pit supplier against supplier, and price becomes a crucial determinant. More than ever, corporate leadership is expected to be inspirational, and CEOs are often expected to be media personalities and deliver measurable benefits. Employees are looking beyond security. They now want personal growth. The views of the corporation have changed over the past century, as shown in Table 11.1.

Every one of the 18 trends identified in the figure calls for more, not less, communication from the corporation. It is very critical for external advertising and other communication agencies to understand the corporate perspective and how and why that perspective has developed. With such

Table 11.1 A century of change for the corporation		
Characteristic	20th Century	21st Century
Organization	The Pyramid	The Web or Network
Focus	Internal	External
Style	Structured	Flexible
Source of strength	Stability	Change
Structure	Self-sufficiency	Interdependencies
Resources	Atoms – physical assets	Bits – information
Operations	Vertical integration	Virtual integration
Products	Mass production	Mass customization
Reach	Domestic	Global
Financials	Quarterly	Real time
Inventories	Months	Hours
Strategy	Top-down	Bottom-up
Leadership	Dogmatic	Inspirational
Workers	Employees	Employees and free agents
Job Expectations	Security	Personal growth
Motivation	To compete	To build
Improvements	Incremental	Revolutionary
Quality	Affordable best	No compromise
Source: Business Week, August 28, 2000.		

an understanding, agencies will be able to go beyond the brief, get to the heart of the issues, and deliver relevant solutions.

Communication is strategic

As stated earlier, if communication is a commitment, then it follows that it has to be strategic as well. Corporate communication, if developed and utilized appropriately, has far-reaching connotations, and can fundamentally impact the business. It can set the tone for the entire corporation. It can be an inspiring rallying point for all stakeholders. It can provide a sense of purpose and direction.

One of the most ignored strategic aspects of communication is the tone of voice. How real is it? How distinctive is it? How recognizable is it? Is it consistent with previous communication efforts and does it build on them?

These are critical questions that need to be answered in the development of corporate communication programs and maintained over time.

The tone of voice actually reflects the attitude of the corporation, and defines what the organization is all about. For example, when Apple Computer says "Think Different," its audience immediately "gets it." When IBM talks of e-business, the tone of the communication says it is knowledgeable, has expertise, and can provide solutions. As earlier mentioned, when GE says "We bring good things to life," it says that they care, are approachable and friendly, and they put the consumer first. In each of these examples, the communication becomes the clarion call of the corporation to all its constituents.

Commenting on the role of the communication executive in the 21st century, Joseph Calahan, Director, Communications and Public Relations, Xerox Corporations has this to say:

> The communication executive's role will be one of leadership. As organizational structure is broken down into small divisions and decentralized business units, entrepreneurial product-development teams are emerging. The Communicator's old role of cascading information down from the top is being replaced by their new job of developing core messages that everyone in the entire company should be communicating with one another. They will have the opportunity to set the communication framework for the entire company. (Calahan, 1995)

Diagnose the problem

Communicators have sometimes been referred to as "doctors of business." While it is important to pay close attention to the corporation's view of the problem, it is necessary to go beyond the brief and diagnose the real situation. Being close to the problem, it is not uncommon for company executives to read the situation differently than do audiences and other stakeholders (that is the "mirror" example).

The best way to test the hypothesis is to talk to the audience or key constituency and gauge their reactions and responses first hand. This can be done through formal research, or even through informal discussions. What is important is not the method, but the fact that the views of the audience are sought before the fact and a clear understanding of the situation determined first. Then, communication can occur.

Reporting on a study done on behalf of McDonald's, Rich Jernstedt, CEO, Golin/Harris Communications highlights the differences in the two views. As he reports:

In a study that ranked each location based on how consumers liked it, it was found that many restaurants received high scores from the company field consultants but received low scores from the customers and vice versa. One reason for the dichotomy was that the company was stressing mechanical perfection, while customers were more concerned with prompt service. (Jernstedt, 1995)

Pick the right tool

Managing communication is a serious responsibility. It often costs a great deal of money to conceive and run communication programs. In today's hyper-sensitive global environment, there are a wide variety of communication tools that can be cost-effectively employed. Be it the use of mass media, public relations, sponsorships, direct marketing, net-based communication, conferences or trade shows, selecting and deploying the right communication tools becomes a serious professional responsibility.

This writer is reminded of the introduction of the Seagram liquor brands into India some years ago. This was a category that had several restrictions on media product portrayals. Surprisingly, the agency employed by Seagram recommended, and the company implemented, a high cost corporate advertising campaign in mass media across the country. The campaign touted the heritage of the Seagram Corporation and alluded to the high quality of its brands. In truth, the heritage of Seagram could be traced back to the 1920s and 30s and liquor bootlegging from Canada into the United States. It was perplexing to see a company that had such a heritage and operating in such a category indulging in corporate advertising in mass media. The campaign perhaps did not yield the desired results, for it was pulled after just a short time.

Resolving this type of issue relates to the wrong choice of communication tool. Picking the right tool demands a sharp insightful understanding of the target constituency, an assessment of its nature, size, and disposition, and the message the organization is about to deliver. The sharper the understanding of the target, the sharper will be the selection of appropriate media, and consequently the more sharp will be the impact of the message. It is the principal responsibility of the outside communications agency to select and recommend the right set of tools to the corporation based on what it is trying to achieve.

Perspectives are different

A common perspective, shared by many people in top management and business, is to view what they do, and indeed what their organization does, as their own private affairs. In fact, many managers are affronted by what they believe are unnecessary and unwanted intrusions into their affairs, and the perceived actions of their companies.

In reality, big business is hardly a private matter. This is particularly true among companies that have raised capital from the stock markets. They become public citizens, living in glass houses, and all their actions are open to scrutiny.

Take the media for instance. The media view business completely differently from company management. They see businesses as having a huge impact on the public. They demand to know, as their right, whatever happens. They will put businesses under the microscope to get at the facts. And in their enthusiasm, they can give a perspective to facts and events that are quite different from that of the company.

Likewise, the perspective of the employees also varies from that of management. The actions of management have a huge impact on their lives. They demand to be included in the deliberations. Even if management does not have a forum for such deliberations, the employees will create their own informal forums. In a world of Intranets and e-mail, rest assured that this forum is online and operates on a 24x7x365 basis.

Proactive communication is the best way for management to align all the differing perspectives. Such an alignment is crucial for the corporate success in the 21st century.

The relevance and difference (R&D) test

Professional managers, particularly at the middle levels, look for external reassurances by way of research among the target audience. Apart from research conducted to identify or define the communication problem, research is also done frequently to test the correctness of the communication materials developed. Time and resources permitting, such research is a good way to make sure that the communication does not go off the rails.

Even before research is embarked upon, it is prudent to ask a few simple questions to evaluate the quality of communication. The R&D test, or the *Relevance* and *Difference* test, raises these questions.

- Is the communication (both content and method) *relevant* to the product/corporation?

- Is the communication (both content and method) *relevant* to the market?

- Is the communication (both content and method) *relevant* to the stake-holders and constituencies who could impact overall business and marketing performance?

- Is the communication (both content and method) *relevant* to the prospect(s)?

- Is the communication (both content and method) *different* from the competition?

- Is the communication (both content and method) *different* from the environmental clutter?

While these questions appear simple enough, it is quite surprising how many communication programs fail to pass the R&D test. For example, in the Seagram case cited earlier, both the content and method employed were not relevant to the organization's background or indeed to the product category. Thus, the communication program was flawed from the beginning.

Relevance can be established only with a clear sense of the corporation's history, values and culture. It calls for a clear definition of the problem, that is, who is being addressed for what reason and with what kind of messages.

Establishing a difference calls for a high degree of knowledge and awareness of the competitive activities as well as the overall communication environment. At a basic level, communication has to break through audience apathy and must be noticed. Communication must be distinct from competition. Beyond that, it must cut through the enormous clutter in the environment to be effective.

The human voice

The moment a company "needs" to communicate to any audience or constituency, chances are that the writing will get formal, and in the process stilted. In adopting the language of impersonality, corporations today all assume a similar character – that of being indistinguishable and somewhat aloof and unapproachable. If this is difficult to appreciate, just pick up any press or news release from a large corporation. It will be filled with passive statements that talk of how "initiatives have been taken to address the situation," "priorities have been identified to strengthen market presence" and so on.

Is it any surprise then that when a Richard Branson (CEO of the Virgin Group in the U.K.) comes along and holds really entertaining press meetings that connect with the audience he gets a disproportionate share of the media's attention, and usually in the most positive way?

Irrespective of all the latest technological advances, people always yearn for human contact. Any company that takes the trouble to be both clear and personal in its communication will score more than a few points with its customers, employees and publics, including shareholders and business analysts.

This business of human contact is not only about verbal communication. It applies equally to visual communication as well. Good visual communication should not be equated to being trendy. Both the words and pictures must be seamlessly integrated under a coherent theme, style and content, to connect with the audience at a human level.

Integrating the communication

We are living in an era where there are a plethora of choices for all constituents of a corporation. Consumers and customers can choose from a wide variety of vendors/suppliers. Shareholders can invest their money in an array of businesses, forms and geographies. Good employees can pretty much choose to work with whomever they want. The basis for choice becomes knowledge, familiarity and likeability of the corporation, and this is driven by communication. It follows then that communication can be, and often is, a source of significant competitive advantage.

Communication works best when it is integrated with the fundamentals of the corporation, and where each part works in harmony with other parts. Then, the overall impact is far greater than the pieces alone. Such integration can be viewed in five parts, as shown in Figure 11.3.

I   Communication must be integrated with the overall corporate mission and values. Therefore this must be articulated clearly so that all internal constituents understand and abide by it. What is the overall corporate strategy? What is the corporation trying to achieve? What is the corporation's attitude toward its various stakeholders? What are its principles by which it will be run? What are its goals vis-à-vis its various

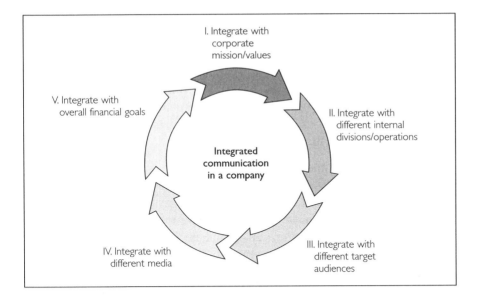

Figure 11.3 Integrated corporate communication

constituents? These are some of the fundamentals that must be articulated. Once that is clearly defined, all other activities and communication must be consistent with these stated objectives and values.

II The communication must be integrated between the various parts and
divisions of the corporation. We live in an era of scale and complexity.
It is not uncommon to witness different parts of a corporation pulling
in different directions. This can be directed in some measure only
when the roles, missions and values of the various divisions and the
product brands marketed are articulated under the overall umbrella
based on the corporate vision. Communication has to harmonize the
potentially conflicting parts of the corporation.

III Communication must be integrated in terms of the messages (both in
content and style) going to the various groups and target audiences. This
may seem obvious but it can easily be divergent. For example, the
corporation cannot be telling its shareholders that it is driving for long-
term value, even as it indulges in frequent and aggressive discounting
and price cuts in its sales and marketing programs. The corporation
cannot claim to be an equal opportunity employer, even as it eschews
suppliers owned by minorities. Lack of integration between the different
groups will result in lack of credibility and failure of communication.

IV Communication must be integrated between the various media used by the corporation. Whether it is a direct one-to-one contact or mass media, whether it is the website or internal communication, the corporation must strive for consistency. This does not immediately mean that the corporation must strive for "one-sight, one-sound" in all its communication programs. This may be neither practical nor necessary. However, it does mean that there are no contradictory messages being delivered in the different media.

V Communication must be integrated with the financial goals of the corporation. If communication is to be treated as an investment, measures must be identified to determine the return on this investment. The discipline must be enforced to outline the measurable outcomes for each identified audience group. Financial integration is often easier when the communication program is focused on a specific product brand. But it can be done for corporate communication programs too. The starting point is to have a measurement orientation and then follow through to ensure that it happens. (We discuss brand measurement in detail in Chapters 12 and 13.)

Integrating the communication from a corporation is not an automatic process. But it is crucial if the full potential of this function is to be harnessed.

Conclusion

As business looks ahead into the 21st century with many hopes and expectations, one thing is clear. Customers, employees, shareholders and the community at large are all looking for a clear understanding of the corporation and its character. If companies do not communicate, these audiences will sort out the information available for themselves. What the company cannot afford to do is project something that it is not. To cut through the clutter, companies will need a coherent and distinctive communication tone. External agencies that can guide and deliver these types and kinds of programs will indeed be making a significant contribution to the success of the corporation in the marketplace.

Texaco: A Shadow on the Red Star

Statement to the shareholders made in the Texaco, Inc. Annual Report 1996:

One of the things we hold in the highest esteem at Texaco is our company's image and reputation. A company's reputation touches many facets of its business – its stock price, its ability to negotiate with companies and governments, the viability of its brand and its bottom line. A strong reputation is registered in the pride of employees and their commitment to uphold the integrity of that reputation ...

If we, as individual companies, are able to clearly communicate the value we add to the world, we will enhance an asset of incalculable worth – our reputation.

Peter I. Bijur
Chairman of the Board and CEO
and Allen J. Krowe
Vice Chairman

Introduction

In the foregoing chapter, we have discussed how corporations are vulnerable given their size, public profile and complexity. The expectation from a corporation is one of flawless behavior towards its various constituents. This is not always possible, given that corporations comprise people at all levels, and human beings tend to make mistakes. The vulnerability of corporations is such that they can be confronted with a crisis from the most unexpected quarters, in the most unexpected manner and at the most unexpected of times.

This case about Texaco is intended to highlight the vulnerability of corporations, and the adversarial relationships between the corporation and its various constituents.

Texaco was suddenly faced with a crisis in 1996 from some unexpected developments, forcing it to make a large settlement in a racial discrimination lawsuit filed by some of the company's African-American employees. This crisis threatened to place the corporation on a collision course with its employees, customers, the government and the community at large. The company took swift action to correct the situation, and by the year 2000 had even emerged as a model corporate citizen in many respects. Critical to this turnaround was vigorous internal and external communication that was undertaken by the company.

This case traces the history of Texaco from its origins in Texas nearly a hundred years ago. It presents the facts about Texaco, how the reputation of

ILLUSTRATION (cont'd)

TEXACO

| 1903 – The Texas Company adopted the five-pointed star of the state of Texas as its symbol | The streamlined star symbol continues till date as one of the most readily recognized symbols anywhere |

Figure 11.4 The Texaco star logo

this proud company was blotted, and, how it came out of the situation. At the end of the case are a few questions that professional communicators can discuss and debate, to determine the role that proactive communications could have perhaps played in averting the crisis in the first place.

From Spindletop to the top of the world

The history of oil in the United States dates back to the time when the first oil well was drilled in western Pennsylvania in 1859. For over four decades, this region held sway over the supplies of kerosene and gasoil to the ever-increasing population and tide of immigrants to the North American continent. The discovery of the Spindletop field, south of Beaumont, Texas in 1901 effectively moved the American "oil patch" from Pennsylvania to the Southwest.

The Texas Company was incorporated on April 7, 1902 by a group of seasoned oilmen and financiers, led by Joseph Cullinan, and this company grew with further discoveries of oil around Beaumont. The unique talent and energy of the founders of this company tamed a turbulent time of blowing oil fields, prodigious waste of crude and raucous boomtowns. The Texas Company ultimately emerged as the only survivor of more than 200 oil companies born at Spindletop.

Right from the beginning, what distinguished the Texas Company was its foresight and understanding of the basics. Even as it discovered oil, the company invested in building pipelines to gather the oil, and tanks to store it in. The company secured contracts with other producers to assure itself crude at favorable prices, and it worked to increase markets by converting locomotives to run on oil and piping gas to business establishments. Conservation was seen as good business. The company worked to plug abandoned wells, and it advocated proper well spacing as opposed to small tract drilling.

The Texas Company saw itself then, and continues to do so even today, as a complete player in the oil, and indeed the energy, business. This includes the *Upstream* activities of exploration and production of crude oil, the *Midstream* activities of trading and transportation and the *Downstream* activities of manufacturing, refining and marketing. Over the nine decades of its existence, the company has innovated in all these aspects, often leading the industry with new methods and sharing these innovations through joint ventures and partnerships.

Upstream activities: Texaco realized that unlocking the earth's secret would be a costly and complex effort, requiring the latest technology and trained experts. After its successful discoveries in the first two decades of its existence in the American Southwest, Texaco ventured overseas to discover oil in the 1930s. Using its new technology of reflection seismography to "see beneath the earth's surface." Texaco discovered oil in geographies as diverse as Colombia, Venezuela and Indonesia. In 1936, it partnered with Chevron to form the Arabian American Oil Company in Saudi Arabia.

The company set up its first geophysical laboratory as early as 1929, and this was expanded to the extensive center in Houston in 1941. Many hundreds of innovations have come out of these labs. Believing in extracting the maximum oil from fields already discovered, the company pioneered methods like steam flooding, horizontal drilling, dual lateral horizontal drilling and 3-D seismic imaging technology.

Offshore drilling was pioneered in 1933 with the industry's first drilling barge – Texaco's *Gilliasco*. The *Gilliasco* drilled in 13 feet of water in coastal Louisiana by providing the stability of a permanent derrick with the portability of the barge. From this humble beginning in offshore drilling, Texaco has moved on and it today operates the complex Tartan platform weighing 37,000 metric tons and towering 335 feet above the water in the North Sea. With a complex sub-sea production pipeline system, the Tartan field is a towering testimony of the engineering prowess of the company.

From its early Spindletop days of producing 15,000 barrels of oil per day, as of 1996 Texaco had grown to producing over 800,000 barrels of crude and over 2000 millions of cubic foot of natural gas per day. This was achieved even as the company expanded its proven reserves to nearly three billion barrels of oil and 6000 billions of cubic feet of natural gas.

Midstream activities: Ensuring the flow of oil to the refineries, and finished products from there to consumers all over the world, is a complex task in logistics. It started in 1902 with a 20-mile pipeline to move crude from Spindletop to Port Arthur, where ocean barges carried the oil to eastern refineries and Louisiana sugar mills. Today Texaco uses a variety of transportation methods ranging from tankers to tugboats and trains to tank trucks to pipelines, to safely and efficiently move hundreds of its products.

Texaco had, as early as in 1905, a fleet of four oceangoing cargo ships to move its crude oil and products, and this was continuously expanded through the years. Emerging from the war, the T-2 cargo ship of 14,000 tons of carrying capacity gave way to the super tankers of 200,000 to 300,000 and then 500,000 deadweight tons bringing crude to Texaco refineries.

There were significant achievements along the way in moving the oil through other methods. In 1942, Texaco helped make possible the construction of pipelines from East Texas to Philadelphia, as an unsinkable way to transport oil as Nazi submarines were seeking to interrupt coastal shipping. In 1950, Texaco helped build the 1000-mile long Trans Arabian Pipeline to move Saudi oil to the Mediterranean, and thus cut the distance of shipping crude by thousands of miles. The company today owns or shares ownership of some 30,000 miles of crude and product pipelines, enabling it to keep its refineries and service stations running without disruption.

Downstream activities: Texaco's manufacturing began at the Port Arthur works in 1903, producing gasoil and kerosene. From this beginning, the company today has built one of the largest, most efficient refining systems in the world, processing over 1.3 million barrels of crude a day. The company's refineries utilize the latest technologies to produce high-value products while meeting all environmental requirements.

Significant Texaco innovations in downstream activities include the industry's first continuous thermal cracking method for refining crude oil which doubled the amount of gasoline that could be produced from a barrel of crude. The company introduced a process for dewaxing lubricating oil thereby improving cold weather starting characteristics. These have become standards throughout the oil industry.

Texaco has over the years moved into petrochemicals with leadership positions in products like ethylene and butadiene, and specialty chemicals like propylene oxide.

In the arena of marketing, Texaco has always been a leader in promoting gasoline, lubricants and other products. Some of the earliest marketing images are of friendly curbside filling stations with a single vacuum pump. This picture has evolved into the System 2000 station first introduced in 1983. The bold design with convenience stores, self-serve gasoline and other customer-oriented facilities, the System 2000 station is recognized as one of the most attractive and efficient in the country. Texaco today markets its products through 22,000 service stations located in the western, southwest and mid-continent areas of the U.S.A., Latin America and in regional markets in Europe and West Africa. Texaco's refined product sales worldwide exceeded two-and-a-half million barrels a day in 1996.

Texaco has expanded beyond producing and marketing petroleum products to explore opportunities in producing alternate energy. The most prominent of the alternate energy efforts are cogeneration (which uses clean-burning natural gas to create electricity and steam) and gasification (which uses coal, other fuels and waste material to produce electricity). In 1996, Texaco operated 12 cogeneration and gasification facilities producing more than 1500 megawatts of electricity.

With shareholder's equity exceeding $10 billion, revenues exceeding $45 billion and net income exceeding $2 billion, the Texaco of 1996 had operations in more than 150 countries. Texaco and its affiliates helped meet the world's energy needs by finding and producing crude oil, manufacturing and marketing high-quality fuel and lubricants, operating transportation, trading and distribution facilities, and producing alternate forms of energy for power and manufacturing. Texaco has indeed traveled a long distance from Spindletop to the top of the world in its over nine decades of existence.

The crisis

By all accounts, Texaco was in good shape in 1996. Out of the blue, in November 1996, the crisis hit the company.

Through most of 1996, Texaco had been involved in defending itself against a discrimination lawsuit brought by some African-American employees. The defense was seen as a routine matter, and in any case the company could not possibly concede to be following any discriminatory practices.

The stupefying news came to the notice of the defense lawyers and company management on the evening of Sunday November 3, 1996. A former top Texaco official had secretly taped meetings about the lawsuit, during which he and his colleagues freely used racial epithets and seemed to be discussing how and when to make some incriminating documents disappear. Worse, the official had supplied copies of the tapes to the plaintiff's attorneys and the *New York Times*, which would be printing the story the very next day, November 4.

The response to the news story was swift and came from all constituents.

- The stock market hammered the stock, as investors fled not knowing how the lawsuit would affect the company. Several major shareholders, including the New York State controller whose state was one of the company's biggest investors, called the management of Texaco and wondered aloud if they should remain invested in Texaco. The stock price plunged more than $3 per share in the days after the tapes became public, wiping out nearly $1 billion from the company's market capitalization.

- The employees of Texaco were horrified and began to question the practices of the company. They were left feeling ashamed, and it was no longer such a good feeling to be carrying a Texaco card. There was also anger and frustration that the company could not handle these issues quietly and privately. How did things get to such a pass? Were we as bad as we were being made out to be? These were the questions employees were asking management in internal forums and meetings.

- The media had a field day. They went on to dig for more malpractice by Texaco. After all here was a big powerful company that was completely exposed by the tapes on a very sensitive matter. Past and present minority employees were interviewed for further exposes. The management was pilloried for looking the other way on the subject of racial discrimination, or even encouraging such behavior.

- The consumers of Texaco products began to wonder if they were doing business with the right company. Some consumer groups, including some minority activist groups, started to call for a boycott of Texaco products.

- The direct trade customers were embarrassed. Consumers at the retail front asked them awkward questions. Worse yet, many started to worry about doing business with a company with questionable practices and reputation.

- The government started to take an interest in Texaco's affairs. Was the company following the guidelines on equal employment opportunity or not? Was there a case for legal violation? Should Texaco be reviewed and punished, and thus made an example, so that other companies are discouraged from similar practices? These were some of the questions raised in various quarters.

The crisis facing Texaco was real and more than just a public relations disaster. In its 94-year history, the company had taken many risks and overcome many obstacles. But in all these years, it had never faced a public crisis of this kind and magnitude that demanded it to seriously review its basic beliefs. As Peter Bijur, the CEO himself said at that time, this was among the "most wrenching and emotional in our company's history."

Responding to the crisis

Right or wrong, guilty as charged or not, company officials knew they were staring at a disaster. Swift response was called for. Peter Bijur called for an immediate settlement. Eleven days after the *New York Times* story appeared, the lawyers agreed on a figure – $140 million in damages and back pay for minority employees, and another $35 million to set up an independent task force to monitor the company's diversity efforts for five years. As Bijur said in a speech four days after the settlement: "It was the reasonable and honorable course of action. It takes the issues we face from the realm of confrontation in the courts into the arena of active cooperation and joint action. It allows the healing process to proceed."

If company officials thought that this was the end of the crisis, they were in for a surprise. A few months later came the after shocks. A book titled *Roberts vs. Texaco* authored by Bari-Ellen Roberts, one of the plaintiffs and a former Texaco African-American employee was published. The book laid out the worst of Texaco's race faults. Among other things, the book unveiled the pay disparities for minorities at Texaco. This was a virtual confirmation of institutionalized discrimination. This time around, people did not even doubt the contents of the book. Since this was about Texaco's racial discrimination practices, the book must be true.

The company management knew that they had to act decisively to address the issue of racial tolerance and diversity in the workplace. Equally important, these actions had to be communicated forcefully and repeatedly inside the company, and outside the company. A firm and quantifiable plan of action was drawn up and communicated with vigor.

Management spent an enormous amount of time meeting with leaders of the NAACP, the Urban League, the Rainbow Coalition, the Southern Christian Leadership Conference and other civil rights groups. One-to-one meetings were held with media where the CEO was queried repeatedly on why people should believe that Texaco would act as per its plans. Internal meetings were held in various Texaco locations to inform people what the company had already done, and was planning to do further to correct the situation.

Over and over again, the message was the same – that Texaco will not tolerate disrespect, and those who act inappropriately will have to leave the company. The company was clear that racial diversity and tolerance was the right thing to do, and that it would immensely benefit the company. Texaco is not just a faceless monolith, the company officials repeatedly said. It is oilrig workers in West Texas and office workers in Westchester ... It is geologists in Kazakhstan and engineers in L.A ... It is small and mid-size entrepreneurs whose businesses bear the Texaco name ... It is 28,000 good and decent people ... They cannot be painted broadly with the brush of racism, since that is just not the case.

The company announced a comprehensive plan to ensure fairness and economic opportunity for its employees and business partners with specific initiatives that could be tracked over time. These included the following:

1. *Recruitment and hiring*

   - Use of search firms with record of recruiting from a diverse range of candidates
   - Undertake scholarship/internship programs to develop minority students for management careers
   - Set a target to increase employment of African-Americans to 13 percent, and employment of women to 35 percent by the year 2000.

2. *Retention and career development*

   - Provide managers with the information and improved skills they need to ensure that promotions are fair and equitable.

3. *Workplace initiatives*

   - Implement diversity learning experience for all U.S.-based employees
   - Include women and minorities on all Human Resource Committees
   - Implement an Alternative Dispute Resolution Process, including the use of an outside counselor.

4. *Accountability and oversight*

   - Implement the company's 360-degree feedback process to include all managers
   - Link managers' compensation to their performance in creating openness and inclusion in the workplace
   - Redesign the employee opinion survey to monitor the success of Texaco's change efforts.

In addition to the above internal initiatives, the company also initiated a number of steps to strengthen its partnering efforts with a broader base of vendors and suppliers of services.

After setting many of these initiatives in motion, Texaco also launched a vigorous external corporate communications program under the theme "Relentless pursuit of energy" which was later modified to "A world of energy." The campaign sought to portray the human face of Texaco, as people with a singular focus of pursuing the worthwhile cause of meeting the energy needs of the world. The company committed significant resources to this process that was overseen by the CEO himself.

Postscript

Reports *Fortune* magazine in its September 6, 1999 issue: "Texaco is in the midst of a remarkable transformation, one that just may turn the company into a bastion of equal opportunity for people of color. In time it may even become a model for any corporation that wants to learn how to become more hospitable to employees of all races."

Questions for professional communicators

1. Could Texaco have averted the crisis at all? What perhaps could have been done in communication terms, both internally and externally, to achieve this?

2. If the crisis was inevitable, what communication practices, if any, should Texaco have followed prior to the crisis to minimize the impact?

3. Once the crisis happened, what communication program should the company have followed to minimize the fallout?

Source: Author.

Vision, values, intellectual property and assets

anders gronstedt and don e. schultz

Facing Up To or Being Faced Down by the Analysts

The following is a true story. But, the names have been changed to protect the participant egos. The story, however, is not unlike others that are occurring daily in management meetings around the world, particularly when senior management and analysts and market-makers face-off in forward-looking discussions.

Mr. Guardo Batista is CEO of Biggo Industries, one of the largest manufacturing organizations in the world. While things are going well in the marketplace, that is, sales are up, profits are meeting expectations, acquisitions are being made with little or no resistance and there have been no strikes, work stoppages or even demonstrations by environmentalists (Biggo has manufacturing plants in many first, second and third world countries), Batista still has a problem.

A couple of years ago, at a regular board meeting, one of the largest shareholding external directors started a conversation that went something like this. "Guardo, you're doing a great job as CEO. We're all happy with the direction the company is going. But, we believe the firm is under-valued. Analysts, investors and the fund managers don't understand what we're doing. Maybe we should try to improve our communication programs. If the analysts and fund managers only knew the 'real story' about Biggo, share prices would probably go up by about 20 or 30 percent."

Batista agreed. The shares were, in his opinion, under-valued. While he felt he had fairly good success in explaining the corporate focus and direction, analysts had not "bought into the Biggo story." Therefore, share prices had not moved as he and the board thought they should. So, he came to the same conclusion that his board had: Biggo Industries needed better communi-

cation with the financial groups. What better way than a corporate advertising program? In that forum, Biggo could communicate its strategy. Show
some neat examples of new products, acquisitions, corporate direction,
vision and so on. In short, really build a fire under the stock price. After all,
folks like BASF, ABB, Mobil, Archer-Daniels-Midland and many others had
done this quite successfully for years.

So, two years ago, Biggo initiated a small corporate advertising program. It
talked about all the things Guardo and other Biggo managers thought were
important. It was placed in the media the agency had recommended. And,
corporate managers were happy with it. It was sure to work.

But there was a problem: analysts thought corporate advertising at that
particular time in Biggo's business history was a bad idea. They challenged
Batista, gently but firmly. Why was he doing this? What was the purpose?
What was the value? How much was Biggo spending? And, why?

Batista answered with all the usual platitudes. The market doesn't know us.
This is our way of communicating with the marketplace. Investors want to
know what we are doing. Jack Welch at GE does this. And so on.

Thinking the problem with analysts was simply one of explanation and illustration, Batista asked Biggo to double the corporate advertising spend for
the following year. That's when the roof fell in. Analysts, as analysts are prone
to do, stepped up their attack on the advertising campaign. They challenged
Batista in every meeting. They asked hard questions. Ones that the corporate
communication director couldn't help Batista answer and ones the agency
simply couldn't field. The true problem, of course, was: it was very difficult to
separate out why the analysts were attacking the corporate advertising for
Biggo Industries. Why they thought it was such a bad idea. And, Guardo, not
being an advertising expert, found it hard to provide useful answers to their
increasingly tough questions. Were the analysts challenging the creative
approach? The media decisions? The amount being invested? Or, was this just
an easy way to prick the corporate ego?

Because there were no immediate answers, Guardo's best way out was to
simply kill off the problem, in other words, get rid of the irritation. So, Batista
ordered an immediate stop to the corporate advertising campaign. The
analysts had won. They had chased the leader of one of the biggest companies
in the world from the field of play.

But, Batista didn't get where he was by running from a fight. He was determined
to find ways to support his decision to conduct a corporate, brand-building,
image-enhancing, share-value-growth-building corporate communication
program. We'll look at his solution at the end of the chapter.

Introduction

The title of this chapter: "Vision, values, intellectual property and assets" may seem a strange title for a chapter in a corporate communication management book. And, even more peculiar is that it comes so late in the text. And, even stranger that this chapter is continued in Chapter 13 concerning measuring corporate brand value. And, it's almost weird that the "vision" comes at the end and not the beginning. After all, isn't it easy to understand values? Aren't they the bedrock of the organization? Intellectual properties are the basic DNA of the firm. And, everyone knows that the quantity of assets controlled by the corporate communication director are generally quite small compared to the managers of the operating divisions. So, what a strange combination and what unusual timing.

But, the timing of this chapter is no accident. It is driven by our initial focus on the major issues facing corporate communication directors in ongoing, current and real time contexts. In other words, short-term communication management issues. As the old saw goes: "If you don't manage the short-term, there will be no long-term." So, we dealt with the short-term issues in the first eleven chapters, that is, crisis communication, marketing public relations, mergers and acquisitions, the CEO as corporate champion and the like. Chapter 11 considered the corporation in its historical and modern context and the need for judicious alliance with appropriate agencies.

But, it is now time to think about the long term, that is, the firm as an ongoing business entity that has value to a broad range of stakeholders and how communication can build or enhance that corporate value over time. That means looking at the firm as an organic system that has values and vision and missions to define and accomplish. Most of all, it means looking at the corporation as an economic entity in which employees, shareholders and management have huge, life-defining stakes. And, trying to determine the value that corporate communication can develop or deliver in this context.

So, how does all this fit within the parameters or the duties of the corporate communication manager? And, most of all, how does it fit under the corporate umbrella? That's what we explore in this chapter.

We start first with the corporate vision and mission and how those define and determine the values, direction, responses and performance of the organization. Most of all, we relate how these elemental corporate building blocks lead to the creation of the corporate brand. We then illustrate how employees and managers, along with customers, prospects and other stakeholders combine to create and define the corporate brand and determine its value to each and all of them.

Then, if we believe the corporate brand has more than intellectual value, that is, some type of financial value, we need to consider the source and structure of that value. That is generally called brand equity. The financial value that makes up brand equity can then be considered an asset of the firm. Assets are forms of value for the firm, shareholders, management, employees, in short, everyone connected to the company. Thus, the corporate communication manager becomes an asset manager of what is often one of the most valuable corporate assets, the corporate brand. (We take up the management of the corporate brand as an asset in Chapter 13.) So, that's the trek we start in this chapter and complete in the following.

The sum and substance of managing a corporate brand

Figure 12.1 illustrates the conceptual framework behind our view of how the corporate brand can be developed and managed. As shown below, we have visualized the four areas covered in this chapter as:

- vision and mission

- internal managers and employees

- customers and other stakeholders

- corporate assets.

These make up the four quadrants of the corporate umbrella. These four elements, when combined, coordinated and properly assembled, serve to cover, protect and nurture the total corporate value, what we will call here, the corporate brand and the resulting corporate brand equity.

Inherent in all our discussion in this chapter is that the corporate communication manager, assuming he/she is truly part of the corporate management team, or hopes to be, by managing the corporate brand and reputation (recall the discussion of corporate reputation in Chapters 8 and 9) often has responsibility for one of the most valuable assets of the firm, that is, the corporate brand. (We discuss the value of the corporate brand and how it might be measured in Chapter 13.)

So, the theme is developed. The corporate communication manager generally has substantial responsibility in helping the organization develop and define the corporate vision and mission. Those corporate commit-

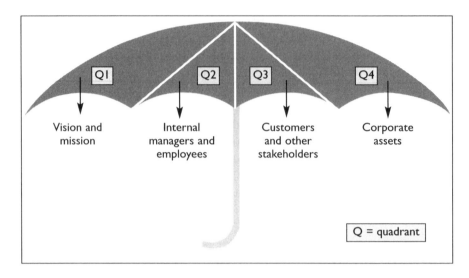

Figure 12.1 Corporate brand value umbrella

ments define the basis on which the firm will operate. They, in turn, influence the actions and activities of the management, employees, suppliers, distributors and other internal stakeholders. Those people and their actions then impact customers and prospects. The organization's customers, prospects and other stakeholders then further define and refine the corporate values, the corporate meaning and, ultimately, the corporate brand. So, whether they formally do so or not, the internal and external stakeholders agree on what the corporate brand is, what it can and what it should be. And, they communicate what they believe the brand to be to the rest of the world through their actions and activities.

As a result of this internal and external agreement or at least consensus among the various stakeholders, the corporate brand develops various forms of value, again both internal and external. (Interestingly, in some cases, the value of the corporate brand is far greater than that of other corporate assets, and in some cases, even greater than that of major operating divisions. We discuss this issue in Chapter 13 as well.) So, as an asset manager, the corporate communication director must rethink his or her role, likely develop new management capabilities and often take on new responsibilities. That's what this chapter is designed to assist in: to prepare the corporate communication manager for the longer-term decisions that increasingly are being required to build and align corporate visions and missions. Bring together and align the internal values of the managers and employees. Meet the external needs and requirements of stakeholders, customers, and prospects. Then, finally, manage the corporate brand as one of the major assets of the organization. It's a large but do-able task as we will illustrate in this chapter and the next.

The vision thing

Inherent in any corporate brand is what the organization, that is the employees, management and other stakeholders, believe the brand to be. That commonly comes from the vision and mission work the organization has defined, developed and communicated over time and to which most managers and employees have agreed or bought into. Most corporate communication directors are intimately familiar with the development of a corporate vision and the structuring and detailing of the various corporate mission statements. Therefore, we will not revisit that ground here. Instead, we will take a different view of what those vision and mission statements are all about and how they might be used to build stakeholder value. In short, we will discuss how the corporate vision and mission are related to generating corporate value through the corporate brand. That is important for it provides tangible, measurable and, hopefully, increasing cash flows and shareholder value far into the future.

In our approach, the future value the corporate communication manager is in charge of managing is clearly the corporate brand. And, in many cases, the corporate brand is really nothing more than a formalized translation of the corporate vision and mission of the organization that has been shared with customers, prospects and other stakeholders (see the discussion in Chapter 3). So, we start first with what we call "the vision thing." Some examples will help make the point:

Fed Ex: ... "Mr. Smith, I have an international question about explaining our service to Europe ..." The question blares from the stereo speakers of a large television set in the center of a Federal Express lunchroom.

Men and women in FedEx uniforms munch on their sandwiches with their heads turned to the television screen as they watch the familiar face of Fred Smith, the venerated founder and chairman of the company. The white-haired figure on the screen sits in a studio setting resembling the *Larry King Live* show. With a pensive look on his face, he waits patiently for the caller to finish her question. He then leans forward and gives a rapid-fire response about how particular international deliveries should be handled. Just as suddenly, he slows down, lowers the pitch of his voice and concludes, "I'll ask Tom or someone on his staff to draft a response that he can get to all of our customer service representatives by tomorrow morning about how to handle such requests. Is that okay with you, Vicky?" Vicky confirms that she is happy with the response.

This is the typical scene at every one of the 1200 Federal Express offices in the United States and hundreds of offices around the world that are reached by *One-On-One*, a call-in show on FedEx's closed-circuit television network. During the show, any employee from around the world can pick up the phone and speak live, on the air with the company's chairman. The calls are not screened. When Fred Smith gets a question he does not know how to answer, one of his senior managers will call in to respond on air. In this sense, the programs serve as corporate town hall meetings where employees and senior managers have an open dialogue and resolve problems.

It is one of many ways in which FedEx communicates its vision of "people–service–profit" to its 140,000-plus workforce. Explains Fred Smith, "When employees are placed first, they will provide the highest possible service, and profits will follow." FedEx sets a "people objective," a "service objective," and a "profit objective" every year. Every employee knows at the beginning of the fiscal year what these three objectives are, and every manager is accountable for specific objectives based on these three corporate objectives. And, that's not all. If the company does not reach the annual employee satisfaction, profit, and service quality goals, the top 300 managers lose their entire bonuses, which are about 40 percent of their salaries.

By putting its money where its mouth is, the board of FedEx sends a clear message to employees and managers that customers and employees are in charge of the operation. "It probably sounds trite, but the people–service–profit credo really is embedded in the culture," attests Gregory Rossiter, public relations managing director. FedEx's management recognizes that its workforce doesn't just deliver letters and packages, it delivers the FedEx brand to the marketplace. By caring for employees and keeping them informed, all brand communication, both corporate and product, can be enforced by employees in their daily contact with customers and other stakeholders (Gronstedt, 1999).

Based on a seven-year study on world-class companies conducted by one of the authors, one common theme clearly stood out – successful global corporate communication starts with a vision of how the organization and its brands adds value to its customers and other stakeholders. The vision provides focus and a sense of purpose to the entire organization. It needs to be anchored in the values and philosophies the company stands for and the mission or purpose of the company (Gronstedt, 1999).

In many organizations, the vision statements are prominently featured in every office, particularly those of world-class companies. They hang as framed pictures in lobbies, coffee rooms, and in the offices. They are featured on the covers of annual reports and prominently featured on the websites. At many companies, when questioned, managers will pull out cards from their shirt pockets that contain the vision, mission philosophy, and annual goals of the company and their part in achieving those objectives. Saturn's public relations manager, Greg Martin, explains the significance of the cards: "Everything we do is done in the context of those three cards. It pretty much ensures that everybody sings off of the same song sheet; everybody is in tune." Although these statements are typically simplistic, they do indeed help energize and focus everyone in the organization. Besides, other people are going to sum up your company in a few words anyway, so you might as well do the job for them (Gronstedt, 1999).

Building a customer-centric vision

The challenge is to develop a vision for the company and its brands that is specific enough to provide real guidance, yet is adaptable enough in today's rapidly changing environment. Some companies make the mistake of crafting exceedingly vague visions that offer the precision of "Make love, not war." On the other hand, a vision that is too detailed, focusing on particular products or technology, will only serve to maintain the status quo.

The classic example of how a vision can paralyze, rather than propel a company forward, is Xerox's failure to capitalize on the personal computer. Xerox's Palo Alto Research Center invented the personal computer in the 1970s, along with its many features, including the mouse, the window concept with pull-down menus, and the computer networking system, Ethernet. These innovations could have made the company a bigger fortune than xerography. But Xerox decided against taking its wonder products to the market because they didn't fit with the company's copying business. Thus, it sat on the truly breakthrough concepts for six years, until a couple of teenage kids named Steven Jobs and Steve Wozniak commercialized them with the Macintosh. The rest, as they say, is history. Xerox had a vision that hampered its growth rather than fostering it, by focusing on products rather than customer needs.

But let's give the management of Xerox credit for partially learning from its mistakes. In recent years, the Xerox brand has been carefully grooming itself to transcend its physical products and instead represent a broad range of document solutions. The firm is now offering professional services such as building digital office networks and even running outsourced printing and copying operations. The onetime maker of photocopiers is now "The Document Company," a one-stop shop for scanning, storing, custom printing, and faxing products and services – the goal is to be a digital powerhouse in the information age. Whether or not Xerox will be able to overcome the accumulated problems of the past years is still to be determined. But, at least it has created the vision that shows they are trying.

As Xerox recognized, the vision needs to be based not only on the firm's core competency – the bundle of skills, technologies and employee capabilities that is central to its strength – but also on opportunities in the marketplace. And, it needs to be a broadly phrased direction for the company rather than a detailed plan, expressed in terms of customer benefits rather than product features. When a division of Danish-based manufacturer Danfoss replaced its vision of "selling air filters" to one that involved "selling clean air," it became more of a service company that offered measurement and advice on dust prevention and other environmental hazards even though it didn't change its culture or its vision or even its mission (Gronstedt, 1999).

The vision of the company is sometimes the brainchild of senior managers. The founders of Volvo scribbled down the vision that the Volvo car would stand for quality and safety in a sauna in 1925 (Gronstedt, 1999). But, this is the exception rather than the rule. In fact, the vision of successful companies is rarely dreamed up by the CEO while taking a hot shower, brainstormed during a retreat by senior managers with bloated bladders, or evoked during a rain dance by a management consultant. Instead, it evolves from an ongoing dialogue among employees and managers of all ranks and, importantly, with customers and other stakeholders. When Carly Fiorina became CEO of Hewlett-Packard, she went on a road show to encourage employees around the world to send her an e-mail with the ten most stupid things the company did. She still reads and responds to thousands of e-mails from employees every month. E-mailing is an effective way for executives such as Fiorina to keep a finger on the pulse of employees and practice virtual "management by wandering around" (MBWA) in such a far-flung global operation.

MBWA was invented by her predecessor and HP founder, Dave Packard, who described it this way: "Straightforward as it sounds, there are some subtleties and requirements that go with MBWA. It needs to be frequent, friendly, unfocused, and unscheduled – but far from pointless. And since its principal aim is to seek out people's thoughts and opinions, it requires good listening." World-class leaders use virtual and actual

MBWA to develop a common future of their organizations and their brands" (Gronstedt 1999).

Moving from vision and mission to brand promises: the heart of the corporate brand

Once a customer-centric, corporate big picture has been developed, it needs to be condensed into a succinct, pithy brand promise that can be communicated effectively to the marketplace and all the stakeholders. The "people–service–profit" vision of FedEx, for instance, is translated into the brand promise of "The World on Time." This promise is made repeatedly in all marketing and corporate communication activities, both internal and external. And every employee is enlisted to live up to the promise and exceed it at every point of customer contact. FedEx even delivers on its promise in its charitable work, through a strategic alliance with the American Red Cross. When a national disaster strikes, FedEx transports containers of cell phones, faxes, and radio equipment to the disaster site, needed for the Red Cross's Quick Response Team. "By sending planes to deliver needed supplies to Chinese flood victims a few summers ago, FedEx cemented its relationship with the community while demonstrating its quick response and global capabilities," says David Drobis (1999), CEO of FedEx's PR firm, Ketchum, adding, "The company seized an opportunity to do good, while gaining added visibility for its value proposition." FedEx also uses its international delivery expertise to aid the Red Cross in the tracking and reuniting of families that have been separated due to war or natural disasters. The company makes a difference in the world by contributing its unique delivery, logistics, and warehousing expertise and capabilities to a broad range of stakeholders. In the process, it's reinforcing its promise of "The World on Time" (Gronstedt, 1999).

The brand promise should not be an afterthought once the product is developed and the price is set. The brand promise of automaker Saturn was developed even before its first car was on the market. It decided early on to put the company before the product: "A Different Kind of Company, a Different Kind of Car." In a refreshing break from the industry tradition of auto-fetishism commercials featuring cars racing in deserts and mountains, the Saturn advertisements showcased real employees and customers talking about their experiences with the Saturn company. Embedding the brand vision in the advertising is only the first step. The message of Saturn being a "Different Kind of Company" is embedded with every brand contact point – every print ad, every interaction with a retailer, and every phone call with a customer service rep. The Saturn sales consultants have all undergone a rigorous one-week training program at the Spring Hill manufacturing plant, to better communicate with each customer how Saturn is a different kind of company. They don't just tour the plant and listen to presentations, they work together building cars or helping the community. The sales people are brought back regularly to Spring Hill to support their jobs as ambassadors of the Saturn brand.

Guided by the internal vision and the external application, Saturn quickly overtook Ford Escort to become the best-selling small car in the United States, capturing an astonishing 10.4 percent share of the small car and sports car market. The following year, Saturn was rated best in overall satisfaction among all car brands, including luxury brands like Lexus and Mercedes-Benz. Ten years after the launch of the new automotive brand, the same brand promise is still featured in all communication. "If we have any legacy at Saturn," proclaims Don Hudler, former Saturn President, "it will be that we built an outstanding brand." The fact the Saturn brand was not built by crafting a façade of smoke and mirrors through advertising imagery and publicity stunts is history. Instead, Saturn focused on every point of contact with customers and stakeholders which it then leveraged to communicate the value proposition of the brand. This change redefines communication with a lower case "c," to Communication with a capital "C" – from a discrete function acting as the sole conduit to customers and stakeholders, to a state of mind of everyone in the organization. In summary, everyone in the organization needs to be involved in creating the brand experience for the customer and other stakeholders (Gronstedt, 1999).

So, that is how the vision and mission relate to the development and articulation of the corporate brand. That's the first quadrant of the corporate umbrella illustrated in Figure 12.1 and it also shows how the internal direction of the firm is related to the other three, managers and employees, customers and shareholders, and corporate assets.

From internal vision to external value – the role of managers and employees

The second quadrant of the corporate umbrella that defines the corporate brand value are, as discussed above, the managers and employees (see Chapters 2 and 3). There is little question that a clearly defined and articulated corporate vision and mission statement are critical to the success of the organization, at least in terms of getting the firm focused and marching to the beat of the same drum. And, those marching are typically the managers and employees of the firm. Those are the people who really define and deliver on the corporate vision and carry out the activities required to accomplish the corporate mission or missions. It is these people who truly determine what the corporate brand is and what it can and/or should be. They are the ones who translate the internal hopes, plans and dreams into the external experiences that customers and prospects receive and respond to over time.

A number of years ago, Ford Motor developed an external advertising program that attempted to redefine their corporate brand. It used the theme line "At Ford, Quality Is Job One." From all accounts, at the time that slogan was developed and was being delivered, "Quality" was not "Job One" at Ford. Far from it. Lots of other things were "Job One" in the hearts and minds of employees and line managers. "Quality," at least in the way the advertising campaign was presented, was not one of them. And, that showed in the way employees and managers acted and reacted both internally and externally. Those were dark days for Ford. By promising something externally to customers and other stakeholders that managers and employees were either not capable of delivering or had no interest in demonstrating simply made many of the problems worse. Of course, Ford did eventually make "Quality Is Job One" a fact in the organization. The external advertising campaign may have had something to do with changing the minds and hearts of internal employees and managers. But, from a customer standpoint, promising "Quality" when "Quality" wasn't being delivered in terms of customer experiences created many problems and challenges that could have been avoided (*Fortune*, 1994). To reinforce our theme, brands are built and maintained based on the experiences received by the customer from those who deliver the brand contacts over time. Indeed, the brand is what employees are and what customers experience. It's that simple. The old saying "What you do is what you are" is never more true than in the arena of corporate brands, corporate branding and corporate brand delivery.

In the past three years, one of the authors has directed two "best practices in brands and branding" studies that involved more than 60 companies in the United States. The firms that were benchmarked ranged from the high tech, high flyers such as Cisco Systems and Dell Computers to more traditional organizations such as Dow Chemical, Sears, Roebuck and BellAtlantic. The one overriding theme that came out of all these branding studies was that the corporate brand starts inside the organization with the managers and employees and then moves out to customers and stakeholders. In other words, brands are created through experiences.

Those experiences are created by managers and employees and their surrogates in the marketplace whether the firm is involved in consumer or business-to-business markets, in service or manufacturing or whether they be local, national or global. Brands start inside and move out. They don't start outside and move back in (APQC, 1998, 2000).

The corporate brand, therefore, is made up of the experiences the managers and employees have internally with each other, with other management, with suppliers and external distributors such as retailers, and yes, with their own customers and prospects. It is these experiences that they in turn deliver to customers and prospects on an ongoing basis. So, the corporate brand is what managers and employees believe it is or at least the experience they create for the organization's external audiences.

It is very clear from the benchmarking studies that the corporate brand doesn't start outside with a brand consultancy or a naming expert or a corporate design firm. It doesn't start outside with signs and slogans and icons and nifty advertising campaigns. Instead, the corporate brand is a reflection of what the people in the organization are. What they believe in. What they can and will deliver to customers and other stakeholders over time. Thus, the core value of the organization is what the employees and managers believe it is, not what customers believe it is or even what they might want it to be. It's the everyday, ongoing view that managers and employees have about the organization that really determines and defines its internal values. And, yes, those values do flow out but, unfortunately, in too many cases, they don't flow back in.

So, the second quadrant of the corporate umbrella that defines the corporate brand value are managers and employees. That now brings us to customers and prospects and all the external stakeholders and audiences that come into contact with the company through its brand contacts. They play a critical role in determining what the corporate brand is and what value it can produce, promise, and deliver. We discuss that next as the third quadrant of the corporate umbrella.

A critical quadrant – customers, shareholders and other stakeholders

We have finally come to what marketing people believe is the acid test of corporate value – the customers, consumers, and shareholders or equity partners of the organization. Marketing people will commonly argue that the understanding of the corporate brand must start with customers and consumers. Many investor relations people will argue just as strenuously that the view analysts, investment bankers, fund managers and even shareholders have are the really critical evaluators of the corporate brand. The truth is, both are right but only partially so. Customers create income flows to the organization just as does the financial community. In today's interlocked and integrated global economies, the firm *must have both*. Customers are important for they furnish ongoing cash flows. Investors are important for they create the resources that allow the firm to maintain or grow those customer income flows. So, customers and shareholders and, ultimately, stakeholders are important in identifying and determining the value of the corporate brand. But, as a reminder, the brand is also what employees and managers believe it is, so it is truly the interaction of all groups that creates the total corporate brand as it exists in the marketplace.

Obviously, companies need to talk with their customers and prospects, their shareholders, their financial partners and the like. They need to ask them such questions as: Who are we? What do we do well? How committed are we? What do you think of our employees? Are you satisfied with our products and our company commitment? But, these questions should come after the organization has asked those same questions internally, among managers and employees. Only by aligning what the organization believes and can deliver with what customers and shareholders and the financial community want can the real value of the organization be determined or even identified.

The challenge of course, is how to take what the corporate brand really is and align that with what customers and the financial markets want and for which they will either pay to receive or accept as the basis for funding. The problem facing managers and particularly the corporate communication director is that what the firm can, will and wants to do, may sometimes be in conflict with what current customers, stakeholders and even shareholders want. That's what really creates the dilemma for the corporate communication manager. Too often we have seen the corporate communication group – and product brand managers as well – forced to develop corporate communication programs that simply aren't related to what the organization can deliver because "this is what the market wants" or "this is what customers want to hear" or "analysts would like to hear that we … ." It is here, in the crucible of what is real and what the organization can deliver and what the customer wants or the analysts desire, that real corporate brands are forged. Unless internal truths and external desires are aligned, the corporate brand is generally nothing more than a logo, an icon or perhaps a corporate color.

A challenging exercise for the corporate communication director might be to consider: would it be easier to get a new set of customers to match the corporate capabilities of what the firm can deliver and the experiences it can provide or would it be easier to get a new set of investors and shareholders that accept the level of growth and return that the firm is capable of generating? Neither is terribly attractive but in some cases, the challenge facing the organization is just that. And, the corporate communication director is right in the middle of that decision. Quite a dilemma.

That's why we argue matching and aligning employees and managers and customers and stakeholders is one of the most critical issues the organization faces and typically, the corporate communication director is the only person who understands and can likely resolve these issues.

We will not dwell further on the subject of matching customer and corporate goals or aligning corporate and financial and investor objectives in greater detail here. Suggestions on how those may be determined and how studies might be conducted are available in numerous texts and research approaches. The key element in this discussion is simply to restate: to understand the corporate brand one must look both inside the organization at the internal forces that are driving the value and potential, that is, employees, managers and the like, and, one must also examine the external influences, that is, customers, shareholders, financial analysts, other stakeholders and so on. It is not one or the other. It is both. As our umbrella analogy suggests, it is all the parts of the corporate umbrella acting together that create the whole that develops and protects the value that is the corporate brand.

The success of the corporate brand evolves to a great extent as a result of the interaction of these two separate but highly influential groups. Most of all, one must remember that brands are created and maintained as a result of the experiences of these groups over time. The internal experiences of managers and employees are translated and transferred to the external customers and stakeholders. So we now have the third quadrant of the corporate umbrella, the influence of customers and shareholders in creating corporate value.

The final quadrant of our umbrella is an understanding of how these customer and employee experiences and the overriding corporate vision and mission translate into something that can be defined as a corporate brand and how that intangible entity can develop, maintain and hopefully grow in value. In other words, how do we turn all the rather soft issues of employee and management beliefs, customer wants and desires into something that has real financial marketplace value? That's the fourth quadrant of the umbrella, turning the corporate brand into a corporate asset.

From soft and squishy to hard and tangible

Many communication people have never been very comfortable with accounting and finance. The so-called "bean counters" have always been the nemesis of the "creative folk." Yet, in today's cash-driven, shareholder-value focused arena, it may well be that accountants and financial managers will be the best friends the corporate communication manager can have. The reason: they control the purse strings and there-fore, the focus of the organization. More importantly, they control the concepts and approaches that communication people must begin using to justify their plans and programs to management and the financial markets in the 21st century.

In this section, we briefly review the accounting and financial theories and practices that we believe make it possible to treat the corporate brand as an organizational asset. Inherent in that approach are topics and elements that may not be everyday language for corporate communication directors. Thus, we will build our case for turning what has traditionally been considered a "soft, squishy" concept like a corporate brand into a hard, tangible, measurable asset similar to the ones that senior manage-ment are most comfortable in dealing with in boardrooms around the world. If the corporate communication director can master the basics, it will be a simple task to add complexity over time.

We cover three areas in this section:

(a) What are assets?

(b) Can the corporate brand be considered an asset?

(c) What's needed to develop a "brand as asset" approach that will resolve many of the current issues facing a corporate communication director?

The ultimate questions of how the corporate brand can be valued and how the firm goes about developing an investment and measurement approach to justify the corporate brand are left for Chapter 13.

(a) What are assets?
The major challenge in treating or even considering the corporate brand as an organizational asset are the GAAP (Generally Accepted Accounting Practices) accounting methodologies currently in place. As important, they are the common practices of financial managers around the world. Unfor-tunately, accountants and their allies, the financial managers, are stuck with a 500-year-old, double-entry bookkeeping system. That system was

developed in a time when hard or tangible assets were primarily such things as land, raw materials, livestock, buildings and the like. Those were the foundations of value for they could be used to create additional hard assets or were, in and of themselves, limited in number, had resale value and were therefore valuable.

That tangible asset system is still in use today. It focuses primarily on hard assets like cash, inventory, accounts receivable, factories, plants, equipment and so on. It ignores the real value-builders in today's market-place, that is, corporate knowledge, employees, skills and most of all, loyal, continuing, profitable customers. In truth, for most organizations, it is the soft, intangible factors such as employee skills, software, know-ledge, experience and alliances that create corporate value today. And, the corporate brand, because it summarizes the commitment and value that managers and employees agree to deliver to customers and prospects, has tremendous value, even though it may be somewhat hard to measure.

In our approach, the major asset of any organization is its customer base. Tangible assets can be bought and sold and can generate cash but only on a one-time basis. Customers, however, are one of the few things an organization has that create ongoing flows of income for the firm. Almost everything else inside or outside the organization is really a cost center. Thus, we argue that the true assets of any organization are its customers for only they create ongoing flows of income for the company.

The problem with this argument in today's corporate operations is that the only instances in which intangibles, such as the corporate brand and other assets such as intellectual property get reported or even considered as a valuable resource for the firm are when they are bought or sold. In those cases, the new owners typically report those values as an unspecified lump sum, using the nebulous term of "goodwill." But, this same value cannot, in most countries, be reported on the balance sheet of the owners who created it and are attempting to maintain it in the marketplace. So, while corporate brands have marketplace value, as evidenced by the fact that they are bought and sold almost every day around the world, the ongoing value of the corporate brand has little or no financial worth to the owning organ-ization on an operating basis. Thus, the challenge is to find ways to identify the value the brand has so that it can be measured over time.

The need, of course, is to be able to measure the corporate brand value on an ongoing basis for that will provide the market value that is demanded of the finance and accounting professions. Thus, if we can define the financial value of the corporate brand, we will have made great strides in treating it as an asset and not part of the nebulous area of "good-will" on the balance sheet (Schultz and Kitchen, 2000).

(b) Can the corporate brand be considered an asset?

There is little question that customers create value for the organization. Like a brand, however, customer value, customer loyalty and customer commitment to the firm are not valued by the organization on an ongoing basis. It is assumed that customers will continue to provide income flows to the firm now and into the future. Obviously, the products and services the firm develops are central to the generation of those ongoing income flows. But, just as the products and services, distribution, pricing, promotional activities and the like all play a part in the generation of customer income flows, we argue the corporate brand plays a part as well. That is, the corporate brand has some real, tangible value to the customer such as providing trust, reliability, a sense of stability and the like. As a result, the corporate brand does provide value in generating and maintaining customer income flows. Further, because the corporate brand becomes an integral part of the product or service bundle the organization is creating and offering, it likely has as much tangible, financial value as the plants, equipment, finished inventory and the like that the company carries on its balance sheet (Schultz and Kitchen, 2000).

The problem of considering the brand as an asset, however, whether corporate or product, is compounded by several factors:

■ Traditional assets, at least in theory, are seen as having an established market and thus, a market value. The corporate brand, unless it is sold, does not.

■ Traditional assets, even with good care, deteriorate over time. If well managed, the corporate brand can appreciate from year to year.

■ The responsibilities for traditional assets can be "departmentalized," whereas the development of the corporate brand, as discussed above, calls for cross-functional efforts by several departments and involves the commitment and attention of most employees and manager to be successful (Schultz and Kitchen, 2000).

The additional challenge is, of course, that the corporate brand has varying value for different companies. For example, in a "house of brands" firm such as Procter & Gamble or Unilever, the corporate brand may have little impact on the acquisition, growth or migration of customers and end-users and their income flows over time. For others such as General Electric, IBM, Sony, Philips, Siemens and the like, in other words, those who manage a "brand house," the corporate brand may be critically important and have much to do with acquiring, growing and migrating customer income flows over time. Thus, like any other asset, the corporate brand has differing values for differing organizations. That is why a generic, off-the-shelf approach to brand valuation has commonly failed.

For these reasons, we argue that the corporate brand is indeed a corporate asset and should be treated as such.

(c) What is needed to value brands as assets?
No one denies that customer equity, that is the ongoing flows of income that customers give the firm in exchange for goods and services, is a real and relevant asset. And, few will deny that the corporate and product brands have something to do with that ongoing customer loyalty. In other words, customers create cash flows for the firm. Those cash flows are generated and to a certain extent influenced by the corporate and product brands the organization uses in the marketplace. Thus, the brands do have current and ongoing value for the organization, the challenge is how to determine that value as the basis for organizational investment and maintenance.

Many accountants contend that intangibles, such as the corporate brand, should not be reported as assets because it is difficult to measure them. If intangible assets really have a value, their argument goes, the results will show up on future income statements as additional profits. This is equally true, however, of the "hard assets" that constitute today's balance sheets. No company today collects buildings, machinery, inventory and other hard assets for any other reason than their potential contribution to future profits. If intangible assets are relevant for future earnings, their value should really be on the balance sheet along with their hard asset parallels, even if both kinds may be less exact than accountants, auditors and others would want them to be. It is better to do something approximately right than perfectly wrong. So, in our view, any method of measuring intangible equity is better than leaving the problem unattended.

While accountants may not know how to value brands, or better said, customer equity, the stock market certainly does. Companies such as Coca-Cola, Microsoft, Cisco Systems, Dell, Nestlé and others have market capitalizations that are often 10 to 20 or more times their book value. Merger and acquisition deal makers value customer equity and corporate brand value as well. For instance, Disney paid more than five times book value of Capital Cities/ABC and IBM paid over six times the book value of Lotus Development to acquire those firms and their brands. The value of those organizations is largely a result of the development of brand equity and brand values. Therefore, if we can find a way to separate out the corporate brand value from the product or service value, then it would likely be possible to treat the brand as a corporate asset (Schultz and Kitchen, 2000).

Summary and conclusion

While some companies have argued that brands are indeed corporate assets and have gone so far as to place them on the balance sheet, that raises a number of issues that are extremely complex and generally beyond the realm of the corporate communication director. We, therefore, leave that topic for the discussion and resolution by accountants, financial directors and chief financial officers. In our view, the case for measurement of brand value can be made, the question is whether or not the organization wants to deal with all the attendant financial and shareholder issues that such a move would entail.

The real challenge, however, is how to determine the value of the brand. Unless and until some type of financial value can be placed on the corporate brand, any discussion of brand investment, brand maintenance or brand value growth is simply a matter of opinion, conjecture and often corporate pride. Thus, we deal with the subject of measuring brand value in the following chapter as the basis for assisting the corporate communication director in answering the three primary questions that senior management will always ask about corporate brand management:

- How much should we invest in building and maintaining our corporate brand?

- What type of returns will the firm receive as a result of those investments, that is, cash flows or shareholder value?

- Over what period of time will those returns occur?

If the corporate communication director can answer those three questions, the challenge of building and growing the corporate brand will be well on the way to resolution.

So, that's the challenge today. What is the value of the corporate brand? How can that value be determined? Unless and until those questions are answered, the corporate communication director will be buffeted by believers and non-believers. This is what we will address in Chapter 13.

Facing Up To or Being Faced Down by the Analysts (continued) ...

As the first step in his "respond to the analysts" program, Guardo assembled a small group of branding management experts. The people he selected were not the typical "brand guys," that is the creative or design or communication people. Instead, he found people who understood the corporate brand as an asset, something that had real value in the marketplace and could relate brand value to corporate value. He asked them to build a "story" he could tell to the analysts.

After a couple of days, the assembled team had developed a list of seven supportable reasons why Biggo Industries was employing a corporate advertising program in support of the Biggo brand. Those reasons were:

1. *Biggo Needs to Explain, Illustrate and Encourage Present and Potential Shareholders to Invest or to Continue to Invest in the Firm*
   Biggo Industries is a complex, global organization that manufactures and sells a very broad assortment of products and services around the world. Many, if not most of its customers, are other businesses. Thus, there is a wide gap between Biggo's business customers, who probably know Biggo products, people and processes quite well, and the firm's shareholder "customers" who may know little about what the firm does and have a totally different value scale when evaluating the organization. With over 800 million shares of common stock outstanding, Biggo has a huge shareholder "customer base" and concomitantly an opportunity for lack of knowledge and understanding by those owners. Communicating with that group through a mass media campaign to either retain their current investment or to encourage others to initially purchase Biggo shares would, on the surface, seem like an appropriate corporate strategy.

2. *Shifting to a Biggo "Brand House" Approach*
   There appears to be a move by Biggo toward rationalizing or at least aggregating some of its brands under some version of a common Biggo label, that is, BiggoBiz, BiggoCapital and the like. In other words, Biggo management has recognized the value of a "brand house" strategy and is taking the first steps in executing that strategy. Thus, there are some valid reasons to build and enhance the corporate Biggo name as it moves from a "house of brands" to more of a "brand house."

3. *Enhance Biggo's Ongoing Acquisition Strategy*
   Over the years, some of the Biggo growth has come through acquisition. One of the critical ingredients in any merger and acquisition strategy is

the importance of and reliance on the knowledge, recognition and acceptance of the acquiring company by those firms being acquired. Those firms being acquired appear to prefer and are often willing to give more attractive terms to organizations they know and understand and have marketplace relevance than to total strangers. Thus, a Biggo corporate branding program delivered through a highly visible advertising campaign would likely help prepare the management and shareholders of organizations that might be acquired in the future to be much more amenable to a Biggo acquisition.

4. *Gain and Hold Biggo Employees and Managers*
The ability of an organization to attract, train and maintain employees is one of management's greatest challenges. Thus, a strong corporate brand is often critical in terms of recruiting new employees and in many cases, retaining existing, valuable ones, in other words, managing the intellectual capital of the organization. Few people like to work for or be associated with an organization that no one knows about or about which little is understood. Thus, the Biggo advertising campaign helps build widespread market knowledge and understanding among present and future employees. Given that Biggo has over 150,000 employees worldwide, the corporate advertising and branding program helps give the Biggo corporate brand meaning and relevance to present and future employees and managers.

5. *Where Biggo Does Business*
A corporate brand has varying values around the globe. In North America, the common branding approach has been that of building a "house of brands." In most of the rest of the world, a "brand house" approach has been used. That is, strong corporate brands dominate and are often the key to success in many non-U.S. markets. For example, in Japan, it is the corporate entity that is important, not the product brand. As Biggo grows its business in external markets, a corporate brand advertising campaign is a sound corporate investment to build knowledge and understanding in those "foreign" markets.

6. *Bundling Biggo Products and Services for Global Customers*
Increasingly, global firms have global customers and global customers have multiple needs across traditional product or category lines. Thus, customers now want "solutions to problems" not just "products and services." Most likely, Biggo business units will increasingly combine Biggo and Biggo-owned brands to provide "customer solutions" although those solutions may include a number of different product names. The only thing that will tie them together is their ability to solve the customer's problem and the fact that their corporate owner is

Biggo. Building a strong corporate brand would enable Biggo to do more of this increasingly important product and service bundling under a common name.

7. *Biggo's Level of Investment in a Corporate Brand Advertising Campaign*
   Critics often suggest that a corporate brand advertising campaign is not a wise use of finite corporate resources and may even be a waste of money. The common reason for this challenge is that the organization is unable to prove that the investment had any returns. Some of those criticisms are justified. Others are not. When Biggo reviewed the costs of its corporate advertising campaign, it found that its investment was only 0.003 percent of sales. As a percentage of Cost of Sales it was only 0.0064 percent. Thus for an organization with nearly $15 billion plus in global sales, the investment in the Biggo corporate brand advertising campaign did not seem out of line.

The final question that Batista and his assembled group of experts were unable to answer, however, was the key one: did the corporate advertising program work? In other words, did Biggo get back as much as it put in? Or, better said, was the corporate advertising campaign a good use of corporate resources, given all the alternatives available to management? If it did produce results, then the critics could be silenced and Batista and Biggo management vindicated.

The problem was that neither Batista nor the analysts really knew for sure. There were opinions but no real facts. The reason: neither side knew the value of the Biggo corporate brand. Thus, without a baseline, it was impossible to tell whether or not the brand advertising campaign increased or perhaps even decreased the customer or brand equity of the Biggo brand.

Thus, the stalemate continued. Batista argued the brand communication program was useful and valuable and the analysts argued that it wasn't. And, no one really knew.

Measuring the value of the corporate brand

don e. schultz

Managing a Major Corporate Asset

What is the value of the corporate brand? How much actual financial worth does it comprise? If we could strip out the value of the corporate brand from all the other corporate assets, both tangible and intangible, would this be a relevant or negligible amount for the firm? The problem is, most managers and most organizations don't know. And, because they don't know the brand's value, they are generally unable to answer the three basic questions posed at the end of Chapter 12.

■ How much should the firm invest in building and maintaining its corporate brand?

■ What type of financial return will the organization receive as a result of those investments?

■ Over what period of time will those results occur if they occur at all?

Because the managers of the organization don't know the financial value of what might be one of its most valuable assets, the common tendency is to either over-invest or under-invest in building and maintaining that brand value or equity. Or, perhaps the worst case of all, is that the corporate brand receives no attention or action simply because its value is unknown or unrecognized. As seen in Chapter 11 and elsewhere, this means essentially that they have passed all control of image into the hands of their stakeholders.

An example will help illustrate the point. (Note: The illustration below is true but the names and figures have been disguised to avoid proprietary values being disclosed.)

Over the past few years, a London-based consultancy, Interbrand, has conducted a number of brand value studies. Based on those studies, they have

	Tangibles assets %	Brand %	Other tangibles %
Utilities	70	0	30
Industrial	70	5	25
Pharmaceutical	40	10	50
Retail	70	15	15
Infor tech	30	20	50
Automotive	50	30	20
Financial services	20	30	50
Food and drink	40	55	5
Luxury goods	25	70	5

Figure 13.1 Brand's contribution to earnings
Source: Interbrand.

been able to develop a series of "rules of thumb" or "norms" about the financial value of the brand or brands to an organization in various industry categories in comparison to their other assets. In other words, they have developed a methodology that allows them to separate the value of the brand from other tangible and intangible assets in terms of contribution to earnings. Figure 13.1 illustrates their current findings.

As shown in the figure, there are wide variations in the contribution of the brand to the firm's earnings. In the Luxury Goods and Food and Drink categories, the brand contributes substantial value. In areas such as Utilities, it contributes very little although this is changing as a result of deregulation and other industry practices. The chart, however, does provide a rough guide for managers in terms of brand values by industry category.

A recent consulting experience will illustrate the challenge of brand value and how senior managers view the corporate brand.

In the pharmaceutical industry, as noted above, the value of the firm's brands generally accounts for about 10 percent of the firm's earnings. Obviously, much of the value of a pharmaceutical firm is contained in plants, factories, manufacturing facilities and the like that manufacture and distribute the products. A great deal of value is contained in the other intangible assets of the organization such as manufacturing know-how, formulae, research and development activities and internal intellectual capital, often in the form of employee knowledge. That has much to do with the value of the products and services that the firms provide. Yet, Interbrand has determined through several studies that the brand or brands a pharmaceutical firm owns or controls can contribute 10 percent or so to the actual earnings of the firm. Think about this scenario.

A major pharmaceutical organization has annual earnings of approximately $35 billion. If we apply the 10 percent value of the brand rule to this organization, that would mean the corporate brand or brands adds approximately $3.5 billion in contribution to earnings. (Annual earnings of $35 billion x 10 percent = $3.5 billion.) If we take the brand only at its earnings value for one year, that is, the $3.5 billion, it becomes a major asset of the firm. As a comparison, if one were to look at the balance sheet of the pharmaceutical company, one would discover that the $3.5 billion in contribution to earnings is more than twice what the firm actually invested in the critical research and development area the previous year. That figure was only $1.5 billion. Further, $3.5 billion in earnings contribution is greater than the total *sales revenue* of three of the firm's five operating divisions for that same one year period. Truly, the pharmaceutical brand(s) owned and controlled by the firm have tremendous value.

When we look at employed capital, the R&D operation and the three operating divisions all had huge amounts of money in place and were continuing to invest on an ongoing basis. One of the divisions has a capital expenditure budget of nearly $1 billion planned over the next three years. In terms of ongoing operating expenses, one of the operating divisions had more than 3000 people employed and another nearly 2500.

Yet, when we look at the firm's brand(s) as a major corporate asset contributing up to $3.5 billion in corporate earnings, we find the corporate brand is being managed by one person and an assistant located in the corporate headquarters. Their total annual operating budget for the year investigated was less than $1.5 million including the advertising and promotion spent on behalf of the corporate brand. And, that manager has to argue strenuously with senior management every year just to obtain that small amount of support.

When the senior management was shown these figures, they were totally surprised. Pharmaceuticals, as all operating managers know, or at least this group thought they knew, is reliant on R&D, patents and a strong ethical salesforce calling on physicians, chemists and pharmacists to generate prescriptions. Those were the things they were managing, not the corporate or even product brands. Yet, increasingly, in the pharmaceutical area as in many other product categories, the corporate and product brands are often one of the major factors in creating total corporate earnings. But, in category after category, we find inattention and insufficient resources as the primary challenges facing corporate communication managers in terms of creating and growing corporate brand value.

As a simple exercise, find your product category in the Interbrand chart above. Do a rough calculation of the earnings value your corporate and product brands provide the company as a percentage of total corporate earnings. Then, estimate the total expenditure by the firm in terms of individual and corporate brand communications. Our bet is you'll find your brand is sadly under appreciated by your corporate management and possibly by you as well.

Source: Author.

Introduction

While the above illustration is likely to prove useful in terms of giving a rough "rule-of-thumb" value to the brand, this is not generally what convinces senior management nor the financial community to make brand investments. What is needed is a practical approach, acceptable to management and the financial community, to brand valuation. That is the basis of this chapter. While some parts of the approach described below may seem technical, we have tried to describe them in layman's terms so that the process is transparent and all the calculations fairly obvious. Perhaps our best advice at this point is to involve financial people from the organization in this discussion at the start. It is they who must agree to the approach and the use of various financial calculations. By having them on board early, much of the later discussions on how the corporate brand might be valued can be avoided. And, you might just find, as we have on a number of occasions, that the financial people are as interested as the corporate communication director in determining the value of the corporate and product brands for investment purposes. We start by considering brand valuation from a managerial perspective.

A basic managerial view of brand valuation

Organizations invest in things that have value or things that create value. And, the more value the item generates or the more value it is believed to have, the greater the attention of senior managers and most commonly, the more the focus of corporate investment. Big plants get more attention than small ones.

Big investments in technology are more closely scrutinized than are small ones. Small acquisitions are made at the end of the board meeting with a voice vote. Giant mergers take weeks, months and sometimes years and thousands of man hours to complete. It's natural and it's common in management. Given limited time and resources, management and the organization must focus on what they perceive to be important and what they believe to be valuable. Since the value of the corporate brand or even the product brands are generally not known, often there is little interest. In truth, the value of the brand is commonly not even estimated unless the organization is planning on selling the brand or purchasing another. Generally, brands are perceived to have low value and thus low management attention. This situation is not true, of course, for those organizations where the brand is the key element in competitive differentiation or where there is clear and present customer preference and value. Managers at Louis Vuitton, Rolex, Calvin Klein, Izod and other luxury goods firms pay close attention to the brand and its standing in the marketplace. The same is true for consumer product companies such as Unilever, Nestlé, Mars and others. But, in a great number of companies, primarily in those categories listed in Figure 13.1 where brand value is less than 25 percent or so of earnings, the brand, while it is known to have value, because that value is intangible, it is difficult to determine how, when, or under what circumstances investments should or could be made and how those investments should or could or might be measured.

The approach we have developed is simple. No one can determine how much to invest in a brand, nor determine what returns might come from that investment or over what period of time unless one knows the basic value of the brand at some point in time. In other words, the key element in brand measurement is having some type of initial base financial value. From that, most managers can, using nothing more than common management calculus, determine the level of investment that could or should be made. The reasoning is simple. If the brand is worth $1 million, rational managers would not invest $5 million to build that value except in unique circumstances. By the same token, few managers would expect a 20 percent return on a $5 million investment if the brand had an initial value of $1 million or less. Senior managers make these types of financial decisions every day. They have managerial calculators in their heads that allow them to assess value, risk and estimated return. The problem with most corporate brands is there are no financial figures to plug into their mental calculators, thus, most senior management has no basis on which to either agree or disagree with recommendations made by the brand and communication people. Awareness, attitudes, share-of-voice and other common communication measurement tools fall on deaf ears, not because they aren't relevant communication measures but only because they don't fit in the financial calculator the senior manager uses to make consistent decisions. That's why we take a strong view that brand values must be presented in financial terms, not communication terms. And, that is why most presentations involving the funding or support of a corporate or even a product branding initiative fail to pass "management level muster." The measures aren't relevant compared to the investments being requested or the returns being promised. So, the typical management reaction is simply to dismiss or ignore the pleas of the corporate communication director, if in fact there is such a person in the organization.

In this chapter, we first review the typical measures that have been used to determine the value of a brand. Since those are primarily attitudinal measures based on some type of survey research that is then projected to the marketplace or some other form of soft measure, we review only the primary approaches. It is not that they are not important to marketing and communication people. They are. It is simply that they aren't very relevant to senior management or financial people. And, after all, those are the persons who hold the purse strings.

We then work through the brand valuation measurement process being used by Brand Finance plc, London (Haigh, 1998). The Interbrand approach is quite similar as may be other methodologies since all are based on the same accounting and financial principles. We favor the Brand Finance approach primarily because it has been developed by accountants and financial managers who have a knowledge and understanding of marketing and management and thus a senior management view. Thus, the Brand Finance approach can withstand the most detailed scrutiny of internal accountants and financial managers, the financial analysts, market-makers and even government, the tax department and the law. Thus, we are on solid ground with the Brand Finance approach and that, in our experience, is critical. Too many times, we have seen corporate communication directors "go down in flames" in a presentation seeking brand funding simply because the approach or concept could not stand the test of financial validity. We know the Brand Finance approach works because we have used it successfully all over the world.

From feelings to financials

There is little question: brands are relationships. Relationships between the marketer and the customer. Figure 13.2 summarizes this relationship view of the brand, using the customer as the primary stakeholder.

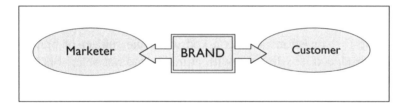

Figure 13.2 How brands create value

Because the marketer–customer relationship has been used as the basis for building, managing or understanding the brand in the past, it is only natural that much of the focus of brand management and brand development has concentrated on the attitudes and feelings of customers and prospects toward the brand. Thus, much brand work has been reliant on traditional attitudinal research for understanding and identification of those attitudes and feelings. And, those research studies have been extremely useful in assisting the marketing organization and its agency partners in understanding the relationship that exists between the brand and its customers or users or advocates. Further, those studies are generally vital in terms of understanding what attributes and elements the brand presently has and how those might be enhanced or improved or sometimes even changed in terms of moving forward. The only problem is, it has been extremely difficult to relate those feelings and attitudes and opinions to the financial value the brand has in the marketplace. And, that value, that is, the financial value, is critical if we are to look at the brand, whether corporate or product, as a corporate asset in which investments can be made and financial value either increased or values returned to the organization over time. Thus, while attitudinal research, valuation and understanding is important, in our approach it is used much more as an explanatory variable than as a predictor. In other words, while attitudes and feelings are important, we use them to explain the consumer behaviors we observe rather than trying to use them to predict what changes in financial value the brand might achieve if attitudes or feelings were changed. And, it is financial value that is important in a valuation model, not attitudinal value.

Therefore, in this section, we briefly illustrate the basis for attitudinal valuations as they are practiced in the world today. We follow that with some of the methodologies currently available to provide an overview of what various alternatives are being used around the world. We then make the transition to the financial value approach used by Brand Finance plc and explain that in some detail with appropriate illustrations and examples.

Why marketers started with attitudinal measures

One of the first questions always asked when the subject of brand valuation is introduced is: why start with attitudes and not behaviors? Behaviors, of course are quite measurable and in most cases, can be translated into financial values, that is, either the customer bought or didn't buy, the purchase price paid was X or it was Y, the incident being measured was either a first time purchase or a repurchase and so on. Thus, it would seem that behaviors would have been the measurement of choice since the beginning. But, they were not.

One must recall the time frame in which these brand and communication systems were developed, generally the 1950s and 60s. One must also remember the organizations and their research and communication suppliers that were most interested in understanding brands at the time the approaches were developed.

Following World War II, most of the marketing concepts developed in the U.S. were focused on fast moving consumer goods (FMCG) such as detergents, cereals, soft drinks, tinned and frozen foods and the like. In most cases, the manufacturer was divorced from the consumer or end-user by very strong and often localized or regionalized distribution systems such as supermarkets. At the same time, regional and national media were emerging, that is, national magazines initially, then radio and eventually television. All those media forms offered substantial cost-effectiveness in terms of the delivery of common messages and incentives to the vast array of customers and end-users and consumers that made up the marketplace. And the focus of the marketing organizations employing the measurement systems was increasingly national in scope. The assumption was that commonly produced products were the most efficient to make, therefore a common view of customers was needed across the continent.

Since technology and the retail system restricted the acquisition and analysis and, of course, measurement of actual consumer or end-user behaviors, the FMCG organizations and their agencies and research suppliers quickly moved to the next best thing. They found they could effectively measure marketplace knowledge such as brand awareness, brand recognition, brand message recall and the like through various forms of survey research. By using statistical analysis, they could sample a small, representative section of the population or the relevant population and then project that to the whole with fairly accurate results. Thus was born the reliance on attitudinal measures.

At the same time, developments in the areas of psychology and psychiatry focused the attention of marketing and communication managers on the development and use of attitudes as influencers in the purchase behavior of customers and prospects. Since behaviors were so difficult to capture or measure, the next best thing was to create an "attitude-leads-to-behavior" mental sequence, that is, make the assumption that attitudes eventually lead to behaviors and use that as the base for customer understanding. The premise then developed was the marketer, by being able to measure such mental elements as awareness, attitudes and intentions, could then build predictive models that would project to and predict the actual behaviors of consumers that might occur at some point in the future. In other words, if the marketer could change the attitudes of the prospect, then purchase behavior would eventually occur. A most intuitively appealing concept.

And, that's exactly what happened. Today, we call the model that was developed the "Hierarchy of Effects" approach. It was developed in 1961 by an academic and a research manager and was named for them, that is, the Lavidge and Steiner (1961) model. A stylized illustration of that basic "attitude-to-behavior" model is shown in Figure 13.3.

As shown, the assumption of the L&S model is that customers or consumers or prospects or shareholders or investment bankers or whoever go through a "learning process" on the way to making a purchase decision. Thus, if we equate this model to the corporate brand, from the standpoint of a prospective customer, they would first become aware of the organization, then develop some knowledge and understanding about it and so on. The end result would be that they would place confidence in the corporate brand for any number of reasons and be supportive of it whether

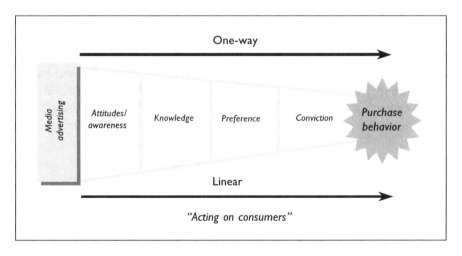

Figure 13.3 Traditional "advertising-based" view of communication

it is linked to a product brand as the "brand endorsement" or as an entity in and of itself. The assumption of the L&S model is, of course, that learning occurs by various corporate-driven initiatives such as advertising, sponsorships, public affairs, social responsibility, promotional activities and the like. In other words, the organization, by investing in various communication programs, helps drive customers or constituencies or publics through the process. The more money invested, the faster or greater the results. Thus, investments in these external activities should help build or maintain the brand in the broad marketplace or marketspace and quite often they do. Thus, investments in advertising, sponsorships, events and the like are often measured in terms of change in awareness, knowledge, preference and the like with the assumption that favorable behaviors will eventually occur. And, it is this basic assumption that many senior managers find so difficult to understand and accept.

The same "attitude-to-behavior" approach is often used with shareholders and other stakeholders. The organization makes the assumption that if the financial analyst or fund manager or investment banker knows about the organization, that good results will occur. While this is sometimes true, it is not always the case. In many instances, organizations may be held in high regard but for any number of reasons investments in the firm's stock may not be made, or recommendations offered by intermediaries may not occur or the advice be taken. For these and a number of other reasons, the use of attitudinal models becomes a less than useful measure when an attempt is made to match those up with financial investments or returns.

This is not to say that attempts are not being made to measure the value of the brand through attitudinal approaches. Indeed, attitudinal models are still the prime methodology used to evaluate the impact and results of brand marketing and communication programs. The problem is, they are fraught with the "connective-ness" issues that have just been discussed. In the spirit of completeness, we describe the primary attitudinal brand measurement tools below before moving to the behavioral model we believe is more relevant, particularly for corporate communication managers.

Some methods of measuring attitudinal value

While a number of customer brand valuation or customer brand equity measures have developed over the years, most all have relied, in one way or another on some variation of the Hierarchy of Effects models. Thus, these so-called "customer brand equity" measures rely primarily on some type of change in brand awareness, knowledge, preference, conviction, intent to purchase or the like. The alternative, provided by some measurement organizations is to offer a variation on the theme, that is, they compare the studied brand with other brands in the category. The assumption is then made that greater success by the brand in attitudinal measures, that is, awareness, preference, intent to purchase or the like, means greater value or greater preference for the brand in the marketplace, at least among those sampled. Again, however, it is quite difficult to connect these attitudinal measures to any type of financial value. Simply liking a brand or admiring a corporation doesn't necessarily translate into product or share purchases. Nor does it say much about customer retention or ongoing business dealings for the products or services the organization is selling.

David Haigh, founder and CEO of Brand Finance, puts the entire subject of measurement into perspective with the following comments:

> Brand strength is based on attempts to access the relevant beliefs, associations and attitude that are in consumers' minds. Our original explanation of the whole branding phenomenon placed considerable emphasis on the meanings and associations that a brand can create in the mind of the consumer, so the obvious place to anatomize the strength of a brand should be in the consumer's mind. (Personal communication, 2000)

David Aaker, Professor at the Graduate School of Business at the University of California, Berkeley, visualizes each brand name as a box in the consumer's mind in which all the bits of information and associations that have to do with that brand are stored (Aaker, 1991). The whole box is in turn stored with positive or negative feelings. It is from this "brand storehouse" that customers, prospects, analysts, shareholders, investment bankers and the like determine their interest in, their relationship with and their involvement in the brand, whether product or corporate. This is as good an illustration as any to summarize the attitudinal approach to measuring brand value, although like all metaphors for how the mind works, it is likely to be too simplistic and probably runs the risk of sometimes being misleading. It will serve however to introduce some basic categories of information that marketers try to gather about what goes on in the consumer's mind as a basis for understanding their relationship with a brand (Aaker, 1991).

- *Awareness* – This determines whether there is a box for the brand at all, or whether the brand box is easy to find given all the other brand boxes that are stored as well.

- *Associations and beliefs* – This is what is in the box. This is a big area in itself with many dimensions to it. (You could imagine smaller boxes inside this box, except that would be too neat and tidy – perhaps we can think of some boxes, some paper bags, some loose items, some broken bits and a couple of bottles that have leaked.)

▩ *Attitude* – This is how the consumer feels about the brand: positive, negative or indifferent.

Each of these areas can be interpreted to reveal an aspect of a brand's strength. One could say a brand is strong because many people have heard of it or spontaneously think of it; one could certainly say it is strong if many people express great loyalty or affection for it, in their words or in their actions. In between, a brand can be called strong if it is strongly associated with imagery or functional benefits that can be interpreted as desirable for consumers, shareholders and other stakeholders. Ultimately the bottom-line relevance of all the perceptual material described in the preceding section is that it somehow translates into some type of consumer or customer or shareholder or analyst behavior – that these feelings or attitudes lead to them buying the brand, staying with the brand, perhaps paying more for the brand or doing any or all of the same with regard to investments in the stock of the organization (Haigh, 1998).

This generalization of how and in what way attitudes are used to attempt to measure brand value or customer brand value, will be helpful in understanding the various processes that have been developed. The key ones are described in the next section.

Some key attitudinally-based methods of measuring brand value

While there are a number of approaches to measuring brand value using attitudes, opinions and other consumer and stakeholder perceptions and beliefs, four primary approaches have received the most attention. Each is outlined in the following sections. It should be noted, all of the measurement approaches rely on some form of survey research for data gathering and all attempt to relate the brand to competitors in the same category and often in other categories as well. All have global capability and the two leading approaches, the BrandAssetValuator and BrandDynamics are in use by a number of organizations around the world.

The four primary attitudinally-based brand equity measurement approaches are briefly described below (see Cooper and Simons, 1997). Please note that these approaches have been designed primarily to gauge consumer or customer views of the brand and generally have little to do with any measures of other stakeholders or of the financial community.

A. Young & Rubicam's BrandAssetValuator is based on a large-scale, quantified consumer survey of brand equity in more than 20 countries around the world. The research study uses the premise that strong brands are built on four pillars: differentiation from competitors; relevance to the needs and wants of the population; esteem, that is, the belief that the brand will live up to its promises, it is of high quality and will do what it claims to do; and knowledge, which is the natural outcome of widespread acceptance and market success among consumers. These elements are then placed in a two-by-two matrix to show movement and also to relate the brand to other brands in the same product category.

B. The EquiTrend approach is based on a small set of questions designed to gauge a consumer's opinions on a wide range of brands. The method is based on measuring three facets of customer brand equity. Those are, "salience" or brand knowledge, that is, the overall quality of the brand. The second measure, "perceived quality" is measured on an 11-point scale which grades consumer reactions to various levels of quality. Finally, "user satisfaction" focuses on the opinion of consumers who buy the brand most often. EquiTrend is an ongoing study of brand equity with waves of research dating back to 1989.

C. BrandVision is designed to measure the depth of consumer commitment to specific brands. It is measured continuously alongside traditional tracking measures such as advertising awareness and brand image. The basic hypothesis of the BrandVision model is that customer commitment is a performance measure that is different from, and far more effective than traditional measures of advertising and marketing performance. The measure uses a small battery of questions to measure four factors which are believed to be involved in the decision-making process:

- Involvement in the category
- Satisfaction with the brands used
- Disposition toward competitors
- Ambivalence of the individual customer toward the brand.

BrandVision constructs a commitment continuum of eight different relationship categories based on its questionnaires. These are placed on a continuum ranging from "most securely committed users" at one end to "non-users who are totally unavailable to competitors" on the other. The value of the model, according to Taylor Nelson Sofres, the sponsors who have developed and promoted the model, is that, for the first time, it is possible to see the effect of marketing activity on latent consumer behavior. Their so-called "Conversion Model" measures the lagged effects of marketing activity and is supposed to help predict when sales will flow from such activities. Some critics have claimed, however, that BrandVision is not a brand equity measurement at all, but rather an advertising/communication observatory, focusing on effective versus efficient marketing communication tracking and measurement.

D. BrandDynamics, offered by Millward Brown, is a system that seeks to measure and explain a brand's customer equity. According to the researchers, consumer equity should distinguish between consumers' predisposition towards a brand and the other factors that contribute to the brand's financial equity, that is, distribution strength, production efficiencies, patents and the like. Each brand is believed to have two key components, the consumer value, that is, a measure of the sales value of each respondent to the brand, and the brand pyramid which is a systematic way of diagnosing the factors driving customer value. Both measures are derived from a proprietary set of questions asked within a survey interview.

It should be noted that all four of these approaches and most of the other attitudinally-based brand measurement systems focus on consumer, end-user or marketplace views of the brand. That is a reflection of the FMCG background of most brand planning and development systems and therefore, the measurement systems that have evolved. Thus, adaptations have to be made to most attitudinal measurement systems to accommodate the different nature of the corporate brand, the differing audiences and the differing involvement of those being measured (Schultz and Walters, 1998).

This is not to say that end-users or consumers are not relevant to the corporate brand. They are. Indeed, Brand Finance bases much of its approach to brand valuation on those same individuals or firms. The difference is, the focus is on behaviors or what people or firms or organizations actually do, not how they feel and what their attitudes are no matter how favorable or unfavorable. That is the basis for the financial evaluation of the corporate and product brand and that is the topic to which we move next.

Financial measures of brand value or brand equity

Five basic approaches to financial valuation of the brand have been developed over the years. They are: historic cost, replacement cost, market value, royalty relief and economic use. We discuss each of the approaches in the following sections but focus on economic use since we believe this is the most relevant method of brand valuation. It is also the one most closely aligned with needs of the corporate communication director and his or her internal and external needs and requirements.

Historic cost

Historic cost is exactly what it says, that is: what did the brand owner invest in the development of the brand over time? This figure would likely include investments in marketing communication, packaging, logotype and icon development, signage, and the like. By adding up all the investments made by the brand owner during the relevant development period, the actual investments made could be determined and from that, the value of the brand could be determined assuming of course that investments are equal to value. There are, of course, major problems with this approach. These range from the difficulty of collecting accurate investment figures to a restatement of the costs in current market values to what can be used as a comparison with like brands. The major difficulty with this type of valuation, though, is that cost or investments made in the brand commonly have little or nothing to do with the current marketplace value of the brand in terms of customer income flows or what it might be sold for. In truth, what is actually being measured is the "output" necessary to build the brand, not the "outcome" or what the brand is actually worth in the marketplace at the time of the evaluation. Further, historic cost has nothing to do with what might be required to maintain or enhance the brand in the current situation. Thus, it is a backward view and of little real value to the corporate communication director.

Replacement cost

Similar to the historic cost approach described above, this valuation methodology relies on development of an estimate of what it might cost in marketing, marketing communication, design and other brand-building investments to replace the brand in the current marketplace. In other words, if the organization were to start over in the current time period, what investment would be required to develop a brand of the same strength and capability for the future. While this approach gets closer to the actual current brand value since it does at least deal with current investment requirements, it is still focused on "outputs," not the "outcomes" or actual marketplace or customer value of the brand. Likewise, given the multiplicative nature of brand development, it is generally difficult to determine what levels of investments might be required for restoration or replacement of the brand in the current marketplace. And, it is also quite difficult to determine the relevant costs that might be required to create the same brand value in the marketplace today or tomorrow. This approach has been borrowed from traditional accounting where the replacement of tangible assets such as plants or factories or rolling stock might be possible to estimate or calculate. In our view, it is generally inappropriate for the measurement of the intangible and dynamic nature of a brand.

Market value

This is a very simple concept. The calculation is based on what the brand might bring the owner if it were sold to another firm or company. Alternatively, it is the value a purchaser might put on the brand should they be the purchaser and not the seller, in other words, what would the purchaser be willing to pay for the brand? The value of the brand, of course, would vary by purchaser. Where one purchaser might find the brand a perfect fit with their present operations, others might not find it so desirable. Thus, the value is dependent on the valuation determined by either the buyer or seller but does not necessarily reflect the actual value in the open marketplace. In addition, this "market value" approach assumes the brand will change hands, that is, it will have a new owner. It says little about how much value the brand has to the present owner in terms of growth or maintenance or continuing income flows. In other words, it does little to help management understand how much value the brand has to the existing owner on an ongoing investment basis. And, that is the key element in any brand valuation model, what is the current value to the owner? Only by knowing that can some sort of financial determination be made as to whether or not investments should be made or whether the brand should be "milked" for value and ultimately disappear.

Royalty relief

This approach gets much closer to the actual ongoing market value of the brand. The basic premise is if the current marketing organization did not currently own the brand, what amount or level of franchise fee or royalty would the firm have to pay the brand owner for use of the brand name and its various appendages for use in the marketplace. In other words, from a brand valuation standpoint, how much could or would the marketing organization save by owning the brand rather than renting or leasing or paying royalties for its use in the marketplace. To determine the royalty rate, the marketing company could use available royalty rate comparisons for similar products or could obtain an estimate of the appropriate rate from an outside expert. The problem, of course, is finding a relevant comparison along with the difficulty of developing the complex rate structures and gaining a transparency of terms to set the royalty rate. Figure 13.4 provides an example of how the royalty relief method of brand valuation might be determined.

As shown, the estimated net sales of the brand being valued is projected out for a period of five years with the base year being taken as Year 0. The royalty rate, here shown as 10 percent, is taken against those sales. This creates a Royalty Income (based on total sales at a 10 percent royalty rate) of 50 in Year 0, growing to 52 in Year 1 and so on. From that, the estimated taxes must be deducted. As shown a rate of 33 percent is used in the

Royalty relief method simplified example		Year 0	Year 1	Year 2	Year 3	Year 4	Year 5
Net sales	a	500	520	550	580	620	650
Royalty rate	b	10%	10%	10%	10%	10%	10%
Royalty income	c	50	52	55	58	62	65
Tax rate		33%	33%	33%	33%	33%	33%
Tax	d	16.5	17.2	18.2	19.1	20.5	21.5
Net royalty	e	33.5	34.8	36.9	38.9	41.5	43.6
Discount rate		15%					
Discount factor	f	1.0	1.15	1.32	1.52	1.75	2.01
Discounted cash flow	g		30.3	27.9	25.6	23.8	21.7
Value to year 5	h	129.1					
Annuity	i	144.3					
Growth	0%						
Brand value		273.5					

Figure 13.4 The royalty relief method

calculation resulting in taxes of 16.5 in Year 0, growing to 17.2 in Year 1 and so on. This provides the Net Royalty (line e). From this Net Royalty, a discounted cash flow calculation must be made to determine the Net Present Value of the royalty income. The figure used in this example is shown as 15 percent. By deducting the Discount Factor (line f) from the Net Royalty, we arrive at a Discounted Cash Flow for each of the five forward-looking years (line g). In this example, the Value to Year 5 total is 129.1 (the addition of each of the five years in line g) shown as line h in the example. In addition, an annuity amount must be added to the Royalty Rate total to account for the future income that will likely result beyond Year Five. In this example, that calculation yields an amount of 144.3. When this is combined with the DCF value of 129.1, this gives a total Brand Value of 273.5. In other words, this is the current value of the brand and can be used not only for internal determination of support going forward, it would also provide a base estimate of the value of the brand to outside prospective purchasers as well (Haigh, 2001).

Economic use

Since this is our preferred method of estimating or calculating the financial value of the brand, and the one we believe to be the most relevant for corporate communication directors, we explain it in some detail. Again, we use the approach developed by Brand Finance plc, a London-based consultancy specializing in brand valuation.

Brand Finance brand valuation methodology

The Brand Finance plc approach to brand valuation is described below. It is an economic use approach based on the premise that incremental earnings for the firm commonly occur and that those are derived as a result of the ownership of the brand. Therefore, the Brand Finance model is primarily managerial rather than tactical and thus, more in line with the approach we believe corporate communication managers need to take. In this example, we will deal with the corporate brand as the overall entity. Product brand valuations can be derived from this general approach but we focus on the corporate brand in this discussion.

As previously noted, the actual value of the brand whether corporate or product, comes from the value the customer or user puts on the brand. In other words the brand value is what the customer or user says it is, not what the marketing organization says it is. Thus, we must be quite clear at this point: while we are attempting to determine the value of the corporate brand, that value is wrapped up in the total bundle that is the product or service the customer buys or uses. Thus, we look primarily at the customer-based value of the brand, not at the market-based value, that is, the shareholders, fund managers, analysts and others' view of the brand in this discussion.

The Brand Finance model is based on the concept of determining a multiple of present and projected future earnings (that is, income flows that are derived from customers) that are then discounted in some way to bring them back to a Net Present Value for the firm. These Discounted Cash Flow (DCF) or Net Present Value (NPV) approaches are the most common and accepted ways of accounting for future income streams. They thus have the benefit of being well established and accepted in accounting and financial circles around the world.

The basic brand valuation model

Figure 13.5 illustrates the basic Brand Finance brand valuation model.

As shown, the model consists of three basic parts or steps. (a) the brand segmentation and business forecast, (b) the brand value added index or

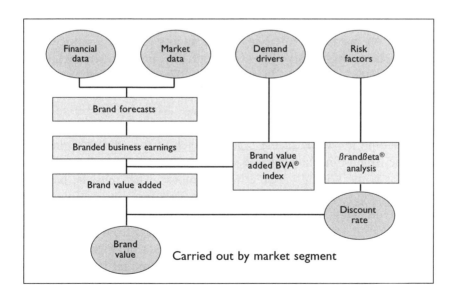

Figure 13.5 Brand valuation approach

BVA and (c) the BrandBeta analysis which is used to determine the discount rate which will be used to account for the risks faced by the organization and the continuation of the current income flows. Each is discussed in turn.

Brand value

In the Brand Finance approach, the financial value of the brand is determined by using the firm's data, generally in the form of historical sales and profit information and combining that with market data using factors such as growth rates, share of market, distribution patterns and the like. From this, as shown in Figure 13.6, Brand Forecasts are determined that include both internal and external firm and market data. These Brand Forecasts are then separated into Branded and Non-Branded Business Earnings based on the amount of products or services sold under the organization's brand. In other words, some organizations may manufacture and sell products that do not have the corporate name or may be manufactured for sale by others under some other brand name. The concern at this point is separating out the branded from the non-branded sales or income flows for additional analysis.

The key to the Brand Finance approach is in finding the right level of segmentation for the brand and the business. Segmentation can be based either on the use of existing company approaches or in some cases, new segmentation approaches must be developed by the analysts depending on the valuation needs. In all cases, the segments must be homogeneous. They can, however, be developed by geography, product, channel, demographics or other identifiers. In many cases, the segmentation approach is defined by the availability of data. That is true simply because the critical ingredients in any segmentation approach are driven by marketing knowledge, market research, financial data and competitor brand information. Understanding the value of the brand to each of the market segments is key to the Brand Finance approach since it is how the customer values the brand that is the critical variable in the process. That must be based on usable and acquirable information and data. The first section of the Brand Finance approach is illustrated in Figure 13.6.

By separating out the Branded Business Earnings from the total earnings of the company, Brand Finance is able to determine what it calls the Brand Value Added. The determination of that amount is generated by using the second step in the process.

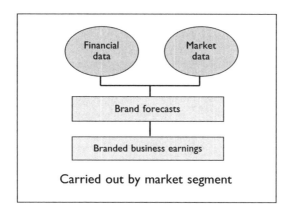

Figure 13.6 1st stage of brand valuation approach (BVA)

Demand drivers and brand value added (BVA) index

The second step in the brand valuation process is to understand the drivers of demand, that is, what factors or elements are responsible for the acceptance, purchase and ultimate value of the brand. Brand Finance calls these the "Brand Value Added or BVA Index" (Figure 13.7).

As shown, when the BVA Index is applied to the Branded Business Earnings, actual Brand Value Added figures can be calculated.

The BVA Index is determined by an analysis of the drivers of demand for the brand, that is, the factors that are important to customers and the

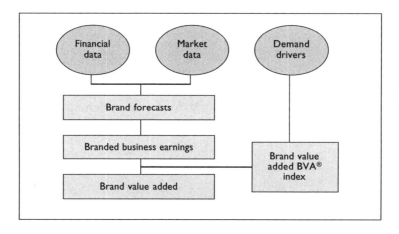

Figure 13.7 2nd stage of BVA

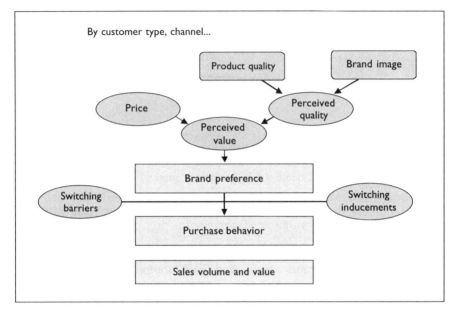

Figure 13.8 Understanding drivers of demand

marketplace that drive sales and purchases to the brand and not to a competitor. An example of this approach is illustrated in Figure 13.8.

As shown, the drivers of demand vary by customer type, channel and so on. Thus, a complete and detailed examination of the drivers for the specific brand in the specific market is required. While we are interested primarily in the corporate brand at this point, it is important to note that, as shown, there are a wide variety of elements that can drive demand ranging from price and product quality to switching inducements and obviously to the reputation, trust and value of the corporate brand over and above the specific product or service elements. The critical ingredient is an understanding of how brand preferences are developed and how those are impacted or influenced by switching barriers and switching inducements, all of which result in purchase behavior that is ultimately illustrated through sales volume and financial value.

Risk factors and BrandBeta analysis

The final element in the Brand Finance brand valuation model is the determination of the risk to the organization that either the historical sales and profits will continue or that elements in the marketplace will change radically and will reduce the value of the organization and its brand. Risk, therefore, can be defined in a number of ways, the most common of which is the risk that historical experience will not continue in the future. The addition of risk to the basic model is illustrated in Figure 13.9.

As shown, the addition of the risk factors to the model using the BrandBeta Analysis determines the discount rate that will be applied to the forecasted future earnings of the brand. An example of the Brand Finance BrandBeta Scoring Template is shown as Figure 13.10.

A total of 10 attributes are used in the Scoring Template. Those range from Time in Market to Price Premium to Brand Awareness. Thus, the Brand Finance model uses both behavioral and attitudinal elements to construct the discount rate. In the example above, the brand is rated on the basis of a maximum of 10 points for each of the attributes with the total points allocated to the brand by the evaluator providing the rating of the brand. It should be noted that the total score is not the actual value but is used instead to develop a comparison rating scheme as illustrated in Figure 13.11.

As shown, two brands are compared in terms of their scoring on the various attributes. The scores are then converted into Ratings ranging from AAA to D.

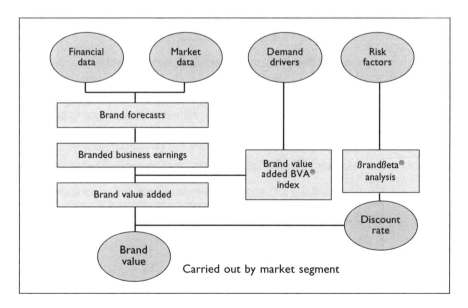

Figure 13.9 Brand valuation approach

Attribute	Score
Time in market	0–10
Distribution	0–10
Market share	0–10
Market position	0–10
Sales growth rate	0–10
Price premium	0–10
Elasticity of price	0–10
Marketing spend/support	0–10
Advertising awareness	0–10
Brand awareness	0–10
Total	**max 100**

Figure 13.10 ßrandßeta® scoring template

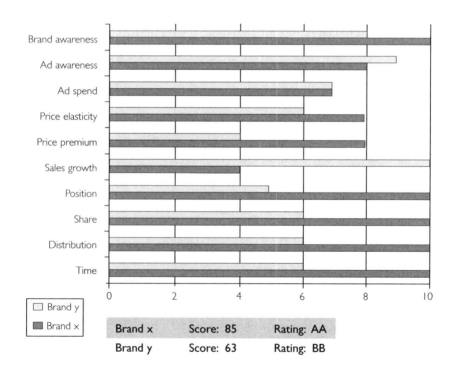

Figure 13.11 ßrandßeta® index: scoring profile

The brand valuation output – discounted future earnings method example

The output of the Brand Finance evaluation is summed up in a calculation called Brand Value determination. An example of the results of the various calculations and their outputs is illustrated in Figure 13.12.

In this figure, the brand value has been calculated based on the Discounted Future Earnings method. As shown, the current year, Year 0, provides the base for the calculation. Net Sales, which are expressed in constant Year 0 money, are then projected into the future, in this case, over the next five years. As can be seen, Net Sales are expected to rise from the current 500 level to 650 at the end of Year 5. It should be noted that Net Sales exclude unbranded and own-label production by the organization or other income sources that are not attributable to the corporate brand. For example, interest or investment earnings would not be included nor would the income from monetary fluctuations or hedging or other financial activities unless they were relevant to the brand value.

Operating Earnings are then determined. In the example above, earnings are estimated to increase 15 percent each year on a compounded basis. Thus, Year 0 earnings of 75 increase to 97.5 in Year 5 with the relevant figures illustrated for the intervening years.

The next step is to calculate the Tangible Capital Employed in the development and production of the product or services the organization is

Discounted future earnings method simplified example		Year 0	Year 1	Year 2	Year 3	Year 4	Year 5
Net sales		500	520	550	580	620	650
Operating earnings	a	75.0	78.0	82.5	87.0	93.0	97.5
Tangible capital employed		250	260	275	290	310	325
Charge for capital @ 5%	b	12.5	13.0	13.8	14.5	15.5	16.3
Intangible earnings	c	62.5	65.0	68.8	72.5	77.5	81.3
Brand earnings @ 75%	d	46.9	48.8	51.6	54.4	58.1	60.9
Tax rate		33%	33%	33%	33%	33%	33%
Tax		15.5	16.1	17.0	17.9	19.2	20.1
Post tax brand earnings	e	31.4	32.7	34.5	36.4	38.9	40.8
Discount rate		15%					
Discount factor	f	1.0	1.15	1.32	1.52	1.75	2.01
Discounted cash flow	g	31.4	28.4	26.1	24.0	22.3	20.3
Value to year 5	h	152.4					
Annuity	i	135.3					
Growth	0%						
Brand value		287.8					

Figure 13.12 Discounted future earnings method chart

vending or for the entity for which the calculation is being developed. Tangible Capital Employed here includes fixed and working capital at current value. In this example, the illustrated company is a manufacturer. Thus, the capital employed to produce the product would consist of the plants, factories, conversion equipment and the like employed in the process. In the example above, this amounts to 250 in Year 0 increasing to 325 in Year 5. This illustrates increasing Tangible Capital Employed by 50 percent of Net Sales compounded annually. To understand the brand value, some rate or remuneration must be paid the firm for the use of this Tangible Capital and the facilities being provided. The premise is that if the organization did now own these resources, they would have to be obtained from another supplier and thus would be a cost to the firm vending the brand. The rate used in this example is a Charge for Capital of 5 percent of the Tangible Capital Employed each year. (Note: this charge for capital is the "real" rate, excluding inflation.) As shown, that amounts to 12.5 in Year 0 increasing to 16.3 in Year 5.

The Intangible Earnings (line c in Figure 13.12) is obtained by deducting the Charge for Capital (line b) from Operating Earnings (line a). In this case in Year 0 Operating Earnings are 75 less the Charge for Capital of 12.5, leaving the Intangible Earnings at 62.5.

The next step is to calculate or estimate the amount of Intangible Earnings that are directly contributed by the brand. In the example, the Brand Finance analyst determined that the brand contributed 75 percent of the value of all Intangible Earnings. This simply means that most of the Intangible Earnings of this firm come from selling branded products and few are sold as private or own label or as basic commodities. For a corporate brand, this calculation becomes quite important since the corporate brand is, in many cases, made up of a number of product brands. As shown in line d, when calculated at 75 percent of Intangible Earnings, the Brand Earnings for this firm amount to 46.9 in Year 0 and are estimated to rise to 60.9 in Year 5.

Taxes, either current or future, must be deducted from the Brand Earnings. The tax rate used in this example is 33 percent, a fairly standard figure for most developed economies. Thus, we deduct the taxes from the Brand Earnings to arrive at Post Tax Brand Earnings (line e). Taxes in Year 0 amount to 15.5 (33 percent of the Brand Earnings, line d) rising to 20.1 in Year 5. That calculation results in the Post Tax Brand Earnings (line e) in our illustrated example. This is the actual value we expect the brand to contribute to the firm over the next five years.

There is, however, another step. Cash today is generally more valuable than cash tomorrow, that is, the idea of Discounted Cash Flow. This approach is designed to accommodate the future value of cash flows, risk, and so on. (See Figures 13.10 and 13.11 and accompanying discussion for the Brand Finance BrandBeta Scoring Template). In this example, a Discount Rate of 15 percent has been established. (Note: the appropriate discount rate is based on a market, sector and BrandBeta analysis by Brand Finance plc.) This creates the Discount Factor (line f) that must be subtracted from the Post Tax Brand Earnings (line e). Line g gives the Discounted Cash Flow for the brand starting with Year 0 at 31.4, decreasing to 20.3 by Year 5. As shown, in Year 1, this amounts to 28.4.

The final step in the process is simply summing to obtain the total of Discounted Cash Flow for this year and the next five as well. In our example, that amounts to 152.4. That is the Discounted Cash Flow for the next five years. That is shown as line h in the illustration.

There is, however, one last step in determining the true value of the brand. Our work above has valued the brand only from the present out to Year 5. Obviously, if the firm continues to own and market the brand beyond Year 5, there must be some ongoing value to the brand owner. This is defined by the Annuity shown in the chart (line i). The Annuity is simply the value of the brand into the future. In most cases, this is determined at a 0 percent growth rate as shown in the illustration above. The Annuity value in this case has been calculated at 135.3 (line i). When we combine the Discounted Cash Flow Value to Year 5 of 152.4 (line h) with the Annuity (line i) the total brand value for this firm is 287.8.

So what does the brand value number mean?

Knowing the Brand Value is interesting and sometimes uplifting for management. It makes them feel good to know they are in charge of something with large market value that is well known and accepted in the marketplace. The more important question, however, is what can the corporate communication director do by knowing the value of the corporate brand or even some of the product brands under management? First, an understanding of the Brand Value can be a major aid to management for it gives them a comparison of the corporate brand with other, more tangible assets that they are managing such as the tangible assets commonly found on the balance sheet. For example, again using our DCF calculation above, if management knew that the value of a tangible asset, say a plant or factory was 25 and the value of the brand was 287.8, it would put the relative value of the importance of the corporate brand in much better perspective. Simply knowing that brands are some of the most valuable assets the firm controls, would provide a much better view of their management to the board and senior operating managers.

Second, knowing the value of the brand provides a basic "rule-of-thumb" by which investments in the brand can be made and measured. If there is evidence that Brand Value is increasing or can be increased by 5 percent or so on a compounded basis each year (the example above shows a roughly 4–5 percent compounded growth in brand earnings each year), then an investment in marketing and brand communication of say 1–2 percent might be a legitimate method of determining a brand investment budget. In the example above, if only 1 percent of the current Brand Value were allocated for marketing and communication investments, that would amount to approximately 2.87 per year, a hefty and totally justifiable investment based on the Brand Value being protected or enhanced. It is certainly more relevant to management than saying the firm should invest 2.7 in a television campaign to "raise corporate brand awareness."

The third reason for determining Brand Value is to provide some basis for measuring returns on marketing and communication investments over the longer-term, that is, more than one fiscal year. If the firm knew that the Brand Value was 287.8, as in the example above, this would then provide a base for determining the return on brand investments. For example, say an investment of 1.0 were made in the brand through a marketing and communication program. While that would have to be deducted from the Discounted Cash Flow in Year 0 and further discounted in Years 1 through 5, if the Post Tax Brand Earnings were to increase by say 2.0, in other words, the marketing and communication program would cover its costs and provide an additional 1.0 at the Brand Earnings line (line d above), that would amount to only a 2 percent increase in Post Tax Brand Earnings to break even. Certainly this would not seem an impossible task but is something that can be evaluated as a financial investment by senior management.

Thus, if we know the current value of the brand, we can then rerun the Brand Value model each year, taking into account investments in marketing and communication programs and thus accurately determining the value that those investments are creating for shareholders on an ongoing basis. So, while such concepts as ability to charge premium prices, creating barriers to entry, reducing marketing costs and the like are interesting methods of valuing the brand, they are not nearly so persuasive or rational as actually determining the increased shareholder value that can be created and most importantly, created over time. And, based on the Brand Finance model, it would seem that this would be possible for most all marketing organizations and all types of corporate brand requirements.

Summing up corporate brand value

With this somewhat detailed explanation of how the corporate brand might be valued, we have provided a basis by which the corporate communication director can develop a rational, supportable and financially feasible approach to investing in building the corporate brand and measuring the returns on the investments made. More important, we have moved the discussion of the corporate brand from the communication-marketing-attitude-only discussion that commonly occurs, to one in which the corporate communication director starts to translate his or her activities into the board or management level concerns and to discuss it in the manner which it deserves. Thus, the corporate brand and the activities of the corporate communication director have immediate and ongoing impact on the success of the corporation.

The corporate brand is obviously one of the most important and valuable contributors to that corporate success. By discussing the corporate brand as a corporate asset, defining the value of investments and returns on those investments, the corporate communication manager leverages him or herself into the most senior level discussions occurring in the firm, those that concern the all-important financial issues. However, even more important is that the corporate brand, in and of itself, is increasingly leveraged into its rightful place in the minds, hearts, and pockets of external stakeholders or constituencies. And that "place" is measured using the tools and mechanisms or proxies for them as described in this chapter.

Undoubtedly, there are many ways to measure and evaluate the corporate brand. But, unfortunately, some of the traditional methods lack the financial requirements we believe are necessary. There is little question that attitudinal and communication research and analysis are needed to help develop effective and efficient brand communication programs. But, in most cases, the information needed to plan and implement a brand communication program falls far short in both the information needed to make relevant choices in investments or the measurement of financial returns on corporate brand and brand communication programs. This chapter has provided the material necessary for the corporate communication director or the team responsible for corporate communication to re-think the approaches and methodologies being used, always remembering of course the comments made in Chapter 11, where external resource and expertise can be brought to bear on these crucial decision areas. Hopefully this discussion will spark a real revolution in terms of how the value of the corporate brand is determined and how that value might be translated to shareholders, employees, management and other stakeholders.

Conclusive note

Brands and branding will be the essence of competitive advantage in the 21st century. Corporations can grow – dynamically, rapidly, and inexorably – if they have the right leadership. Not that there is anything new in that statement – it was made originally by Ted Levitt in 1960. Business growth and profitability globally are no longer just a matter of products, prices, and promotion. Instead the business itself, the corporate entity, spread in space and time, is under the microscope. Not just its products, processes and profitability – the so-called tangible assets – but also its personalities, positioning, and performance. For these latter P's, raising the corporate umbrella will undoubtedly be a major corporate endeavor in the 21st century.

ILLUSTRATION

Brand Building and Brand Leverage

While the marketing world is just now beginning to see the emergence of available textbooks and articles on the subject of brand measurement (either corporate or individual), the field continues to change and evolve. For example, there appears to be a switch from brand building only to brand leveraging as well – that is extending the brand, maximizing its value, and building its presence in one or more product categories throughout the global marketplace. But leveraging also means *building*. Few global corporations are about to rest on their laurels of past and current success. Instead, all are assiduously engaged in looking to future prospects, future growth, and future development.

In order to build and maintain corporate success at least four organizational elements must be in place, according to Court, Leiter and Loch (1999). These are brand stewardship, brand leveraging, developing support capabilities, and putting appropriate metrics into place. We have adapted these from Court et al.'s original paper.

1. Overarching brand stewardship

Successful corporations and businesses such as Coca-Cola, General Electric, Procter & Gamble, Nestlé and many others regard their brand or product brands as a treasured asset and treat it as such. The communication of such a brand is not left to chance or left to stakeholders to define. Instead CEOs, corporate communication teams, and external agencies are engaged in communicating brand benefits to all stakeholders. Note, however, that:

- brand communication must be in line with corporate heritage (see P&G illustration in Chapter 1)

- leaders must lead or everything goes downhill (see The Warehouse illustration in Chapter 2)

- external measurement or evaluation must be continuous and ongoing and strategic communication adjusted where necessary (see opening illustration in Chapter 3)

- clear differentiation must be made between communicating values that rest on a solid foundation versus those based on spin doctoring (see The Body Shop illustration in Chapter 4). Our recommendation is to stay with a solid foundation rather than obfuscation, spin, and rhetoric, and if that foundation is not already in place, to find ways and means to build it up

- other differentiation factors and supportive mechanisms are exhibited in illustrations throughout this text.

Accepting stewardship for the corporate brand is a commitment that runs through all that the entity is and that which it communicates to the varied stakeholders.

2. Embed brand leverage issues in planning

Brand leverage needs to be considered, in our view, at every level of corporate planning. The organization, the corporate entity, must continually be searching for ways to leverage the benefits and core principles associated with the corporate brand and permeate these throughout the strategic business units and individual brands within its portfolio. We noted earlier in Chapter 11 that branding is both an art and a science. Thus, it is not enough to be creative, the organization needs to be creative in the face of ongoing competitive realities in the global marketplace. Moreover, what the brand stands for – in the minds and hearts of publics, stakeholders, and constituencies – must be accurately understood. The mirror analogy drawn by Swamy in Chapter 11 must be Janus-faced – looking inwards (corporate identity) and outwards (corporate image). The strategic gap between these two structures can be closed, by a close adherence to and application of principles and concepts contained in this book.

3. Develop supporting capabilities

As we have discussed elsewhere (see Schultz and Kitchen, 2000), it is not enough to have the will or desire to develop communication programs that can be termed "integrated." Integration spells organizational change. Organizational change implies developing the necessary organizational structures that are needed to manage corporate communication and marketing communication on an inclusive interactive basis. And, this has to take place in national, international, and global scenarios. Employing or using even the best external agency to develop corporate communication without internal change is very much like adopting rhetoric as a substitute for real learning. Real learning is about changing mindsets, organizational infrastructures, personalities and teams if necessary (even the CEO), and developing real relationships with key constituencies. In our view real relationships involve two-way (not one-way) communication. That is very difficult for many organizations, who may have proclaimed the doctrine of marketing for many years, only to find that what they may have are the trappings, but not the substance, that allows corporations to develop old and new businesses and simultaneously reshape and strengthen the global brand.

4. The missing metrics

As seen in this, and in our previous book, the most under-developed area of brand communication in terms of leveraging corporate brand benefit are the missing metrics. In this chapter we have drawn on a number of current metrics to facilitate valuation of the corporate brand. However, these metrics are still embryonic in nature. In text after text, there is still the old alliance between marketing and corporate communication and attitudes. We have, however, not suggested throwing out the attitudinal baby with the hierarchy of effects bathwater. What we have recommended is the development of financial analyses in conjunction with marketing and corporate communication. Only when this is done, and done consistently and well over time, will corporations begin to reap the benefits of raising the corporate umbrella and measuring the direct commensurable benefits.

Acknowledgement and note

The material in this chapter is used with the kind permission of Brand Finance. Readers are reminded that the Brand Finance methodology is continually being developed. Brand Finance are in the process of developing Brand Value Trackers which assesses brand value *and* brand health over a period of time.

Closing and re-opening the corporate umbrella

don e. schultz and philip j. kitchen

The Global PR Crisis

In June, 1999, some 200 people in Belgium and France began to complain of digestive illnesses apparently caused by drinking Coca-Cola products. Within days, it was alleged that bottles had been infused with defective carbon dioxide at a Coca-Cola plant in Antwerp, Belgium. Further, it was alleged cans produced in Dunkirk, France, were contaminated with a fungicide from pallets used to ship products. As a result of these allegations, government officials in Belgium, France, The Netherlands, Germany, Luxembourg, Switzerland, and Spain issued bans or partial bans on Coca-Cola products (Holsendolph, 1999a, 1999b).

Coca-Cola lost no time in sending out a response team to counter these allegations and to restore confidence among government leaders, consumers, and its own employees. CEO Douglas Ivester met with government officials and health agencies in Belgium to express apologies. Full-page advertisements were placed in major European newspapers. Ivester and other Coca-Cola officials met with all employees in Belgium and sent memos to some 57,000 more employees around the world to reassure them that everything possible was being done to resolve the problem (Roughton and Unger, 1999).

Despite these overt actions, Coca-Cola was criticized on several fronts. As one reporter noted:

> As the hours fly by, the precious Coca-Cola brand is threatened, with one country and then another registering levels of concern about the beverages. (Liu, 1999)

Even with the above meetings, the bans remained in place for several days until officials could implement investigations of the plants and be assured that the problems were truly resolved. At least partly because of the crisis, company officials expected a loss of six to seven percent in overall sales in the second quarter (Liu, 1999). By the end of July, stock prices for Coke were down 28 percent from the previous year (Farrell and della Cava, 1999).

So, what went wrong with Coke? Some crisis management critics argued that although the company did initiate a few responsible actions, its efforts were too late and insufficient. For example, Ivester was criticized for not speaking up sooner – his first public communication did not come until more than four days after the first allegations were made. He also did not travel to Europe to offer any symbolic display of concern until a week after the crisis began. Even the company's global communication officer and president of European operations (who apparently was based in Atlanta) failed to make it to Europe until several days had passed (Holsendolph, 1999a). Paul Holmes, editor of *Reputation Management Magazine*, was quoted as saying:

> In an age of global media, when any threat – whether true or unfounded – is aimed at your brand's reputation, you must react immediately from the highest levels within the organization, no matter where in the world the threat is being launched. In Coke's case, waiting several days to issue a response from corporate head-quarters in the United States raised serious questions about the company's sens-itivity to customer safety concerns. (Holsendolph, 1999b)

Additional issues haunted Coca-Cola's efforts to repair its image. As Newsom et al. have argued, the most important facet of crisis management and communication is anticipation (Newsom et al., 1996). Coca-Cola graded poorly not only in anticipating the crisis but in actually recognizing and acting upon its explosive context. A public health crisis related to dioxin and agri-cultural products was already blooming in Europe, and particularly in Belgium, the heart of the European Union and origin of the allegations against Coca-Cola. As a European crisis expert explained, "Coca-Cola did not give due weight to the context in a climate of wild imaginings about food safety" (Kempner, 1999). Other reports suggested that Coca-Cola actually had a chance to curtail this crisis long before it occurred. Similar allegations against the company had arisen four weeks before this incident broke. After its own investigation, however, the company dismissed these earlier concerns.

Aside from ignoring the immediate context, Coca-Cola also failed to properly gauge some long-term issues related to the differences between conducting business globally versus the U.S. domestic market. The first concern centered on attitudes toward large U.S. firms operating around the world. The second was based on structural flaws within the organization itself.

Sometimes U.S.-based multinationals face problems in other countries strictly because they represent Americana. Nationalism can easily surface among those who resent the "cultural imperialism" of the U.S. As Iritani (1999) suggested in the *International Herald Tribune*, "From Singapore to Toronto to Paris, a rising chorus of voices questions whether openness to

Hollywood blockbusters, MTV and Gap clothing spell the end of their indigenous, but less marketable, ways of life." McDonald's learned this the hard way when Serbian nationals in Yugoslavia, angered over U.S.-led NATO bombing, ransacked and burned a McDonald's restaurant in downtown Belgrade because it was a symbol of the hated American culture.

An article in the *Financial Times* pointed out problems in Europe specific to Coca-Cola:

> Coke's difficulties may ... be more to do with how it is regarded in France and Belgium. Not long ago, its bid for Orangina was blocked by French authorities. It is seen by some as one of the most powerful global corporations exporting an alien brand of Americana. (Peters, 1999)

Peters further contrasted this image to the multinational's great reputation in Atlanta, where it is based and where it invests heavily in civic and community causes:

> Coke needs to address two issues: the rising tide of opinion against powerful global corporations and deep concerns, among some, about Americanisation. (Ibid.)

The failure to anticipate the problems noted above suggests a certain arrogance by Coca-Cola executives in the way they conduct business around the world. Indeed, in a national conference of the Public Relations Society of America (PRSA), one company official participated in a panel on managing a global reputation. His opening comments indicated that the company does not do much with reputation management because it has no real reputation problems. As a result, the attention of top management is focused mostly on "brand promotion."

If arrogance is not the issue, then maybe the company, as large as it is, does not really understand the corporate communication or public relations implications of the global marketplace. This is where structural issues alluded to earlier come in. Certainly, public relations at Coca-Cola seems to take a back seat to marketing, as sensed by the original writer of this piece (Wakefield, 1999). In a visit to Romania last summer, he reviewed a global guidebook that all public relations people in Coca-Cola were required to follow. In 100-plus pages, the manual addressed only one stakeholder group – namely – consumers! The comment by the Coca-Cola executive at the PRSA conference parallels this philosophy.

A strictly consumerist view seems short-sighted in a global context. The groups who would observe and possibly act against the interests of a company like Coca-Cola run the gamut, from local, regional or global media to government regulators, local communities, competitors, environmentalists, and consumer, human, or animal rights activists, to name just a few. For a multinational to truly protect its reputation, it should communicate not only with customers and potential customers, but with key stakeholder groups such as those mentioned. If it chooses not to communicate with any one of these groups – a risky proposition in itself – it should at least monitor their activities as related to corporate interests.

Nevertheless, armed with this consumer orientation, when the European crisis heated up the public relations staff of Coca-Cola seemed powerless to help resolve it; instead, the company sent its "trusted fix-it man," as one reporter noted – marketing chief Charles Frenette (Holsendorph, 1999b). That is a strange way to handle a public relations problem, but it suggests that, in the global arena, anyway, public relations only supports marketing, rather than emphasizing stakeholder scanning and issues anticipation. With these critical roles missing, a crisis outside of Coca-Cola's home territory becomes not only possible but also entirely predictable.

Source: Wakefield, 1999; used with permission.

Introduction

It seems only appropriate that a book that began with a metaphor, should end with one. In Chapter 1, we referred to the premise developed by Charles Handy that the present-day corporation could be likened to an empty raincoat, with nothing underneath in terms of values, responsibilities, trust or relationships. While there are doubtless many organizations seeking corporate gain at whatever the cost, in our experience there are many others that are solid combinations of enlightened management, interested and dedicated workers, useful and honest channel members and supportive shareholders that are interested in building for the future, not just maximizing immediate corporate returns. The challenge, of course, is separating those who "proclaim" and those that actually "perform." And, that has a lot to do with communication, both corporate and stakeholder.

From the view of the corporate communication director, it is much easier to provide useful and valuable strategic direction and tactical execution in communication programs to the latter than the former. The challenge, of course, is sorting the two for organizations do change, sometimes for the worse but often for the better. One of the key tasks of the corporate communication director is to be able to anticipate when such changes are occurring and either try to do things to increase positive changes or perceptions or to mitigate the impact and effect of those issues and crises that are negative as described in the opening vignette. In this role, the corporate communication director becomes the conscience of the corporation. Reflecting what is useful and valuable to be communicated and trying to control or limit those forms of communication that are either false or may have the potential to deceive or mislead.

Thus, we see the future role of the corporate communication manager changing dramatically in the 21st century organization. Where formerly, in too many cases, the corporate communication director was viewed as the person who "fixed things with the media when the coverage was negative" or was responsible for "spinning some corporate value out of nothing" or was viewed simply as a "PR bunny" whose primary task was to organize the corporate parties and create some type of "buzz" about the organization, we see tomorrow's communication director as someone who works at the senior management and boardroom level, creating communication strategies and giving corporate focus and direction to all the ways the organization touches its myriad stakeholders around the world.

Let there be no doubt, communication is and will be critical to every organization in the 21st century marketplace. In fact, it may well be the most important thing the organization does or can do, even more so than the products or services it has developed and marketed. Perceptions, beliefs and feelings of the various stakeholders will have a major impact on the current and ongoing success of the company. Communication will drive the corporate organization in the 21st century as has been discussed in previous chapters. The reason: if the organization can't communicate its vision, mission, brands or values, some other organization, entity, stakeholder, or irate public with the communication capabilities can and will. And that will have a major impact on the top, bottom and middle lines of the balance sheet. So, whether it is a merger or acquisition, a crisis, a misunderstanding with shareholders or just run of the mill corporate, marketing and sales communication with customers and prospects, communication is something every organization must master or else it will master the corporation.

The real issue today and tomorrow is not really marketing or sales or financial or stockholder or employee communication, that is, the traditional functional communication elements that have been the mainstay of communication managers for years. Instead the corporate challenge in the 21st century will be the management of brand contacts. In a best practices in branding study done a few years ago, Mobil Corporation (now Exxon/Mobil) described its view of communication through a visual chart. That is shown as Figure 14.1.

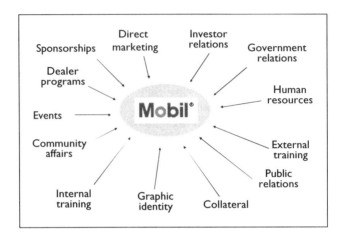

Figure 14.1 Mobil communication contact chart

As shown, Mobil looked at its corporate communication programs in a comprehensive and all inclusive way. That view included internal and external audiences, customers and government, distribution channels, communities, the media and so on; in short, every way Mobil came in contact with any corporate stakeholder was considered and, if not managed, at least identified and some accommodation made. And, Mobil also recognized that there were a number of corporate brand contacts it couldn't manage. For example, Mobil had little control over the media, environmentalists, corporate raiders, unhappy shareholders and so on. But, it could recognize and try to deal with those publics on a proactive, rather than a reactive basis.

It is this understanding and consideration of all the stakeholders and publics and the varied communication forms that the corporate communication director must observe and respond to by going forward in a positive way. That is what we mean by "brand contacts," that is, each and every way the organization touches a stakeholder has an impact now and into the future and helps build and sustain ongoing relationships with those persons, groups, businesses, government, or whatever. There are no "unimportant" contacts, just as there are no unimportant "stakeholders."

The key, of course, is to understand and communicate with those audiences in ways they want to communicate, not just the ways the organization wants to communicate. Increasingly, that will be driven through interactive communication, that is, the Web, the Internet and other new electronic media and distribution forms and formats. But, at the same time, the corporate communication director cannot forget the traditional media communication forms such as advertising, press releases, direct mail and the like. The challenge is managing the convergence of these forms and formats of communication, as illustrated in Figure 14.2.

As shown, traditional and electronic communication forms are converging. And, they are converging at the customer, consumer, and stakeholder level. In too many instances, we have seen corporate communication programs that separated the communication approaches. Electronic on the right. Traditional communication on the left. Yet, they both converge at the consumer or customer or stakeholder level. So, one of the critical ingredients in managing a 21st-century corporate communication program is to make sure that all forms of communication are aligned and integrated. That is one of the major challenges of the next several years.

But, managing brand contacts is only half the game. Assembling and delivering external and even internal communication programs is important. But, monitoring the results, that is the performance of the organization in those communication arenas is just as critical. Cigna Insurance, a corporation born out of the merger of Continental Insurance and Insurance Company of North America a few years ago struggled mightily with corporate structure, corporate culture and with corporate communication. It wasn't until the organization developed the concept of the "Tree of Life" that summarized both the internal and external vision, mission and meaning of the corporation and the corporate brand was the organization able to

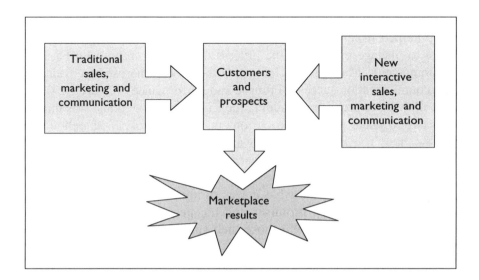

Figure 14.2 Convergence chart

Figure 14.3 Cigna Tree of Life

make strides in effectively communicating both internally and externally. Figure 14.3 shows the visual graphic that was used in this program.

The "Tree of Life" became both the internal and external integrating concept that allowed the members inside the organization to come together and it gave the external audiences and stakeholders a quick, concise and meaningful short-hand idea of the vision, mission and values of the firm.

The communication program Cigna developed included all employees, managers, customers, channels and other stakeholders under the branches of the "Tree of Life" message. It was then that the organization truly began to come together and rose as one of the major players in the areas of the insurance business in which it chose to compete.

Part of the Cigna success was the result of a clear and concise focus on monitoring the impact and effect of its communication activities. That really helped in terms of adjusting and adapting the messages and the media to manage throughout the process of difficult change. Ed Farulo, Communication Manager at Cigna calls the process he used to evaluate their communication success "Promise and Performance" (Figure 14.4).

Farulo's basic premise in building the Cigna corporate brand was that it was easy to make promises to customers, agents, brokers, shareholders and the like. The key ingredient was whether or not the organization actually performed in the marketplace on those promises. Therefore, he matched promise to performance in the communication area, that is, was Cigna really delivering on what it was promising customers and other stakeholders? When the promises and the performance were aligned, Cigna made great strides and those then spilled over into all the other areas of the Cigna operation.

What Farulo did at Cigna does much to put bones and flesh and yes, even heart inside the raincoat of the corporation and to raise the corporate umbrella of communication in a meaningful and significant way. It helps

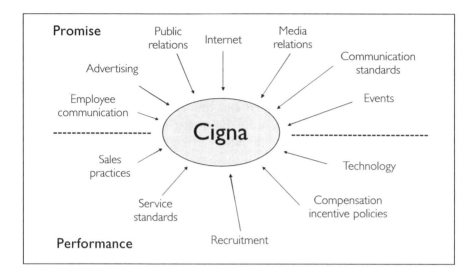

Figure 14.4 Cigna promise and performance chart

provide the substance that is needed in all the ways the firm interacts with stakeholders and other relevant populations and communities. The challenge, of course, is change. Change not just in how the corporate communication director and other key communicators do things but change in what they or he or she does and does well. And, as we all know, change is not easy and it is generally not pleasant and it is not something people or organizations or managers always embrace. But, change is necessary and for a number of very good reasons (Farulo in a presentation at Northwestern University, Fall, 1998.)

The closing corporate communication umbrella

In the section below, we review what we consider to be the key factors that have traditionally influenced the development of corporate communication programs. Those illustrate how businesses have operated during the Industrial Age or as Shekar Swamy described in Chapter 11, during the era of "sledgehammer capitalism" that occurred 100 or so years ago. These are the assumptions businesses and business leaders have always made about the organization, how it operated, what was important, who the publics were and by inference, how the firm could and would communicate with the generally quite separated and specific audiences.

These are, of course, the same assumptions the corporate communication manager has commonly used when developing communication programs. These were the "marching orders" for the functional job of corporate communication director or manager. So, the "corporate rules" were followed and the programs put in place and everyone was happy. Or, at least the people who developed and implemented and delivered the programs were happy for they were following the rules and they were doing things by the book. Since so little was known about the audiences, they were considered unimportant. If there was no reaction or resistance, it was assumed the audiences either agreed or didn't care or couldn't be made to understand.

In short, the following communication drivers, which we refer to as the "ribs of the corporate communication umbrella" were the ways corporations saw themselves in the marketplace and how they saw the role of communication, no matter what level and no matter what audience.

Perhaps most important to our discussion, however, is these are the areas in which corporate communication managers commonly are well versed and perhaps are the basis for their present-day successes. And, that is likely the greatest challenge, that is, some of these factors are still in place and some of them still work. Therefore, senior managers still accept them and the industry still applauds them or at least lauds them with awards and citations and gimmicky hardware. Unfortunately, as long as the assumptions aren't challenged and they continue to appear to work, communication managers will be loath to give them up even if they are in the twilight years of their relevance. So, while we list these as areas and concepts that will likely disappear we must recognize that they have served the corporation well, but in our view, their days are limited.

We identify each of these corporate beliefs or assumptions or "managing rules" with a few brief statements that we believe every corporate communication director will recognize as the inherent truth. And, those managers will be able to quickly and easily relate them to the warp and woof of current-day corporation communication development and management.

In the areas listed below, we argue that this type of umbrella is closing or being furled, not necessarily by choice, but by the changing environmental circumstances in which corporations compete and communicate. These concepts and approaches have had their day and while they, like a used umbrella, will continue to provide some coverage of corporate value, they are getting rather tacky and torn. Like a weakened umbrella in the raging storm, the concepts and approaches are sure to be "turned inside out" through the strong winds of change.

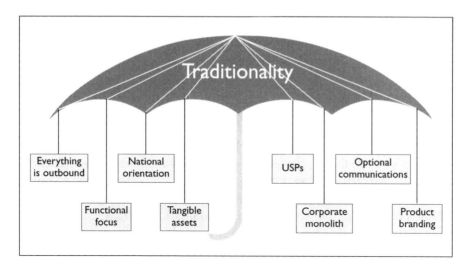

Figure 14.5 Closing eight-section umbrella

Figure 14.5 illustrates what we believe is the rapidly closing umbrella of traditional corporate communication assumptions and approaches.

As shown, we have identified eight major assumptions or driving forces that have directed or guided corporate communication management for at least the past 40 years. Starting at the top, the corporate assumptions included the following areas and operating principles each of which in turn has influenced their corporate communication programs.

1. Everything is outbound

For the most part, traditional corporate communication programs reflected the views, needs and wants of the corporation. These were the things or ideas or concepts or beliefs the firm wanted to deliver to the audiences the organization had selected. For the most part, these messages were developed to inform, educate, persuade or influence the various audiences and stakeholders identified by the firm and which the firm felt needed to be communicated to. Communication and messages were directed toward those external audiences and success was measured by the successful distribution of those messages under the assumption that "more messages delivered" was better than "fewer messages delivered." Internal communication, if it were used at all, was developed by the human resources group and consisted primarily of keeping employees and other interested groups informed about what their company was doing and how it would impact and affect their lives and how enthused they should be about corporate direction.

2. Functional focus

Communication programs were developed and implemented by communication specialists, that is, people or groups with functional communication expertise. Advertising people ran the advertising programs. Public relations people ran the public relations programs. Employee communication people ran the employee communication program. Each was budgeted separately. Each program was developed separately. Each activity was evaluated separately. There was no need for the functional specialists to talk to each other for they were conducting functional programs about which the other functional managers knew or cared little. And, as a result of this functional focus, there was always the internal battle for turf, position, power and money with the winner claiming victory each fiscal year at budget time.

3. National orientation

With limited exceptions, the multinationals being the primary ones, organizations focused on their own national market. And, even among multinationals, the approach was commonly the same, organized and focused on the national market. Since each country often operated separately and independently in terms of products, services, production, distribution and so on even though they might share common borders, the result was the same. Communication programs were constrained and limited to the specific geographic areas in which the firm or its divisions or business units were located. Communication seldom crossed borders and if it did, it was developed and executed by international specialists, often from the headquarters, who knew communication systems but often knew little about the cultures and countries to which and in which they were communicating.

4. Tangible assets

From the boardroom to the delivery dock, the focus was on the balance sheet and the balance sheet focused on tangible assets and the use of those assets. Thus, the measures of the use of tangible assets such as outputs, plant capacity, share of market and the like were the key financial measures for the organization. The corporate communication director took cues from the senior management and the board in terms of what was important. Therefore, the communication focus was generally on the implementation, application and results of the use of the tangible assets. The balance sheet was king and what the financial markets wanted to hear was uppermost in everyone's mind. Customers and brands were nice to have, particularly for FMCG organizations, but they didn't really have much to do with the success of the organization, for success was measured by the distribution and sale of goods and services the organization produced, not the customers it served. Communication therefore was about product attributes, features, differences, uses and the like. The corporate message was about sales increases and competitors routed from the field, and the value of the organization. So, to a certain extent, one might consider the communication programs self-serving, except to the senior management and the communication director to whom they were "informative and useful."

5. Unique selling propositions

Along with the focus on tangible assets as the organization's primary valuation tool, came the belief that it was the products and services that the organization produced and sold that were important, not the customers the organization served. In other words, product positioning, product benefits and product brands were the most valuable communication values the organization had to deliver. When the corporate brand was considered, it was thought of only as something in which the financial community had an interest. And, until recently, that primarily North American view prevailed. Few saw the value of the corporate brand, particularly those at General Motors, Unilever, Emerson Electric and the like. As a result, product brands dominated the marketplace and most organizations believed that a "house of product brands" structure was the logical choice of not just the marketer but the marketplace as well. Thus, because product brands dominated, at least in North America, the corporate communication area became the backwater of the communication industry. Little activity. Little funding. Little value. And, little attention except when there was a corporate crisis such as the well-known "problems" of Tylenol, Union Carbide, Exxon, Perrier and most recently Ford and Firestone. Then, all the focus was on the organization and as demonstrated in this text, some did respond well and some not so well. The primary point, however, is that for the most part, the product brands have dominated organizational interest and financial support rather than the corporate brand.

6. The corporate monolith

Traditionally, most organizations attempted to be monolithic. That is, with some exceptions, the organization wanted to own everything. Thus, few focused on affiliations, alliances or even joint ventures unless and except when they were required to do so in overseas markets by government decree. The corporation was seen as a single, stand-alone unit for which, although it might have a number of divisions or business units, the goal was corporate integration. And, that integration ranged from the totally integrated automobile manufacturing organizations of pre-World War II to the integrated oil companies that had a brief flourish in the 1960s and 70s. Every organization tried to own everything and thus benefit from their ability to create revenue all along the "value chain." There was, therefore, little interest in bringing organizations together, developing alliances, or trying to find ways to cooperatively build markets or even to build brands. Communication was the last place most senior managers believed value could be built on a cooperative basis. They proclaimed: "we are who we are!" "They are who they are!" "We're competitors and we're out to take their markets," "capture their customers," "establish beachheads in their areas of strength" and other various war-like analogies. The focus was on corporate gain, not corporate cooperation and the various forms of communication reflected this view. Corporate communication programs tended to be related almost entirely to "telling the corporate story to the financial market" in the hopes that would impact or influence share prices, and influence competitors in some way.

7. Communication as an option

Communication in any form has traditionally been seen as a corporate option. That is, management at their sole and total discretion, could either fund or not fund communication programs, certainly at the corporate level. Since measurement or evaluation programs were few and far between, most corporate managers couldn't notice any difference in the firm's performance as a result of their communication decisions. If they invested in corporate communication, things stayed about the same. If they didn't invest in corporate communication, things were "samer." Thus, corporate communication could be funded this year and not the next or funded next year but nothing allocated the following year or whatever. Communication was treated as an organizational expense. The accountants said it had to be. Thus, communication was seldom viewed as an investment by either the firm or the customers or the stakeholders. It was an expense, pure and simple. Thus, when the time came to cut expenses, the corporate communication program was typically at the top of the list. Thus, in many cases, the corporate communication allocation was often held as a bottom-line reserve that could be accessed whenever the rest of the corporation wasn't operating up to expectations. Thus, there was little commitment to communication, particularly at the corporate level. Great plans were laid but often not executed.

8. Brands and branding

Emanating primarily from North America and from FMCG organizations, each and every product was branded and thus each and every product attempted to become a brand. The individual brand concept, developed and perfected by Procter & Gamble (P&G) in the 1930s through the 1950s, was focused on building entirely separate product brands with separate organizations, activities, budgets and the like. That concept reached its peak in the era of mass marketing and mass media in the 1960s and 70s. Brand managers flourished. Each brand had a place in the market and each brand position was communicated separately and independently. The same company could bring four to six detergent brands to market, each with its own formulae, packaging and distribution system and of course, with its own advertising and marketing communication program. The corporate organization was a detail, a nonentity. In fact, the product brands worked to keep the corporate brand out of sight. The less connection between the various product brands, the better. Thus, the corporate brand became like the "empty raincoat" that Handy epitomized in his writings in the 1990s. P&G was a shell. So was Unilever. Corporate meant nothing. The product brands meant everything. And, along with this focus on product brands, there grew up a whole mythology of how brands were built and maintained. The focus was on mass communication, primarily television, to mass audiences with a common message that was driven home to the target market through huge investments in media and promotion. The problem was, the model only worked for P&G and Unilever and a few others. When it was tried by other corporate organizations, it failed, often miserably.

Thus, senior management began to believe that the corporate brand had little value, it couldn't be built and developed at any reasonable cost and therefore, there was no use trying. And so, today, we have corporate brands that are not managed at all, except by their stakeholders. Yet, there is a recognition that the corporate brand is important. Global firms such as Sony, Samsung, LG, Schneider and others have shown that corporate brands can indeed have value and provide a differentiating force in the marketplace among all levels of corporate stakeholders. Yet, the perception persists, certainly in North America, that corporate brands are nice to have but not really equal to the product brands. And, that perception generally persists until the organization breaks its pick in the global arena. The result has been that in many organizations corporate branding or corporate communication when it was used, was used primarily to support the product brands in some way. And, it appears that practice still continues.

There may well be other organizational beliefs and operating principles that have had an impact on the development of corporate communication programs over the years but these seem to be the key ones. They have driven the manner in which companies and firms have communicated and have been instrumental in guiding the development of media systems and supplier organizations. Most of all, they appear to have worked. They worked for they were developed for a specific type of marketplace, a specific type of communication delivery system, and a specific type of corporate focus. The problem is, that corporate focus is changing and has been doing so for the past decade. Much of that change has been driven by technology that has radically altered the communication landscape. A great deal has resulted from the development of new forms of corporate value systems and the attempt to include, not exclude social priorities, concepts and ideas. And, much has come as a result of knowledge and learning. The old ways worked and they worked well but there are now newer and better approaches on the horizon. We discuss those in the next section.

Opening the new corporate umbrella

There is little question that communication is changing, sometimes for the better, sometimes for the worse. But, it is changing. And the changes we see occurring are having and will continue to have a major impact on the way corporate communication programs are designed, developed and delivered in the 21st century. In the following pages, we outline the changes we believe are the most important. If one looks closely, it can be seen that they are the counterpoints to the traditional approaches just described. But, that

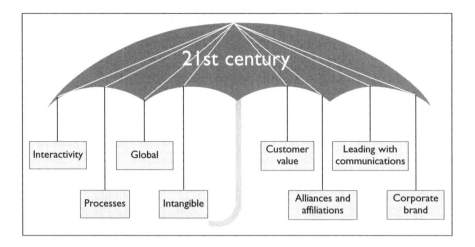

Figure 14.6 Opening eight-section umbrella

is as it should be. The new sometimes replaces the old and sometimes just adapts the old to a different model. But, as we are reminded in the New Testament analogy, new wine just won't go into old bottles. The challenge, of course, is when to change, when to adapt and when to stand pat. That is what this section hopes to provide, a guide to the best choices.

As we used the metaphor of the corporate umbrella in the earlier section, we repeat the concept here. The difference is we believe this is the opening of a new corporate umbrella based on the activities, concepts and approaches that are visible now and most likely will grow over time in the 21st century (see Figure 14.6).

As before, we have identified the eight most important changes or factors that will drive the organization and particularly communication in the 21st century. Those are reviewed in some detail below. As before, these are not prescriptive and each corporate communication manager and those responsible for corporate communication will have to review them and see how they fit his or her specific organization, or can be configured in relation thereto.

1. Interactivity–interactivity

There is little question that the whole area of interactivity is and will continue to have a major impact on the corporate organization. While the focus in communication has been on the Web, the Internet and the like, the real change the electronic systems are having on organizations is through "connectivity," that is the hooking together, the sharing and the increasingly close relationships organizations are forming with customers, suppliers, alliance partners, in short any and everyone and any and every group with which the firm has some type of dealing. The electronic interchanges that provide updates on inventory, manufacturing scheduling, parts supplies and the like are a prime example of this interactive connection. From a communication standpoint, communication in today's corporation never stops. It is continuous and ongoing. Thus, communication is not something the organization "does." It is, instead, something in which the organization is involved. The result will likely be the rise in dialogs and conversations between people in the corporation and the firm's suppliers, partners, customers and other stakeholders. This will also likely lead to a decline in traditional outbound, directed communication in which the corporation says its piece or delivers its message and then sits back and waits for a reaction. The impact of interactivity on the organization is now and will, in the future, be incredible for it forces the organization to begin listening and not just talking. Outbound communication will not disappear but it will certainly be swamped in the future by interactivity.

2. Processes

There is little question that the functional structure of the organization is being challenged. Hand-offs, piece work, silos and separated units are being replaced by processes and systems. Everything is being connected or integrated into everything else, around the world. The integration of the organization is one of the key management goals of the 21st century with the focus on "just-in-time," "efficient customer response" and "electronic data interchange" driving how organizations are organized and how they operate. Even the time-honored strategic business unit or SBU is under attack as it becomes increasingly difficult for senior management to separate the activities of one unit from another. Certainly this process approach is impacting and will affect communication. The attempt to integrate all forms of communication has now reached almost total acceptance in most enlightened organizations with only the most recalcitrant functional managers and firms valiantly attempting to stem the tide. While some functional specialists will likely be needed in the future for there are always substantial differences in various forms and types of delivery systems such as advertising, public relations and the like, there is little question that the development of communication processes will grow and expand. Thus, the corporate communication director becomes not just a "communicator" but a "process manager" as well, with all the inherent change that type of activity will require.

3. Global – every organization is now global

There is no choice for there is no way to limit the flow of information, products, services, activities and the like. Organizations that formerly operated on a strict geographic basis, that is, on a country by country approach are rapidly finding that their customers are driving the change to global, and they are helpless to stem the tide. Differential pricing or distribution schemes set up for customers in individual countries are no longer acceptable. One solution, one price, one distribution method, one billing system are the basis on which organizations will operate in the future. The impact of this global approach is only now beginning to be felt by the communication groups. The need for cross-cultural, cross-border, cross-language capabilities in communication groups is increasing at a rapid rate. The requirements for instantaneous communication around the world are increasing. The ability of the firm to plan, develop and deliver communication programs becomes less important as the switch to developing an ability to sense communication needs, adapt communication messages, and respond to customers, markets, and stakeholders on a real-time basis becomes mandatory. This sense–adapt–respond model will increasingly be the key element for ongoing corporate success. Thus, many of the communication planning approaches that have historically been used must give way to new, innovative research methodologies that are just emerging, as must the old, established communication systems give way to ones that not only span the globe but allow the manager to drill down into local situations as needed or required.

4. Intangible

As the value of the organization moves more and more to the intangible areas of intellectual property, brands, patents, know-how and the like, the focus of the firm must move more and more toward the management of these intangible assets and away from the traditional focus on plants, factories, inventory, distribution systems and the like. Thus, senior management will need to be able to manage the new "corporate value," much of which will be bound up in new methods and approaches to management that are just now emerging. Chief among the new skills that will be needed by management will be the capacity and capability to communicate the new corporate value to all the stakeholders. Where once the balance sheet spoke for itself with hard, verifiable, tangible assets as the value base, as the organization shifts to the intangible, more difficult to measure values of the future, communication becomes the key element. The ability to explain, illustrate, teach and even persuade becomes a key tool in the corporations' management toolkit. Obviously the corporate communication manager will and must play a key role in all these tasks. Communication, like the new corporate assets, is often believed to be intangible. Therefore the capability of the corporate communication director to put "substance" inside the presently empty raincoat that is the corporation becomes the key contribution to the ongoing success of the organization.

5. Customer value

There is little question that many corporations are beginning to understand that the real value of the corporate organization is its ability to gain, retain and grow customers and their income flows over time. Products and services are just the means by which the organization gains income and ultimately profits from customers. The same is true of the financial community. It is not the current share price that is important, it is the confidence and acceptance of shareholders for the longer term. It is not the number of employees the organization has, it is their capability to gain and maintain customers and their income flows that will count. Thus, the focus of the communication programs must shift from that of products and services and plants and corporate "stuff" to customers and prospects and shareholders and stakeholders and income flows and the like. That is a radically different approach to communication by the organization because it requires the communication to be focused on external customers and stakeholders and not on internal managers and products. Getting information about the corporation is relatively easy. Most of the required knowledge is already inside. Getting information about the external stakeholders whether they be customers or governments or environmentalists or communities is much more difficult and requires an entirely new skill set. But, that will be the task of the new corporate communication manager. So, new skills, new tools, new approaches. All will be critical in the management of 21st-century corporate communication programs.

6. Alliances and affiliations

Traditionally, senior managers have focused on managing employees and maybe a few distribution partners. In most cases, the management had control or power over those individuals or groups so the task was relatively straightforward based on command and control. Employees could be coerced or fired. Channels could be restricted or their franchises canceled. But, in the new world of alliances, partnerships, joint ventures, affiliations and the like, the situations are commonly ones of equal power or at least shared power. Thus, managers must become negotiators, referees, consensus builders and the like. That's a new role for many of the "hard-nosed" managers of the past. It requires different skills, capabilities and even emotions. These are not areas where edicts, directives or even "strong management recommendations" carry much weight. It is here that the corporate communication director will likely find many new challenges. Historically, internal and cross-company or cross-SBU communication has not been something in which corporate communication directors have had much of a hand. That fell to other internal people. Yet, in the 21st-century arena we see developing, corporate communication directors will likely play a key role in assisting senior managers with the often delicate communication tasks that keep an alliance or affiliation or other rather fragile relationships not just functioning but thriving. While this may be a new role for the corporate communication director it will not be a new one in every sense. It is simply that the communication skills will have to be applied in a new arena and in most cases, on a much larger and more delicate stage.

7. Leading with communication

Where in many companies, communication has been an after-thought, in the 21st-century arena we envision, communication will be the lead element. Investments in communication will be one of the top priorities of many firms and the corporate communication director will be working and perhaps sometimes even directing senior managers. As organizations move more and more into the management of customers and customer groups as their primary focus, rather than the operation of plants and factories or internal employees, communication becomes one of the key skills the corporation will employ. As before, the ability to listen, learn and respond becomes critical for the firm. Similarly, the ability of the organization to create and maintain an ongoing dialog with all stakeholders becomes the primary way in which the organization is able to gauge its marketplace success. Inherent in this is the need for the organization to develop new, different, and more relevant methods of measuring the impact and effect of the communication programs it chooses to implement. As was discussed in Chapters 12 and 13, communication must become an investment by the firm and treated like any other asset. In this sense, the ability of the corporate communication manager to identify, value, determine investment levels and measure results becomes just as important as the role strategic planners and chief financial officers fill today. Make no mistake, communication must become a key skill in the corporation of the 21st century and for the most part, it must lead rather than follow the strategic directions and actions of the firm. In many cases, this will be a totally new role for the corporate communication director but one that must be filled.

8. Corporate brand

Much of the last half of this book has focused on the corporate brand. The changes here are enormous. As the firm moves from a focus on product brands to that of the corporate brand, major risks are incurred and major advantages gained. By operating under a corporate brand, the firm obviously risks total marketplace annihilation should things go wrong as they did in the case of Firestone. By the same token, the advantages of corporate identification, affiliation and value are increased. There is little question that strong corporate brands such as Microsoft, FedEx and Cisco Systems have done much to build the value of the organization on a global basis. IBM, Hewlett-Packard and UPS don't have to explain what they do. All the relevant stakeholders know. By the same token a strong corporate brand such as Virgin or Kraft or Nestlé allows them to move into new and exciting areas where the recognition of their name often paves the way for instant or near-instant success. Corporate brands have value for they communicate a mass of values to customers and consumers and shareholders and stakeholders and other interested parties. Managing a corporate brand is not an easy task, however. In many cases, interested parties try to crawl under the corporate umbrella to take advantage of its coverage and reputation when they are not deserving of that blanket coverage. In other cases, business units or product managers refuse to take on the corporate cloak believing that their name, their recognition, their history and their future is greater by going it alone. One of the key skills of the corporate communication director of the 21st century will be the capability and capacity to recognize what belongs under the corporate umbrella and what does not. To invite in those who are deserving and to keep out those who are not. And, quite honestly, when all is said and done, that may be the most critical skill of the corporate communication directors of the 21st-century organization.

With this view of the furling corporate umbrella of the past and the re-opening of the new corporate umbrella of the future, we close our discussion of "Raising the Corporate Umbrella." We believe there is value to the corporation. As Shekar Swamy identified in Chapter 11, the corporation has been one of the most important and impactful concepts in human history. Much has been written about the corporation in the past, both good and bad, and much will be written in the future. It is our belief that the corporation must move beyond the "empty raincoat" days of the latter part of the 20th century. It is our hope and our belief that the corporate communication director of the 21st century will play a key role in "filling the corporate raincoat" and that corporate communication will have much to do with allowing the organization to toss away the raincoat and raise the corporate umbrella through effective corporate communication. The opportunity is there. All corporate communication directors, as authorized by CEOs, need do is seize the handle and open the umbrella.

Summary and conclusion

Well, now we draw the strands to a close. An old adage comes to mind that is appropriate in this setting:

> The sermon had ended,
> The priest had descended.
> Delighted were they …
> *But they preferred the old way.* (Anon; italics added)

In this book we have described a way forward. We have not advocated throwing away the old worn-out umbrella of the 20th century, *yet*! We recognize that most torn corporate umbrellas, whose handle, ribs or cloth may have become damaged, torn, or even collapsed under the slings and arrows of outrageous fortune, do indeed end up forced into the dustbin of history. Corporate communicators, communication teams, and CEOs will do well to examine the focus of their activities. For example phrases and words such as *outbound, functional focus, national orientation, tangible assets, USPs, corporate monolith, optional communications,* and *individual brands* are already moving into the economic and social history and marketing books of the 20th century. They are not dead, just dated, outworn, somewhat shop-soiled, and unsuited for the bright corporates of the 21st century.

Instead the stars of the 21st century would do well to examine the terminology their people use. Words and phrases such as: *interactivity*, *processes*, *global*, *intangible*, *customer value*, *alliances* and *affiliations*, *leading with communication*, and *corporate brand* are the new buzzwords of corporate success. All are forward looking, all are interactive, all are synergistic, all involve communication with the various stakeholders that could impact on performance, share value, and profitability. "Raising the corporate umbrella" is a suitable metaphor for it generates questions concerning leadership, structures, processes, systems, and values. Such a metaphor is not concerned with rhetoric or spin, for these tactics of communication rebound eventually on their users whether they be corporations, or individuals with corporate-size egos.

Thus empty raincoats are relegated. Battered and torn umbrellas are thrown away. Living flesh and bones have been placed in the raincoat. The storms are upon today's corporations. But with the stem in the hands of excellent CEOs, aided by able corporate communication directors, and with all the communication ribs fully extended, the stretched unbroken cloth of the corporate umbrella can do much to assuage the storms of corporate life.

ILLUSTRATION

Vignette Montage

Over recent months there have been several hundred articles and papers concerning corporate communication issues. Below are just a few extracts to stimulate attention and interest in this area. All suggest the need for corporate communicators to effectively develop communication in relation to the needs of varied stakeholders:

> The race to find an ideal merger partner in the pharmaceutical industry may subject corporates to an unpredictable market *and* force them to dig deep in their pockets. Warner Lambert's near-merger with American Home Products (AHP) and subsequent hostile takeover by Pfizer are discussed. Despite the acrimony, the Warner Lambert and Pfizer merger will create the world's largest pharmaceutical company. AHP was paid the largest ever kill fee, $1.8 billion, and still retains a strong if battered [losing] position. Glaxo Welcome and SmithKline Beecham, and Pharmacia & Upjohn and Monsanto have also merged, and are seeing their shares traded up above the market average. (Tully, K., 2000, italics and brackets added)

Michael Parker who has recently taken up the position of President and CEO of Dow Chemical Company has recently stated:

> I think you'll see our industry ... respond by consolidating their product lines so they have better offerings. Globalism is another key word because a company like Unilever wants to do business with the *same people all over the world.* (Jarvis, L., 2000)

Monsanto continues to encounter almost daily battles in the world press (see Anon, 2001; Bown, 2000). Notably, unproven allegations still impact on major distributors. Friends of the Earth, a major environmental watchdog and invidious stakeholder recently alleged that:

> two kinds of genetically modified corn produced by Monsanto, *neither approved for sale in Europe,* have been detected in three brands of tortilla chips sold in the UK.

> Supermarket chains [such as] Safeway, Sainsburys, Tesco, and Asda [Wal-Mart] [all major UK supermarket retailers], which buy tortilla chips from companies that used Monsanto corn say they have not withdrawn the affected products from sale as of *Chemical Week's* press time. (Bown, 2000)

Finally, a warning voice, is raised by Larry Foster. Larry had been head of PR for Johnson & Johnson for 30 years and during the Tylenol crises. He should know what he is talking about:

> There are some dark and disturbing clouds on the horizon. The darkest is the tendency of many large multinational companies to make international public relations management the victim of benign neglect.

> As a result of this neglect [this function] has not developed in large corporations as it should. While this may seem to bode well for the public relations agencies and consultancies that are filling the void, *I believe that over the long term it can spell trouble.* (Foster, 1999; cited in Wakefield, 1999)

Mergers, acquisitions, corporate unpredictability, globalization, partnerization, consolidation, allegation, government interest, stakeholder and environmental vigilance, suppliers, agencies, consultancies, potential neglect and trouble. A mixed montage of factors – one potential resolution! Raising the corporate umbrella – not the battered, torn, and windswept version of the 20th century, but the new structured, responsive, interactive, and above all protective umbrella of the 21st-century corporation is needed. That's what this book has been about ... Keep watching this space!

Acknowledgement

We gratefully acknowledge the kind permission of Robert I. Wakefield to cite segments of his Bled Symposia paper concerning the recent Coca-Cola crisis in Europe.

References

"Dentsu restructures Head Office to quicken response time" (1998) *Ad Age International Online*

"Reaching consumers amidst global change" (1999) *IAA Perspectives*, a publication of the International Advertising Association, New York, June

"Shell taps *Reader's Digest* for global ads" (1999) *International Advertising Age*, June 01, p. 21

"Sorrell says agencies should offer more strategy" (1996) *Ad Age International Online*, June 11

"The arguments: finally fixed down by figures" (1999) *M&M Europe*, July, pp. vi–vii

Aaker, D. A. (1991) *Managing Brand Equity: Capitalizing on the Value of a Brand Name*, New York, Free Press

Albert, S. and Whetten, D. A. (1985) "Organizational identity," in Cummings, L. L. and Staw, B. M. (eds) *Research in Organizational Behaviour*, Greenwich, CT, JAI Press

Alsop, R. (1999) "The best corporate reputations in America," *The Wall Street Journal*, September 23, p. B1

Anderson, L. and Varey, R. J. (2000) "Explaining communication effectiveness as a management competence: personal constructs and social construction," working paper presented to the "Managing Across Boundaries" Conference of the British Academy of Management, Edinburgh School of Management, 13–15 September

Anonymous (2001) "Monsanto gets experimental use permits for GM corn crop," *Chemical Market Reporter*, January 29, **259**(5): 25

Ansen, D. (1999) "The hyping of *Star Wars*," *Newsweek*, May 17, pp. 56–66

APQC (American Productivity and Quality Centre) (1998) *Integrated Marketing Communications*, Houston, APQC International Benchmarking Clearinghouse

APQC (American Productivity and Quality Centre) (2000) *Brand Building & Communication: Power Strategies for the 21st Century*, Houston, APQC International Benchmarking Clearinghouse

Ardrey, R. (1967) *The Territorial Imperative*, London, Collins

Bartlett, C. A. and Ghoshal, S. (1998) *Managing Across Borders: The Transnational Solution*, 2nd edn, Boston, Harvard Business School Press

Bass, B. M. (1985) *Leadership and Performance Beyond Expectations*, New York, Free Press

Bastien, D T. (1987) "Common patterns of behavior and communication in corporate mergers and acquisitions," *Human Resource Management*, **26**(1): 17–33

Beckett, A. (2000) "Is Coke still it?: It's the top-selling drink and the biggest brand in the world – but for how long? Image problems, bad PR, tumbling share prices, health

398

scares, and a flood of smoothies and energy drinks are threatening to burst the Coca-Cola bubble," October 2, *Guardian*, Guardian features pages, p. 2

Belch, G. E. and Belch, M. A. (1997) *Advertising and Promotion: an Integrated Marketing Communications Perspective*, 4th edn, Boston, Irwin/McGraw-Hill

Berk, T. G. (1996) "Sending the right merger message to all employees," *Mergers & Acquisitions*, **30**(4): 30–3, January–February

Bhattacharya, C. B., Rao, H. and Glynn, M. A. (1995) "Understanding the bond of identification: an investigation of its correlates among art museum members," *Journal of Marketing*, **59**: 46–57

Biggar, J. M. and Selame, E. (1992) "Building brand assets," *Chief Executive*, July/August pp. 36–9

Birkigt, K. and Stadler, M. M. (1986) *Corporate Identity: Grundlagen, Funktionen, Fallbeispiele* [*Corporate Identity: Foundations, Functions, Case Examples*], 3rd edn, Landsberg am Lech, Verlag Moderne Industrie

Bown, J. (2000) "Monsanto in GM corn flap," *Chemical Week*, **162**(43): 44

Brabbs, C. (2000) "Can Coke and IPG truly 'think local'?," *Marketing*, December 7, p. 7, Haymarket Publishing Services

Bridge, K. and Baxter, L. A. (1992) "Blended relationships: friends as work associates," *Western Journal of Communication*, **56**: 200–25

Brown, A. D. and Starkey, K. (1994) "The effect of organizational culture on communication and information," *Journal of Management Studies*, **31**(6): 807–29

Brown, P. and Levinson, S. C. (1987) *Politeness: Some Universals in Language Usage*, Cambridge, Cambridge University Press

Brown, T. J. and Dacin, P. A. (1997) "The company and the product: corporate associations and consumer product responses," *Journal of Marketing*, **61**(1): 68–84

Burns, J. M. (1978) *Leadership*, New York, Harper & Row

Business Week (Asian Edition) (2000), McGraw Hill Companies, August 28, p. 47

Butler, R. (1991) *Designing Organisations: A Decision-Making Perspective*, London, Routledge

Calahan, J. (1995) "The shifting paradigm in communications," in Garone, S.J (ed.) *Integrating Business Strategies with Communications*, Conference Board Proceedings, Conference Board, New York, p. 27

Campbell, A., Goold, M. and Alexander, M. (1995) "Corporate strategy: the quest for parenting advantage," *Harvard Business Review*, **73**(2): 120–32

Cartwright, S. and Cooper, C. L. (1992) *Mergers and Acquisitions: The Human Factor*, Oxford, Butterworth Heinemann

Chatman, J. A., Bell, N. E. and Staw, B. M. (1986) "The managed thought: the role of self-justification and impression management in organizational settings," in Sims, H. P. and Gioia, D. A. (eds) *The Thinking Organization*, San Francisco, CA, Jossey-Bass, pp. 191–214

Choo, C. W. (1998) *The Knowing Organization*, New York, Oxford University Press

Clemente, M. N. and Greenspan, D. S. (1999) "M&As: preventing culture clash," *HR Focus*, **76**(2): 9–11

Cookson, C. (2000) "Double size, double complexity," *Financial Times*, survey of Life Sciences and Pharmaceuticals, April 6

Cooper, A. and Simons, P. (1997) *Brand Equity Lifestage: An Entrepreneurial Revolution*, London, TBWA Simons Palmer, September

Coulter, P. (1996) "A merger is nothing but a 'planned' crisis," *IABC Communication World*, December–January, pp. 22–4

Court, D. C., Leiter, M. G. and Loch, M. A. (1999) "Brand leverage," *The McKinsey Quarterly*, **2**: 101–10

Craig, S. P. and Douglas, C. S. (1995) *Global Marketing Strategy*, New York, McGraw Hill

Cutlip, S. M., Center, A. H. and Broom, G. M. (1994) *Effective Public Relations*, Englewood Cliffs, NJ, Prentice Hall

Davidson, D. Kirk (1998) "Consumers really don't care about brand products owners," *Marketing News*, **32**(24): 5

Daft, R. L. and Weick, K. E. (1984) "Toward a model of organizations as interpretation systems," *Academy of Management Review*, **9**(2): 284–95

Datta, D. K. (1991) "Organizational fit and acquisition performance: effects of post-acquisition integration," *Strategic Management Journal*, **12**: 284–97

Daymon, C. (2000) "On considering the meaning of managed communication: or why employees resist 'excellent' communication," *Journal of Communication Management*, **4**(3): 240–52

de Chernatony, L. and McDonald, M. (1998) *Creating Powerful Brands in Consumer, Service and Industrial Markets*, Oxford, Butterworth Heinemann

Deetz, S. A. (1992) *Democracy in an Age of Corporate Colonization: Developments in Communication and the Politics of Everyday Life*, Albany, NY, State University of New York Press

Deetz, S. A. (1995) *Transforming Communication, Transforming Business: Building Responsive and Responsible Workplaces*, Creskill, NJ, Hampton Press

Dietrich, J. (1999) "U.S. multinationals," *Ad Age International*, June, pp. 39–44

Dixon, T. (1996) *Communication, Organization and Performance*, Norwood, NJ, Ablex Publishing

Dowling, G. R. (1986) "Managing your corporate image," *Industrial Marketing Management*, **15**(2): 109–15

Dozier, D. M., Grunig, L. A. and Grunig, J. E. (1995) *The Manager's Guide to Excellence in Public Relations and Communication Management*, Mahwah, NJ, Lawrence Erlbaum Associates

Drobis, D. R. (1999) "Communication: the essential ingredient in the value equation," *Raglan's Public Relations Journal*, March/April, p.14

Druckenmiller, B. (1999) "Brand vs. reputation," *Inside PR*, April 17, p. 2

Ducoffe, R. and Grein, A. (1998) "Strategic responses to market globalization among advertising agencies," *International Journal of Advertising*, **17**(3)

Duncan, R. (1979) "What is the right organisation structure? Decision tree analysis provides the answer," *Organisational Dynamics*, Winter, pp. 59–80

Dunning, J. H. (1993) *Multinational Enterprises and the Global Economy*, Wokingham, Addison Wesley Publishing Company

Dutton, J. E. and Dukerich, J. M. (1991) "Keeping an eye on the mirror: image and identity in organizational adaptation," *Academy of Management Journal*, **34**: 517–54

Dutton, J. E., Dukerich, J. M. and Harquail, C. V. (1994) "Organizational images and member identification," *Administrative Science Quarterly*, **39**: 239–63

Eales, R. (1990) "Multinational report: multinational corporate communications, a growth sector," *Multinational Business*, **4**: 28–31

Economist, The (1989) "Corporate eyes, ears, and mouth," March 18, pp. 105–6

Eisenberg, E. M. (1984) "Ambiguity as strategy in organizational communication," *Communication Monographs*, **51**: 227–42

Elliott, S. (1999) "Ford goes global in effort to control the clock," *The New York Times*, Late edition, Section C, October 27, p. 1

Fahey, L., and Narayanan, V. K. (1986) *Macroenvironmental Analysis for Strategic Management*, St. Paul, West Publishers

Fairclough, N. (1992) *Discourse and Social Change*, Cambridge, Polity Press

Fairclough, N. (1995) *Critical Discourse Analysis: The Critical Study of Language*, London, Longman

Fairhurst, G. T. and Sarr, R. A. (1996) *The Art of Framing: Managing the Language of Leadership*, San Francisco, Jossey-Bass

Farrell, G. and della Cava, M. (1999). "Coca-Cola boss: company's flat days are over," *USA Today*, July 23, p. B1

Farulo, E (1998) Presentation to the Integrated Marketing Communication Department students, Northwestern University, Evanston, IL, Fall

Feldman, M. S. (1991) "The meaning of ambiguity: learning from stories and metaphors," in Frost, P. J., Moore, L. F., Reis, L. M., Lundberg, C. C. and Martin, J. (eds) *Reframing Organizational Culture*, Newbury Park, CA, Sage

Financial Times (1998) "The global FT," special insert, November 6, p.1

Fisher, R. J. and Wakefield, K. (1998) "Factors leading to group identification: a field study of winners and losers," *Psychology and Marketing*, **15**(1): 23–40

Fortune (1994) special advertising section, September 19

Fortune (2000) November 22, pp. 153, 185

Foster, L. (1998) "1998 Atlas award lecture on public relations," *PRSA Inter-national Section Monograph Series*, New York, p. 1; cited in Wakefield (1999)

Freiberg, K. and Freiberg, J. (1996) *Nuts! Southwest Airlines' Crazy Recipe for Business and Personal Success*, Austin, TX, Bard Press

Friedman, T. L. (1999) *The Lexus and the Olive Tree: Understanding Globalisation*, New York, Farrar, Strauss, and Girouox, pp. 93–119

Frost, P. J., Moore, L. F., Reis, L. M., Lundberg, C. C. and Martin, J. (eds) (1991) *Reframing Organizational Culture*, Newbury Park, CA, Sage Publications

Fulop, L. and Linstead, S. (eds) (1999) *Management: A Critical Text*, London, Macmillan Business – now Palgrave

Gardner, W. L. and Avolio, B. J. (1998) "The charismatic relationship: a dramaturgical perspective," *Academy of Management Review*, **23**: pp. 32–58

Gardner, W. L. and Cleavenger, D. (1998) "The impression management strategies associated with transformational leadership at the world-class level," *Management Communication Quarterly*, **12**: pp. 3–41

Garritty, J. (1999) "The power of branding," a presentation to the Charlotte Chapter of the PRSA

Gordon, G. (1985) "The relationship of corporate culture to industry sector and corporate performance," in Kilman, R. H., Saxton, M. J., Serpa, R. et al. (eds) *Gaining Control of the Corporate Culture*, San Francisco, CA, Jossey-Bass

Gould, S. J. (2000) "The state of IMC research and applications," *Journal of Advertising Research*, **40**(5): pp. 22–3

Gronstedt, A. (2000) *The Customer Century: Lessons from World-class Companies in Integrated Marketing and Communication*, London, Routledge

Grunig, J. E. and Hunt, T. (1984) *Managing Public Relations*, Forth Worth, TX, Holt, Rinehart, Winston

Gurciyan, T. (2000) Communicating change as part of merger and acquisition strategies: a cultural and sense making approach. Unpublished MBA dissertation, School of Management, University of Salford

Habermas (1984) *Theory of Communicative Action*, Vol. 1 (trans. T. McCarthy), London, Heinemann

Haigh, D. (1998) "Brand valuation: understanding, exploiting, and communicating brand values," *Financial Times* (Retail and Consumer), p. 19

Haigh, D. (2000) "Current practice in brand valuation," *The Financial Fact Brand Bulletin*; No. 16, July, London, Gee Publishing

Haigh, D. (2001) T*he Brand Finance Report: The Case for Brand Value Reporting*, London, Brand Finance plc

Halal, W. E. (1996) T*he New Management: Democracy and Enterprise Are Transforming Organisations*, San Francisco, CA, Berrett-Koehler Publishers

Halal, W. E. and Varey, R. J. (1999) "Recognizing the emerging 'third way'," *The Christian Science Monitor*, February 3, p. 9

Hamel, G. and Prahalad, C. K. (1994) *Competing for the Future*, Cambridge, MA, Harvard Business School Press

Hamill, J. and Kitchen, P. J. (2000) "The Internet: international context," in Kitchen, P. J. (ed.) *Marketing Communications: Principles and Practice*, London, International Thomson, Ch. 22

Handy, C. (1993) *Understanding Organizations*, 4th edn, London, Penguin

Handy, C. (1995) *The Empty Raincoat*, London, Arrow Books, (first published by Hutchinson, London in 1994)

Harris, C. (1997) "Theorizing interactivity," in *Fit for the Global Future? New Approaches in Marketing, Advertising, and Market Research in Response to a Changing Business Environment*, Amsterdam, ESOMAR

Harris, T. (1993) *The Marketer's Guide to Public Relations*, New York, John Wiley & Sons

Harris, T. L. (1998) *Value-added Public Relations*, New York, Wiley & Sons

Hayek, F. (1990) *The Fatal Conceit: The Errors of Socialism*, Chicago, IL, University of Chicago Press

Heath, R. L. (1994) *Management of Corporate Communication: From Interpersonal Contacts to External Affairs*, Hillsdale, NJ, Lawrence Erlbaum Associates

Hochschild, A. R. (1983) *The Managed Heart: The Commercialization of Human Feeling*, Berkeley, CA, University of California Press

Hofstede, G. (1991) *Cultures and Organizations: Software of the Mind*, New York, McGraw-Hill

Holmes, P. (2000) "Brand is personality; reputation is character," *Inside PR*, June 12, p. 3

Holsendolph, E. (1999a) "'Owning up' can cut the damage," *The Atlanta Journal – Constitution* (www.ajc.com), June 18

Holsendolph, E. (1999b) "Firm sends trusted fix-it man to restore faith," *The Atlanta Journal – Constitution* (www.ajc.com), June 22

Hubbard, A. (2000) "The boss too good to be true," *Sunday Star Times*, April 2, p. 11

Hubbard, N. (1999) *Acquisition Strategy and Implementation*, London, Macmillan – now Palgrave

Hucker, C. (1991) "Restating old values at Hallmark," in Caropreso, F. (ed.) *Communication Strategies for Changing Times*, New York, Conference Board, p. 13

Hunger, J. D. and Wheelan, T. (1993) *Strategic Management*, 4th edn, Reading, MA, Addison-Wesley

Ind, N. (1998) *Making the Most of Your Corporate Brand*, London, Financial Times Management,

Iritani, E. (1999). "Hong Kong asks: Is Mickey Mouse the club to join?," *International Herald Tribune* (www.iht.com), June 16

Jarvis, L. (2000) "Hydrocolloid producers consolidate despite demand," *Chemical Market Reporter*, November 6, pp. 5, 14

Jemison, D. B. and Sitkin, S. B. (1990) "Corporate acquisitions: a process perspective" in *Mergers and Acquisitions: Organisational and Cultural Issues*, working document, Barcelona, Centre for Organizational Studies

Jernstedt, R. (1995) "Billions and billions served," in Garone, S. J. (ed.) *Integrating Business Strategies with Communications*, New York: Conference Board Proceedings, p. 19

Joachimsthaler, E. and Aaker, D. A. (1999) "Building brands without mass advertising," *Harvard Business Review*, January/February

Johnson, G. and Scholes, K. (1989) *Exploring Corporate Strategy: Text and Cases*, London, Prentice Hall

Jones, J. P. (2000) *International Advertising Realities and Myths*, London, Sage Publications

Kammerer, J. (1989) *Beitrag der Produktpolitik zur Corporate Identity* [Contribution of product policy to corporate identity], München, SIBI-Verlag

Kapferer, J .N. (1992) *Strategic Brand Management*, London, Kogan Page

Kapferer, J.N. (1996) *Marketing Magazine*, interview with Kapferer, J. N., March

Keegan, W. J. (1999) *Global Marketing Management*, 6th edn, London, Prentice Hall

Keller, K. L. (1993) "Conceptualizing, measuring and managing customer based brand equity," *Journal of Marketing*, January, **57**: 1–22

Kempner, M. (1999). "Coke slow on the uptake in Europe, critics say," *The Atlanta Journal – Constitution* (www.ajc.com), June 19

Kets de Vries, M. F. R. (1993) *Percy Barnevik and ABB*, Fontainbleau, France, European Case Clearing House, p. 17

Kitchen, P. J. (1995) "Toward the integration of marketing and public relations," *Marketing Intelligence and Planning*, **11**(11): 15–21

Kitchen, P. J. (1997) *Public Relations: Principles and Practice*, London, International Thomson

Kitchen, P. J. (1999) *Marketing Communications: Principles and Practice*, London, International Thomson

Kitchen, P. J. and Moss, D. (1995) "Marketing and public relations: the relationship revisited," *Journal of Marketing Communications*, **1**(2): 105–19

Kitchen, P. J. and Papasolomou, I. D. (1997) "Marketing Public Relations," in Kitchen, P. J. (ed.) *Public Relations: Principles and Practice*, London, International Thomson, Ch. 20

Knapp, G. (1991) "Nurturing and motivating employees with communication that sells," in Caropreso, F. (ed.) *Communications Strategies for Changing Times*, New York, Conference Board, p. 38

Kotler, P. (1991) *Marketing Management*, Englewood Cliffs, NJ, Prentice Hall, pp. 621–48

Kotler, P. (2000) *Marketing Management*, 10th edn, Englewood Cliffs, NJ, Prentice Hall

Kouzes, J. and Posner, B. Z. (1987) *The Leadership Challenge: How to get Extraordinary Things Done in Organizations*, San Francisco, Jossey-Bass

Laforet, S. and Saunders, J. (1999) "Managing brand portfolios: why leaders do what they do," *Journal of Advertising Research*, January/February, **51**: 51–66

Lauer, L. D. (1995) "Integrated communication," *Communication World*, August, pp. 26–7

Lauzen, M. M. (1991) "Imperialism and encroachment in public relations," *Public Relations Review*, **17**(3): 245–55

Lauzen, M. M. (1992) "Public relations roles, intraorganizational power, and encroachment," *Journal of Public Relations Research*, **4**(2): 61–80

Lavidge, R. J. and Steiner, G. A. (1961) "A model for predictive measurements of advertising effectiveness," *Journal of Marketing*, October, **61**

Leitch, S. (1999) "From logo-centrism to corporate branding? The (r)evolution in organisational identity," *Australian Journal of Communication*, **26**: 1–8

Leitch, S. and Motion, J. (1999) *Managing Multiplicity: a Corporate Identity Perspective*, Department of Management Communication Working Paper Series

Levitt, T. (1960) "Marketing myopia," *Harvard Business Review*, **38**(4): 45–56

Levitt, T. (1983) "The globalization of markets," *Harvard Business Review*, May–June, **61**: 92–101

Levitt, T. (1983) *The Marketing Imagination*, New York, Free Press, p. xxii

Lightcap, K. (1984) "Marketing support," in Cantor, B. (ed.) *Experts in Action: Inside Public Relations*, White Plains, NY, Longman, pp. 124–9

Liu, B. (1999). "Coca-Cola faces 6% sales fall in Europe," *Financial Times*, July 1, p. 15

M&M Europe Survey (1999) Edited by Crowe, C. (July)

Maathuis, O. J. M. (1999) Corporate branding: the value of the corporate brand to customers and managers. Unpublished dissertation, Rotterdam, Erasmus University

Mael, F. and Ashforth, B. E. (1992) "Alumni and their alma mater: a partial test of the reformulated model of organizational identification," *Journal of Organizational Behavior*, **13**: 103–23

March, J. G. (1988) *Decisions and Organizations*, Oxford, Basil Blackwell

Mardiks, E. R. (1999) "The next big deal," *Reputation Management*, November/December, p. 31

Martin, D. (1998) "Chain reaction," *Financial Times*, November 17, p. 32

Massaro, E. (1991) "Westinghouse, no longer the best known, unknown company," in Caropreso, F (ed.) *Communication Strategies for Changing Times*, New York, Conference Board, p. 35

McDonald's Corporation Annual Report (1999) p. 6

Melewar, T. C. and Saunders, J. (1998) "Global visual corporate identity systems: standardisation, control and benefits," *International Marketing Review*, **15**(4): 291–308

Melewar, T. C. and Saunders, J., (2000) "Global visual corporate identity systems: using an extended marketing mix," *European Journal of Marketing*, **34**(5/6): 538–50

Mellor, V. (1999) "Delivering brand promises through people," *Strategic Communication Management*, February/March

Micklethwait, J. and Wooldridge, A. (1997) *The Witch Doctors*, London, Mandarin

Milne, J. (1995) "Mill owner says he'll pay workers for a month," *The Boston Globe*, December 12, p. B50

Mintzberg, H. (1983) *Power In and Around Organisations*, Englewood Cliffs, NJ, Prentice Hall

Mintzberg, H., Quinn, J. B. and Ghoshal, S. (1998) *The Strategy Process*, London, Prentice Hall

Mitchell, R. K., Agle, B. R. and Wood, D. J. (1997) "Toward a theory of stakeholder identification and salience: defining the principle of who and what really counts," *Academy of Management Review*, **22**(4): 853–86

Molenaar, C. (1996) *Interactive Marketing: The End of Mass Marketing*, London, Gower Hill Publishing Company

Mosser, T. (1993) "Building corporate brands and reputations through public relations," *A.N.A/The Advertiser*, Summer

Narisetti, R. (1997) "P&G, seeing shoppers confused, overhauls marketing," *The Wall Street Journal*, Europe, January 20

National Business Review (19 May 2000) Stephen Robert Tindall, 49. (Retrieved from http://tiki.knowledge-basket.co.nz/mags/ 17 December 2000)

Nauert, P. W. (2000) "Telling the right deal story to employees," *Mergers & Acquisitions*, May

Newsom, D., Turk, J. V. S. and Kruckeberg, D. (1996) *This is PR: The Realities of Public Relations*, 6th edn, Belmont, CA, Wadsworth

Ogilvy & Mather/Houston (1998) "Does corporate advertising pay?" *Corporate Images*, **1**(2)

Ogilvy & Mather/Houston (1998) "There is a correlation between advertising and stock price," *Corporate Images*, **1**(1)

Olins, W. (1989) *Corporate identity: Making Business Strategy Visible Through Design*, London, Thames & Hudson

Papone, A. (1994) Speech to the IAA World Advertising Congress, Cancun, Mexico

Peters, G. (1999) "Putting a stopper on bad publicity," *Financial Times*, July 1, p. 10

Pettis, C. (1995) "The relationship of corporate brand strategy and stock price," *US Investment Research*, June 13

Porter, M .E. (1980) *Competitive Strategy: Techniques for Analysing Industries and Competitors*, New York, Free Press

Porter, M. E. (1985) *Competitive Advantage: Creating and Sustaining Superior Performance*, New York, Free Press

Prahalad, C. K. and Hamel, G. (1990) "The core competence of the corporation," *Harvard Business Review*, **68**(3): 79–91

Puranam, P., Singh, H. and Zollo, M. (2000) "Bringing some discipline to M&A mania," *Financial Times Mastering Management* supplement, 30 October

Rankine, D. (1998) *A Practical Guide to Acquisitions: How to Increase Your Chances of Success*, Chichester, John Wiley & Sons

Rawlins, W. K. (1989) "A dialectical analysis of the tensions, functions, and strategic directions of communication in young adult friendships," in Andersen J. A. (ed.) *Communication Yearbook 12*, Newbury Park, CA, Sage Publications, pp. 157–89

Raynaud, M. and Teasdale, M. (1992) "Confusions and acquisitions: post-merger culture shock and some remedies," *Communication World*, **9**(6): 44–5

Reis, A. and Reis, L. (1998) T*he 22 Immutable Laws of Branding*, New York, Harper Books, Ch. 3

Risberg, A. (1997) "Ambiguity and communication in cross-cultural acquisitions: towards a conceptual framework," *Leadership & Organization Development Journal*, **18**(5): 257–67

Roberts, K. cited in Webber, A. M. (2000) "Trust in the future," *Fast Company*, September, p. 214

Roddick, A. (1992) *Body and Soul*, London, Vermilion

Roughton, B. Jr. and Unger, H. (1999). "Multifront effort seeks to restore confidence," *The Atlanta Journal – Constitution* (www.ajc.com), June 22

Schein, E. (1993) "On dialogue, culture and organizational learning," *Organizational Dynamics*, **22**(2): 40–51

Schultz, D. E. (1998) "Branding the basis for marketing integration," *Marketing News*, **32**(24): 8

Schultz, D. E. and Gronstedt, A. (1998) "Making Marcom an investment," *CTAM Quarterly Journal*, Spring, pp. 36–45

Schultz D. E. and Kitchen, P. J. (2000) *Communicating Globally: An Integrated Marketing Approach*, Chicago, NTC Business Books, and London, Macmillan – now Palgrave

Schultz, D. E., Tannenbaum, S. L. and Lauterborn, R. E. (1994) *Integrated Marketing Communications, Pulling it Together and Making it Work*, Chicago, NTC Business Books

Schultz, D. E. and Walters, J. S. (1998) *Measuring Brand Communication ROI*, New York, Association of National Advertisers

Schultz, D. E. and Schultz, H. F. (1999) cited in *Brand Building and Communication: Power Strategies for the 21st Century*, Best Practice Report on a Consortium Benchmarking Study, Houston, TX, conducted by the American Productivity and Quality Center

Schultz, H. (1999) *Starbucks Inc Annual Report*, USA

Schumacher, E. F. (1973) *Small is Beautiful, Economics as if People Mattered*, New York, Harper & Row

Seeger, M. W. (ed.) (1994) *I Gotta Tell You*, Speeches of Lee Iacocca, Detroit, Wayne State University Press

Shepherd, A. D. (1997) "Communication in organisations operating internationally," *Journal of Communication Management*, **2**(2): 158–66

Sheth, J. N., Gardner, D. M. and Garrett, D. E. (1988) *Marketing Theory: Evolution and Evaluation*, London, John Wiley & Sons, pp. 1–33

Shimp, T. A. (2000) *Advertising, Promotion, and Supplemental Aspects of Integrated Marketing Communications*, Fort Worth, TX, The Dryden Press, Harcourt Brace College Publishers, p. 4

Siegel, A. (1993) "Corporate image: one unique voice," in Laborde, A. (ed.) *Corporate Image: Communicating Visions and Values: Conference Board Proceedings*, New York, Conference Board, p. 24

Smeltzer, L. R. (1991) "An analysis of strategies for announcing organization-wide change," *Group & Organization Studies*, **16**(1): 5–24

Smidts, A., van Riel, C. B. M. and Pruyn, A. T. (2000) *The Impact of Employee Communication and Perceived External Prestige on Organizational Identification*, Rotterdam, ERIM Report Series Research in Management

Soderstrom, J. (1999) "Rising up to tomorrow's challenges: the power of integration," *The Advertiser*, June/July

Spencer, H. (1897/1968) *Principles of Sociology*, New York, Appleton & Co/Macmillan – now Palgrave

Spencer, H. (1971) *Structure, Function and Evolution*, London, Michael Joseph

Stefl, A. (1999) Videotaped interview on branding, courtesy of First Union Corporation

Sterngold, J. (1999) "Low-key thrills at Legoland," *The New York Times*, May 19, p. 10

Sullivan, M. (1990) "Measuring image spillovers in umbrella branded products," *Journal of Business*, **63**(3): 309–29

Suss, D. (1996) "The acquisition tango," *IABC Communication World*, September, special supplement on "Building credibility in time of change," pp. 30–2

Swan, W., Langford, N., Watson, I. and Varey, R. J. (2000) "Viewing the corporate community as a knowledge network," *Corporate Communications: An International Journal*, **5**(2): 97–106

Tapsell, S. (1998) "Stephen Tindall: a leader by example," *Management*, **45**(3): 24–8. (Retrieved from http://proquest.umi.com/pqdweb on 20 December 2000)

Thayer, L. (1997) *Pieces: Revisioning Communication/Life*, London, Ablex Publishing Corporation

Tully, K. (2000) "New strategies in mergers and acquisitions," *Corporate Finance*, London, November

Ulmer, R. R. (2000) "Consistent questions of ambiguity in organizational crisis communication: Jack in the box as a case study," *Journal of Business Ethics*, **25**: 143–55

Ulmer, R. R. (in press) "Effective crisis management through established stakeholder relationships: Malden Mills as a case study," *Management Communication Quarterly*

Unger, H. and Leith, S. (2000) "One agency gets Coke Classic ad: Interpublic is chosen," *The Atlanta Journal – Constitution*, Business, December 2, p. 1D

van Rekom, J. (1998) Corporate identity: development of the concept and a measurement instrument. Unpublished dissertation, Rotterdam, Erasmus University

van Riel, C. B. M. (1995) *Principles of Corporate Communication*, London, Prentice Hall, pp. 26–7

van Riel, C. B. M. (1997) "Protecting the corporate brand by orchestrated communication," *Journal of Brand Management*, **4**(6): 409–18

van Riel, C. B. M. (2000) "Corporate communication orchestrated by a sustainable corporate story," in Schultz, M., Hatch, M. J. and Larsen, M. H. (eds) *The Expressive Organization: Linking Identity, Reputation, and the Corporate Brand*, Oxford, Oxford University Press, pp. 157–81 van Riel, C. B. M. (2000) *Strategic Corporate Communication*, Belgium, Samsom

van Riel, C. B. M. and van den Broek, M. J. E. (1992) "Besluitvorming over concerncommunicatiebudgetten bij twintig Nederlandse beursgenoteerde ondernemingen" ["Decision-making on group communication budgets in twenty Dutch companies quoted on the stock exchange"] *Massacommunicatie*, **4**: 267–86

Varey, R. J. (1996a) A broadened conception of internal marketing. Unpublished Ph.D thesis, Manchester School of Management

Varey, R. J. (1996b) "The future of marketing," *The Business Studies Magazine*, **8**(3): 2–4

Varey, R. J. (1996c) "Conscious corporate communication: a conceptual analysis," *Journal of Communication Management*, **1**(2): 134–44

Varey, R. J. (1998) "Locating marketing within the corporate communication managing system," *Journal of Marketing Communications*, **4**(3): 177–90

Varey, R. J. (2000) "A critical review of conceptions of communication evident in contemporary business and management literature," *Journal of Communication Management*, **4**(4): 328–40

Varey, R. J. (2000a) "The Social Constructionist Approach to Human Communication: Social Theory, Communication Theory and a Normative Basis for Management and Learning," paper presented to the "Knowing the Social World" Interdisciplinary Conference on Social Theory, Methodology and Method, Institute of Social Research, University of Salford, July

Varey, R. J. and Lewis, B. R. (eds) (2000) *Internal Marketing: Directions for Management*, London, Routledge

Varey, R. J. and Mounter, P. (1997) "Re-configuring and organising for strategic communication management: the BP oil experience," *Journal of Communication Management*, **2**(1): 11–23

Varey, R. J. and White, J. (2000) "The corporate communication system of managing," *Corporate Communications: An International Journal*, **5**(1): 5–11

Wakefield, R.I. (1999) "World-Class Public Relations: A Model for Effective Public Relations in the Multinational," presentation at the 6th Annual International PR Research Symposium, Slovenia, July 2–3, 1999. Subsequently published in the *Journal of Communication Management*, August 2000, **5**(1): 59–71. (Symposium version used here with permission of the author)

Weick, K. E. (1995) *Sensemaking in Organizations*, Thousand Oaks, CA, Sage Publications

Wilber, K. (1995) *Sex, Ecology, Spirituality: The Spirit of Evolution*, Boston, MA, Shambhala Publications

Wilber, K. (1996) *A Brief History of Everything*, Boston, MA, Shambhala Publications

Wreford A. (1995) "Planning for corporate communications," in Hart, N. A. (ed.) *Strategic Public Relations*, London, Macmillan – now Palgrave, pp. 10–23

www.johnsonandjohnson.com

www.kelloggs.com

www.pg.com

Yankelovich Monitor Trend Reference Books (1997) "Sticking with what works" **2**: 71

Yankelovich Monitor Trend Reference Books (1997) "Unfamiliar brands" **2**: 73

Yip, G. S. (1996) *Total Global Strategy, Managing for Worldwide Competitive Advantage*, Business school edn, Englewood Cliffs, NJ, Prentice Hall

Young & Rubicam (1994) *Brand Power Study*, London

Zorn, T. E. (1995) "Bosses and buddies: a constructive/dramaturgical analysis of simultaneously close and hierarchical relationships in organizations," in Wood, J. T. and Duck, S. (eds) *Understudied Relationships: Off the Beaten Track*. Newbury Park, CA, Sage Publications, pp. 122–47

Index